The American Revolution
and Righteous Community

The American Revolution and Righteous Community

SELECTED SERMONS OF BISHOP ROBERT SMITH

Edited by Charles Wilbanks

The University of South Carolina Press

© 2007 University of South Carolina

Published by the University of South Carolina Press
Columbia, South Carolina 29208

www.sc.edu/uscpress

Manufactured in the United States of America

16 15 14 13 12 11 10 09 08 07   10 9 8 7 6 5 4 3 2 1

Library of Congress Cataloging-in-Publication Data

Smith, Robert, 1732–1801.
   The American Revolution and righteous community : selected sermons of Bishop Robert Smith /
edited by Charles Wilbanks.
       p. cm.
   Includes bibliographical references and index.
   ISBN-13: 978-1-57003-665-1 (cloth : alk. paper)
   ISBN-10: 1-57003-665-9 (cloth : alk. paper)
       1. Smith, Robert, 1732–1801—Sermons. 2. United States—History—Revolution, 1775–1783—
Sermons. 3. South Carolina—History—Revolution, 1775–1783—Sermons. 4. Sermons,
American—18th century. I. Wilbanks, Charles. II. Title.
   E297.S67 2006
   973.3'1—dc22   2006022267

This book was printed on Glatfelter Natures Book, a recycled paper with 50 percent
postconsumer waste content.

Contents

Introduction

South Carolina and the Revolution

In the early morning hours of January 15, 1778, a fire broke out in the kitchen behind a bakery on Union Street in Charlestown. It was discovered quickly, and strenuous efforts were made to extinguish it, but all efforts were futile. Before two hours had elapsed, much of the city was in flames. Some reports indicate that the flames rose so high that they could be seen from as far away as James Island.[1] In another hour even more of the city was being threatened with annihilation. When it was over more than 250 buildings were destroyed or severely damaged (almost 20 percent of the city).[2]

According to some early accounts of the fire, as efforts were being made to fight the flames, at least some inhabitants took advantage of their less-fortunate neighbors and pilfered their unprotected property.[3] Other accounts of the fire's aftermath, however, paint a more positive picture of the citizens of Charlestown. For example, in an April letter to Henry Laurens, John Lewis Gervais offered his appraisal of his neighbors struggling to overcome their losses:

> I expected to find the Town in Mourning & in distress & my house being received some of my distressed neighbors—on my arrival the sight of the devastation affected me, but I did not find the inhabitants cast down, as it might be supposed it would, & I didn't hear of anyone being rendered to poverty by it.[4]

In fact, Gervais reported that of "real objects of Charity by this Catastrophe I know none."[5] Where did this resilience and optimism come from? In the face of such tragedy

---

1. Letter from Joseph Kershaw to Henry Laurens, January 23, 1778, in *The Papers of Henry Laurens,* 16 vols. (Columbia: University of South Carolina Press, 1990), 12:332.

2. George C. Rogers, *Charleston in the Age of the Pinckneys* (Norman: University of Oklahoma Press, 1969), 28.

3. Letter from Kershaw, 12:332.

4. Letter from John Lewis Gervais to Henry Laurens, April 19, 1778, in *The Papers of Henry Laurens,* 13:153.

5. Ibid., 13:154.

and hardship, where did the citizens find the spirit to pick themselves up from such loss? Where did they find the resources to protect those who were left homeless from the catastrophe? The fire occurred while Charlestown was engaged in war. It was a time of great uncertainty, and the tremendous disruption created by a catastrophe of this magnitude could have destroyed the resilience of the town. There was, however, an unmistakable unifying community spirit. Where did it come from?

Perhaps it came from an emerging common identity, a sense of unity evident in the town since the beginning of the hostilities with Britain. Robert Weir has described the celebration of independence in Charlestown just little more than a year earlier:

> On August 5, 1776, the independence of the United States of America was proclaimed in Charleston. At twelve noon the town regiment of militia was drawn up under arms in Broad Street. Forty-five minutes later President John Rutledge, Major General Charles Lee and his chief subordinates, members of the privy and legislative councils, members of the lower house, and officers of the army appeared in a procession which halted at the front of the regiment. The Declaration of Independence was read. The procession then moved slowly east on Broad Street to the Exchange where the Declaration was read a second time. The multitude responded with cheers; the cannon at the bastions along the Cooper River with salutes.[6]

Fire and war are life-altering events that sometimes, in themselves, bring people together in common cause. In South Carolina, however, they were many reasons to expect disintegration of community. The celebration that occurred in response to the Declaration of Independence illustrates an important, if unexpected fact: that there was a remarkable unity in evidence in Charlestown. There is no doubt that loyalists abounded in the town, but that day they were conspicuously out of sight. The celebration was important. It certainly reflected a growing majority, if not unanimity, in support of the American cause. What were the sources of that unity? One of the purposes of this volume is to offer some answers to that question.

An important participant in the emerging support for independence was the Reverend Robert Smith, rector of St. Philip's Church, the largest and most important Anglican church in South Carolina. Robert Smith was forty-four years old and one of the most respected men in Charlestown. He did not sit by and watch his neighbors go to war without him. He joined them in spirit and in action. Robert Smith reflected his community's values. He joined in their unity of purpose, and he shared their community allegiance. This volume will reveal the motivation for Smith's actions.

Charlestown played a critical role in the fight for independence in South Carolina. It also played an important role in constructing the widespread consensus of opinion supporting the Revolution. The extent of the unity in the state's movement toward

---

6. Robert Weir, *"A Most Important Epocha": The Coming of the Revolution in South Carolina* (Columbia: University of South Carolina Press, 1970), 77.

independence is in some ways difficult to fathom. Charlestown and South Carolina were propelled toward revolution for reasons that differ from those of their New England counterparts.

There have been several notable attempts to explain South Carolina's enthusiasm for the war. One such explanation was offered by Robert Weir in 1970 and 1983. Weir's explanation for South Carolina's unity is four-fold: (1) philosophical ideas pertaining to the natural rights of man that had been offered by the British political opposition during the early eighteenth century became popular especially in the South; (2) in the face of the institution of slavery, southern patriots realized that liberty is what distinguished men from beast or slave (in other words, the exposure to a system of enslavement heightened the sensibilities of the southern slaveholder to the human dignity attendant to freedom); (3) an ideological fusion occurred between the notions of personal independence and the acquisition and the retention of property; (4) American colonists came to believe that governments were tolerable only if they served to protect that property and, by extension, their personal liberty.[7]

Of course, the philosophy of the liberty based on the natural rights of man has long been touted as the motive force behind the revolutionary impulse in all corners of colonial America. Weir has suggested that it also informed and fueled the move toward war in South Carolina and that, given the peculiarities of the economic structure and the institution of slavery, the impulse in the state gained a momentum behind a priority of property rights. He has maintained that these factors led to unified support for war in the state despite significant religious, ethnic, economic, and regional differences.[8]

Eugene Sirmans has also maintained that the South Carolina colonists' unified resistance to the British can be found in the perceived economic threats to the colony posed by British tax and import policy.[9] George Rogers has posited that, instead of coalescing to protect their economic largesse, the rising merchant and planter class became self-assured and aggressive in asserting all their prerogatives.[10] Rogers's argument seems to be that prosperity fed a self-confidence that allowed the leadership class to believe they could attain independence. What all these explanations have in common is the premise that the motivation of this unity for independence was based on economic and social status, on a desire of the planter class to protect its wealth.

Certainly Weir and others have always cited reaction to the onerous policies of the royal government, such as importation duties, the Stamp Act (1765–66), the Townshend Acts (1767–70), and the utilization of placemen (1767) as reasons for disparate groups in the state to coalesce. Those were, in combination, the impetus for South

---

7. Ibid., 6–7.

8. Robert Weir, *Colonial South Carolina: A History* (Millwood, N.Y.: KTO Press, 1983).

9. Eugene Sirmans, *Colonial South Carolina: A Political History, 1663–1763* (Chapel Hill: University of North Carolina Press, 1966).

10. Rogers, *Charleston*, 40.

Carolina patriots to take up arms. The underlying reasons for opposition to these British actions are less clear.

I will not deny that progressively oppressive British policies led to the growing support for independence. My position, however, is that while this unity was fueled by the planter class, what Weir has called the "planters' ethos"[11] did not entail a desire primarily to protect wealth and property. It was, in fact, based on a reaction to a perceived threat to a paternalistic-patriarchal social structure that viewed as anathema any expression of autonomy from above or below.

At least for the lowcountry aristocracy, who dominated political life of the province, the protection of this paternalism and the society built around it compelled the move toward independence. Robert Smith shared this view of society. In his sermons he articulated how important it was to him and to his patrician congregants to maintain the social fabric. His rhetoric represents the philosophical and theological bases of their paternalistic community. As we shall see, however, the backcountry shared philosophical and political tendencies with the North. In many ways the lowcountry and the backcountry held widely different views. To strengthen South Carolina's support for independence, these divisions had to be bridged.

Prior to their actions to rein in the precocious behavior of the colonies, the British were rather benign overseers. The colonists were, for the most part, left to govern themselves. That was especially true in South Carolina, where the Commons House of Assembly had great power and the royal government went almost unnoticed. Under such circumstances, the paternalism of the planter class was secure, especially within their own communities. There was no reason for the South Carolina planter aristocracy to rebel. Their status and their autonomy was not threatened. They never wanted independence as a natural right, but, in view of the British unrelenting condescension, it became the only alternative to protect their patriarchal system from a "foreign" usurper.

It is problematic to argue that the powerful South Carolina planter class supported war because they feared economic loss. Perhaps no other colony in the Americas had fared so well as South Carolina under British control. Agriculturally, economically, and politically, the colony had more reasons than not, it seemed, to support the king and the colonial government. At first glance then, it is puzzling to observe that not only did South Carolinians join in the revolutionary fervor sweeping across America in the 1770s, but their unifying impulse was remarkably strong. Unlikely patriots were prominent, particularly in Charlestown. Rogers asked, "Over such tumult would rich men dare to revolt and open up the seams of society?"[12] It is my view, however, that their goal in supporting the rebellion was precisely to keep the seams of their society from unraveling. In the end, war was their only recourse. The society of the city was dominated by the rising merchant class, leaders of the community and respected as such

11. Weir, *Colonial South Carolina*, 173–74.
12. Rogers, *Charleston*, 42.

by others in the city. The story of how these men came to lead a revolution, seemingly in opposition to their own private interests, is critical in understanding why South Carolina was as unified as it was in its war efforts.

The Placemen Controversy

Perhaps the quintessential example of the perceived encroachment by the royal government on the paternalistic prerogatives of the Charlestown aristocracy—a telling parable about the dangers of official arrogance—was the crisis that ensued over the appointment of Daniel Moore as customs collector in 1767. Weir has reported that Moore began to enforce trade regulations "so strictly and venally" that even the letter of the law was probably violated.[13] Most of the planters in the region relied on free navigation of vessels to transport their product. Merchants also relied on the rather open trade of an earlier period in colonial South Carolina history. They bristled at Moore's heavy-handedness, which led to a tumultuous confrontation that had the disputants engaging in a war of pamphlets and clashes in the courts. According to Weir:

> Technically, coasting vessels were required to clear each voyage at a customs house; normally, however, this provision was waived in cases where compliance was clearly impracticable. Apparently wishing to make an example of a leading local merchant, Moore unexpectedly ordered his underlings to seize two plantation schooners belonging to Henry Laurens, and a trial ensued in the court of vice-admiralty, which operated without a jury. At this time, the judge was Egerton Leigh who was not only related to Laurens by marriage but also a personal friend. Leigh attempted to arrange a compromise by ordering one of the vessels forfeited and the other returned to Laurens. In addition, he neglected to declare that reasonable grounds existed for believing the discharged schooner had been operating in violation of the law, and this omission permitted Laurens to recover his losses on the one vessel by suing for damages in the case of the other.[14]

Leigh's clumsy attempt at walking the line between his self-interest and his reputation led to more turmoil. When Laurens sued and won, the customs searcher was unable to pay.[15] Leigh then had another of Laurens' schooners seized and held in an attempt to persuade Laurens to release his claim on the award. Laurens angrily refused. Personal feelings and resentment grew not only among the principals but throughout the planter and merchant community. Rogers has pointed out that the situation almost grew out of control: "Irked, [Laurens] twisted Moore's nose one day while walking on the Battery. A pamphlet war ensued, in which Henry Laurens, Gabriel Manigault, and their friends were pitted against the placemen, Daniel Moore and Egerton Leigh."[16]

13. Weir, *Colonial South Carolina*, 299.
14. Ibid., 300.
15. Ibid.
16. Rogers, *Charleston*, 42.

The issue that generated such rancor and resentment, however, was not the loss of a schooner or the execution of a court judgment. It was the assault by Moore, a government appointee, on the prerogatives of the planters to conduct their business as they chose—a way that not only benefited them but supported the entire community. Laurens and Manigault's resistance was not designed to protect their wealth; it was designed to protect their status and the duty they believed they had to their community. Duty and status were indivisible. The protection of the wealth that they enjoyed was secondary to the protection of the structure of their society. They felt that their duty to their community was paramount. They were not going to transfer that status voluntarily to an intruder, which they considered Moore to be.

Paternalism

To some extent, all persons of wealth exhibit some degree of paternalism, a self-aggrandizing view of their self-importance. In the South, however, paternalism was not just an attitude but a way of life. An example of its pervasiveness can be seen in the institution of slavery.

Even early in the eighteenth century there was debate about the morality and the wisdom of slavery. Eighteenth-century slaveholders viewed the kinship community in which they lived as populated with people who had reciprocal responsibilities and obligations. While clearly not egalitarian, these slaveholders communicated that their responsibility to the plantation community was one of father to children, protector of the vulnerable. In exchange for the protection and provision of their master, slaves were obligated to labor so that the enterprise could prosper and the community could be strengthened.

Even those South Carolinians who had moral reservations about slavery were nonetheless unwilling to abandon this social structure, which defined their role in the community. The leading aristocracy had certain obligations, and expectations were placed on them that they could not ignore. They conformed to those expectations, but not because it was to their economic benefit to do so; in many instances it was not, and in others planters expressed a willingness to relinquish financial gain for "higher" considerations. Nor was such conformity always consistent with all their ethical and moral proclivities; the evidence suggests that in many instances it was not. They conformed to their community's expectations simply because they were inextricable participants in the life of their community, and to them there was no higher obligation but to serve it.

There is little doubt that one of the wealthiest planters in Charlestown, Henry Laurens, had serious moral reservations about the continuation of slavery. He harbored these feelings and sometimes expressed them to his neighbors, but at the same time he continued to own slaves and to expand his slave population. It is clear from his own words that his slaveholding was not motivated by economic gain. In an August 16, 1783, letter to Richard Oswald, Laurens discussed a transaction for the purchase of slaves, writing:

I perceive in a moment your humane views in favor of the poor East Florida Negroes and altho' I had advised Mr. Owen and Mr. Gervais of the proposed consignment I cannot but approve of your subsequent Determination and will therefore write to Mr. Clay and inclose my letter with this submitting the disposal of it yourself. We feel for those Wretches the Negroes and wish to make them as happy as their condition will admit of; We forgo our own interest in part by keeping them together in families, but how long will this continue?[17]

Laurens was torn between his duties to the enterprise he led, to his legacy, to his community and his duty to the human bondsmen he held. His reservations were clear, but he chose to continue his slaveholding. It is commonplace to assign the thirst for profit as the motive of the southern slave owner of this era. While that may have been true for some, for the ruling planter class in Charlestown—and particularly for Henry Laurens —it was not true. In the same letter, he described his motives:

In these few words my Dr Sir you learn my opinion of your Plan, which I do not mean to discourage, my own feelings restrain me, partial happiness is acceptable & desirable. I had rather lose a large annual profit by keeping my Negroes comfortably together in families than avail myself of Gain by violent Seperations of Man & Wife, Parents & Children, my practice has ever been consistent with this Declaration, I see nevertheless Evils which will arise after my Death unless something for prevention shall be done in the meantime hence I ardently wish to be once more among those who are committed to my charge in order that I may take measures for cutting off, in some degree if not wholly, the Entail of Slavery. Successors may improve upon my foundation. What does it signify Whether We are possessed of a few thousands more or less in the hour of Death; or what comparison in that hour will Money bear to a tranquil and satisfied Mind.[18]

While he rejected a motive of enrichment, he was concerned about his duty to those who would follow after.

Likewise, there were those who had fewer reservations about their slaveholding but nevertheless expressed a paternal obligation to those they held in bondage. An example of this plantation-class paternalism may be found in the words of Georgia planter and sometime South Carolina resident James Habersham. Consider the following poignant description of the death of one of his slaves:

Oronoko's wife dyed last Night, and the poor fellow is inconsolable, and as she was a favourite of my dear deceased wife and nursed two of my Daughters, I must own the sight of her has affected me more than all the negroes I have ever lost; by bringing to

17. Henry Laurens to Richard Oswald, in *The Papers of Henry Laurens,* 16:267.
18. Ibid., 16:267–68.

my remembrance those dear Innocents and their now happy Mother, that I have really been obliged to lay down my pen several times to give Vent to those Feelings only known to a tender Husband, and Parent.

The sentiment of affection that is apparent in the Habersham and Laurens letters is typical of the eighteenth century. It communicates a sense of the slave's humanity and of the legitimacy of the plantation community. Moreover, Habersham apparently viewed his obligation to his slaves mostly as a spiritual father, responsible for their instruction in the gospel. In fact, for Habersham religious instruction was the greatest good that could come from slavery. In a 1770 letter he stressed that responsibility: "It is to me unaccountable, that any people calling themselves Christians, should have any objections against having their Servants instructed, unless it is their Inattention to, or Ignorance of, the eternal Importance of the Christian Revelation." A half century later, supporters of slavery virtually rejected the worthiness of slaves to receive salvation. Habersham, however, believed that slaves were as deserving of God's grace as any human. In a letter to the Reverend Thomas Broughton of London, Habersham wrote,

> Some ignorant people would <u>foolishly</u> insinuate that they [slaves] are scarcely reasonably Creatures, and not capable of being instructed in the divine Truths of Christianity; an absurdity too obvious to deserve any refutation, and I am ashamed to have occasion to make this observation, as daily Experience evinces, that there are many ingenious Mechanicks among them, and as far as they have had Opportunity of being instructed, have discovered as good abilities, as are usually found among people of our Colony; but making them good tradesmen is immediately profitable, and the Reward of making them good Christians is at a Distance.[19]

Habersham's paternalism, while not universal in the eighteenth-century South, was nonetheless common, especially among the aristocracy.

Dr. David Ramsay, the son-in-law of Henry Laurens, also continued and expanded his slaveholding despite misgivings about the institution. Again, the justification for his continued slaveholding was not protection of wealth but protection of a social structure based on paternalism. Joanna Bowen Gillespie has described Ramsay's justification for his slaveholding:

> Despite lives totally intertwined with slaves and slavery, white citizens in Martha's [Ramsay's wife] hometown preserved an all-but-total eclipse of the topic in both written record and public utterances during the post-war decades. If slavery appeared in personal letters, it was most often treated as an integral component of an

---

19. James Habersham, *The Letters of the Hon. James Habersham, 1756–1775* (Savannah: Georgia Historical Society, 1904), 23, 100–101.

elite society's gracious self-image which northern criticism of it was dismissed as ill-informed and unaware.[20]

Undeniably, cruelty and inhumane treatment of slaves were to be found, as were slave owners who were motivated not only by financial gain but by racism and the exercise of power and brutality. Josiah Quincy, who visited Charlestown in 1773, wrote of attitudes he detected about slaveholding: "The brutality used toward slaves has a very bad tendency with reference to the manners of the people, but much worse with regard to the youth."[21] Evidence indicates that for the most part, however, the Charlestown aristocracy not only opposed such treatment on principle but actively resisted it.

This resistance to brutality in the eighteenth century was based in a moral code that was a characteristic of the Anglican religion of the South Carolina aristocracy. According to Frederick Bowers, the Anglican message was a call for active piety:

> In thus narrowing Christianity to a moral code and ignoring its spiritual potency the Anglican Church did not, however, assume a passive role. Rather it preached an active religion, one to be followed in daily life and exemplified in visible good works—caring for the poor, the sick, the helpless and the distressed. By its literal interpretation of the scriptural injunction regarding charity the church helped [create] a humanitarian spirit of which the S.P.G. itself was an expression.[22]

The charity demanded by the church certainly extended to slaves. An incident that seemed to fix the attention of Henry Laurens (who wrote several letters to his son describing the situation) also brought other community leaders to intervene on behalf of a condemned slave, Jerry. In August 1775 Jerry was condemned on the questionable testimony of another slave, Jeremy. Apparently, not a few of the leading men of the community worked to free Jerry or at least to save his life. In the end the efforts failed, and Jerry was executed, but the extraordinary measures taken by many Charlestown leaders reinforces the notion that the ruling planters were motivated—if not by a commitment to equality and universal liberty—by a rather more humane paternalism than has been generally recognized.

So, while many in the colony held views more closely allied with republicanism of the middle or northern states and while others had a more pecuniary, racist, and power-driven motive for their activity, the South Carolina aristocracy harbored a patriarchal and paternalistic attitude about their role in their community. This attitude came to define the political impulses of the entire province. Josiah Quincy recognized the dominance of the elite on the identity of South Carolina:

20. Joanna Bowen Gillespie, *The Life and Times of Martha Laurens Ramsay, 1759–1811* (Columbia: University of South Carolina Press, 2001), 149.

21. Josiah Quincy, *Memoir of the Life of Josiah Quincy* (1825; New York: DeCapo Press, 1971), 89.

22. Frederick Bowers, *The Culture of Early Charleston* (Chapel Hill: University of North Carolina Press, 1942), 29.

It may well be questioned whether there is, in reality, any third branch in the constitution of this government. It is true they have a House of Assembly, but whom do
they represent? The labourer, the mechanic, the tradesman, the farmer, the yeoman?
No, the representatives are almost, if not wholly, rich planters. The Planting interest
is, therefore represented, but conceive nothing else as it ought to be.[23]

Quincy also recognized an equally important of aspect of aristocratic paternalism. His
observation speaks to the very reason that the South Carolina aristocracy seemingly
acted against their own interests in supporting independence. The elite leadership of
the colony would not brook encroachment of their prerogatives, nor the usurpation of
their obligations either from above or below. Quincy reflected on the exclusion of the
common man from the mechanism of power:

At present the House of Assembly are staunch colonists. But what is this owing to?
Bad policy on the other side of the water. The members of the House are all very
wealthy and such men have, in general, little solicitude about the interest or concern
of the many. . . . Such extravagant disproportion of property is to the last degree
impolitic and dangerous.[24]

On the other hand, Quincy properly recognized the total disdain of the aristocracy for
those who illegitimately attempted to usurp their rightful place in the life blood of the
community. Quincy pointed out:

The Council, Judges, and other great officers are all appointed by mandamus from
Great Britain. Nay, even the clerk of the Board, and Assembly! Who are, and have
been appointed? Persons disconnected with the people and obnoxious to them. I
heard several planters say "We none of us when we grow old can expect honours of
the State; they are all given away to worthless, poor sycophants!"[25]

The elite wanted to remain just that, not primarily because they wanted to retain power,
but because exercising that power was a duty they felt morally bound to exercise, precisely because of their status. They refused to transfer that duty to those for whom they
had responsibility or to those who illegitimately attempted to take it from them.

Unity Challenged

Based on the lead of the planter elite, opinion in South Carolina was by the mid-1770s
coalescing in favor of independence. It was clear by that time that Robert Smith had
joined with it. There were some leading citizens, however—such as Alexander Garden
(the physician and botanist), Robert Perroneau, William Wragg, Robert Cooper (rector
of St. Michael's Church), and Miles Brewton—who openly opposed the American

---

23. Quincy, *Memoir*, 87.
24. Ibid., 87–88.
25. Ibid., 88.

cause. By the time fighting had started in the state in 1776, it had become apparent that the loyalists among the elites were growing fewer and fewer. Rogers maintained that the few existing loyalists were opposing a near-unanimous citizenry.[26] This unanimity, according to Rogers, came at a price. Charlestown leaders had to do something to reduce the discontent from the increasingly vocal upcountry representatives, who were demanding more from the Charlestown elite than they had ever been willing to give before. According to Rogers,

> The first state constitution, written in 1776, did not satisfy these new men. Therefore, in 1777, it was rewritten to bring about some of the reforms desired, particularly the disestablishment of the Anglican church. A new constitution of 1778 appeared with these concessions, the price that the merchant oligarchy [of Charlestown] paid for the help of the new men and an extension of Carolina solidarity to the upcountry. It was at a time of these constitutional changes, in February 1777, that an oath was prescribed as a sign of loyalty to the new state.[27]

Those who refused to sign the oath were banished. The disestablishment of the Anglican Church had a fundamental and permanent impact on the political fortunes of South Carolina. It also altered the social structure of the society. The connection of the move toward independence and the disestablishment of the Anglican Church, makes Robert Smith's patriotism all the more remarkable and puzzling.

Charlestonians who were abroad at the time, felt an urgency to return so that they could defend their home. The confusion that surrounded the situation of the Carolinians in England has been explained by Rogers:

> Gabriel Manigault sent off ominous news to [Francis] Kinloch on March 12, 1778: "I am informed (but I do not know how true it is) that they have resolved in our Province to confiscate the estate of every Carolinian above the age of twenty-one, and who does not return there; as they think that those who have any Property there, ought to help defend it." Kinloch answered on March 30 from Edinburgh that he would like to know "for certain, whether or no the South Carolina Assembly has entered into any resolution respecting the estates of absentees." Spurred on by this rumor, Carolinians in England began feverish preparations to return to America. In May, Manigault wrote his grandfather that he would soon be the only Carolinian in London except those who had been banished.[28]

Whether the rumor was true, or exaggerated, it reflected two important aspects of the struggle: those who had been caught abroad when hostilities erupted found it difficult

---

26. Rogers, *Charleston,* 43.

27. Ibid., 45.

28. Rogers, *Evolution of a Federalist: William Laughton Smith, 1758–1812* (Columbia: University of South Carolina Press, 1962), 83.

to keep up with events at home, and all property owners felt a duty to defend their community. Those who were fortunate enough to own property had an obligation to defend those who did not.

South Carolina supported the Revolution in action and in spirit. South Carolinians joined the fight despite their discomfort with the call for universal liberty and despite the fact that the interests of the aristocracy were in opposition to independence. They joined primarily because their community was under assault, an assault not so much against property as on the moral code that made their society what it was.

Robert Smith is a wonderful example of this thinking. He was Anglican and English. He was a clergyman, a planter, and a businessman. He did not take up arms against his native country because he wanted to protect his wealth—he risked it all. He did not become a revolutionary because he wanted to solidify his leadership position within the church. He, in fact, joined those who wanted to disconnect the church from government subsidy. He did not act in order to protect his life; he fought as a regular soldier during the siege at Fort Sullivan. He certainly did not decide to become a revolutionary because he agreed with the republican politics that spawned the war—he was not a republican. He fought for the same reason as other Charlestonians of his class, because he was duty bound to protect the integrity of his community.

Smith's Sermons

Not much has been written about the delivery of Smith's sermons. No description of his delivery style by a contemporary parishioner has been uncovered. A visiting clergyman, however, the Reverend Josiah Quincy, did write of his reaction to Smith's preaching. On March 7, 1773, Quincy wrote,

> Went to St. Philip's Church; very few present, though the first part of the day is the most full. A young clergyman read prayers with the most gay, indifferent and gallant air imaginable. A very elegant piece of modern declamatory composition was read by another clergyman [obviously Robert Smith], by way of sermon, from these words in Job: "Acquaint now thyself with God; that good may come of it." Having heard a young church clergyman very coxcomically advance a few days before, that no sermon ought to exceed twenty-five minutes, I had the curiosity to see by my watch whether our clerical instructor was of the same sentiments, and found that he shortened the space above seven minutes and a half. This divine, after showing that avocations, business, etc. precluded a certain species of acquaintance with God, very sagely said, "I come now to show that there is a certain allowable acquaintance with God." Qu[estion:] What kind of acquaintance can the creature have with the Creator which is not allowable?[29]

---

29. Quincy, *Memoir*, 75–76.

As far as I have been able to determine, Quincy's is the only contemporary description of Smith's pulpit delivery. In 1775 Henry Laurens described Smith's address before the Commons House of Assembly, writing to his son on February 18: "Yesterday, was observed as a Day of Prayer & humiliation & there really appeared a more general Seriousness & Solemnity than I remember to have seen upon any other Fast—the Reverd. Mr. Smith preached an occasional Sermon at St. Philip's, the best I ever heard from his Reverence."[30] If Laurens had been more specific, perhaps we could surmise in what ways the assembly address was better than others. It is clear from the comments, however, that Smith commanded a great deal of respect.

It appears that Quincy was bemused at the brevity of Charlestown homilies. Perhaps there were other "peculiarities" of Smith's worship routine. If so, they have not been recorded. We do know something of the Anglican worship practices of the time. Bowers has written,

> By the time Charleston had reached its period of cultural maturity, the local aristocracy was comfortably settled in the Anglican faith. The church served them well for a generation and had established itself firmly in the thoughts and affection of the upper class. No great effort was henceforth needed to maintain this position, for Anglicanism was essentially a gentleman's religion and made no extravagant demands on the credulity of its members. Rather, the Church of Locke and Tillotson scorned enthusiasm of any kind and kept steadily to the middle way. It neither discarded Revelation for Reason with the Deists nor indulged in the emotional faith of the Wesleyites. Its emphasis was on practical morality, which suited perfectly the temper of the Carolina aristocrat, as its decorous service satisfied his sense of dignity and propriety.[31]

Despite the localized adaptation that Charlestown clergy, and Robert Smith in particular, may have made, Smith's sermons conform nicely with the expectations of two of the most widely read treatises on pulpit eloquence of the day: George Campbell's *Philosophy of Eloquence* (1776) and Hugh Blair's *Lectures on Rhetoric and Belles Lettres* (1783). These works were widely used in seminary training at the time, and as the writings of Anglican ministers, they carried an unmistakable credibility. Without a much more complete record of Smith's delivery skills and his reception by his parishioners, it is difficult to make confident judgments about the extent to which he may have met the standards of these treatises. Nevertheless, some conclusions can be made pertaining to the quality of Smith's eloquence.

---

30. *The Papers of Henry Laurens,* 10:71.
31. Bowers, *Early Charleston,* 21.

Pulpit Eloquence in the Eighteenth Century

George Campbell produced the more philosophical of the two treatises, Blair the more practical. Campbell recognized the difficulty of the preacher's task:

> Arising from the nature of the profession, it will not admit a question, that the preacher hath in this respect the most difficult task [of any profession]; inasmuch as he hath a character to support, which is more easily injured than that either of the senator, or the speaker at the bar.[32]

Campbell's most ardent standard for pulpit discourse was moderation and temperance in content and delivery. He insisted,

> First, then, it [a minister] is a character of some authority, as it is of one educated for a purpose so important as that of a teacher of religion. The authority, however, from the nature of the function, must be tempered with moderation, candour and benevolence. The teacher of the gospel as the very terms import, is the minister of grace, the herald of divine mercy to ignorant, sinful, and erring men.[33]

Although we do not have nearly a complete picture of Smith's public persona, it appears from the evidence we do have that he conformed to Campbell's standard of moderation.

The most useful of the two works for our purpose is Hugh Blair's, because of its practical instructions. Blair presented four requisites: (1) the preacher must have a just and fixed view of the end of preaching; (2) the preacher must be a good man; (3) his subject must have gravity and warmth; and (4) it should be the point of greatest importance to him.[34] One may assume that Smith's preaching met these requisites even though, for the most part, such judgments more properly should have been made by his contemporaries.

Smith did seem to have had a fixed view of the end of preaching. A cursory review of his existing sermons and a reading of his other writings pertaining to religion and natural philosophy give the distinct view that Smith had carefully thought through his task as minister, as opposed to his roles as educator and businessman. The subjects chosen for his sermons appear to be typical of the time and in accord with Anglican principles, and they carry sufficient import and gravity to meet the third of Blair's requisites. We cannot be certain what subjects were most important to Smith, but it is a logical conclusion that Smith preached on subjects that were important to his theological view.

---

32. George Campbell, *The Philosophy of Rhetoric* (1776; Carbondale: Southern Illinois University Press, 1963), 99.

33. Ibid., 100.

34. Hugh Blair, *Lectures on Rhetoric and Belles Lettres,* 2 vols. (1783; Carbondale: Southern Illinois University Press, 1965), 2:105–8.

Blair also suggests five rules for the construction and delivery of sermons. The preacher should (1) attend to the unity of the sermon, (2) draw the subject more precise and particular, (3) not say all that can be said on a subject (which Blair considers the greatest error a preacher can make), (4) place himself in the situation of a serious hearer and make the sermon interesting, and (5) not adapt to the model of preaching that may happen to be in fashion. In general Blair believed that the preacher should adopt a presentation style "calculated for the instruction of all sorts of hearers, plainness and simplicity should reign in them." He went on to caution, "All unusual, swoln, or high sounding words, should be avoided; especially all words that are merely poetical, or merely philosophical."[35] Smith seems to have conformed to these standards.

Unity. Smith certainly followed the organizational conventions of the day, and his sermons have an internal and logical unity. A Smith sermon is consistent with tradition by beginning with the text on which its message is based. It then offers a brief summary of the meaning of the text—a sort of context within which his hearers should understand the rest of the sermon. For example, a sermon on the duty of magistrates (1761) begins thus:

> These words are variously rendered and as variously applied by different men: Some with a little change of the version understand and expound them with relation to God himself, and connect them with the preceding verses, as a part of his glorious title and attributes, whereby his absolute dominion and sovereignty is particularly expressed over just men and those that fear him. Others without any change of the version, explain the text, and that not unjustly as a part of the character of the promised Messiah and the anointed son of God: for he properly is, as well as his Almighty Father, the Rock and Support of Israel, a most just and holy ruler over men, and one that rules in the fear of God that so rules his subjects by his blessed Spirit, that they may learn from a true fear of God, to study and practice piety and holiness of life, according to the great end of which he laid down his life, viz., that he might purchase to himself a particular people, zealous of good works.[36]

Smith articulated the approach he was to take within this context and outlined the points he was to make in illuminating the meaning of the text, saying, "And in this acceptation of the words, I shall consider them on this present occasion. First, by pointing out the necessity and advantages of Government in general. And secondly, the useful and necessary qualifications of a good magistrate."[37] Finally, after fulfilling the promise of the organizational preview, he applied all that he had said to the actual lives of the congregation. For example:

---

35. Ibid., 2:108–15.
36. Robert Smith (1761), Smith Sermons Collection, St. Philip's Church, Charleston, S.C.
37. Ibid.

But if these considerations will not prevail, I shall desire you seriously to consider how sharply the Apostle reproves those that despise government, that are presumptuous, self-willed, and are not afraid to speak evil of dignities: And let the Apostle's reproof excite us to behave, as to deserve none. Yea, rather let it excite us so to behave, as may entitle us to those great rewards which are reserved in heaven for all those, who live in obedience to the just laws of man, and the holy laws of God. For to such, will the great judge eternal at the last day pronounce well done good and faithful servants; enter ye into your Masters joy—which may God of his infinite mercy say to us all through.[38]

The internal structure of Smith's sermons appears unified. So too the logical integrity of his discourse.

Particular Subjects. A review of the sermons in the St. Philip's collection reveals that, for the most part, Smith carefully focused his subjects. There are many notable sermons with quite pointed subjects; for example: "On Evil Speaking," "On Swearing Oaths," "The Efficacy of National Virtue," "The Knowledge of Human Conscience," and "On Death." Other examples, fewer in number, have rather broad targets such as "On God's Providence," "The Justice of God," "The Fruit of the Spirit," and "The Victory of Faith."

Condensed and Refined Treatment. Blair's most important rule was his insistence that the preacher should refrain from presenting all there is to say on a particular subject. If one is to take Josiah Quincy's criticism of the brevity of one Smith sermon as representative of all, then Smith certainly met this rule. A reading of the sermons also supports this conclusion. Most often, Smith organized his discourse in three or four main points. Blair would probably have been pleased with Smith's pulpit eloquence.

Search for Common Ground. It was not difficult for Smith to put himself in the place of his congregation. In many ways he was in their place. Members of St. Philip's were the elite and the leaders of the community. Smith was counted among them. He understood their concerns, their values, their joys, and their goals. That made his task of reaching them and instructing them on a moral plane less difficult.

Avoid Fashion. Blair's last two rules are in some ways at odds. Smith certainly understood his audience well. He adapted to their peculiarities and characteristics. As South Carolina moved toward war, Smith evidently made his message fit the particular concerns of the community, and he did it well. There is no evidence, however, that Smith adapted his preaching in other respects to the fashion of the times. Other than Quincy's complaint about the length of his sermons, Smith seems to have been a fairly traditional Anglican preacher of his time.

The Collection

The collection held at St. Philip's Church in Charleston includes a total of 283 sermons. Some are not complete, and about ten are little more than fragments. Another eight to

---

38. Ibid.

ten were not written by Smith, as their authorship predates his ministry, although it is possible that he delivered them. Most of the sermons are numbered and labeled with the date and location of each delivery. Most were delivered multiple times (as many as twenty-four); a few were delivered but once. The sermons are not titled, but the text is sometimes truncated as a sort of title.

Editorial Perspective

This selection of 27 sermons from the 283 in the St. Philip's collection, is based on the identification of those that focus primarily on issues of public morality, specifically civic duty, citizenship, charity, universal love, and national virtue. The identification was initially based on the scriptural reference and the cataloguer's annotations, but the final selection was made by a careful analysis of each text. A few otherwise appropriate sermons were not included because of the incomplete or poor condition of the original manuscript, which made useful transcription nearly impossible.

Copy Text. The sermons were obviously written to be delivered. Therefore, my editorial decisions have been made with that in mind. To me, the value of the sermons is not to be found in their literary qualities, although they are artfully composed, but in the rhetorical force they had on the audience who heard them. That is important as it impacts my editorial treatment of revisions Smith often made to the sermons. All the sermons included in this volume had at least a few authorial revisions, some were liberally altered, and in a few even the biblical texts were changed in subsequent delivery. Since the likelihood is that these revisions were made prior to the delivery of the sermon or to successive deliveries, I have assumed that they were incorporated into Smith's oral presentation. Therefore, I have incorporated Smith's revisions into the final edited text, always including the revision that was used in the final delivery. I consider the sermons works in progress. As such, the latest versions are included in this volume. They are more telling of the *application* of Smith's theology, the primary interest of this analysis.

Other editorial decisions are driven by this assumption. All editorial interventions are guided by two principles: that the oral character of the sermons be preserved when possible and that readability of the text should be afforded without sacrificing the historical or personal character of the sermons.

Editorial Method

Since the sermons were written to be delivered and were progressively revised for subsequent delivery, the copy text for each sermon is the manuscript itself. None of Smith's sermons has been previously published. On the other hand, the sermons were certainly written to be delivered publicly. In that sense, Smith intended for them to be "published." The final transcription of the sermons is accordingly a clear text. If these examples were intended as personal documents, such as letters or a diary, then the choice of genetic text would be more appropriate. The process of generating a clear text of the manuscript required an intervening step of transcribing a genetic text.

Authenticity of the Texts. The manuscripts likely represent, to some degree, the contributions of sermons written by others. Smith acknowledges these contributions either on the manuscript itself or on his index, or list, of the sermons. These have been noted when applicable. It appears that not many of the sermons were written in Smith's own hand. Subsequent revisions, however, were almost always made by Smith himself. It is also clear that Smith was careful to record the date and place of delivery of each sermon, so the authenticity of its delivery is assured. The sermons included in this volume were delivered by Smith, and the extent of authorial contributions by others notwithstanding, their organization, style, and theology consistently reflect that of Smith.

Textual Notes. Textual notes indicate instances of Smith's insertions, deletions, and substitutions, both strikethroughs and overwrites. The section containing the textual notes includes a fuller explanation of how the notes were constructed.

Silent Emendations. Silent emendations include citation of biblical texts, expansion of abbreviations, regularization of numbering, regularization of punctuation, regularization of capitalization, and regularization of spelling.

1. Citation of biblical texts. References to biblical sources have been regularized: for example, Jam (James), Matt (Matthew), Prov (Proverbs).
2. Abbreviations have been expanded; for example, & (and), wd. (would), procur'd (procured), pge. (page), ver. (verse), no. (number).
3. Numbers are regularized: for example, 9 (nine), 1st. (First).
4. Missing or inadvertently misplaced punctuation has been regularized; for example, Smith's sermons occasionally contain slashes instead of periods, especially at the end of paragraphs. Those have been changed to periods.
5. Capitalization has been regularized.
6. Inadvertent or inconsistently misspelled words have been regularized; for example, "agreable" (agreeable), "reverance" (reverence).

Reported Emendations. Reported emendations include strikethroughs and overwrites, cancellations and insertions, conventional misspellings, inadvertent omissions, and illegible words or phrases.

1. Strikethroughs and overwrites. Since such substitutions were likely made prior to delivery, in every case the text includes the word that has been substituted for one struck through. Likewise, the text includes the word that appears above one initially written. The changes are reported in the textual notes.
2. Misspellings that are consistent throughout the sermons are emended but reported in the textual notes. Misspellings due to historical convention are likewise noted.
3. Inadvertent omissions or illegible words that can be confidently provided have been emended and reported. Omissions and illegible words that cannot be determined with confidence are indicated by the word *illegible* enclosed in brackets, [illegible].

PART ONE

Robert Smith and His Community

Chapter 1

The Americanization of Robert Smith

T HE REALITY OF THE WAR hit Charlestown hard in the summer of 1776. On June 28, British forces under the command of Peter Parker began an assault on Fort Sullivan at the entrance of Charlestown Harbor. Largely because of miscalculation and blunder on the part of British commanders, the patriots successfully repelled the attackers, but ten provincial defenders were killed. The news further stoked the passions of an already volatile populace. It seemed now certain that no Charlestonian could avoid taking sides in the growing conflict.

Following the battle, existing divisions within the Anglican community became even deeper. The pulpits of St. Michael's and St. Philip's were set apart by competing loyalties and strident political partisanship. The day after the battle, the Reverend Robert Cooper, the rector of St. Michael's, offered prayers for the fortunes of the king's army and for the success of their mission against the rebel enemies. He prayed for God to "strengthen him that he may vanquish all his enemies."[1] It is likely that many from his own congregation, or their loved ones, were among the defenders at Fort Sullivan. Cooper's prayers had, in essence, called on God to vanquish many of his own communicants. It was too much for the vestry to abide. They met two days later, just before Sunday services were to begin, and approved the following resolution:

> That the bells of St. Michael's Church are not to be rung today to summon the People to divine service. That the sence of the Parishioners be taken on Mr. Cooper's conduct, & That the Church Wardens do by Advertisement summon the Parishioners to meet at St. Michael's Church on Tuesday, 2 July at 10 O'Clock in the forenoon—and that the Clerk do acquaint Mr. Cooper with these resolutions.[2]

1. Frederick Dalcho, *An Historical Account of the Protestant Episcopal Church in South Carolina* (Charleston, 1820), 202.

2. George Williams, *St. Michael's Charleston, 1751*–1951 (Columbia: University of South Carolina Press, 1951), 37.

Cooper, perhaps rightly, interpreted the resolution to mean that he had been dismissed. In any event the Friday prayers marked the last time that Cooper addressed his congregation with its consent. On July 2, 1776, Cooper was formally dismissed by the vestry.

Nearby, another Anglican pulpit served as a dais for political advocacy. The Reverend Robert Smith addressed his congregation, still stirred by the battle at Sullivan's Island. His message could hardly have been more different from Cooper's. Speaking of the apparent victory of the Americans, Smith told his congregants,

> May this prove to be an auspicious omen to the cause of liberty. May the spirit of freedom, even of that glorious freedom, which we are now contending for, pervade the whole state. May every man engaged in this most noble cause think that our safety, and his own depend on his single aim, and may every man be determined to act accordingly.
>
> The present moment calls on us for all our vigor, all our exertion.[3]

The response of the congregation at St. Philip's was as enthusiastic in support for Smith as St. Michael's was against their rector.

What led Smith to oppose his king? Why was Smith moved to act against the oath of his ordination?[4] How was it possible for Smith and Cooper—alike in so many ways and cooperative and collaborative in ecclesiastical matters—to come to oppose each other on such an important and fundamental issue affecting their community? The answers to these questions are indeed central to understanding Robert Smith, and I will argue that they are primary in understanding South Carolina's unity in support for the American Revolution.

Robert Smith arrived in Charlestown from England on November 3, 1757. He came to replace a giant in the history of the Anglican Church in South Carolina, Alexander Garden, who had died in September 1756. Garden had been the commissary for the bishop of London and had become widely known for his very public clashes with the revivalist Anglican preacher George Whitefield. Garden had also been given credit for the phenomenal growth and success of the Society for the Propagation of the Gospel in Foreign Parts (S.P.G.), which had been used to evangelize Native Americans on the frontier and the slave population throughout the colony. Both the Whitefield controversy and the activity of the S.P.G. helped to shape the nature of Smith's early tenure at St. Philip's.

Community Divided

The revivalist-establishment confrontation (epitomized by the clash between Whitefield and Garden) was rooted in one fundamental issue—justification by faith. Or, put

---

3. Robert Smith (1776), Smith Sermons Collection, St. Philip's Church, Charleston, S.C.

4. On ordination, Anglican clergy swore an oath to the king, the titular head of the church. For this reason they could not be ordained abroad, a cause of friction between the colonial churches and the bishops in England.

another way, which path or paths to salvation are allowed by scripture? Whitefield's anti-Arminian theology was not only antagonistic to established Anglican teaching, but it threatened the legitimacy of Garden's ecclesiastical office.

Whitefield's impact on the Anglican community in Charlestown was rooted, without a doubt, in the circumstances surrounding his second visit to the city in the spring and summer of 1740. Preaching that the Anglican clergy were hypocritical, or worse, in their teaching of salvation or justification, Whitefield accused the establishment clergy of teaching their congregants that faith alone was not sufficient to attain salvation. He claimed that such Arminianism was in contradiction to traditional church interpretation and was at its core an evil doctrine.

As overseer of the faith in South Carolina, Alexander Garden had taken Whitefield's charges personally, and when the revivalist arrived in Charlestown in March of 1740, Garden was not gracious in receiving the young Whitefield. In fact Whitefield reported in his diary that Garden ordered him out of his house.[5] For months afterward Garden and Whitefield exchanged charges, and public debate was carried on over the theological issues that fueled the controversy. The dispute between the two men became personal. Whitefield charged that the current "masters of Israel" were deliberately misleading their congregations.[6] Garden, meanwhile, accused Whitefield of gross misapplication of scripture and of hopeless contradictions in his theology.[7]

Beyond the doctrinal objections, most established Anglicans observed with alarm other aspects of Whitefield's preaching. The emotionalism that always characterized Whitefield's revivals was in itself a matter of concern for local churches and their clergy. Many believed that religious ritual and doctrine needed to be viewed with a degree of decorum and reverence that the revivalists seemed to dismiss. Leonard Labaree has written,

> Contrary to the practices of most organized churches, which held that a minister was set as pastor over a particular flock and charged with the protection of its spiritual life, the revivalists, either neglecting their own parishes or without assuming responsibility for congregations of their own, moved from place to place interfering with the charges of the regularly settled ministers in every parish where they entered.[8]

These local ministers took their responsibilities seriously. They viewed their duties as much aimed at their community as to their church. To see an "outsider" intrude on that relationship so as to undermine the sense of mutual community connections was

---

5. George Whitefield, *George Whitefield's Journals* (London: Banner of Truth Trust, 1960), 401.

6. Whitefield, *The Works of George Whitefield*, 6 vols. (London: Edward & Charles Dilly, 1772), 5:362.

7. Alexander Garden, *Six Letters to Reverend George Whitefield* (Boston: T. Fleet, 1740), 5.

8. Leonard W. Labaree, "The Conservative Attitude toward the Great Awakening," *William and Mary Quarterly* 4 (October 1944): 335–36.

a threat not only to them but also to their neighbors. So, while Whitefield and other revivalists were often successful in stirring the faithful, they sowed the seeds for a philosophical transformation that justified the rejection of traditional religious authority and eventually the political establishment. This would become even more apparent after the war, when the struggle to reorganize the American church took place, and disputes over the consecration of bishops raged.

Not only did Whitefield urge a change in doctrinal teaching, he attacked the very morality of local clergy. As he suggested in his dispute with Garden, he preached that his revival worshipers were likely more worthy of grace than their own local ministers.[9] In questioning the legitimacy of the Anglican leadership, Whitefield stoked the simmering discontent that many already fostered against British institutions. Even though he himself was ordained an Anglican and had sworn allegiance to church leaders, Whitefield attacked his own church without reservation. William Howland Kenney has written that Whitefield's assault was calculated to exploit already significant antiestablishment sentiment:

> Despite his actual willingness to cater to dissenter animosities, George Whitefield liked to profess a broadly latitudinarian piety, deploring the "bigotry" of allegiance to any one earthly institution. But even before his arrival in America in 1739, the colonial press had established that, according to Whitefield, the Anglican Church was worse than the least Protestant religious institution.[10]

So, not only did Whitefield challenge the cohesion of the religious community, he directly questioned the legitimacy of the clergy as spiritual leaders of their parishes. The very identities of their communities were at risk of unraveling. Alexander Garden, in the face of such challenges, was remarkably successful in holding his communion together. The danger of the revivalists' radical teachings was not Garden's only concern in the years just prior to Robert Smith's arrival in South Carolina. Garden also faced the intensifying uneasiness that accompanied the growth of the S.P.G. and its success in instructing slaves in the doctrine of salvation.

The religious instruction of slaves in South Carolina became a controversial issue as Garden's health and vigor declined. Garden, however, continued to promote the activities of the S.P.G.[11] For the slaves to be converted, thereby making their salvation possible, they had to be taught not necessarily to read but to understand and accept basic theological doctrine. Even those who supported slave conversion harbored racist—

---

9. Ibid., 337.

10. William Howland Kenney, "George Whitefield, Dissenter Priest of the Great Awakening, 1739–1741," *William and Mary Quarterly* 1 (January 1969): 78.

11. For a fuller explanation of the S.P.G. and Alexander Garden's activities in support of it, see *Publications of the Dalcho Historical Association of the Diocese of South Carolina* 2 (1953): 22–35.

albeit relatively benign—attitudes toward enslavement. This prejudice led to a sense of suspicion. William Knox, for example, who served the S.P.G., wrote in 1768,

> The dull stupidity of the Negroe leaves him without any desire for instruction. Whether the creator originally formed these black people a little lower than other men, or that they have lost their intellectual powers through disuse, I will not assume the province of determining; but certain it is, that a *new Negroe,* (as those lately imported from Africa are called,) is a complete definition of indolent stupidity, nor could a more forcible means than setting one of these creatures before him, as an example of man in a state of nature, *unbiassed* by revelation or education. Their stupidity does not, however, authorize us to consider them as beasts for our use, much less to deny them all knowledge of their common salvation.[12]

Certainly, Knox was no egalitarian. It is clear that he viewed the black man as inferior and saw the slaves' intellect to be less than that of other humans. He seemed to reject, however, the notion that whites, as a consequence, are entitled to keep blacks enslaved as beasts for purely selfish reasons or to deny them the riches of salvation.[13]

In that sense Knox's position was not totally reflective of most eighteenth-century American attitudes toward slaves. He was British but nonetheless generally held the pre-Revolutionary American outlook on the institution of slavery. Most proslavery rhetoric of the period cast the slave, as did Knox, as an unfortunate creature and less than capable of independence. It is easy, however, to discern the humanity that Knox recognized in the slave. Defenders of slavery at the time viewed masters as the patriarchal overseers of a plantation community—protectors of the vulnerable, providers for the helpless. Whether the reality came close to such benevolence did not change the nature of their rhetoric. This perspective led inevitably to a desire to educate slaves in the gospels. From this perspective, slaveholders had a moral responsibility for the spiritual well-being of the slave.

Whitefield attempted to justify his own slaveholding with the same kind of rhetorical device. Despite Whitefield's stern condemnation of the mistreatment of slaves, which was published in 1740, he never condemned the practice of slaveholding, as did Jonathan Edwards and John Wesley. Just a few years later, Whitefield purchased slaves for his Bethesda School for Orphans in Georgia. He justified his acquisition by declaring, as did many southern slaveholders of the time, that the benefit of slavery was "to make their lives comfortable and to lay a foundation for breeding up their posterity."[14]

---

12. William Knox, *Three Tracts Respecting the Conversion and Instruction of the Free Indians and Negroe Slaves in the Colonies,* tract 2 (London: J. Debrett, 1769), 14–15.

13. Ibid., 15.

14. Whitefield, quoted in Alan Gallay, "The Origins of Slaveholder's Paternalism: George Whitefield, the Bryan Family, and the Great Awakening in the South," *Journal of Southern History* 53 (August 1987): 392.

As disingenuous as Whitefield's denials may have been, he rejected the notion that he had changed his position on slavery. He wrote, "I had no hand in bringing them into Georgia; though my judgement was for it. . . . let us reason no more about it, but diligently improve the present opportunity for their instruction."[15] In a more fully expositive statement about his views on slavery, Whitefield wrote directly to slaves in 1743:

> And though he [God] hath now called you into his *own Family,* to be his *own Children and Servants;* he doth not call you hereby from *the Service of your Masters according to the Flesh;* but to *serve him* in *serving them,* in obeying all their lawful Commands, and submitting to the *Yoke* his Providence has placed you under. And oh remember, it is CHRIST's *yoke now;* the Yoke that is put upon you by your REDEEMER's *Hand,* that his *Love,* his *Law,* calls you, binds you to wear. Oh *take it on you freely:* The *Love* of CHRIST will make it so *easy,* that it will not *hurt your Necks;* and by your chearful and constant *Obedience, put to Silence the Ignorance of foolish Men,* of your nominal *Christian Masters;* who having never felt the constraining Power of Christ's Love in their own Souls, have thought, and said, "That if you, their *poor Slaves,* were brought to *Christianity,* you would be no more *Servants to them.*" Oh never let this Calumny be cast upon Christ's Holy Religion, by the disagreeable Behaviour of any of you *believing Negroes!*[16]

Whitefield's rhetoric seemed to be rather benevolent toward blacks, although nonetheless supportive of their enslavement. More-explicitly racist rhetoric, so common in the nineteenth century, was not as prevalent in pre-Revolutionary South Carolina. It may have been because the eighteenth-century attitude toward slaves was more paternalistic than racist.

Nevertheless, opposition to the propagation of the gospel to the slaves began to grow as the S.P.G. and others started to succeed with their work. Knox recognized the objections and attempted to diffuse them. Even though Knox seemed uncomfortable with the continuation of slavery, he saved his most ardent rhetoric for his main purpose: to extend the opportunity for salvation to the slaves of America. He also took pains to support the paternalistic vision of the southern slaveholder. He admitted,

> It is a good speculative position, that no man ought to be bound by conditions to which he never personally consented, yet we shall find no government existing where the child would not be punished for refusing submission to the constitution handed down to him by his ancestors; and indeed the permanency of all government rests upon the acknowledged right in their past to decide the political condition of his offspring.[17]

15. Ibid.

16. Whitefield, *Letter to the Negroes,* in Stephen J. Stein, "George Whitefield on Slavery: Some New Evidence," *Church History* 42 (June 1973): 254.

17. Knox, *Three Tracts,* 20.

Knox believed and argued that, if slavery were to continue, then the instruction of the slave in matters necessary to bring them to redemption was essential. Knox recognized, "Our planters objections to their Negroes being instructed is simply this, that instruction renders them less fit or less willing to labour."[18] So, the S.P.G. that Smith inherited was a tangled problem for anyone without the great stature of a seasoned and respected cleric, such as Garden, who was able to diffuse major concerns about the S.P.G. Knox argued, as a matter of fact, that proper religious instruction would have to yield, to a degree, to the objections of the slaveholders:

> No planter is so grossly barbarous as not to wish to have his Negroes do his work with a good will; and very few would be so brutal or ignorant as not to perceive, that were their Negroes interested in religion, and taught to serve their masters for conscience sake, that they would be much better served by them; but it is surely the height of folly to expect of any owner of Negroes to permit them to be told, that he violates all divine and human laws by restraining them in his service or to allow them to have any notions of a religion, whose sanctions he must appear to them to condemn by making them his slaves. Until, therefore, the lawfulness of continuing these people in perpetual servitude be determined, it will be in vain to expect that our American planters will permit their Negroes to be instructed, much less contribute toward their instruction.[19]

It was the very success of the S.P.G. that was most alarming to many slaveholders. An incident not far from Charlestown, illustrates the problem. Hugh Bryan was a follower of George Whitefield and a slave owner who lived near Beaufort. A true believer, Bryan not only supported Whitefield's theological enthusiasm but also actively promoted religious instruction of slaves. Bryan's efforts to teach slaves brought stiff opposition from some of the neighboring planters. He was battered by criticism of his community and threatened by his government. An incident in 1740, however, convinced him that he was doing God's work. On November 18 a fire consumed more than three hundred buildings in Charlestown. The Reverend Josiah Smith proclaimed that such was the "Burning of Sodom."[20] Bryan was apparently convinced, for he redoubled his missionary efforts after the fire.

Bryan, whose brother John eventually became a neighbor of Robert Smith in Berkeley County, pursued his Christian-training program aggressively and did not escape notice of other slaveholders the colonial government. Many people believed that Bryan was not just educating his own slaves but gathering slaves from neighboring plantations. They were probably right. There was a growing fear—probably an overreaction—

18. Ibid., 15.
19. Ibid., 25.
20. Harvey Jackson, "Hugh Bryan and the Evangelical Movement in Colonial South Carolina," *William and Mary Quarterly* 43 (October 1986): 601.

that, instead of offering mere religious training, Bryan was promoting or encouraging insurrection.[21] In February 1742 the Commons House of Assembly passed a law providing that "however commendable" it may be to instruct slaves in "the Principles of Religion or Morality in their own Plantations," anyone who encouraged slaves "from different plantations" to congregate together should be punished for endangering the "Safety of the Province."[22]

Bryan became so aggressive in his teaching that fears continued to rise in response. He was a fugitive for a time, avoiding prosecution and the reaction of his neighbors. Harvey Jackson has written of the Bryan affair:

> Thus evangelicals found themselves fighting fears that their doctrine promised, or threatened, physical as well as spiritual freedom and were pressed to allay concerns that some in their movement might encourage slaves to hasten then process along. Seizing the initiative, the Anglican clergy and gentry closed ranks, hung the albatross of slave insurrection around the necks of Whitefield and his followers, and took much of the momentum away from the evangelical movement in South Carolina.[23]

Bryan's aggressiveness and persistence, coupled with the growing reach of the S.P.G., touched a discordant nerve among the planter class of the lowcountry. It was not such a leap to blame the S.P.G.—and by extension the Anglican leadership—for the dangers they saw in slave instruction. It was, after all, a point of agreement between Whitefield and Garden, the Anglican representative in the province. The fear fed an existing suspicion of the church. So, by the midpoint of the century, there was a growing distrust of church authority and institutions. The distrust was strong, based in theology, religious practice, and experience. Even before the confrontation with Britain began, the church's authority was beginning to weaken noticeably. This was the tense and suspicious atmosphere that greeted Smith as he disembarked at Charlestown.

The divisions that were beginning to become visible within the Anglican Church were being added to a clash with the theology, politics, and philosophy of the increasingly powerful backcountry. By the mid-1760s the underdeveloped reaches of the Carolina backcountry were characterized by a general lack of religious organization. What religion there was could be described as a collage of many sects, most of which were influenced by leaders outside the province. As a result, a significant difference in political perspective between the elite of Charlestown and backcountry inhabitants began to widen. According to Charles Woodmason, an Anglican itinerant preacher of the day, the most zealous and most oppositional sects of the upcountry were the

21. Gallay, "Slaveholder's Paternalism," 386.
22. Ibid.
23. Jackson, "Hugh Bryan," 612.

Anabaptists and the Presbyterians.[24] The Presbyterians, with their ministers being supplied by Scotland, were particularly influenced by "foreign" cultural values.[25] As a result, many of the religiously devout in the backcountry seemed to share more of New England's political views than those of the Charlestown aristocracy. This difference was an important obstacle later in achieving unity toward revolution.

It was not only religious and philosophical differences that seemed to drive a wedge between Charlestown and the less-developed country. Some viewed the Charlestown ruling class as being rather arrogant in treating the economic interests of backcountry planters and merchants. Woodmason reported that, because backcountry inhabitants had no choice but to travel to Charlestown with their goods, the aristocracy there showed no interest in improving their ability to do so, assuming that they would fend for themselves:

> At least in the Back Country without Law, Gospel, or the least Advantage, of Civil or Religious Life—No Churches, Ministers, Schools, Order, Discipline No Roads Cut—Bridges built—Causeys made for them—But Strangers and Pilgrims they must execute ev'ry thing themselves—The People below will do nought for them—All which is owing to this Circumstance—There is but one Good Harbour or Port in this Country—where the Merchants are fix'd—which is Charlestown—altho Port Royal is larger, deeper, and Safer—But it is too remote from the Back Country. Charlestown owes its Advantages, not to the Goodness of its Harbour, but its Centr[ali]ty to the Province, as being Equidistant from North Carolina on the one and Georgia on the other Side of it—This obliges the Back Country People to come to it—Not from Choice, but Necessity—Which the Charles Town Inhabitants are so sensible off That they will not mend a Road, or even a Bridge leading to the Metropolis for benefit of Commerce and Travellers but leave all things to be done by those who travel, as knowing that they must come to them for Goods and can go nowhere else—All things propos'd for the Good of the Back Settlers, has therefore all along met with the strongest Opposition from the Inhabitants of Charlestown.[26]

Thus, simmering discontent and potential divisions existed not only within the Anglican community but also between the regions and the social classes of the province. Whether Smith knew, or could have known, of the importance that these divisions would have just a few years later, is impossible to determine, but he surely could have observed at least some of the more palpable disputes soon after he arrived. They should have concerned him.

---

24. Charles Woodmason, *The Carolina Backcountry on the Eve of the Revolution,* ed. Richard Hooker (Chapel Hill: University of North Carolina Press, 1953), 80.
25. Ibid., 74.
26. Ibid., 239–40.

The Early Years

When he arrived in Charlestown, Robert Smith was a young priest, barely twenty-four years of age. He had been born in Worstead Parish, County Norfolk, England, on August 25, 1732, to Stephen Smith and the former Hannah Press. The Smith family of Norfolk was not wealthy. Stephen Smith was a grazier and likely lived modestly at best. He was, however, able to provide a living for his family, which included two sons, Robert and Press.

Robert Smith's education was most likely typical for the area. He attended Norwich Grammar School, studying under Timothy Bullimer. Smith apparently impressed those around him, because at the age of eighteen he began studies at Caius and Gonville College, Cambridge, under a subsidy recommended by William Mason, M.P.[27] He graduated in 1754 and was appointed a fellow the following year. He continued to reside in Cambridge after graduation and prepared for the life of an Anglican minister. He was ordained a deacon on March 7, 1756, and as a priest the following December by the bishop of Ely, Matthias Mawson. Again on a recommendation by William Mason, he was appointed assistant minister at St. Philip's Church in Charlestown, South Carolina. As he sailed toward the colonies, Smith was facing his first appointment as a minister in an unfamiliar community with unfamiliar customs.

Thanks to Garden's leadership, Smith found the state of the Anglican Communion in South Carolina strong and dynamic, if a bit uneasy. The establishment church was growing within an atmosphere of dynamic dissension and, although uncertainty was high, it must have been an exciting time for the young cleric. The emotions and controversies that had been created by the revivals of twenty years earlier were still surely felt, but probably less keenly, and the antiestablishment attitude was growing but not yet threatening the church. The congregation at St. Philip's included some of the most-prominent citizens of Charlestown. For example, there were the Draytons, Heywards, Laurenses, Manigaults, Middletons, Motteses, Pinckneys, and the Shubricks. All these families already had played, or would soon play, important roles in the history of South Carolina. When he faced the congregation that first Sunday, it is likely that he looked into the face of a twenty-year-old John Rutledge, who eventually became the first governor of the State of South Carolina. Indeed, the number of community and colonial leaders, military officers, and all manner of social elite whom Smith found in the pews of his new church was rivaled only by St. Michael's.

The theological and philosophical remnants of the revivalist controversies still lingered, and Smith found the Anglican community somewhat divided on the validity of the charges that Whitefield had leveled against his church and torn between the rituals of the establishment and the enthusiasm of the revivalists. While some agreed with both Whitefield's theology and his enthusiasm, others admired his fervent faith but dismissed

---

27. *Dictionary of American Biography* (New York: Scribners, 1936), 9:336.

his specific doctrinal positions. In the years since Whitefield's first visit to Charlestown and in the time since Alexander Garden's death, the emotions of the revivalist controversy had waned, but not the theological debate. It is undeniable that public sentiment toward disestablishment had never been greater. Garden had been able to keep it in check, but it was unclear whether it could continue to be constrained without Garden's able stewardship.

In the sixteen years that had intervened between the Whitefield-Garden dispute and Smith's arrival, emotions had subsided, but the theological debate had not been settled. Particularly in Charlestown, the doctrine of justification by faith and the implications that flowed from it were a divisive issue within the church. It continued to play a significant role in the history of pre-Revolutionary South Carolina.

Smith's first few years at St. Philip's are hard to re-create. It must have been a difficult task for such a young minister to adjust to a new church, perhaps the most important Anglican parish in the entire colony and certainly the largest. The evidence indicates that he took to his new community with relish and confidence. Within a year of Smith's arrival, he was offering lectures to the young men of Charlestown. A public notice published in the *South Carolina Gazette* described the lectures as being on moral and natural philosophy and offered three mornings a week.[28] His partner for this enterprise was the Reverend Charles Martyn. Martyn had arrived in Charlestown in 1752 as an S.P.G. missionary. He had been ordained a priest in 1748 and had become the rector of St. Andrew's Parish in 1753.[29]

Smith and Martyn promised the instruction to be "in such an easy and familiar Way as may serve both an Entertainment and Improvement."[30] We do not know how successful this offering was, or the precise nature of the curriculum. About this time Smith likely wrote a rather substantial study that he called "Observations on Nature," which included six sections, or "books," with several separate studies contained within each. The manuscript is included in the Smith Family Papers held by the South Carolina Historical Society, and its authorship has been attributed to Robert Smith. If Smith did write this work, it must have been written shortly after he arrived in Charlestown or not long before. It appears that the material in it might be consistent with the content of his lectures. Yet, there is an aspect of the manuscript that could raise doubts as to the attribution of authorship to Smith. In a closing paragraph of the section titled "On Education," the author speaks of disappointment. He apparently is "dejected" that he has not acquired a "rural spot" so that he could have composed his observations on nature there. He has "another source of regret," which is his "misfortune of not having

28. *South Carolina Gazette*, November 10, 1758.

29. Dalcho, *Protestant Episcopal Church*, 341.

30. *South Carolina Gazette*, November 10, 1758.

marked to his lot" a wife and children.[31] That would be an unusual statement by a man of just twenty-five (which was his age at marriage). However, the contents of the work, seem to be consistent with his views on nature and divine providence and the virtue that he articulated in his sermons. So despite the odd comment about marriage, the attribution of authorship of this manuscript to Smith may be valid.

Soon after the beginning of the lecture series, Smith became associated with a more-traditional school. In December 1760 the *Gazette* reported that the Provincial Free School, with Robert Smith and Gabriel Manigault as directors, had displayed its considerable merits to visitors.[32] The lectures, the composition of "Observations on Nature," and his directorship of the free school marked the beginning of Smith's life-long interest in education.

Since his arrival, Smith had served as the assistant to the rector, the Reverend Richard Clarke, who resigned in 1759. Smith was elected to replace him. In fewer than three years since his ordination, Smith assumed full responsibilities as rector. Speaking of the tremendous challenge Smith faced, Albert Sidney Thomas, a modern historian of the Episcopal Church, pointed out that "at a very early age he assumed a position of great responsibility as rector of the mother parish, and much the largest, of the colony."[33] Since Garden had not been replaced by another commissary, many of those responsibilities also fell to the rector of St. Philip's.[34] The spiritual health of the community that Smith had apparently found so inviting was now largely his responsibility. Even as capable as Smith seemed to be, he must have seen his new position as a daunting task.

If the year 1759 was an important one in Smith's professional life, the year before had marked the most important event in his personal life. On July 9, 1758, he married Elizabeth Paget, daughter of the late John Paget and the former Constantia Hassel. Elizabeth Paget was the heir to a large estate. Her mother had remarried and Elizabeth had title to her father's plantation, Brabant. John Paget had bequeathed to his only child about 3,600 acres with a rather large and handsome plantation house. It is not known how the couple met, but Thomas related a story about Elizabeth's first glimpse of Robert Smith: "A romantic story is told of his first landing in Charlestown. Robert Smith was a very handsome young man; and, as he walked along the Bay, Miss Paget saw him from her window, and then and there made up her mind that he was the man she wished to marry."[35] On their marriage Elizabeth deeded the plantation to her new husband. The Smiths now had a home in Charlestown and a country estate, which soon

31. Smith, "Observations on Nature" (n.d.), Smith Family Papers, South Carolina Historical Society, Charleston, S.C.

32. *South Carolina Gazette,* December 16, 1760.

33. Albert Sidney Thomas, "Robert Smith—First Bishop of South Carolina," *Historical Magazine of the Protestant Episcopal Church* 15 (March 1946): 16.

34. Ibid., 16–17.

35. Ibid., 17.

grew to about four thousand acres.[36] He began to spend time at Brabant whenever his duties at St. Philip's allowed it.

The acquisition of Brabant marked the unusual and unexpected elevation of Smith into the elite strata of Charlestown society. Before his marriage, he was becoming a prominent figure in the community, a budding spiritual leader to the privileged and powerful. After the acquisition of his country estate, he became a member of the landed elite. The son of a lowly grazier was now the master of one of the largest plantations in Berkeley County, the equal to any in his congregation, in both spiritual and material matters. He could relate to his congregation not only by participating in the activities of his community as a respected clergy and academician but by virtue of being one of them, a planter and a businessman.

The marriage also tied Smith to another extremely wealthy and influential family in the community. Elizabeth's great-uncle was Gabriel Manigault. By some accounts, Manigault was the wealthiest merchant in Charlestown. It has been reported that Manigault amassed more than eight hundred thousand dollars, an enormous fortune for the time.[37] He also owned the largest plantation, utilizing nearly three hundred slaves, in St. Thomas Parish, located not far from Brabant in Berkeley County. Manigault had served as treasurer of the Province of South Carolina and had represented the city in the Commons House of Assembly. During his early years in Charlestown, Smith managed not only to connect with his community but to become inextricably part of it. That intimate participation was important later as his loyalties and his patriotism were severely tested. Through his marriage, Smith also became related to another prominent family, the Ashbys. The marriage also fulfilled a personal longing for Smith.

In the first few years after he became rector, Smith dealt with the lingering problems of the S.P.G. and the education of slaves. As it had been in the final years of Commissary Garden's tenure, the S.P.G. was a thorny issue for Smith. It would have been so for any new clergy assuming the responsibilities that faced Smith. By 1762, however, it was clear that Smith had virtually abandoned the S.P.G. The lack of funding for missionaries, the growth of permanent parishes, and the controversial nature of its work had made the society difficult to justify any longer. There is evidence, however, that Smith continued to operate the "negroe school" within St. Philip's Parish that Garden had established and struggled hard to maintain. By allowing the S.P.G. to wither, Smith offered a gesture to those in his congregation who had reservations about its missionary reach. By continuing his commitment to the education of young slaves within the parish, he honored the memory and the nurturing idealism of Alexander Garden. Shortly afterward, however, in 1764, the school was closed because of lack of space and the want of qualified teachers.

---

36. Brabant eventually grew to more than six thousand acres by the time of Smith's death in 1801.
37. See http://www.famousamericans.net/gabrielmanigault/ (accessed April 27, 2005).

In 1762 Smith helped to form the Society for the Widows and Orphans of the Clergy of the Church of England. The first meeting of the society was held on April 21. There were eleven ministers in attendance: Alexander Garden (the commissary's nephew and rector of St. Thomas in Berkeley County), James Harrison, Robert Baron, Winwood Serjeant (rector of St. Georges in Dorchester County), Robert Smith, Albert Cooper, John Tonge, Abraham Imer, Joseph Dacre Wilton (assistant rector at St. Philip's), Joseph Stokes, and Offspring Pearce (rector of St. George in Winyah). They announced the purpose of the new society as follows:

> We the above taking into various considerations the distressed and melancholy situa-
> tion that Widows and Children are every day left in, particularly the Widows and
> Children of our deceased Brethren the Clergy of the Church of England, in Province
> of South Carolina and being moved with compassion as well as with a sense of our
> most holy Religion and the obligations we the undersigned do the exercise of Christ-
> ian Charity have agreed to enter into a Society to be hereafter forever called, *The
> Society for the Relief of the Widows and Children of the Clergy of the Church of England
> in the Province of South Carolina.* And for the better furthering the End & Design of
> this Society have agreed upon and signed a certain set of rules and orders.[38]

There is no evidence that Smith had any encouragement from the leaders of his church for this enterprise, and certainly he had no monetary subsidy from anyone as the new society was formed. In its early years the society floundered with barely enough money to justify its existence. From the beginning the younger Reverend Alexander Garden was an active member, providing a symbolic bridge from the church's past. Smith served as treasurer of the society from its inception until long after the Revolution. The establish-ment of this society was later recognized as perhaps the most noble charitable achieve-ment of Smith's professional life.

Sometime in late 1767 or early the following year, both Robert and Elizabeth fell ill. Apparently their conditions worsened, and Smith believed that a change of climate might prove curative. It was a reasonable assumption. About that time, a traveler to the city wrote of Charlestown's unhealthy climate: "There are but few country seats near the town, & many people move to considerable distances up into the country to spend the summer and avoid the intense heats & confin'd air of the town: the winds gener-ally blowing during the summer months from the south and S.W. from off the hot sands of Florida and Georgia are much warmer than the Westindia breezes which come from the sea."[39] Smith apparently decided that they could more easily recover abroad,

38. *Journal of the Proceedings of the Society for the Relief of the Widows and Orphans of the Clergy of the Church of England in the Province of South Carolina,* 2, online at http://www.clansinclair.org/society/journal/1762.htm (accessed February 12, 2005).

39. Pelatiah Webster, "Journal of a Voyage to Charlestown," ed. T. P. Harrison, *Publications of the Southern History Association* 2 (1898): 137.

and also wished to visit his aging and widowed mother one last time. He determined to ask the vestry for leave so he could visit England for a few months.[40] The vestry approved, and the couple sailed in mid-May 1768.[41]

While there, the Smiths recuperation did not require idleness. Indeed, he preached at least on several occasions in and around Bath, among other locations. He also acquired the appointment of an assistant rector for St. Philip's. The position became vacant as a result of an unusual and untimely departure and death of the previous assistant, the Reverend Crallan. Dalcho explained what happened:

> The Rev. Mr. Crallan resigned his office in St. Philip's Church April 25, 1768. He was occasionally deranged in his mind, and had made an attempt upon his life by throwing himself out of a window at the Rev. Mr. Smith's. On his passage to England, he threw himself overboard and was lost.[42]

Smith soon sent back the Reverend Robert Purcell to assume the duties of assistant rector. Smith decided that he and Elizabeth would remain in England longer than previously planned.

Instead of returning after a few months, Smith did not return to Charlestown for more than a year and a half. They sailed aboard the vessel *Nancy* and landed in Charlestown on December 29, 1769. The change of climate seems to have been beneficial.[43] On their return journey, the Smiths had shared passage with Charlestown merchant Samson Neyle and the Reverend James Pearce.[44]

Sadly, Elizabeth relapsed, and she died on June 11, 1771. The marriage had produced no children, and Robert Smith was alone again. Yet, he had charge of the most prestigious parish in the colony, had the growing respect of his community, and had ownership of Brabant. During the next few years his focus turned to the society he had founded. For the first few years of its operation, the society met but was unable to assist those in need because the treasury was anemic. In 1770 the society changed its rules and allowed membership to nonclergy. This important change not only allowed a new stream of support for the organization but "connected" the welfare of the clergy with the sensibilities of the secular community. Almost immediately there was a significant infusion of money into the society, and it began to grow. As Charlestown and South Carolina headed toward revolution, the society boasted membership of some of the most powerful men in the colony: Henry Middleton, John Huger, Charles Cotesworth

40. Thomas, "Robert Smith," 17. Smith's father died in 1763.

41. *South Carolina Gazette,* May 16, 1768.

42. Dalcho, *Protestant Episcopal Church,* 198–99.

43. Apparently, the community was aware that the Smiths had gone to England to recoup their health. On their return it was reported that all passengers were healthy. *South Carolina Gazette,* January 4, 1770.

44. Ibid.

Pinckney, William Gibbes, Hugh Rutledge, and Thomas Shubrick. Its new vitality and support from the community also helped the society to counter a strengthening anti-establishment impulse.

Smith also extended his reach into the society of Charlestown and of St. Thomas Parish, within the bounds of which Brabant was located. He became friends with Thomas Shubrick, an aging sea captain turned merchant, whose plantation was not far from Brabant and whose business was a short walk from Smith's study at St. Philip's. Thomas Shubrick was a towering figure in colonial Charlestown. Besides his substantial wealth and his successful businesses, he had served as fire master of Charlestown from 1748 to 1750; he had represented St. Philip's Parish in the assembly in the early 1760s; and he was the director of Cherokee Trade, 1762–64. He later served in the Second Provincial Congress, the Legislative Council, and the First General Assembly of South Carolina.

It was a fortunate friendship. On February 17, 1774, Robert Smith married Sally (Sarah), the daughter of Thomas Shubrick. The Shubrick union further established Smith's connection to his new community. Through his two marriages, Smith was now related to several of the most powerful and influential families in the colony: Pagets, Manigaults, Shubricks, Ashbys and Mottes, the family of Sally's mother.

As Smith and his new wife began their marriage, they were about to face what would be the most important time of their lives and a momentous era for South Carolina as well. Tensions between the colonies and Britain had been growing, and the uneasy peace that once favored Charlestown and much of South Carolina seemed to be on the verge of disintegrating into partisanship and division. Patriots and loyalists feared and suspected each other. Neighbor hesitated to trust neighbor, and even the religious institutions of the city could not be counted as sanctuaries from political intrigue.

From the moment he arrived in South Carolina and made an impression on the young Elizabeth Paget, Robert Smith began his journey to becoming an American. It was an unlikely journey. He was the product of a typical British upbringing and education. His ties to England were strong, and his commitment to the king and to the leadership of his church had been reinforced by his solemn and sacred oath of ordination. Even before the life-changing events of the Revolution, Smith had demonstrated that he was becoming more American than British.

Chapter 2

Unlikely Patriot

O N AUGUST 14, 1774, the assistant minister at St. Michael's, the Reverend
John Bullman, took his pulpit with a keen sense of anxiety. He was troubled by the tensions that were palpable in his community. To Bullman his
duty was to persuade his parishioners to calm their emotions and to step
away from the questions of government and politics, with which—in his opinion—
they had no business. He proclaimed, "To this duty of Peace making, it is highly requisite that we avoid pragmaticalness; that is, the needless intruding ourselves to meddle
with, and to pass our censures upon other men's business." The temper of the times, he
continued, led neighbor to oppose neighbor and in the process damaged the fabric of
the community. He complained that "we pry into our neighbour's secrets, that we may
censure and find fault, and are exceedingly rash and precipitate in passing our judge-
ments, and do not a little mischief by these uncharitable censures, exposing our neighbour to the contempt of others, and so, often injuring his interest and his reputation,
and sowing the seeds of lasting discourse and division." It must have been an unusual
service, to have a minister suggest that the unmistakable movement of a country
toward war was an enterprise that his congregants should not only refrain from dis-
cussing but also virtually ignore. He was not finished. The agitated spirit of the community, he complained, was so much the more dangerous,

> because it is commonly restrained within no bounds of decency, reason or religion;
> no sacredness of subject, no dignity of person, no want of Intelligence and due
> Information, no evil consequences of exposing authority, restrains persons of this
> pragmatical spirit, from pronouncing their opinions boldly of the greatest mysteries
> of Religion, of the most deliberate actions of the State, of the greatest secrets of War
> and Peace, of the fitness or unfitness of all persons in power and authority. In short,
> it is from this unhappy temper, that every idle Projector, who cannot, perhaps, govern
> his own household, or pay the debts of his own contracting, presumes he is qualified

to dictate how the State should be governed, and to point out means of paying the debts of a nation.[1]

This scolding lecture was not well received by the congregation. No one now knows who Bullman had in mind when he questioned the financial acumen of certain citizens. Within his congregation, after all, were some of the most-successful businessmen of the province. It was an odd argument to make in that particular parish, and the vestry objected. To them, his attempt to persuade the congregation to refrain from politics had—more clearly than any words of the congregants—advocated a particular political position, and from the pulpit. Before the week had ended, the congregation had voted overwhelmingly to remove Mr. Bullman.[2] On August 18, the vestry dismissed him. While Bullman had his supporters, and some efforts were made to reinstate him, he never again served St. Michael's.

Winds of War

History is silent on Robert Smith's specific response to Bullman's sermon. Just five months later, however, on February 17, 1775, Smith addressed the Commons House of Assembly which had walked en masse to St. Philip's to hear Smith speak. The fact that they chose to come to him on a day they had designated for prayer, fasting, and humiliation, spoke volumes about their anticipation of his remarks.

Smith began his address by reminding the assembly that, regardless of the righteousness of their politics, Providence remains as their benefactor. He suggested:

> We form schemes of happiness, and deceive ourselves with a weak imagination of security, without ever taking God into the question; no wonder then if our hopes prove abortive, and the conceits of our vain minds end in disappointment and sorrow. For we are inclined to attribute our prosperity to the wisdom of our own councils, and the arm of our own flesh, we become forgetful of him from whom our strength and wisdom are derived; and are then betrayed into that fatal security, which ends in shame, in misery and ruin.[3]

In this sermon Smith gave sanction to the expected actions of the assembly in the just cause "in sole defense of undoubted rights." Unlike Bullman, however, Smith's address does not begin as accusatory. It does not put his hearers in a state of defensiveness, but of reflection. His rhetoric is not as much instructive as reverent. In a later passage Smith warned against arrogance in spirit or action: "God hath declared his power over, and

1. Frederick Dalcho, *An Historical Account of the Protestant Episcopal Church in South Carolina* (Charleston, 1820), 201–3.

2. There is some dispute as to how many parishioners finally voted to remove Bullman, but at no time did a majority wish to retain him. For a fuller discussion of this incident, see ibid., 203–7.

3. Robert Smith (1775), Smith Sermons Collection, St. Philip's Church, Charleston, S.C. (hereafter SSC).

government of the world; instructing us, that apart of his blessing, vain is the counsel and the help of man: that with it the most improbable means can administer happiness, and afford security." Fear God, he told them, "keep all his commandments always," and "it should be well with them, and their children forever."[4] The difference in Bullman's rhetoric and Smith's could scarcely be more divergent. The former is clear in denying his audience God's blessing if they fail to change course. The latter suggests that whether their efforts are worthy of God's blessing depends, not on man's specific schemes, but on his righteous conduct. In other words, neither side in the political battle necessarily will have God's approval. They must take care to check the arrogance of their actions.

The response to his address was quite different from the community's reaction to Bullman's months earlier. The assembly received his sermon with grateful praise. Later, he was cited by the assembly with these words:

> The readiness, Sir, with which you complied with the request of the people; and the suitable manner in which you acquitted yourself, carry the strongest evidence that, no illiberal, narrow principles influence your conduct, but, on the contrary, that you are actuated by a truly benevolent heart, and a real love of mankind; the good and welfare of whom, is the ultimate end of all institutions, religious as well as civil.[5]

By 1775 Smith had clearly decided his loyalties lay with his community and not with his king. This was a gradual and difficult transition for Smith, and we can, to some degree, follow it in the development of his sermons. The sermon he delivered to the assembly in February 1775 was closely modeled after a sermon he had composed fourteen years earlier. The revisions he made to the text of the later version are telling of his changing political perspectives or least of his growing sensitivity to the feelings of his congregation. The most significant difference in the two versions seems to be the absence in the latter of references to a duty to submit to one's superiors and to authority. In the 1761 version of the sermon, Smith wrote, "In acknowledging the absolute power of God, our dependence on his mercy; and unworthiness of it, we have acted a proper and becoming part; but let us remember this; that we have ill answered the intentions of our superiors, if we rest the duty here. . . ." In the sermon before the assembly, he replaced "answered the intentions of our superiors" with "answered the intentions of this public call." Later in the 1761 sermon, Smith identified several human shortcomings that have negative impacts on a society:

> We have many follies to restrain, many vices to subdue; and though there appears not that daring impiety of which some complain; yet the religion hath lost much of its force amongst us is very plain; from that disregard for worship, that contempt of

---

4. Ibid.
5. Dalcho, *Protestant Episcopal Church*, 219.

authority; that love of dissipation and of pleasure, and that dissoluteness of manner which is daily before us.[6]

In the 1775 version he revised the sentiments significantly:

Let us take this opportunity to begin our amendments, we have many follies to restrain, many vices to subdue; and though there appears not that daring impiety of which some complain; yet that religion has lost much of its force amongst us, is very evident: from that disregard of worship, that love of dissipation and of pleasure, and that dissoluteness of manners which is daily before us.[7]

Again, Smith excised the reference to rejection of authority. Given the political climate of the time and, especially, the audience hearing his message, it was a reasonable change. That Smith's political views were sincere is hardly arguable, but the adaptations for the 1775 version of the sermon illustrate the extent of the transformation in his political beliefs. As hostilities became inevitable, hardly anyone in Charlestown could remain neutral. The decision that almost everyone faced was difficult. For those such as Smith, born in England and owing his position to the king, it must have been a tortured choice.

On the one hand, Robert Smith was British by birth. He owed the government, through its subsidy, for his Cambridge education. He even owed William Mason for his appointment at St. Philip's, a position through which he was able to acquire his fortune and his family. He had sworn a solemn oath of allegiance to the king and a sacred pledge to his church. It was an oath that Smith could not have taken lightly.

On the other hand, in the sixteen years he had been in Charlestown, he had become one with his community. He had become related through marriage to the very leaders he would have to oppose if he decided to honor his oath of ordination. He had relied spiritually and materially on his American neighbors and now had an American family. In fact, his marriage to Elizabeth had filled a personal void in his life. He had felt the support and the comfort of his congregation when he buried Elizabeth four years before. He had rejoiced in his community's enthusiasm when he had married Sally the previous winter.

The choice he faced was between an institution and a monarchy to which he had undeniable legal obligations and a community and a family to which he owed an inescapable moral debt. For Robert Smith the choice was inevitable and not really ever in doubt. He chose his community, his wife, and his family. He chose to violate his oath of ordination. Even though it was a clear choice, it could not have been made without agony. In a way the choice that confronted Smith was faced by many others in the colony. It was a reflection of one difficulty that many had in coming to terms with the war.

6. Smith (1761), SSC.
7. Smith (1775), SSC.

In his address to the assembly, Smith gave support for the revolutionaries but urged them to look to God, not to man, as their eventual benefactor. Smith knew that the road ahead would be difficult. He sensed that the difficulties facing them were more dire than anyone could predict. He knew that the coming war could end in catastrophe for him and for his community.

As an indication of the esteem in which his neighbors held him, Smith was elected to represent St. Thomas Parish (where Brabant was located) in the Second Provincial Congress in 1775. He did not take his seat, giving it up to devote all his energy to his ecclesiastical duties. He was elected again, however, to fill a vacant seat from St. Thomas in September 1776. The Second Provincial Congress was then sworn in and became the First General Assembly of South Carolina. So, after addressing the assembly in February of 1775, he took a seat among them the following year.[8]

The situation festered during the ensuing year. British troops were massing for an invasion of South Carolina, and most predicted that it would come from the sea. As the provincial army raced to complete the fortifications at Fort Sullivan, the British were preparing for their attack. After the fateful confrontation, Smith gave his Sunday sermon and praised the defenders at Fort Sullivan. Before that sermon, however, Smith was among the enlisted privates defending the fort. He had not only lent rhetorical commitment to the patriots' cause, he had taken up arms and actively participated in his community's defense. He must have had reservations about going to battle against his native country, but he surely had no reservations about defending his home and his family.

The attack on Fort Sullivan had made the conflict—and the choice—more than simply a political dispute. Ten of their own had died. Smith had supported them with his prayers, and he had joined them in battle. He had seen not only the duty to pronounce his patriotism but also the necessity to claim it through action—direct participation in his community. He was not so much motivated by politics—because he most likely disagreed with the politics of the New England revolutionaries—as by the duty to act in defense of his community. Long after the war, Alexander Garden wrote of Smith's courage in battle at Fort Sullivan: "The late Bishop Smith shouldered his musket, and amidst scenes of the greatest danger, both by precept and by example, stimulated to intrepid resistance."[9]

Smith did not remain a regular soldier for long. He was quickly made chaplain of an artillery company. Later he served as chaplain of the First South Carolina Regiment.

---

8. *Journals of the General Assembly and House of Representatives 1776–1780,* edited by William Edwin Hemphill, Wylma Anne Wates, and R. Nicholas Olsberg (Columbia: University of South Carolina Press, 1970), 59–60, 301–7.

9. Alexander Garden, *Anecdotes of the Revolutionary War in America* (Charleston: A. E. Miller, 1822), 199.

He also served as chaplain of the Continental hospital in Charlestown. For a time he served the hospital without commission and without pay. He received his commission in 1779 as chaplain-general of the Southern Department of the Continental Army. During the early years of the war, Robert Smith certainly established himself as a patriot and further endeared himself to his community.

Unfortunately, personal tragedy again visited Smith. On July 7, 1779, Sally died after only five years of marriage. Smith was left with the responsibilities of St. Philip's, the duties of chaplain-general during wartime, and a three-year-old daughter, Sarah. The grief and the pressure must have been enormous.

Imprisonment, Banishment, and Separation

As 1780 approached, the war was not going well for the Americans in South Carolina. The fall of Charlestown was imminent. In May the city fell to the British, and the citizens of the city were subjected to rather stringent rules of occupation. Although technically the entire state was under British control, their hold on Charlestown was especially onerous. Walter Edgar has described the occupation this way:

> In occupied Charleston the British did not establish civilian government, although Lt. Gov. William Bull and other former royal officials had returned. The military commandants of Charleston appointed a Board of Police (mostly former royal officials) to perform quasi-judicial functions and give them advice. The board's authority was unclear, and before the end of the occupation many of its actions had been undercut by British officials. In the eyes of South Carolina patriots, its members were collaborators who were involved with the implementation of a variety of punitive actions.[10]

As the occupation there took hold, General Charles Cornwallis, who had taken over from General Horatio Gates, issued a list of patriot property to be seized. Brabant was near the top of the list. The property was quickly taken, and its contents were appropriated or sold. We know, in some detail, the totality of Smith's property loss because shortly after Smith returned to Charlestown the following public notice appeared in the *Gazette:*

> When the subscriber's estate was sequestered, and himself and Child exil'd by Cornwallis, Balfour, and adherents, his Household Furniture, consisting of bedsteads, feather beds, mattrasses, mahogany dining, sideboard, breakfast, tea, dressing, and night tables, wash-stands, chairs, dressing-glasses, small pier, and a remarkable octagon inlaid frame looking-glass; blue and white table china, glass ware, fire dogs, shovels and tongs, kitchen furniture of all Sorts, &c., &c., was made use of, or lent out by British commissioner, John Cruden, and as few of the above articles have been

---

10. Walter Edgar, *South Carolina: A History* (Columbia: University of South Carolina Press, 1998), 237.

recovered he requests all persons having furniture, &c., left in their houses by the British, to inform him thereof, or those who have purchased, to inform him of who purchased.[11]

Cornwallis used Brabant as a headquarters for a time. Once the occupation was underway, the British sought to fortify their position. While the British were headquartered at Brabant, they heard that Smith's overseer, an Irish immigrant named Mauder, had hidden the silver from St. Philip's and Brabant somewhere on the property for safekeeping. The British were keen on seizing anything of value to help finance their operation. In an attempt to intimidate Mauder into disclosing the location, they hanged him from a large tree. Mauder resisted, even after three hanging attempts by his tormentors. They never found the hidden valuables, and Mauder survived the ordeal.[12]

Apparently, the British attempted to send Smith to St. Augustine with other prisoners. Only the intervention of General William Moultrie prevented his transfer. A congressional document outlining Smith's service puts it this way:

That your memorialist was in Charleston during the siege of that place and confined there after the capitulation in May 1780, contrary to the repeated efforts of the British to send your memorialist to Augustine which was only prevented by the spirited remonstrances of General Moultrie, that your memorialist continued doing duty in the Hospital till such time as the Continental Soldiers were diminished in number by death, and enlistment into British Regiments.[13]

Not only did Smith lose his property, but he was imprisoned along with other Continental officers. He was kept under constant guard while in Charlestown. It appears that Smith's outspoken and eloquent support for the American cause was viewed as particularly dangerous by the British occupation forces. Despite Smith's betrayal, however, he was given an opportunity to regain his freedom. He was offered release if he took an oath of loyalty to the crown. He could regain his freedom, his pulpit, and his property, but he refused, declaring, "Rather would I be hanged by the King of England than go off and hang myself in shame and despair like Judas."[14]

In mid-April Smith joined other Continental officers who had been detained and taken to Haddrel's Point, located near what is now Mount Pleasant. They remained there until June 1781, when they were transported to Philadelphia. In the span of a few months, Smith had lost his wife to death and his pulpit and his fortune to the British. In what must have been especially galling for Smith, the Church of England assigned the Reverend Robert Cooper, the previously dismissed loyalist, to assume Smith's position

11. *South Carolina Gazette,* July 12, 1783.

12. For a more complete discussion of this incident, see Henry A. M. Smith, *The Baronies of South Carolina,* 3 vols. (Spartanburg, S.C.: Rupert, 1988), 1:178–80.

13. Smith Family Papers, South Carolina Historical Society, Charleston, S.C.

14. *Dictionary of American Biography* (New York: Scribners, 1936), 9:336.

at St. Philip's. What happened to Smith's daughter, Sarah, during his imprisonment at Haddrel's Point is unknown. It is likely that she was left in the care of Sally's family, the Shubricks. Sarah apparently accompanied Smith to Philadelphia.

Evidence suggests that Smith stayed in Philadelphia a short time, perhaps a few months. His banishment could not have been easy, being separated as he was from his home and family. He could not move freely about the city as he was technically a parolee and was required to remain close to the British compound. In 1782 he was released from parole and began to venture into the city, at least once delivering a sermon at Christ Church and another at St. Peter's. Soon he met others and forged new friendships. One such person was the widely respected Edward Tilghman. The Tilghman family had come from Maryland, where Edward had been a member of the Maryland Assembly and its speaker. He had also served in the militia as a colonel. Edward's son, also named Edward, was a leading lawyer in Philadelphia. The elder Tilghman's wife, Elizabeth, was the daughter of the equally distinguished Benjamin Chew. Smith eventually met Anna Maria Goldsborough, daughter of Edward and Elizabeth Tilghman and the young widow of Charles Goldsborough.

Robert Smith and Elizabeth Goldsborough were married in Philadelphia sometime in 1782. Most likely through the assistance of the Tilghmans, Smith received an appointment to serve as rector of St. Paul's Parish in Queen Anne County, Maryland. Although he served the church only a short time, probably less than a year, he made a positive mark on his parishioners. The following letter was written by the vestry on their learning of his impending return home:

Rev. Smith,

Your obliging letter of the 8th ultimate was handed to us by Mr. Earle. We sincerely congratulate you on the important event of the evacuation of Charles Town and truly lament that the deranged situation of your affairs there makes it indespensably necessary for you to leave this Parish. You have our grateful thanks for your affectionate respectful behavior to the good people of this Parish during your residence among them and the painful regret you express at being obliged to leave them. You have our unfeigned wishes and we persuade ourselves of every Parishioner that your journey to your long wished for home may be agreeable and that you may find your own private concerns and those of the State of South Carolina in a better situation than from the Horrors and calamities of war you have a right to expect. Accept our acknowledgements for your assiduity and care in discharging the Duties of your office during your residence here. We have already set to work at shall use our utmost endeavors to collect all we can from our parishioners to compensate you for the essential services you have rendered to the Parish. Believe us to be with the greatest esteem and respect. BJ Earle, Ant. Emory Jun., Thomas Emory of Arthur, J Gibson. Vestrymen of St. Paul's Parish in Queen Anne's County, Maryland, March 3, 1783.[15]

15. Smith Family Papers, South Carolina Historical Society, Charleston, S.C.

By June 1, 1783, Smith had returned to Charleston.[16] On that date he gave a home-coming sermon. He had given the same sermon the year before in Philadelphia's Christ Church, not long after he had been released from parole and shortly before accepting the appointment as rector of St. Paul's. The sermon suggested the connection between righteousness and prosperity not of self but of society. He stressed the importance of religion and to society:

> By righteousness in this place, must be signified a due sense of the religion; that is, an acknowledgement of an overruling Providence, the Rewarder of good men and the Punisher of the evil. If the words of the text be thus explained and understood; the subject naturally resulting from them will be the importance of religion to society. [17]

Just as he had in his address before the Commons House of Assembly, seven years earlier, Smith admonishes his hearers not to depend on the success of human labor, but on God's grace:

> In the first rudiments indeed of civil society, if the expression may be allowed, open and intended violence, when apparently so, may be restrained; the insolent may be quelled, and the outrageous crushed. But this is by no means sufficient to secure the safety of any community whatever. For in time, fraud and artifice will take place in place of open and avowed violence, and whatever mischievous designs, though carried on in secret, though attended with the utmost danger to society, may not only escape public opposition, but even public observation. For it is certain, there is a great weakness and inefficacy in every human society simply and abstractedly considered. For strip it of its dependencies on matters which at first may seem foreign to it and it will be found hardly equal to the task of enforcing an obedience to the moral duties.[18]

For his first sermon back at St. Philip's, Smith chose not to speak of the victory of the Americans in the war, not to lament the cruelties the British occupation visited on the city or himself, and not to take for granted the praise of his friends, but to warn his congregation of the necessity to place all their victories and their wounds into perspective. Just as he had before the war began, he wanted to fix his hearers attention on the power of Providence and the importance of the community, not on their own affairs.

Anna and Robert had two sons, Robert (born in 1783) and William Mason (born in 1784), and a daughter, who did not survive infancy. At the age of fifty Robert Smith was back home with his family and in the loving embrace of his community. He once again assumed the pulpit at St. Philip's. His homecoming sermon was a powerful statement of his views on the necessity of maintaining a righteous community. His insistence

16. After 1783 the city was known as Charleston rather than the colonial name of Charlestown.
17. Smith (1782), SSC.
18. Ibid.

on the importance of community was not simply a rhetorical device, it was a fundamental aspect of his theology. The persistence of his reference to community is the thread that constructs his justification for the Revolution.

Return, Readjustment, and Rededication

It did not take long for Smith to come face to face with the difficulties of his position. The war had devastated the state of South Carolina. Since disestablishment in 1778, the church was no longer being subsidized by the state, and the attention to the internal affairs of the church and even the maintenance of the buildings had to be set aside for a time.

It was not long before the reorganization of the American church was urged by the leaders in almost all parts of the country. The differences, particularly regional ones, soon led to a crisis. In 1784 a group of representatives from Connecticut, Massachusetts, and Rhode Island led the opposition to a reorganization plan suggested principally by the southern states. The southern regional representatives believed fervently that the selection of bishops should be tied directly to the approval of the state conventions with the active participation of the laity. The distrust the southern laity harbored against the leadership of the church had lingered from the early days of the S.P.G., and they wanted to be certain that any new organization would recognize the prerogatives of the nonclergy. Some representatives of the northern colonies—the above-mentioned three most aggressively—opposed any control by the laity of the episcopate. This objective has been explained by Robert Prichard:

> Representatives from Connecticut, Massachusetts and Rhode Island had attended the organizational meetings in 1784, but they did not attend the general convention of 1785 or 1786. They objected in principle to the approach taken by the clergy of the middle and southern states, drawing on Anglican covenant arguments that S.P.G. missionaries had been advancing in New England for three-quarters of a century, they believed that the churches essential nature came from the historic episcopate and not from the voluntary association of clergy and laity.[19]

The dissenting northern representatives refused to participate in the conventions of 1785 and 1786 and, instead, selected one of their own, Samuel Seabury, to become bishop. He sailed for England for ordination. The church leaders in London, however, refused to endorse the election. He then traveled to Scotland and was consecrated by bishops of the church there, with the stipulation that he maintain the doctrine of complete separation of the episcopate and the laity. This, of course, was unacceptable to the southern representatives.

---

19. Robert W. Prichard, *A History of the Episcopal Church* (Harrisburg, Pa.: Morehouse, 1991), 87.

At the convention of 1786, opponents of Bishop Seabury, led by Robert Smith, tried to pass a resolution rejecting the validity of Seabury's consecration.[20] William Manross reported Smith's attempts to invalidate Seabury's elevation at the 1786 convention:

> The motions for this purpose were made by the Rev. Robert Smith of South Carolina and were supported by South Carolina, New York and New Jersey. The first motion was to require the clergy present to show their letters of orders or tell by whom they were ordained, the object being to challenge those ordained by Seabury. Debate on this proposal was shut off by a moving of the previous question by William Smith, seconded by White, and the motion was defeated.[21]

Eventually a compromise was struck whereby Seabury kept his position, but individual state conventions retained the freedom to refuse acceptance into their jurisdiction of individual bishops who had not been ordained in a manner acceptable to that particular convention.[22] The major problem with Seabury's consecration, as far as the southern representatives were concerned, was that the agreement Seabury had made with the Scottish bishops placed bishops completely beyond the control of the laity.

Pritchard noted that the southern states were also interested in changing some of the order of worship. That also was opposed by other state representatives. According to Pritchard,

> The participants in the middle and southern states' conventions were attempting to deemphasize some of the distinctive elements of their tradition. Elements that they dropped from the *Proposed Book,* such as the Athanasian Creed, the word *priest,* and the use of *regeneration* to refer to baptism, were unfamiliar to most other American Protestants. In New England Seabury followed the opposite course. The presence of a bishop enabled New England Anglicans to develop their covenant theology in ways that further distinguished them from the Congregational establishment.[23]

Clearly the theological disputes that generated the clash between the revivalists and the conservatives more than a generation earlier were still being felt. In many ways the dispute would not be much diminished in the lifetime of Robert Smith.

As the decade of the 1780s came to a close, many questions remained for the church, and the aging Robert Smith was struggling to return to his routine as rector of St. Philip's. He turned his attention to other matters, such as his love of education. Now that the war was over, he had an opportunity to devote more time to it.

---

20. William Wilson Manross, *A History of the American Episcopal Church* (New York: Morehouse-Gorham, 1959), 197.

21. Ibid.

22. Ibid.

23. Prichard, *Episcopal Church,* 89.

The Later Years

Smith had long expressed an interest in education. His public lectures, his writing on natural philosophy, and his early involvement with the Provincial Free School were precursors to his commitment to the establishment of a college in Charleston. Although many others deserve credit as well, it was Smith's leadership, vision, and resources that made it a reality. What later became the College of Charleston was established by an act of the General Assembly on March 19, 1785. While his elevation to bishop has been cited as his most notable professional achievement, Smith's participation in the founding of the College of Charleston represents his most enduring legacy.

By most accounts, the forerunner of the College of Charleston was the Charlestown Library Society, established in 1748. The original purpose of the society was to encourage reading as a recreational pursuit.[24] The society apparently grew in popularity and held many public exhibitions. Later, the society enlarged its purpose to include promoting the study of science, even sponsoring William Johnson's exhibit of electrical experiments.[25] It was widely known as a cultural center and attracted the support of some of the most prominent men of the area.

Eventually, as the society grew, its scope of interests and its ambition grew as well. The society announced in 1759 that it intended to examine the prospects for the establishment of an academy and appointed a committee to report after careful study.[26] The committee responded quickly but concluded that the cost of such a venture outstripped the resources of the organization. The idea was abandoned.

The goal of establishing a provincial college remained alive, however, and several attempts were made to persuade the assembly to subsidize such an institution. An essay that appeared in the *South Carolina Gazette* on November 9, 1769, outlined one resident's justification for a state academy:

> At a time when a general plan of economy is promoted for the benefit of a community and every person in it, is giving or wishing to give, assistance for the prosecution of a system which, in its nature, must be replete with divers great advantages to individuals as well as the public. I take leave to point out one branch of economy which I think is necessary to be practiced in this flourishing colony. I am induced to point out at this juncture, because as we are prosecuting an economic plan, I think it is the duty of every one to endeavor to contribute something to make that plan as complete as the nature of it will permit. To enlighten the mind of man, and free it from the thick mists of native ignorance, is the greatest and best work, which human nature is capable of performing. It is this enlargement from darkness, which enables her to

---

24. J. H. Easterby, *A History of the College of Charleston* (Charleston, 1935), 4–5.
25. Ibid., 4.
26. Ibid., 5–6.

discern the dignity of her nature, and to possess a faint idea of the sacred majesty of her Creator![27]

If it were not known that Robert Smith was still abroad at the time the essay appeared, one could easily ascribe the sentiments expressed in it to him. The anonymous writer connected education to the prosperity of the province and to religion as a justification of official sanction. The mechanism to achieve the fulfillment of this ideal was the establishment of a provincial college. The essayist wrote,

> Many parents in this country, has so far done their duty as to have sent their children abroad for an education, which they could not have received at home. And of course large sums, very large sums of money have been and are actually remitted to maintain them, which in effect is so much money lost to the province. The Northern colonies for some time, used the same practice, but some of them have prudently discontinued the custom, and have had their youth as well instructed in their colleges at home, as they could have been in colleges abroad. Besides that their present mode of education is attended with more satisfaction, and less expense to the parties, and but little charge to the province. Why cannot we imitate so successful an example?[28]

Public support for such a college grew, and on January 30, 1770, Lieutenant Governor William Bull recommended to the assembly the establishment of a provincial college. It was finally approved. The plan for the college approved by the assembly called for a president drawn from the clergy of the Church of England and instruction in divinity, moral philosophy, Greek, Hebrew, civil and common law, physics, anatomy, botany, natural and experimental philosophy, history, and modern languages. The institution was to be known as the College of South Carolina.[29]

The first meeting of the trustees occurred on August 26, 1785. They included many of the most respected and the most powerful men of the city. They were John Lloyd, Daniel DeSaussure, David Bordeaux, Dr. David Oliphant, Arnoldus Vander Horst (governor, 1794–96), Joseph Atkinson, John Rutledge (governor, 1776–78), John Mathews (governor, 1782–83), Richard Hutson, Thomas Heyward Jr., Thomas Bee, Dr. David Ramsey, Arthur Middleton, Gabriel Manigault, Ralph Izard, William Loughton Smith, Charles Pinckney (governor, 1789–92), Richard Beresford, Charles Cotesworth Pinckney, Hugh Rutledge, and the Reverend Robert Smith.[30] Those who served on the first board were also, for the most part, members of the Library Society and had served the American cause in the war. Some had been trustees or directors of the Provincial Free School, and others had been instrumental in the formation of the Library Society. Still

27. *South Carolina Gazette,* November 9, 1769.
28. Ibid.
29. Easterby, *College of Charleston,* 12.
30. Ibid., 20.

others had been active members of the Society for Widows and Orphans. Four had been or later became governors of the State of South Carolina.

The board did not meet again until February 6, 1786. At that meeting Robert Smith was elected the first president of the board of trustees. Having been established, the college needed impetus to become a functioning reality. Although the board did not meet again for four years, Robert Smith was not idle. In 1789 he received a doctor of divinity degree from the University of Pennsylvania. He was also busy establishing an academy of his own, appealing to students younger than college age. J. H. Easterby has suggested that Smith surreptitiously created the academy or at least worked beyond the notice of the trustees:

> Meanwhile, though the fact seems not to have been recognized by anyone at the time, there was being brought together through the efforts of President Robert Smith a body of teachers and students who were to form the first College classes. With the idea of supplying in some measure the place of schools which had been forced to close during the war, Doctor Smith had undertaken to conduct an academy for the instruction of youth. . . . The school was opened July 3, 1785, and met with immediate success, being resorted to by parents of all ranks and condition in life.[31]

Smith operated this new academy out of the parsonage of St. Philip's. Easterby has reported that on March 14, 1789, steps were taken to join the academy with the college. The merger took place officially on January 1, 1790, and the College of Charleston had its first students, about sixty in number. With actual students now enrolled, Smith became, in addition to president of the trustees, the principal of the college.

Students were moved into buildings that had been used as barracks for soldiers during the war. Plans were made to erect new buildings, and the movement toward operation of the college gained momentum. Without Smith's vision and the single-minded efforts, the college might not have commenced operation as soon as it did.

After a brief period of operation, it became apparent that the barracks buildings were not sufficiently functional, or in sufficient repair, to serve the students adequately. It was decided that the facilities would have to be enlarged and refurbished. The treasury of the college, however, was inadequate to meet the costs of the renovation. Nonetheless, Smith and a contractor, a Mr. Cannon, devised a plan for the renovation of the buildings. Smith agreed to pay for some of the materials and for the brickwork. Cannon agreed to accept a bond from the trustees for the rest. In the end, Smith also insisted that the roof be replaced at his expense. The cost of the project exceeded ten thousand dollars with most if not all, coming from Smith's personal resources.[32]

As he was beginning to become involved in educational administration, tragedy battered Smith for the third time. On December 6, 1792, Anna died at Brabant. Later the

---

31. Ibid., 27.
32. Ibid., 29.

same month, Smith's infant daughter also died. The deaths must have left him with deep wounds, but he persevered and was surely kept busy by his many responsibilities.

The controversy that swirled around the consecration of bishops—the elevation of Samuel Seabury in particular—and the regional divide that had existed over the power of the laity was much less contentious by the early 1790s. Passions had subsided, but the dispute had not been resolved. Ultimately the question arose about the appointment of a bishop for the state of South Carolina. Even within the state delegation, unanimity could not be achieved. The relative powers of the laity and the bishop were again the point of greatest tension. As one recent history of the Episcopal Church in South Carolina reports:

> On October 16, 1794, when the subject of giving bishops an absolute negative or veto on the proceedings of the clergy and laity in General Convention, came before the Diocesan Convention, the unanimous opinion of the convention was that no such power should be granted. Feelings grew very strong. It was even suggested that schism might follow and, therefore, immediate action should be taken to secure the consecration of a bishop that the Church in South Carolina be not left without power to ordain much-needed clergymen and to confirm.[33]

The state of South Carolina, therefore, would not be left without power within the larger church structure.

On February 10, 1795, Robert Smith was unanimously elected the first bishop of the Diocese of South Carolina. In September, at the following General Convention, which was held in Philadelphia, Smith was consecrated. The consecration took place at Christ Church, the same church he had blessed with a sermon during his banishment thirteen years earlier. Smith served as South Carolina's bishop until his death in 1801.

The task of its first bishop was made more difficult by South Carolina's inherent distrust of church hierarchy and official authority in general. Some still viewed the church as a vestige of British oppression. Smith's prelacy has been summarized by Bishop Howe as mainly an attempt to heal suspicions and divisions:

> And when the honor of the first episcopate did come to him in 1795, I seem to see, in Bishop Smith's after-administration of the diocese, a care, first of all, to remove prejudices against the episcopate. Knowing these prejudices in the minds of his people against "My Lord Bishop" he kept "My Lord" out of sight altogether, and let the bishop appear only on rare occasions. Probably he was too considerate of popular prejudices. I have turned the leaves of the Episcopal register back to Bishop Smith's day, and find no record of visitations, or of confirmations in the six years of his episcopate. Eleven ordinations are carefully recorded of names by tradition only—that is

33. "A Short History of the Diocese of South Carolina," in *Publications of the Dalcho Historical Society of the Diocese of South Carolina* 2 (1953): 50–51.

all. If South Carolina had a resident bishop he did not obtrude himself or his prelacy upon her.[34]

Bishop Howe's assessment that Smith was perhaps too sensitive to the prejudices of the community disregards at once the depth of feelings in Charleston against absolute authority and the extent to which Smith was integrated into the life pulse of his community.

Robert Smith had distinguished himself as a leader of his church and as a leader of his community. He had proven that his neighbors and his congregation could depend on him to support and protect them. There is less evidence to draw conclusions about his personal life. There are two glimpses we have into it, however.

The first relates to his relationship with his brother, Press. In an undated letter, Smith responded to what was obviously a request from Press for some financial assistance. Smith wrote of his heartfelt emotions concerning Press's problems. He then explained that the only solution to his brother's predicament appeared to be the sale of some of the inherited land that was in his possession. Robert then clearly refused to send his brother any money, explaining he had already loaned him money that had not been repaid.[35] There is no further evidence indicating the outcome of this particular incident. In Robert Smith's will, however, he indicated that he still respected Press and released him from his previous debt (in the amount of about four hundred pounds). He also appointed his brother as one of the executors and one of his son's guardians. Obviously, Smith's relationship with his brother was not overly sentimental but did not appear to be strained.

The same could be said of Smith's relationship with his sons. Both Robert and William Mason spent considerable time away from their father. They were only teenagers when their father died and had been away from Charleston at school since they were very young children.[36] In an undated letter written to one of his sons, Robert Smith reminded the recipient of the value of diligence in studies and seriousness in attitude. Before closing, however, he made the point that his words of caution were not meant to convey a lack of confidence or trust.[37] Again, Smith was not overly sentimental with his children, but clearly he was a loving and supportive parent.

Bishop Robert Smith died quietly at his home in Charleston on October 28, 1801. His obituary appeared in the *City Gazette and Advertiser* on November 3:

34. Ibid., 53.

35. Smith to Press Smith, undated letter, Smith Family Papers, South Carolina Historical Society, Charleston, S.C.

36. In the 1790 census, at which time Robert would have been seven and William Mason would have been six, they were not listed in the household.

37. Smith to his son, undated letter, Smith Family Papers, South Carolina Historical Society, Charleston, S.C.

Died on Wednesday afternoon, after a short illness, the Right Reverend Robert Smith, D.D., Bishop of the Episcopal Churches in South Carolina in the 73 year of his age, 45 of which he has performed the duties of minister at St. Philip's Church. His remains attended by his weeping relatives, the Society of Cincinnati, and a most numerous train of friends and fellow citizens, were conducted last evening, to St. Philip's Church, where they were interred. It may be said with great truth, that his upright conduct through life drew upon him the regard of all good men, and no other proof need be given of the love and esteem he was held in by all ranks of society, than the many tears which were shed when his dust was deposited in the silent grave.[38]

He was buried in the cemetery next to the church. Quoting from a private letter, Albert Sidney Thomas has report that subsequent renovations of the church have created an interesting fact about Smith's legacy:

There is a pleasant touch to link Bishop Smith with the present. The present St. Philip's Church was built after his death, the first building having been destroyed by fire. But yet another fire having damaged the chancel, the restoration [1921] was made with a lengthening of the chancel over the spot where the bishop was buried. It was found that he had been buried in a vault with a heavy masonry arch over it. The architect said nothing could make a better foundation for the new chancel wall than this arch. So the bishop rests in peace, taking part as he did in life in the welfare of the church.[39]

Not only was Robert Smith willing to proclaim his allegiance to his community, but he demonstrated that allegiance by going to war. He was transformed from a loyal defender of the king to a loyal American, neighbor, and community representative. The choices forced on him by events beyond his design hastened the transformation.

It is initially puzzling why he chose to become an active participant in the struggle for the liberation of his state. It is surprising that a man of peace and refined eloquence unhesitatingly took up arms in battle. The answer lies not in the calculation of worldly gains and losses. It lies in considerations of the heart and the soul. It was less his acquisition of wealth than his felt obligation to his community that led inevitably to the struggle against his homeland. He had become rooted in the community-rich society of Charlestown; he had established ties of affection, of duty, of friendship, and of obligation.

Robert Smith was not simply a resident of Charlestown. He was an active participant in the life of the community. Engaged in strengthening its spiritual health, he was a leader in the instruction of its youth, a mediator among disputants, a philanthropist

38. *Charleston City Gazette and Advertiser,* November 3, 1801.

39. Albert Sidney Thomas, "Robert Smith—First Bishop of South Carolina," *Historical Magazine of the Protestant Episcopal Church* 15 (March 1946): 29.

to the vulnerable, and a defender of his neighbors. Robert Smith enjoyed an enviable reputation in his community, and he had no morally acceptable option of abandoning it to appease the requirements of any oath.

History has largely overlooked the magnitude of Robert Smith's accomplishments and sacrifices. His becoming bishop and his role in the establishment of the College of Charleston do not begin to define his stature. He served as a soldier not just in title, but in heroic action. He served a legislator and risked not only his life, but his fortune. The real value of Smith's contributions to his church, his community and his country has not been treated with the seriousness it deserves. It is time that the oversight is corrected.

Chapter 3

Faith and Good Works

I N MARCH OF 1740 the young and brash revivalist preacher George Whitefield arrived for his second visit to Charlestown, South Carolina. He soon went to the residence of the commissary of the bishop of London, Alexander Garden, who had received him so graciously two years earlier. This time, however, his reception was decidedly less cordial. Whitefield had been attacking most of the Anglican clergy for teaching false doctrine regarding salvation, and Garden responded with anger. He demanded that the young Whitefield clarify his charges. Instead of backing down, Whitefield coolly responded that as far as the charges were concerned, he "had scarce begun with them." As Whitefield started his attempt to instruct the commissary of the error of established preaching, Garden stopped him. He shouted at Whitefield, "What, must you come to catechize me?" Then, "in a very great rage," he ordered Whitefield, "Get you out of my house."[1] Three days later, Garden wrote a letter to Whitefield exposing what he believed to be contradictions in the younger preacher's doctrine. In closing the letter Garden wrote, "Please to untie this knot, if you can and you may hear further from [me]."[2] Garden wrote five more letters to Whitefield during the spring and summer of that year.

What disturbed the Anglican Church in the 1740s was the growing intellectual and religious ferment brought about by the Great Awakening. Whitefield was a prominent actor in those events, and eventually the religious ideas of Whitefield and other revivalists fueled the sociopolitical notion of universal liberty. This ideology was the most compelling philosophical force of the American Revolution. That the war was

---

1. George Whitefield, *George Whitefield's Journals* (London: Banner of Truth Trust, 1960), 400–401.

2. Alexander Garden, *Six Letters to the Reverend George Whitefield* (Boston: T. Fleet, 1740), 5.

rooted in the Puritan and revivalist rhetoric of the Great Awakening is not particularly controversial. Typical of the scholarship that identifies the period of revivalism with the revolutionary impulse is the work of Jerald Brauer, who has written, "Revivalism, along with Puritanism, helped to prepare and sustain an attitude in the American colonies which eventuated in rebellion and revolution." The sermons of Jonathan Edwards and George Whitefield reflect as clearly as any the nature of Puritan theology. This theology elevated the ideal of individual rights at the expense of the value of community. The Revolution's deification of the individual became over time the driving force behind a newly formed societal cohesion. This new national identity was civil and religious in character. Sidney Mead has explained "that the religion of a society is whatever system of beliefs actually provides cosmic legitimation for its institutions, and for the activities of its people."[3] The "religion" of the individual that emerged from the Great Awakening and its philosophical foundations not only transformed theological thought but changed how the new republic viewed itself.

Central to the rise of the individual was the Puritan-revivalist notion of regeneration. Unlike their conservative counterparts, revivalists argued that people are justified through faith in Christ, *and by faith alone.* They argued that faith was separate and prior (both temporally and spiritually) to the acceptance of good works or righteous conduct. This was not a subtle difference. It was critical to the Christian's understanding of the proper path to salvation. It also defined faith as seeded in the heart only, not requiring human action or demonstration. More important, if the path to salvation was only that of faith, without works or human action, grace was an object that must be obtained entirely outside any consideration of the community or righteous conduct. To the Puritan mind, people might act altruistically within the community, and perhaps they should, but whether they did had no bearing on their eventual salvation.

To religious conservatives of the time, this separation of human action and salvation represented a misreading of scripture and suggested a devaluation of the community. Robert Smith attempted to remove the passion from the dispute by pointing to the danger of drawing too tight a theological context around the issue:

> There are extremes in this case, which are equally dangerous; and, therefore, ought to be equally avoided; for some have become so intemperate in their assertions as to declare good works to be in themselves pernicious and utterly <u>destructive</u> of salvation; and, according to them, we ought to <u>glory</u> in the character of being unprofitable servants; and, we should best answer the <u>ends</u> of religion, by contradicting the <u>commands</u> of it.

---

3. Jerald Brauer, "Puritanism, Revivalism and the Revolution," in *Religion and the American Revolution,* edited by Brauer (Philadelphia: Fortress Press, 1976), 19; Sidney Mead, "Christendom, Enlightenment, and the Revolution," in *Religion and the American Revolution,* 35.

Others, so <u>magnify</u> works, as to make them meritorious, and oblige God to <u>regale</u> them, even by the laws of strict justice.

It is not easy to determine which opinion carries with it the most mischievous consequences; since the former has in it, a proper tendency to render us careless and dissolute; and the latter, arrogant and presumptuous; the one teaches us to overlook all duty as superfluous; and the other to overvalue it as meritorious.[4]

To Puritans, community interest was spiritually and socially separated from that of the individual. No matter how carefully he drew the distinction, Smith saw community interest, salvation, and good works as inseparable. The practical implication of revivalist separation was that the motive of mutual obligation, which was necessary in building strong communities, was undermined or destroyed.

The revivalist notion of regeneration and its attendant doctrinal refinements, such as predestination and original sin, led to the rise of individualism, which not only weakened ties to England but justified the rejection of authority. The Puritan basis for the Revolution, separatist individualism, which was so pervasive in New England, was never as popular in the South. Smith represented a reticence to accept this Puritan standard.

Justification by Faith

Whitefield was perhaps the greatest revivalist preacher of the period. He was certainly the most celebrated. The itinerant preacher made several tours of the southern colonies and made a huge impact everywhere he went, especially in South Carolina. There is evidence that his preaching made at least some conservatives rethink their understanding of the proper path to salvation. The dispute that raged between Whitefield and Garden was remarkable. To Whitefield, Anglican Arminianism, which Smith articulated a generation later, was a contradiction to the clear teaching of the gospel. In a sermon called "What Ye Think of Christ?," Whitefield spoke of the contradiction: "This doctrine of our free justification by faith in Christ Jesus, however censured and evil spoken of by our present Masters of *Israel,* was highly esteemed by our wise fore-fathers; for in the subsequent words of the aforementioned article, it is called a most *wholesome doctrine,* and very full of comfort: and so it is to all that are weary and heavy laden, and are truly willing to find rest in Jesus Christ."[5] Speaking specifically against the Arminianism of the church leaders and inviting the bitter responses that came his way, he charged,

But I think it proper to premise something farther, because this text [Matt. 18:3] is the grand strong-hold of *Arminians,* and others. They learn of the devil to bring texts

---

4. Robert Smith (1766), Smith Sermons Collection, St. Philip's Church, Charleston, S.C. (hereafter SSC).

5. *The Works of George Whitefield,* 6 vols. (London: Edward & Charles Dilly, 1772), 5:362.

to propagate bad principles: when the devil had a mind to tempt Jesus Christ, because Christ quoted scripture, therefore Satan did so too. And such persons, that their doctrine and bad principles may go down the better, would fain persuade unwary and unstable souls, that they are founded upon the word of God.[6]

Whitefield argued that, not only did the leaders of his church speak doctrine that was counter to traditional teaching, but also that the established clergy actually propagated an evil doctrine. The implication was that contemporary church theology went beyond interpretive error; it constituted deliberate miscalculation and was meant to lead congregations away from Christ. Whitefield was not suggesting intellectual error as much as intellectual dishonesty.

Whitefield's charges were not received well by the clerical establishment of the Anglican Church. Neither was Whitefield ignored, certainly not by Alexander Garden. Responding to the sermon quoted above, Garden was pointed in his rebuttal:

passing over your using the word cause for condition; pray how is it possible for you, after setting down the article at large in the next preceding page, thus to explain it into a contradiction to your own doctrine? As if good works are the Fruits of Faith and pleasing to God, did not precede Justification, but follows after it only. For as true and lively faith, you admit must precede Justification; so good works, teaches the latter part of this article do spring necessarily out of a true and lively faith. Now, if good works do necessarily spring out of a true and lively faith, and a true and lively faith necessarily precedes Justification, the consequence is plain, that good works must not only follow after but precede Justification also. And therefore your explaining the article so, as to separate a true and lively faith from good works, admitting the one to go before, and the other only to follow after Justification, is explaining the article into a contradiction to your own doctrine.[7]

The theological dispute in this exchange is not insignificant. It is foundational, as it questions how salvation is to be received—earned or given.

To Whitefield the doctrine of salvation was not vague. He argued that "faith is the instrument whereby the sinner applies or brings home the redemption of Jesus Christ to his heart. And to whomsoever God gives such a faith (for it is a free gift of God) he may lift up his head with boldness, he need not fear; he is a spiritual son of our spiritual David; he is passed from death to life, he shall never come into condemnation."[8] Whitefield believed that faith was the *only* instrument that could be used to apply for redemption; the issue was not debatable. Whitefield explained, "If any man or angel preach any other gospel, than this of our being freely justified through faith in Christ

6. Ibid., 5:339.
7. Garden, *Six Letters*, 5–6.
8. *Works of George Whitefield*, 5:362

Jesus, we have the authority of the greatest Apostle, to pronounce him accursed."[9] Garden responded, "I firmly believe, and have always taught, that good works do as necessarily spring from and accompany a true and lively faith, whether before or after Justification, as light and heat do the sun; or that as the body without the soul is dead, so Faith without Works, whether before or after Justification, is dead also."[10] Garden disputed the scriptural interpretation that Whitefield believed was indisputable. Smith also attempted to teach a more complex understanding of the doctrine. He maintained,

> We are called upon, to be always abounding in the work of the Lord; God commands it, our own interest prompts us to it, and the good of our neighbor requires it from us. They therefore are great <u>enemies</u> to Christianity, who set up faith in opposition to practice, and throw themselves wholly upon <u>Christ</u>, that they may be free from any personal obligation of their <u>own</u>. For we thankfully acknowledge His merits, and confess our own unworthiness, or want of desert. We entirely acquiesce in his obedience; not as it makes <u>ours useless</u>, but as it renders it more <u>acceptable</u>. We do not <u>presume</u> upon our works, but humbly beg of God to regard them, through the merits of His Son. And though we <u>must</u> be unprofitable, our prayer, is, that we may be found faithful servants, and, then, we shall enter into our Master's joy.[11]

What perhaps angered Garden the most, however, was not the nature of the doctrinal dispute but the suggestion that he and the clerical establishment were deliberately misleading their congregations. The fact that most of the established clergy were themselves condemned by Whitefield may indicate the likelihood that most disagreed with Whitefield's theology. As it gained prominence, the reductionist interpretation of the proper path to salvation that Whitefield and other revivalists preached inevitably led to a fundamental challenge to the traditional conception of community. Whitefield was not the only widely effective revivalist of the time. Jonathan Edwards also had a tremendous impact on the doctrinal debate about salvation.

In many ways, Edwards was even more articulate than Whitefield in making the anti-Arminian attack. Edwards seems to rely more on logical argument than on emotion and confrontation, as Whitefield seems to have done. For instance, Edwards argued,

> The doctrine of the forgiveness of sins is a capital doctrine of the gospel. As it is much insisted on by other writers of the New Testament; so it is above all, by the author of this epistle. In our text, he asserts that we are forgiven *according to the riches of grace;* not merely in the exercise of *grace,* as the very term *forgiveness* implies, but to the exercise of *the riches of grace;* importing that forgiveness is an act of the most

---

9. Ibid.
10. Garden, *Six Letters*, 7.
11. Smith (1766), SSC.

free and abundant grace. . . . The scriptures also teach the absolute *necessity* of the atonement of Christ, and that we can obtain forgiveness and salvation through that only.[12]

His insistence on the notion of grace as the only path to salvation is not vague. It places Edwards in the same theological camp as Whitefield. With these two preachers leading the way, the Puritan point of view had a formidable army of orators. On the one hand, Whitefield became the missionary, extending the revivalist point of view into the frontier. In Edwards, the Puritans had the interpreter of doctrine, the academic, whose almost logical explanations for his positions appealed to others who may not have been moved by Whitefield's enthusiasm.

For example, in Edwards's attempt at a logical approach of the doctrine of grace, he explained,

We could not make atonement of our sins by *repentance* or *reformation*. Repentance and reformation are a mere return to our duty, which we ought never to have forsaken or intermitted. Suppose a soldier deserts the service into which he is enlisted, and at the most critical period not only forsakes his general and the cause of his country, but joins the enemy and exerts himself to his utmost in his cause, and in direct opposition to that of his country; yet after twelve months spent in this manner, he repents and returns to his duty and his former service; will this repentance and reformation atone for his desertion and rebellion?[13]

Edwards seems to have relied on a much less emotional rhetoric to justify his anti-Arminian theology, than did Whitefield. Just as Whitefield, however, Edwards rejected the notion that anything humans might do could ever lead to salvation. To Edwards, the only path to justification was through the free gift of God's grace. He concluded this way:

Thus it clearly appears, that we could never have atoned for our own sins. If therefore atonement be made at all, it must be made by some other person; and since as we before argued, Christ the son of God hath been appointed to this work, we may be sure, that it could be done by no other person of inferior dignity. It may be inquired of those who deny the necessity of the atonement of Christ, whether the *mission, work and death* of Christ were all *necessary* in order to the salvation of sinners.[14]

12. *The Works of Jonathan Edwards,* 14 vols. (New Haven, Conn.: Yale University Press, 1957), 2:11–13.

13. Ibid., 18.

14. Ibid., 19–20.

The Puritan notion of justification by faith characterized the differences between religious conservatives and the growing revivalist fervor of the time. Even John Wesley, who had his own differences with the Puritans, especially Whitefield, was clear in his acceptance of the revivalist doctrine of justification by faith. He maintained,

> All the blessings which God hath bestowed upon man are of his mere grace, bounty or favour, favour altogether undeserved, man having no claim to the least of his mercies. It was free grace that "formed man out of the dust of the ground, and breathed into him a living soul," and stamped on that soul the image of God, and "put all things under his feet." The same free grace continues to us, at this day, life and breath, and all things. For there is nothing we are, or have, or do, which can deserve the least thing at God's hand. "All our works thou, O God, hast wrought in us." These therefore are so many more instances of free mercy: and whatever righteousness may be found in man, this also is the gift of God.[15]

Although Whitefield had created the greatest turmoil in South Carolina, it was John Wesley who perhaps had more of an impact on actual adherents. It is certainly true that Wesley had a more profound impact on the state after the Revolution. Wesley's point of view on this particular doctrine lent support for the anti-Arminian position. Although Wesley diverged from the revivalist doctrine on election, on justification by faith he was consistent.

Closely connected to the doctrine of justification was the belief in election or predestination. This idea is most important in determining the eighteenth-century perspective of community. It was the belief that only God could determine who was saved and who was not that undermined the perceived value of good works. If good works could not lead to salvation, then there was no reason for the community to recognize anything other than the virtue of the individual. Community virtue was virtually meaningless.

Predestination and Good Works

The belief in the predetermination of God's grace and the utter uselessness of human action to gain redemption at once fed the new ideology of the individual and undermined the once-strong kinship basis of the southern conception of community. To Edwards it was illogical to deny the truth of election. Edwards believed that scripture was unambiguous in supporting it and that it was virtually unfathomable for anyone to deny it:

> Thus if we allow that Christ came to save all men from an endless punishment, we must not only give up the moral rectitude of God and of his son Jesus Christ, but

15. *The Works of John Wesley*, 22 vols. (Nashville, Tenn.: Abington Press, 1984), 1:117–18.

must impute to them the grossest oppression and iniquity. Nor is there any way to avoid these shocking consequences, but by granting that an endless punishment is justly threatened against all mankind, and may justly be inflicted.[16]

The matter is not arguable for Edwards. He continued his analysis, however, by pointing out that to deny the truth of predestination is to deny that no man can suffer a deserved punishment. If that be the case, Edwards believed it denies that Christ is the source of grace:

Thus I have attempted to show that if all men are saved, they are not saved by Christ; because if we suppose all are saved by him, they are saved either from an endless, or from a temporary punishment. But it cannot be supposed that all men are saved by Christ from an *endless* punishment, unless it be allowed that they were justly liable to such a punishment; that it may be inflicted consistently with all the attributes of God; that all the arguments against endless punishment, drawn from the attributes of God are to be relinquished; that no man can suffer a punishment proportioned or equal to his deserts; and that sin is an infinite evil, as by the present supposition it deserves an endless punishment; which things are utterly denied by those who hold to the salvation of all men, and are entirely inconsistent with their system.[17]

Justification by faith and predestination are founded on the belief that only God determines who is saved and who is not. While Edwards eloquently challenged the internal logic of the Arminians and those who believe in universal salvation, Whitefield ridiculed them and injected the notion of worthiness into the dispute.

Whitefield argued that grace comes only as a gift from the hands of God. If this gift is bestowed beyond the influence or actions of any human, then those who have it necessarily are separated from those who do not. They are separated in the eyes of God (one viewed as worthy and the other reprobate) and in the eyes of other believers. If no human action could influence the gift, there would be no reason for the saved to be much concerned with the health of the community or any of their neighbors. Those who have grace are worthy of it, while those who do not are clearly unworthy. For Smith, since no one is worthy of God's grace, any notion of community must be constructed without regard to worthiness.

Smith rejected the idea that human action is useless as a means to salvation. The revivalist insistence that duty and piety follows after faith clashed with conservative Anglican theology of Garden's day. It seemed to be in opposition to Smith's teaching as well. He professed that pious behavior "promotes" faith, clearly arguing that faith and human action are at least temporally adjacent, if not that faith follows after good works:

16. *Works of Jonathan Edwards*, 2:429–30.
17. Ibid., 433.

It is true, these and many other passages of like import, in the New Testament are chiefly to be understood of the times when they were first spoken, the infant age of Christianity, when the standard of the cross being set up, all they who repaired to it, were engaged in a continual opposition to the powers of this world, and persecutions, afflictions, distresses, attended in every step of their conflict. And the sufferings of Christians were designed to promote the faith of Christ, and the seed of the Word sown, was to be made fruitful by the blood of martyrs.

Then indeed was it most remarkably, most imminently true, that the Christian state and profession was a state of suffering.[18]

Smith connected faith and good works in time and in spirit. One cannot adhere to the doctrine of predestination and follow Smith's point of view. To Smith faith and good works supported and strengthened each other. In a statement of the matter that casts no doubt of Smith's rejection of the revivalist notion of predestination, he said,

And, surely there cannot be a greater reproach cast upon our faith, than by supposing it to be lazy and inactive in its nature; from hence springs a shameful neglect of all moral goodness; and if I may so speak, men nail their <u>virtues</u> to <u>that</u> cross, where their sins only should be fastened. <u>They</u> talk much of the efficacy of faith; and, so far, there is no harm, if they did not advance it to <u>such</u> a degree, as to destroy that <u>love</u>, by which it should work; and by their doctrine and example, make others very indifferent, whether they preserved the power, as long as they retained the <u>name</u> of Christianity.[19]

Smith believed that faith was not alive without the power of human action. Pious human action was not something merely admirable to Smith; it gave the Christian faith its strength. To Smith, salvation had to be based in part on human piety; thus, predetermination of grace was not possible.

Closely connected theologically to the doctrine of predestination, of course, is the notion of good works or charity. Consistent with his Puritan theology, Whitefield endorsed good works with less than enthusiasm and did not apply it universally. Whitefield reflected his reservations about universal charity when he asked, "Is that true charity, when we give anything to our fellow-creatures purely to indulge them in vice: this is so far from being charity, that it is a sin, both against God, and against his fellow-creatures." If charity were to be extended to those who might misuse it, or would unfairly benefit from it, then Whitefield claimed that a double sin would be committed, because one should never encourage another to sin.[20] In that case, Whitefield believed

18. Smith (1776), SSC.
19. Smith (1766), SSC.
20. *Works of George Whitefield,* 6:235, 235–36.

that the greater sinner is the person offering the charity. According to Whitefield, we are to determine the worthiness of the recipients of our charity *before* we offer it.

This is not consistent, however, with conservative Anglican theology. Robert Smith articulated the establishment view of charity in 1766:

> It is as gross an abuse of our own reform, as of God's mercy, to form a larger indulgence for sinful men, out of <u>that</u> pardon, which is only allowed to the penitent; and then, to deny the necessity of good works, when we are by the assistance of God's grace, enabled to perform them. For though we have redemption through Christ, the forgiveness of sins, according to the riches of His grace; yet, there are conditions requisite on our part, to make that benefit effectual; and St. John has briefly comprehended them in his saying; if we walk in the light, as He is in the light, the blood of Jesus Christ, His Son, cleanseth us from all sin.[21]

Smith saw a *necessity* of good works in order to achieve salvation. To Smith, believers are not to determine the worthiness of those to whom the good works should be directed. Charity was necessary, not because of the needs of the recipients, but because it was the duty of those who would offer it.

Whitefield was consistent in arguing that the charity that Christians are obliged to give was directed at the spiritual well-being of one's neighbor, and not so much to his physical needs. He stated, "And is not the soul more valuable than the body? It would be of no advantage, but an infinite disadvantage, to obtain all the world, if we were to lose our souls. The soul is of infinite value, and of infinite concern, and, therefore, we should extend our charity whenever we see it needful, and likewise should reprove, rebuke, and exhort with all godliness and love." Whitefield also virtually rejected any Christian obligation to the community if it meant a sacrifice in one's own comfort or that of one's family.[22] Smith's approach is clearly different. In the following passage he eloquently endorsed good works *as sacrificial:*

> Christ has enjoined us in our daily petition, to pray that God's will may be done on earth; that is, the <u>commands</u> as cheerfully <u>performed</u> as the <u>afflictions suffered</u>, which He is pleased to send, here is an absolute obligation to duty; since by virtue of another precept, our light so to shine before men, that they, seeing our good works, may glorify our father which is in Heaven; there is <u>as</u> pressing an engagement upon us to set a good example to our neighbor; and, if we are tempted to vanity by an overweening conceit of our own performances, the Apostle's interrogation will soon abate the honor of our pride; who hath first <u>given</u> to him, and it shall be recompensed to him again.[23]

21. Smith (1766), SSC.
22. *Works of George Whitefield,* 6:233, 227.
23. Smith (1766), SSC.

To Smith, personal sacrifice was not something to avoid or to weigh against a recipient's worthiness. It was a duty. Later he explained, "It is a matter of our bounty, that we are able to do <u>anything</u>; and, because as St. Paul speaks of Philemon, we owe even <u>ourselves</u> to God, who made us, and hath wrought all our <u>works</u> in us, it is impossible we can oblige him, when, in every act that we discharge, we must of necessity be his debtors."[24] Smith maintained that it is for God, not for the recipients of our good works, that we must offer of ourselves and of our resources. It is the insistence that good works and faith together lead to salvation that separates Smith theologically from the revivalists.

Contrary to Smith's theology, Whitefield believed that charity was to be made out of duty but should not be offered at one's own expense. Moreover, he did not view the community as an extension of a kinship structure but as existing in opposition to it. In this regard there is certainly a large and important difference between the scope of Whitefield's charity and that of Robert Smith. Smith insisted that we should extend charity to everyone, "not only those whom we know, but those whose distresses we are acquainted with, though their persons are strangers to us."[25] Smith's conception of love is important to this issue. To him, love was expansive. Consider the following passage:

> Now the nature of love will be best known by its acts and its objects. As to the acts of love, it comprehends all those things whereby men may be beneficial and useful to one another. It reaches not only to the body but to the soul of man, that nobler and better part of us; and is conversant about those things whereby we may be serviceable to the temporal or spiritual good of others, to promote either their present, or future and eternal happiness. In short it resolves the doubtful minds, comforts the weak, heals the broken-hearted, relieves the afflicted, weeps with those that weep, and mourns with them that mourn.[26]

Smith's rhetoric, which is reflective of generations of Anglican conservatives, was in pointed opposition to the revivalists. While Whitefield and Edwards turned the Christian obligation inward to one's own soul and then cast narrowly to one's family first, Smith made no distinction between family and community, or between the worthy and the unworthy. While Whitefield envisioned man as living *in* communities, the church establishment viewed men as living *as* communities—a fundamental difference. Moreover, Smith seemed to view the place of sacrifice in acts of charity differently than Whitefield did. While Whitefield's theology seemed to focus on the individual and a narrow vision of kinship, Smith's focused on the collective and viewed the community as an extension of the family. To Smith, helping a neighbor was helping a family member. Smith's rhetoric thus universalized filial love.

24. Ibid.
25. Smith (1756), SSC.
26. Ibid.

The revivalists' approach devalued the community, or at least conceived of it as antagonistic to the Christian's proper role in society. They believed that salvation was available only to those worthy of it, the elect, so charity should be extended only to the worthy. From the southern conservative point of view, Christianity universalized kinship. Smith preached,

> But our Savior has restored this law of laws, this duty of love, to its natural and original extent. And the Christian is not allowed to count any sort of people his enemy. He has commanded us to bear an amiable and friendly disposition to all men, and taught us that our brethren are not only those of our own kindred and nation, but those of the same nature. The old law taught us to love our neighbors, but the new law teaches us that all the world are our neighbors; not only those whom we know, but those whose distresses we are acquainted with, though their persons are strangers to us. . . . He may cease to be our friend but cannot cease to be our brother; for all are descended from the same loins.[27]

Smith urged his listeners to look beyond their circle of family and friends and to consider everyone as part of their family. To Whitefield, kinship was constrained, proprietary, and narrowly conceived. Whitefield's philosophy leads to a decidedly individualistic point of view. Smith's philosophy is one of universal community.

Faith and the Sacralization of Man

Emile Durkheim has written of two kinds of individualism: one that is utilitarian and one that is founded on a belief in human equality. According to Durkheim, the latter view of individualism leads men to seek out commonalities rather than differences:

> This is far indeed from the apotheosis of comfort and private interest, the egoistic cult of the self for which utilitarian individualism has justly been reproached. Quite the contrary: according to these moralists, duty consists in averting our attention from what concerns us personally, from all that relates to our empirical individuality, so as uniquely to seek that which our human condition demands, that which we hold in common with all our fellow men.[28]

Durkheim described a deification of the individual, *applied to every individual.* He called the sacralization of man as a "transcendental majesty which the churches of all times have given to their Gods."[29] To Durkheim, the sacralization of the individual impacts the resulting morality to such an extent that it is in itself religious. He explained,

27. Ibid.

28. Emile Durkheim, *Durkheim on Religion: A Selection of Readings with Bibliographies,* ed. W. S. F. Pickering, trans. Ephriam Fischoff (London: Routledge & Kegan Paul, 1975), 61.

29. Ibid., 62.

Whoever makes an attempt on a man's life, on a man's liberty, on a man's honor inspires us with a feeling of horror, in every way analogous to that which the believer experiences when he sees his idol profaned. Such a morality is therefore not simply a hygienic discipline or a wise principle of economy. It is a religion of which man is, at the same time, both believer and God.[30]

The distinction between an emphasis on the individual and one on community informs our understanding of the Puritan-conservative confrontation as it reflects the fundamental divergence of the doctrines.

The dispute between revivalists and the Anglican establishment was not just a matter of arguing around the edges of scriptural interpretation, which might interest only clerics and theologians. What Whitefield and other revivalists were suggesting was a fundamental transformation of how society constructs its sense of morality and its identity. Is our conception of morality rooted in the individual, or does it emerge from the cohesiveness of community? Smith and other conservatives offered very different answers to the question than did revivalists.

Max Weber's analysis of religion in society may be instructive in our understanding of how Puritan and conservative philosophies diverged in their conception of morality and community. Weber investigated the impact of the rationalization of salvation religions on the evolution of society. He compared the transformation of pure mystical religious belief to the "Puritanized" version of Christianity. The divergence of the two religious doctrines on the issue of "good works"—and the resultant separation of the worthy and the unworthy—also represented an important, albeit less fundamental, transformation. Weber illustrated how the impact of predestination in particular has led our society further away from the mystical past:

Mystical religions had necessarily to take a diametrically opposite path [from salvation religion] with regard to the rationalization of economics. The foundering of the postulate of brotherly love in its collision with the loveless realities of the economic domain once it became rationalized led to the expansion of love for one's fellow man until it came to require a completely unselective generosity. Such unselective generosity did not inquire into the reason and outcome of absolute self-surrender, into the worth of the person soliciting help, or into his capacity to help himself. . . . In mystical religions, the individual for whom the sacrifice is made is regarded in the final analysis as unimportant and fungible; his individual value is negated.[31]

The conservative Anglican could not be regarded as mystical, but as the Puritan doctrine of predestination gained adherents, Christianity certainly moved toward a more

---

30. Ibid.
31. Max Weber, *The Sociology of Religion*, trans. Ephraim Fischoff (Boston: Beacon Press, 1963), 221.

rationalist perspective. Moreover, as Weber's final thought suggests, the value of the individual increases as religion moves from its mystical foundation. That is an essential shift, which can hardly be overstated.

Certainly, what revivalists were promoting was not an individualism that is utilitarian but rather a new religion of sorts, a religion of humanity. Durkheim argued, "This religion of humanity has all that is required to speak to its believers in a tone that is no less imperative than the religions it replaces."[32] He was not speaking of the glorification of the individual but of the glorification of man. He explained,

> Now all that societies require in order to hold together is that their members fix their eyes on the same end and come together in a single faith; but it is not at all necessary that the object of this common faith be quite unconnected with individual persons. In short, individualism thus understood is the glorification not of the self, but of the individual in general. Its motive force is not egoism but sympathy for all that is human, a wider pity for all sufferings, for all human miseries, a more ardent desire to combat and alleviate them, and a greater thirst for justice.[33]

This was the struggle. It was a battle over what ideal would impel social cohesion, or if such cohesion was a legitimate societal goal at all, and what values would define the identity of the new nation. Would it be based on a traditional Anglican value of community, or on a new religion of humanity, a new individualism?

While Durkheim maintained that utilitarian individualism neglected the force of moral beliefs, the individualism that leads to the deification of man supplies a new morality.[34] It was indeed a battle over the birth of a new identity, or in Durkheim's terms, a new "organic solidarity." It was not greed that motivated the eighteenth-century individualist but the belief in the inherent value and equality of every human being. What motivated the southern conservative was the value of the collective and the reciprocal obligation each person had to everyone else within it.

Predestination Politics and the Community

Robert Bellah's seminal work on civil religion broke ground not only in identifying the force of Puritan values to the American Revolution but also to the development of America's national character.[35] It is undeniable that the impact of such figures as George Whitefield and Jonathan Edwards did indeed transform the divergent American colonies into a collective force. At least in New England, the Puritan influence was substantial.

32. Durkheim, *Durkheim on Religion,* 63–64.
33. Ibid., 64.
34. Charles E. Marske, "Durkheim's 'Cult of the Individual' and the Moral Reconstruction of Society," *Sociological Theory* 5 (Spring 1987): 2.
35. Robert Bellah, "Civil Religion in America," *Daedalus* 96 (Winter 1967): 1–21.

One of the legacies that the Puritans left was the notion of the separation of church and state. Bellah was right to suggest that this notion has become almost a religious tenet in America. Within a religious view that elevates individual responsibility and the notion of predestination to sacred heights, it is understandable that the realms of religion and politics not only could coexist separately but, in fact, should operate that way. Indeed, the Puritans led many of our founding fathers to embed the notion into our national religious world view.

It must be remembered, however, that the Puritan influence, while significant, was not universal. There were other significant religious movements and other sets of ethical values that competed with the Puritans, especially in the southern colonies. In the South non-Puritan Protestant churches had much impact on society, and Anglican influence was significant, particularly in South Carolina and Virginia. The difference in the religious development of New England and the South is critical in understanding what I think was a unique vision of community expressed in the South, which was different from New England's. The treatment of two doctrines illustrates the difference with the greatest clarity: predestination and community. Predestination offers the greatest divergence theologically while the notion of community, more philosophically, is understood within a cluster of issues that includes the path to salvation, good works, and the meaning of Christian love.

Central to Puritan theology, the notion of predestination logically followed from the beliefs that only faith in God can lead to salvation and that God alone determines eternal destiny. No human action can alter it. The adherence to the doctrine of predestination had tremendous and fundamental impact on the interest that the Puritans had in the political sphere. It was also the most obvious counterpoint to Smith's theology of community. If no human action could alter the predetermined course of mankind, then there was no reason for the religious to be concerned with the schemes and machinations of nonreligious human activity and no reason to pay much attention to the health of the community. Therefore, the rhetoric based in Puritan tradition has a separatist inclination—not only keeping separate the religious and the political but also the individual and the collective.

Bellah has stressed this idea in his discussion of the separation of church and state as being central to the American civil religion:

> The principle of separation of church and state guarantees the freedom of religious belief and association, but at the same time clearly segregates the religious sphere, which is considered too be essentially private, from the political one. . . . the separation of church and state has not denied the political realm a religious dimension.[36]

According to Bellah, the religious dimension of the political sphere is the central element of American civil religion. He did not discuss the counterpart. That is, what about

36. Ibid, 3.

the political dimension of the religious sphere? If, as Bellah has claimed, civil religion grew out of Puritan and pioneer mentality and values, it would appear that the theological assumption of predestination essentially precludes the possibility of any political advocacy from the pulpit. It also precludes the importance of "good works," which was at the heart of Smith's righteous community. If only God determines salvation and if no human action can alter God's predetermined eternal plan, then no number of good works can lead in any way to salvation.

From the Puritan perspective, there is only a need to preach grace and salvation through faith in Christ. This view has profound impact on how a society views community. From the viewpoint of Puritanism and the doctrine of predestination in particular, the theological perspective toward community is divisive. Some are saved, and some are not. If we are to seek grace, those who have it necessarily are preferred to those who do not, so a real-world separation occurs. But the separatist impulse is much more pervasive than even that.

Kenneth Burke suggested that the proclamation of predestination logologically sets apart many of those to which the doctrine is understood:

> If I say "the furniture in the room," I have merged many objects under a single head. However different from one another, they are terminologically at rest in a kind of Edenic bliss. If I now break my expression into components (listing so many chairs, tables, rugs, curtains, etc., of such and such sorts), I shall have introduced distinctions —and these are like a "fall" from the "unity" of the overall usage by which they were previously classed together. They are now "set apart" from one another, with that such separation implies.[37]

Some are selected, and some are not. The language, the rhetoric of predestination, does not create community—just the opposite. Such rhetoric undermines community and increases the capacity for rationalization, which in turn increases the tension between the religious and the political sphere. It appears that in the Puritan tradition the select and worthy are certainly separate from the unworthy. More than that, since human action is irrelevant to the gift of grace—and, since it is predetermined based outside human action, it is a gift—the select have no moral or ethical obligation to those who have been set apart.

For community to be strengthened, an ethical construct that is based on mutual obligation and responsibility to a collective is essential. A theology that not only allows the existence of good works but believes in good works as a path to salvation is requisite. The Puritan tradition could never provide that foundation. In such a tradition, the individual, not the community, is preeminent.

---

37. Kenneth Burke, *The Rhetoric of Religion* (Berkeley: University of California Press, 1970), 265–66.

Smith's success is directly related to his ability to base his ideal community solidly upon a theistic foundation, but at the same time it is suggestive of active engagement in the political process as well. In an eloquent justification for the connection of the religious and the political sphere, Smith outlined the problems inherent in a political system vacant of religious values:

> Most men, in political nations, look on nature with indifference. They are surrounded with human grandeur. What sham after all can render the history of man so interesting? It has to boast of vain objects of glory alone, of uncertain opinions, of bloody victories, or at most, of useless labors. If nature sometimes finds a place in it, we are called upon only to observe the ravages she has committed, and to hear her charged with a thousand calamities, which may be all traced up to our own imprudence.[38]

Smith believed that the arrogance of man leads us to ruin. Respect for nature and God's providence is the way to understand and to live in the world. Our vision of the world would be vastly different if we did:

> If we would form a just idea of the order of nature, we must give up our circumscribed ideas of human order. We must renounce the plans of our own architecture, which frequently employs straight lines, that the imbecility of our visionary organs may be able to take in the whole extent of our domain at a glance and which symmetrizes all our distributions.[39]

Smith was specific when he condemned the ambition found in the realm of politics. Ambition, he charged, was inconsistent with virtue:

> Virtue and ambition are absolutely incompatible. The glory of ambition is to mount, and that of virtue is to descend. Observe that Jesus Christ reprimanded his disciples when they inquired of him who should be the first among them. He takes a little child, and places him in the midst. . . . Ah! when He recommends the humility so suitable to our frail ambitions, it is because he was confident that even power supreme is not capable of constituting our happiness in this world.[40]

The Puritans' adherence to the notion of predestination had necessarily excluded the possibility of cohesive community and virtually mandated the forced separation of the political and religious spheres. Their theological positions, especially predestination and the rhetoric of separation, increased the tension between the religious and political spheres that even Smith recognized. The difference, of course, is that while Puritans

---

38. Smith, "Observations on Nature" (n.d.), Smith Family Papers, South Carolina Historical Society, Charleston, S.C.

39. Ibid.

40. Ibid.

suggested separation of the spheres as the solution, Smith suggested their more thorough integration.

This choice of separatist language and emotion offers the starkest contrast between the Puritan tradition and Smith's more-accommodating rhetoric, at least as it relates to community. Roderick Hart has faulted Bellah for his failure to demonstrate the ability of the civil religion he envisioned to integrate religious factions—to say nothing of competing value spheres—into a cohesive community.[41] Marcela Cristi complained that Bellah was wrong in saying that communities are based on values in the first place.[42]

I believe that all three are wrong. Bellah suggested that ritual and temporal symbols (such as monuments and buildings) and personages that engender reverence (such as George Washington and Abraham Lincoln) forge the cohesion of community, or the integration of society. Hart claimed that the language, the rhetoric of the American political realm, brings us together. Instead, the integration implied by the idea of civil religion is more like the *poetic meaning* that Kenneth Burke discussed in *Symbols and Society,* where he suggested that the poetic meaning, extended here to imply a poetic community, is understood metaphorically.[43] If we think about integration of a community, we view it semantically as "physically" integrated. A poetic conception of community is one in which the community is no less real but is felt rather than actually viewed:

> Instead of being taken for the description of man's essence, it [poetic meaning or metaphor] would be considered simply for its value in revealing certain important things to look out for in any attempt to plead for a more satisfactory communicative or cooperative structure.[44]

According to Burke, poetic meaning would consist of much more than pragmatic values; positivistic and futuristic values are possible. If one views the course of the community in pragmatic terms, the fullness of a moral act could not be appreciated at the moment of the act. Burke pointed out that from a poetic view a fully moral act is a *total* assertion at the time of the assertion. Put another way, Burke wrote that the semantic avoids drama, the poetic envisions a vocabulary that goes through drama:

> The first [semantic] would be aside from battle, stressing the role of the observer, whose observations it is hoped will define situations with sufficient realistic accuracy

41. Roderick Hart, *The Political Pulpit* (West Lafayette, Ind.: Purdue University Press, 1977), 33–36.

42. Marcela Cristi, *From Civil to Political Religion: The Intersection of Culture, Religion and Politics* (Waterloo, Ont.: Wilfrid Laurier University Press, 2001), 75.

43. Kenneth Burke, *Symbols and Society* (Chicago: University of Chicago Press, 1989), 91.

44. Ibid., 92.

to prepare an adequate chart for action; the second [poetic] would contend, by implication, that true knowledge can only be attained through the battle stressing the role of the participant, who in the course of his participation, it is hoped, will define situations with sufficient realistic accuracy to prepare an image for action.[45]

It may have been impossible to integrate fully the divergent viewpoints active in colonial Charleston. But through a rhetoric of community, Smith attempted to integrate them in at least poetic terms—a felt community that was no less rhetorically powerful. As Burke explained,

> The semantic ideal would attempt to get a description by the elimination of attitude. The poetic ideal would attempt to attain a full moral act by attaining perspective atop all the conflicts of attitude. The first would try to cut away to abstract, all emotional factors that complicate the objective character of meaning. The second would try to derive its vision from the maximum heaping up of all those emotional, playing them off against one another, inviting them to reinforce and contradict one another, and seeking to make this active participation itself a major ingredient of the vision.[46]

The "semantic" rhetoric, characterized by the rational, Puritan-based ideal of individualism, cannot possibly lead to a real sense of community. Burke's poetic ideal, represented by the southern-conservative sense of community, offers a real contrast to the revivalist-republican notion of separation.

Smith's rhetoric was not necessarily a precursor to actual integration, but it allowed the feeling of a collective morality, a recurrent theme of his sermons. This morality perhaps means something different to different people but leads to the same general moral and ethical construct, which works to overcome the increased tension pulling them apart.

To Smith, the necessity of good works underlay the public duty that each member of the community had for every other member. For those, such as Smith, who had been blessed with fortune and with status, duty was even more pronounced. Their obligations to the community were inescapable. Smith and his community did not share the sense of individualism spawned by revivalist doctrines of faith and election. It was an essential difference.

45. Ibid., 94.
46. Ibid., 92.

Chapter 4

Civic Conscience and the
Evolution of a Righteous Community

Robert Smith's banishment must have been difficult to bear. On his homecoming and his resumption of his pulpit on June 1, 1783, his congregation might have forgiven him if he was bitter. They would have understood if he expressed anger toward his tormentors. They would have joined in his vitriol if he had railed against the occupiers who had devastated his home. Robert Smith, however, did none of that. He did not speak of the depravity of his enemies. He did not seek vengeance and retribution. He spoke instead of the congregants' duty and how they must conduct themselves as Christians and as a new nation. He chose for his text that day a simple passage from Proverbs: "Righteousness exalteth a nation." He chose to remind his listeners—as he did eight years earlier, on the brink of war, when he spoke in front of the Commons House of Assembly—that it was their conduct, their righteousness, that should consume their thoughts. Whether God had sanctioned their victory was of no consequence unless they acted according to divine principles.

In his first opportunity to address his congregants in three years, Smith chose to admonish them to take care to remember the importance of religion to the community:

> let us only well observe that even though virtue be in its own nature ever so amiable, yet considering the great and flagrant corruption of human nature, its power would by no means suffice without that of religion. For to be guided by the rules of right reason; to be influenced by the charms of moral excellence, undoubtedly requires a more elegant and refined taste, than can possibly be attained by the general herd of mankind.[1]

---

1. Robert Smith (1782), Smith Sermons Collection, St. Philip's Church, Charleston, S.C. (hereafter SSC).

The critical importance of this topic to Smith is obvious. He chose the topic of Christian duty and society as his very first message to his community on his return. The sincerity of his views is unquestionable.

Natural Law and Social Contract

Robert Smith was a product of his century. He was a student of the philosophy and the thinking of the Enlightenment. His concepts of man and of government were based in part on his understanding of those writers of the time who had revolutionized how men viewed their governors. He could not have escaped his Cambridge education without learning of the philosophy of John Locke and others in his day, who talked of the relationship between man and nature. As the impetus toward war was gaining speed, talk of natural rights and natural impulses was popular. Within this climate, Smith, however, developed his own ideas. He could not have done that without understanding the philosophies of his day. We know that Smith was familiar with the teaching of John Locke and his ideas about social contracts, natural rights of man, and boundaries of government.

Locke believed that political power was not based on any paternalistic justification. He argued that only three reasons could support the legitimate use of political power. First, political power could be asserted to protect property legitimately obtained. Second, governments could legitimately assert power to protect a society from injury perpetrated by a foreign power. Finally, all this could be done only if, it had as its end, the public good.[2] This view of the power and boundaries of government served as the basis of the republican call for independence. It was an important philosophical force that helped to shape the American response to British colonial rule.

Basing his argument partly on Richard Hooker, Locke asserted that political power *rightly conceived* was based on nature, which was such as to render all mankind perfectly equal. He believed that if any man had power over another, it had to be exercised only with the consent of those to whom it was directed. It was this idea that created such opposition in the colonies to the taxation and regulations of late British colonial rule. Natural law defined the proper role of government.

Even Locke, however, saw a limit to the natural rights of man, and coincidentally, he recognized another proper role for government. He argued,

> The state of nature has a law of nature to govern it, which obliges everyone, and reason, which is that law, teaches all mankind, who will but consult it, that having all equal and independent, no one ought to harm another in his life, health, liberty, or possessions for men being all the workmanship of one omnipotent, and infinitely wise maker; all the servants of one sovereign master, sent into the world by his order,

---

2. John Locke, "An Essay Concerning the True Original Extent of the End of Civil Government" (1690), in *Social Contract,* ed. Ernest Baker (Oxford: Oxford University Press, 1960), 4.

and about his business; they are his property, where workmanship they are, made to last during his, not another's pleasure: and being furnished with like faculties, sharing all in one community of nature, they cannot be supposed any such subordination among us, that may authorize us to destroy one another, as if we were made for one another's uses, as the inferior ranks of creatures are for ours.[3]

Locke wrote of the liberty that man enjoys from the *intrusion* of others. He pointed to a liberty derived from the natural state of man, a perfect equality. If each human has a natural right to be free from the unwanted interference from others, then, to Locke, the only way that government could legitimately be tolerated is by the consent of the governed—a social contract among equals, whereby one agrees that others may construct and implement laws for the public good. To Locke, this natural law did not grant license to injure or wrongly interfere with others.

Robert Smith did not adhere to Locke's vision of natural right. He was no republican. The liberty that Smith identified was more spiritual—a liberty to exercise one's duty to others unfettered. It was a liberty not from *intrusion* of individual prerogatives but from the prerogatives of the community. Smith's freedom was not based on a natural dictate to refrain from harming others but on a freedom to do good positively to others.

Locke believed that one of government's critical functions was suppling reason to a rather chaotic society.[4] While Locke believed that government's proper role was to prevent injury to others by supplying reason, Smith believed that the role of government was not to supply reason but to represent divine law, to remind us of our Christian duty, on which government is (or should) be based.

Unlike Locke and the republicans, Robert Smith viewed nature not as the source of individual liberty but as the reason for the existence of human government. For Smith, nature was not the spring for man's virtue but the source of the corruption and the chaos that always characterizes societies of men. We need governments, Smith insisted, to protect us from each other. To Smith, it was not reason that man and governments should strive to obtain, but virtue:

As man has formed his intellect on that of nature he has been obliged to regulate his moral sense by that of her author. He felt that in order to please him who is the principle of all good it was necessary to contribute to the general good; hence the effort made by man in every age to raise himself to God, by the practice of virtue. This religious character which distinguishes man from every sensible being, belongs more properly to his heart than his understanding. It is in him not so much an illumination as a feeling, for it appears independent even of the spectacle of nature, and manifests

---

3. Ibid., 5–6.
4. Ibid., 7–8.

itself with equal energy in those who are most remote from it, as in those who are continually enjoying it.[5]

So, to Smith, it was virtue not reason that brings order to chaos and is manifested in the public good. He did not reject reason, however, and believed that Christians did not have to abandon reason to justify their faith: "We profess ourselves rational beings and to act upon rational principles. Our faith is not founded upon enthusiasm, but upon the most solid basis of reason itself; and we apprehend we can give a sufficient reason of the hope that is in us."[6]

The difference between Locke's view of legitimate government and Smith's is more than marginal. The source and the end of political power both define their divergence. To Locke, the consent of the governed—the social contract—was the source of political power. To Smith, the source was nature and God. In this regard, Smith is consistent with the views of John Wesley, who said that "there is no power but from God."[7] To Locke, the establishment of reason was the end of government action. To Smith, collective virtue was the grand goal of government.

The Necessity and Advantages of Government

Smith's justification for the existence of human government was based on his belief in "the natural proneness of man to sin."[8] Smith clearly believed in the doctrine of original sin and insisted that the natural depravity of man necessitated instituted law. Left to his own devices unrestrained, man would not behave constructively, which is essential to healthy societies. He also believed that man must obey the laws of man because they are or should be based on divine law. He insisted that "as the Apostle informs us, and we find by experience, that we have a 'law in our members,' continually warring against the law of our mind, which hurries us on with a much stronger bias toward evil, than toward good."[9] This war is between the natural tendencies of man toward evil and chaos and the intellectual understanding of the need for righteousness. Human law guides us in the paths of righteousness and helps us to win the battle against nature.

Specifically, Smith argued that God provided us with rules so that we could overcome the "deceitfulness and depravity of our hearts" and, out of his infinite mercy, to follow them. This, Smith insisted, was the only way for us to achieve happiness, for it was the only way that we will turn against the natural tendencies of sin.[10] Smith put it this way:

---

5. Smith, "Observations on Nature" (n.d.), Smith Family Papers, South Carolina Historical Society, Charleston, S.C.

6. Smith (1766), Smith Family Papers, South Carolina Historical Society, Charleston, S.C.

7. John Wesley, *Political Writings of John Wesley* (Bristol: Thoemmes Press, 1998), 46.

8. Smith (1761), SSC.

9. Ibid.

10. Ibid.

Wherefore, because the law of nature shone with a dim and feeble ray, it pleased the most high God, by an express declaration of his will, enforced by the most glorious rewards promised to the obedient and the most dreadful punishments denounced against the disobedient, to oblige us to do justly, to love mercy, and to walk humbly with him.[11]

The final thought, "to do justly, to love mercy, and to walk humbly with God," was almost a mantra for Smith; it was the underpinning of his conception of the Christian citizen. It permeated his approach to government, both for the governed and the governors.

Smith was consistent in stating that the absolute force of divine law does not release anyone, no matter what status he may hold in the community, from his obligation to live under the dictates of human law. Human law, Smith reasoned, is also of divine origin:

Neither doth this obligation we lie under from the divine, supercede or evacuate the necessity of human laws: For all human laws are, or ought to be, founded upon, and to be the interpreters, and asserters of the divine; for the maintaining and enforcing of which, they are not only proper but highly necessary; because since man is more apt to walk "by sight, than by faith" and to be governed with respect to his thoughts and desires, his hopes and fears, by those things which are present and visible, more than by those which are future and invisible; the sufferings of bodily pain, and terrors of present death, which are some of the severest sanctions of human laws, may, and do oftentimes keep those in awe, whom neither the hopes of eternal life, nor the fears of eternal death, which are the sanctions of the divine law, can persuade to the practice of virtue, or restrain from the commission of vice.[12]

Thus, Smith believed firmly in the necessity of human government. It is necessary, not because we need it to guarantee our liberty based on natural law, but to protect us from our natural tendencies toward evil. To Smith, government was an extension of the divine dictates of God. Simply put, the natural state of man necessitates the existence of the government.

Not only is government necessary, but to Smith, it allows for the enjoyment of other advantages as well. Those advantages are twofold. First, government protects man from the unavoidable evils of living in society. Referring to his previous point that, for man, the state of nature is a state of war between good and evil, Smith insisted that without human law we would not be secure from the "degeneracy of human nature."[13] Without human law, he insisted, the entire community would be in jeopardy:

11. Ibid.
12. Ibid.
13. Ibid.

So that the whole foundation of justice, and all other moral virtues, would be out of course and overturned, the weak would be injured and insulted by the strong; the ignorant and unwise would be over-reached and undermined by the crafty and subtle; each man, according to his abilities, would be no better than a sort of beast of prey to another.[14]

This passage indicates how strongly Smith believed that the laws of a community were instituted to protect the integrity of the community itself, not simply the prerogatives of an individual or a group of individuals. Smith's view is that all members of the community need to be protected so that they can enjoy the fruits of their collectivity. The wealthiest, the smartest, the most eloquent, or the most fortunate cannot be allowed to prey on the relative vulnerabilities of others. This is indeed the foundation of Smith's concept of community.

Smith continued his discussion of the advantages of government by pointing out that all our blessings are protected by a fair and uniform administration of justice. As a general statement he said, "Whereas all those mischiefs are in great measure restrained and prevented, and all the contrary benefits procured and safely enjoyed, by a uniform and regular administration of justice."[15] He was clear when he said,

For to a just and good Government, next to the protection of the divine providence, we owe the secure use and possession of all those blessings which we enjoy, either with respect to our civil, or religious affairs. To that we owe the safety of our persons, and the property of our estates; to God we owe our improvement in the several arts and sciences of this life and even in the knowledge of our great Creator; and are indebted to that for having the freedom and liberty of worshipping him, according to the merciful declarations of his own good will and pleasure, continued to us.[16]

To Smith, the natural state of man was corrupt and chaotic. He believed that divine providence protects us from the corruption, and the laws of man strengthen our resolve of virtue and protect us from the tendency of humans to undermine the relationships we have with one another.

Smith saw government, not as a protector of individual rights, but as a mechanism to strengthen communities. He saw the just and fair administration of laws as a way of protecting the more vulnerable from the powerful. He saw government as the mechanism by which the weak and the powerful, indeed all species of man, can live together as communities.

14. Ibid.
15. Ibid.
16. Ibid.

The Duty of Those That Govern

To Smith, there was no separation between the church and the state. There was no division of the obligations we have to God and the responsibilities we have to each other. Those who have been entrusted by their neighbors to govern need to be zealous guardians of God's honor and at the same time committed to a "conscientious and prudent execution" of the laws of man. He equated the duties of the least of the community to those of the highest status. He implied, though, that those who are powerful have an even greater responsibility to those who may be vulnerable. The idea that communities are formed to protect everyone is consistently reinforced in Smith's rhetoric, but the protection of the vulnerable was especially important to him.

Underlying this philosophy is Smith's steadfast belief that the duty of government is the same as that of the individual, to exercise virtue. Accordingly, Smith insisted, "It is therefore in the power, and consequently the bound and duty of the magistrate, to be a faithful and zealous guardian of God's honor, in the support of his sacred laws, by conscientious and prudent execution of the wise and just laws of men."[17] Speaking specifically of the magistrate, Smith said, "He rules in the fear of God." In particular, the magistrate

> "must be just, ruling in the fear of God," the fear of God being the fountain or foundation, not only of justice, but of all other moral virtues whatsoever; for that magistrate that fears not God, whose vicegerent he is, must of necessity want those good principles from which alone all virtues do proceed, and on which alone all virtues do depend.[18]

This idea of the duty of a magistrate differs sharply from Locke's. It is clear that, to Smith, the magistrate should reflect virtue, not only in his judicious execution of the law, but in his behavior.

Smith was specific in delineating the qualifications of a magistrate. Flowing from this underlying notion that a magistrate should reflect virtue is the requirement that he should be just. For example, he said, "He that ruleth over men must be just; and must execute all those particular statutes or laws, which he may or shall have frequent occasion to execute, without prejudice or partiality."[19] To Smith, this meant that the magistrate should defend the just petition of a poor man "against a rich and powerful invader of his right" and likewise should not defend it out of pity or public feeling.[20] Virtue that should be defended no matter who presents the case.

Smith insisted that the magistrate must fear God. The full import of that admonition is that the magistrate should not fear man:

17. Ibid.
18. Ibid.
19. Smith (1771), SSC.
20. Smith (1761), SSC.

Now to rule in fear of God, implies that the magistrate should rule with courage and resolution; He must fear God and not man. And as he must expect to meet with rich and powerful, as well as poor and weak offenders; so must he arm himself with resolution to subdue and humble the pride and insolence of the one, as well as punish the transgressions of the other. Nay he will think it his honor, no less than his duty, to dare to curb <u>him</u>, how great soever he be, that shall dare to offend; like a good shepherd, he will protect the people, which are his flock; And like David, will smite even a lion, that shall presume to break into his hold.[21]

A more eloquent statement of the magistrate's role in maintaining paternalistic community would be hard to devise. Smith believed that the magistrate must reflect God's will for the community and must protect that righteous community from invaders no matter how powerful.

Finally, the magistrate should be wise. Smith did not share with Locke and other republicans the notion that government should impart reason to the chaos of society. Wisdom, in the sense that Smith meant it here, is a "natural depth of the mind" rather than intellect or an academic logic. Smith explained that by wisdom and knowledge he did not mean

a vast stock of human learning, the being well read in history or politics so as to be able to give a plausible account of the reasons of things, the design of governments, and the interest of nations; nor a skill in the more difficult and abstruse cases of law. The first, though an ingenious and laudable accomplishment, being not so absolutely necessary for men of this character and station. And the second may and generally is supplied by the assistance of those whose proper business and profession it is. But by knowledge I mean such a natural foresight and depth of mind, as may dispose them to comprehend and achieve working designs; such a quickness and sagacity as may qualify them for the management and conduct of business; such a wise decorum and becoming gravity as may support their own reverence and authority in [illegible] government into the love and affections of the people and yet keep up the just respect and grandeur of magistracy.[22]

To Smith, the magistrate was the agent of a government whose purpose was to reflect virtue and to protect the righteousness of the community.

In essence Smith's virtuous magistrate holds allegiance first to God and then to the community that he serves. The magistrate acts from a premise built on divine law. While Locke's magistrate protects the community from physical harm and injury from the evil acts of others, Smith's magistrate exercises a duty not only to protect the body from

21. Ibid.
22. Smith, "Observations on Nature" (n.d.), Smith Family Papers, South Carolina Historical Society, Charleston, S.C.

injury but, more important, to shield the community from the corruption of the natural tendencies of man. Smith's magistrate has a duty to foster the righteousness of the community.

Smith was clear in arguing that the most important characteristic for the civil magistrate is virtue. He asserted that the state and the church are inseparable and that the only way for the laws of man to be effective is to use them in the pursuit of God's glory:

> The most effectual method of doing which, is for the magistrate to give countenance to piety and virtue, and to rebuke with all authority, irreligion and profaneness; to put the laws of man in force against all those that violate the laws of God, and to protect his sacred religion, and all that belongs to it from the virulent tongues of lewd and presumptuous libertines: and by thus advancing the honor and glory of God, he will advance his own; for God will honor those that honor him; whereas they that despise him shall be lightly esteemed.[23]

The difference between the republican vision of acceptable government and the view of the virtuous magistrate shared by Smith and the religious conservatives of the time is important. That Smith was not a republican is clear. That his support for the revolution had to be based on something other than the natural rights and universal equality of man cannot be dismissed. Smith had a vision of government that was intertwined with his conception of community—a righteous community.

Other than virtue, or perhaps connected with it, are additional qualities that Smith maintained were necessary in the magistrate. Among them were a generous spirit, love of justice, affability and condescension, and compassion.[24] To Smith, however, it was not only the magistrate who had Christian duties related to the community. Everyone who shared in the benefits of society had an obligation to its well-being, and what should be certain by now is that the well-being that was most important to Smith was the spiritual well-being of the collective. Although the congregation to which Smith addressed his homecoming sermon in 1782 included many political leaders and officeholders, his remarks were meant for everyone. His admonition for righteousness was not meant only for those who held political power.

Duty of the Governed

In a statement that characterizes Smith's paternalism as clearly as any and illustrates his antirepublican attitudes unambiguously, Smith gave voice to his belief that a citizen must act in "ready and cheerful compliance to all just commands of your superiors; and to excite in your hearts a spirit of gratitude towards God; and those whom he has commissioned to bear rule over you."[25] This general attitude of the righteous citizen is

---

23. Smith (1761), SSC.
24. Ibid.
25. Ibid.

the principle that supports Smith's vision of government: duty first to God and then to the community. He insisted that the righteous citizen must humble himself first to God and then to those whom God has ordained to further his glory. Humbling ourselves means to amend our ways. Being a citizen is not just an attitude; it requires the fulfillment of an active obligation to the community. As Smith explained,

> If then we are serious in thus humbling ourselves before God for our past offences, and if engaging his blessing by a future amendment of life; If we mean well to our country and are in earnest in our wishes for its happiness we must, in the language of scripture cease to do evil, and learn to do well; we must acquire those virtuous habits and dispositions, which alone can recommend any people to the God of uprightness, and effectually secure them his protection.[26]

Smith was convinced that the righteousness of a community was nothing other than the righteousness of "individuals collected."[27] Therefore, to Smith, it was clear that each and every citizen had a Christian duty to act righteously and in harmony with divine law "lest his misconduct, joined to the misconduct of others, be the fatal bar to the divine protection."[28] It was not enough, however, just to act accordingly. To Smith, real virtue was to be found not only in our behavior but also in our hearts. The citizen must mean what he says and does. Sincerity is an essential characteristic of the Christian citizen. Smith asked, "Are my pretensions to virtuous and religious practices, sincere and real; or being the daubings only of outward garnish, do they hide the deformity of a fool heart, of iniquitous deed, and base design?"[29] It was not easy to be the citizen in Smith's vision. The ideal individualism touted by Locke and other republicans simply had no place in Smith's ideal community. We are not free to act as we choose as long as we injure no one. We have a duty to others and to the community, not only to avoid harming others but, more important, to exalt others to righteousness. Citizens have this duty, not because we owe it to the community, but because we owe it to God. Smith reminded his congregants that the blessings they enjoyed were not a result of their toil or their neighbors' benevolence but because of God's grace, for which they should give thanks. According to Smith, "As we of America were long blessed with signal marks of God's forbearance; our gratitude to heaven should have borne some proportion to the mercies vouchsafed. Disobedience under our circumstances was doubly heinous, and will greatly increase the offences punished."[30]

The prosperity of any society, according to Smith, depends on the degree to which its members are virtuous. It is religion, not government devoid of it, that will lead to

26. Smith (1775), SSC.
27. Ibid.
28. Ibid.
29. Ibid.
30. Ibid.

virtue. Smith maintained, "It is genius of true religion to inspire the mind with every noble virtue; the love of our country, generosity, fortitude, temperance."[31] In another clear explanation of his paternalism, he admonishes especially those with wealth and influence, that theirs is the greatest duty:

> Men of large fortunes and extensive influence lead the way, and thousands will catch the fashion from them. Let them be examples of every noble and virtuous require-ment, of love for their community, temperance, moderation, fidelity and honor, let them reverence that Almighty Being on whom they depend for all things; and they will find the advantage of so wise a conduct—they will find it in the willing obedi-ence of their children; in the duty and faithfulness of their dependents; in the con-stancy of their friends; in the proud approbation of their country; and the admiration and fear of their enemies.[32]

Smith's vision of community was one in which every person had a sacred obligation for the well-being of everyone else. Those who were blessed with wealth or influence had a greater obligation because they served as examples to the rest. If the powerful were not virtuous, then their dependents would likely fall short as well.

But the wealthy and the powerful were not alone in shouldering responsibility to their community. Smith insisted that even the lowliest of those among them had a Christian duty to act according to God's will. "Even the beggar, though clothed in rags," Smith preached, "can have his mind adorned with the robes of righteousness."[33] Smith viewed the righteousness of the community as everyone's responsibility because the "sins of a community are made up of the sins of individuals."[34] The community reflects righteousness as the individuals within it act with virtue. Christian duty to the com-munity is not just a benevolent attitude or kind words, it requires or actions, positive and virtuous. No matter if we are magistrates or beggars, our responsibilities to our neighbors are real and sacred.

Smith's Ideal Society

In his homecoming sermon, Smith proclaimed that there are no better guidelines for moral conduct in private and well as public affairs than those contained in the Prov-erbs of Solomon. The basis for their usefulness is, according to Smith, they are based on a single solid principle, "the fear of the Lord."[35] By this Smith clearly meant that an "overruling providence" was the source of our blessings and should be the reason for

31. Ibid.
32. Ibid.
33. Ibid.
34. Ibid.
35. Smith (1782), SSC.

our humility. The ideal society was based on the due sense of religion, an acknowledgment that there is a power superior to any that anyone on earth can exert or bestow. Humility underlay the ideal society. Arrogance of power and arrogance of the individual were the corrupters of the virtuous community. To Smith, the advantages of such a society is that, while it performs the functions of all societies—that is the protection of the inhabitants against the evils of others—it provides a morality that is not found in communities devoid of religion.

For Smith, while social institutions were necessary to secure the safety of the community, they were insufficient to provide all the security that was needed:

> In the first rudiments indeed of civil society, if the expression may be allowed, open and intended violence, when apparently so, may be restrained; the insolent may be quelled, and the outrageous crushed. But this is by no means sufficient to secure the safety of any community whatever. For in time, fraud and artifice will take place in place of open and avowed violence, and whatever mischievous designs, though carried on in secret, though attended with the utmost danger to society, may not only escape public opposition, but even public observation.[36]

To Smith, the value of public institutions are undeniable, but they are insufficient to protect us because much of what undermines the health of a community occurs outside the notice of the public. A higher tribunal is necessary. A greater force than human institutions is needed. Smith argued that human beings are motivated by the lure of reward and the deterrent of punishment. He maintained that this is the "the master hinge on which every form of government amongst men must turn" and that without it, societies would unravel. The reason that human institutions are inadequate is precisely "because society must in many respects be ignorant of many dark frauds, many secret villainies, which may be committed."[37] Smith believed that such dangers could be prevented only if protection comes "from a much higher tribunal, than an earthly one."[38] All injury cannot be prevented simply by the threat of punishments. Even if all crimes are discovered and punished, however, something more is needed. To Smith, a conscience of the community was required. A conscience that was derived not from human law but from divine law and an active and sincere fear of God. The ideal community is one with a collective conscience.

Civic Conscience

To Smith, it was unarguable that "men must fear some superior power" and "must be restrained either by their own consciences, or not at all."[39] Smith implored, "By what

36. Ibid.
37. Ibid.
38. Ibid.
39. Ibid.

force, let us ask, can conscience have in a state where no religion, no sense of over-ruling providence prevails?"[40] Even if some, or most, individuals possess the right moral rectitude, what of the larger community? To Smith, there must be a collective conscience. That is the real shield against evil. That is the only effective force to protect the community—a civic conscience.

The source of Smith's conception of civic conscience was undoubtedly based on his theology. His conservative religious orientation certainly served as the foundation of his approach. Another unlikely patriot of the time, John Witherspoon, the Scottish president of the College of New Jersey (later Princeton), had a similar view of civic obligation. Witherspoon, the only clergy to have signed the Declaration of Independence, wrote of his vision of a duty of citizenship rooted in faith.

Explaining that such duty was based on the development of a moral sense, Witherspoon believed that the development of a moral sense, or conscience, was impossible without the belief in divine providence; that is,

> the moral sense carries a good deal more in it than merely an approbation than a certain class of actions as beautiful, praiseworthy or delightful, and therefore finding our interest in them as the most noble gratification. The moral sense implies also a sense of obligation, that such and such things are right and others wrong, that we are bound in duty to do the one, and that our conduct is hateful, blameable, and deserving of punishment if we do the contrary; and there is also in the moral sense or conscience an apprehension or belief that reward and punishment will follow according as we shall act in the one way or in the other.[41]

There is no evidence that Smith was influenced in any way by Witherspoon. They both may have been influenced by shared sources—perhaps by Anthony Ashley Cooper, third Earl of Shaftesbury—but the convergence of their views, about civic conscience, are striking.[42] Witherspoon was convinced, and it appears no less so than Smith, that duty or obligation is what elevated the virtue of right conduct to higher nobility. Witherspoon explained "that indeed the beauty and sweetness of virtuous action arises from this very circumstance—that it is a compliance with duty or supposed obligation. Take away this, and the beauty vanishes as well as the pleasure."[43] Duty to others is virtuous and more noble than any other right conduct.

Christian duty, Witherspoon and Smith seem to have insisted, involve affirmative action to promote the public good. Witherspoon wrote that "promoting the public

---

40. Ibid.

41. John Witherspoon, *Selected Writings* (Carbondale: Southern Illinois University Press, 1990), 163.

42. For discussion of Witherspoon's sources on civic conscience, see his *Selected Writings*, 7.

43. Ibid., 163.

good seems to be so nearly connected with virtue that we must necessarily suppose that universal virtue could be of universal utility."[44] He was even clearer when he wrote:

> True virtue certainly promotes the general good, and this may be made use of as an argument in doubtful cases to determine whether a particular principle is right or wrong, but to make the good of the whole our immediate principle of action is putting ourselves in God's place and actually superseding the necessity and use of the particular principles of duty which hath impressed upon the conscience.[45]

Witherspoon saw the connection and the mutual necessity of both individual and public interest as "they should be made to assist and not destroy each other."[46] This belief, certainly shared by Smith, is yet another reason for his insistence that religion and the affairs of state could not be separated.

Likewise, the development of a civic conscience is impossible in the thinking of both Smith and Witherspoon without a solid faith. Witherspoon argued,

> Nor is this all, but we have all certainly a natural sense of dependence. The belief of a divine being is certainly either innate and necessary or has been handed down from the first man and can now be well supported by the clearest reason. And our relation to him not only lays the foundation of many moral sentiments and duties, but completes the idea of morality and law by subjecting us to him and teaching us to conceive of him, not only as our Maker, preserver and benefactor, but as our righteous governor and supreme judge. As the being and perfections of God irrefrangibly established, the obligation of duty must ultimately rest here. It ought not to be forgotten that the belief or apprehension of a future state of rewards and punishments has been as universal as the belief of a deity, and seems inseparable from it, and therefore must be considered as the sanction of the moral law.[47]

It is easy to see that the notion of predestination or election would undermine this sense of reward and punishment in the ultimate sense.

Robert Smith not only conceived of a civic duty that reflected a due concern for the good of the community but saw it as a result of a collective conscience based on religious belief. Without this belief that extended to the acceptance of divine providence, the nobility of such a duty was undermined. So the beauty of right action toward the community was not just a matter of the public good and public interest, it was a path to the satisfaction of the private interest as well. To Smith, Christian duty and civic conscience were inescapably bound.

44. Ibid., 167.
45. Ibid., 167–68.
46. Ibid., 168.
47. Ibid., 169.

The Pursuit of Virtue and Righteous Community

When John Witherspoon wrote, "Civil society is distinguished from domestic in the union of a number of families in one state for their mutual benefit," he meant much more than the impact of such union on the mere comfort or wealth of the collective.[48] Witherspoon, as well as Smith, believed that ensuring the mutual well-being of a community was a spiritual act, one that bestowed as much benefit to those who were exercising such duty as to those who were the recipients.

Robert Smith did not embrace the enlightenment idea of social contract, nor did his aristocratic brethren. Smith was not an adherent of the popular notion of individualism, nor was he a republican. He believed that we were obligated to serve our community. Our individual well-being was not only subordinate to that of the community; it was dependent on our due exercise of our duty to our neighbors. Smith rejected the republican belief in the separation of church and state, insisting that the ideal government was inseparable from religion.

This belief led Smith to argue that Christians should exhibit a sense of community that was based solidly on the theology of good works. Christian duty, then, was intertwined with a civic conscience. The civic conscience that Smith envisioned should mandate that the Christians defend, above all, the public good. Private gain, personal comfort, individual rights and prerogatives were clearly subordinate to the duty to one's community.

While others were motivated in their revolutionary action by the compelling force of natural universal rights and individualism, Smith and his neighbors were motivated by a very different philosophy. Their motivation was not even similar to that of their northern revolutionary comrades, but it was no less compelling. It was not the rights of the individual that Smith was fighting for, it was for the righteousness of his community. That was more important than any other consideration.

48. Ibid., 199.

PART TWO

The Sermons

I

"Ruling in the Fear of God"

2 Samuel 23:3
He that ruleth over men must be just ruling in the fear of God.

THESE WORDS though variously rendered and as variously applied by different men: some with a little change of the version understand and[1] expound them with relation to God himself, and connect them with the preceding verses, as a part of his glorious title and attributes, whereby his absolute dominion and sovereignty is particularly expressed over just men and those that fear him.

Others without any change of the version, explain the text, and that not unjustly as a part of the character of the promised Messiah and the anointed Son of God: for he properly is, as well as his Almighty Father, the Rock and Support of Israel, a most just and holy ruler over men, and one that rules in the fear of God that so rules his subjects by his blessed Spirit, that they may learn from a true fear of God, to study and practice piety and holiness of life, according to the great end of which he laid down his life, viz., that he might purchase to himself a particular people, zealous of good works.

Others are yet in the general acceptation of these, more particularly applied to David, the pious and glorious king of Israel; and that either as a promise or prediction of him, in which sense they signify that David the son of Jesse should be a just ruler over men, and that he should rule in the fear of God; or else as a precept or command given to King David agreeable to which he shall rule and govern his people; and consequently the text in this sense may be conceived, as useful and obligatory, not only to <u>him</u>, but to all other things and inferior magistrates whatsoever.

And in this acceptation of the words, I shall consider them on this present occasion. First, by pointing out the necessity and advantages of Government in general. And secondly, the useful and necessary qualifications of a good magistrate. As the first of these, the necessity and advantages of Government in General.

The former is founded upon the natural proneness of man to sin and the latter is the necessary consequent of that just restraint, which good government lays upon that proneness. Was man in the same condition now, wherein he was at first created, had he a [illegible], like that of [illegible] enlightened with the brightest reason and adorned with the beauty of holiness and virtue, possibly these might be no occasion for any law to instruct him in, or to persuade, or to compel him to the practice of his duty; because in such a case, the "the law written in his heart," might be a law, a very perfect law for the conduct of his life: But since as the Apostle informs us, and we find by experience, that we have a "law in our members," continually warring against the law of our mind, which hurries us on with a much stronger bias toward evil, than toward good; it was necessary for us, that God, who knew the deceitfulness and depravity of our hearts, should out of his infinite mercy prescribe us such wholesome rules, as might direct and excite us to walk in the paths of wisdom and happiness, and fright us from the ways of folly and perdition.

Wherefore, because the law of nature shone with a dim and feeble ray, it pleased the most high God, by an express declaration of his will, enforced by the most glorious rewards promised to the obedient and the most dreadful punishments denounced against the disobedient, to oblige us to do justly, to love mercy, and to walk humbly with him. Neither doth this obligation we lie under from the divine, supercede or evacuate the necessity of human laws: For all human laws are, or ought to be, founded upon, and to be the interpreters, and asserters of the divine; for the maintaining and enforcing of which, they are not only proper but highly necessary; because since man is more apt to walk "by sight, than by faith"[2] and to be governed with respect to his thoughts and desires, his hopes and fears, by those things which are present and visible, more than by those which are future and invisible; the sufferings of bodily pain, and terrors of present death, which are some of the severest sanctions of human laws, may, and do oftentimes keep those in awe, whom neither the hopes of eternal life, nor the fears of eternal death, which are the sanctions of the divine law, can persuade to the practice of virtue, or restrain from the commission of vice.

It is therefore in the power, and consequently the bound and duty of the magistrate, to be a faithful and zealous guardian of God's honor, in the support of his sacred laws, by a conscientious and prudent execution of the wise and just laws of men. The advantages of which we may cultivate, partly from those unavoidable evils, from which such a[3] conscientious and prudent execution of the wise and just laws of men, doth deliver and secure us; and partly from those great benefits, which do necessarily accrue to that body or community, wherein such a regular administration of justice is observed; the advantages of which we may estimate, first, from those unavoidable evils, from which a conscientious and prudent execution of the laws of men doth deliver and secure us: for without it such is the degeneracy of human nature, that taking a survey of it, not from its original beauty and perfection, but from its ruin and decay, we should have too much reason, to infer, that a state of nature is a state of war; wherein it would be truly said of every man, what the angel of the Lord said of Ishmael, "his hand will be against every man, and every man's hand against him." So that the whole foundation of justice, and all other moral virtues, would be out of course and overturned, the weak would be injured and insulted by the strong; the ignorant and unwise would be over-reached and undermined by the crafty and subtle; each man, according to his abilities, would be no better than a sort of beast of prey to another. Whereas all those mischiefs are in a great measure restrained and prevented, and all the contrary benefits procured and safely enjoyed, by a uniform and regular administration of justice.

Which is another thing, whereby we may estimate the advantages thereof: and these advantages are a great and many, but so very common and familiar, that like health and strength to a sound and vigorous constitution of body, they are either not all observed, or else[4] (which shows our base ingratitude) not esteemed by us as they deserve to be. For to a just and good Government, next to the protection of the divine providence, we owe the secure use and possession of all those blessings which we enjoy, either with respect to our civil, or religious affairs. To that we owe the safety of our persons, and the property of our estates; to God we owe our improvement in the several arts and sciences of this life and even in the knowledge of our great Creator; and are indebted to that for having the freedom and liberty of worshipping him, according to the merciful declarations of his own good will and pleasure, continued to us. For the preservation of which happy inestimable privileges, there is no national establishment in the world, better provided with laws, both wise and excellent, through kingdoms and provinces to which we belong and yet even these[5] might have been useless to us, had it not pleased the Almighty in his good providence, to place the crown on the head of a protestant prince, whose heart we beseech Almighty God so to dispose and govern, that he may always strenuously defend the faith of the Church, and impartially execute the laws of the state; that in all his thoughts, words, and works, he may ever seek God's glory and honor, and study to preserve the people committed to his charge, in wealth, peace, and godliness: To shall all inferior and subordinate magistrates learn from his great example, as well as from the words of the text, what qualifications are not only expedient, but necessary, if they hope to discharge the important trust committed to them with honor to themselves, and benefit to those over whom they preside.[6]

Which leads to the second particular to be considered, viz., the necessary qualifications of a good magistrate; He that ruleth over men must be just, ruling in the fear of God. First, He that ruleth over men must be just; and must execute all those particular statutes or laws, which he may or shall have frequent occasion to execute, without prejudice or partiality.[7]

The wise and good magistrate therefore, will observe an impartial distribution of justice, without any respect of persons—interest—or opinions and will strenuously defend the just cause of a poor man, against a rich and powerful invader of his right; and yet will not, through pity or popularity, countenance any person in a bad one. Neither can the unworthy treatment he may have received from his enemy, provoke him to pervert justice that he might satisfy his own revenge. Nor can all the endearing offices of Love and Kindness so far bribe his judgment, as to make him turn the seals of justice that he might gratify his friend; But will, whoever be the unjust aggressor, correct him by his authority, chastise him with the sword of justice, which, he knows is his bounden duty not to bear in vain. And will on the other hand, whoever be the party injured, redress and support him by the same authority, which he is assured was therefore given him, that he might protect and comfort those that do <u>good</u>; and terrify and restrain only those that do <u>evil</u>. Nevertheless this qualification of impartiality is not sufficient for the magistrate, or rather the magistrate is not sufficient for it: Unless, secondly, he rules[8] in the fear of God: "He must be just, ruling in the fear of God," the fear of God being the fountain or foundation, not only of justice, but of all other moral virtues whatsoever; for that magistrate that fears not God, whose vicegerent he is, must of necessity want those good principles from which alone all virtues do proceed, and on which alone all virtues do depend.

Now to rule in fear of God, implies that the magistrate should rule with courage and resolution; He must fear God and not man. And as he must expect to meet with rich and powerful, as well as poor and weak offenders; so must he arm himself with resolution to subdue and humble the pride and insolence of the one, as well as punish the transgressions of the other. Nay he will think it his honor, no less than his duty, to dare to curb <u>him</u>, how great soever he be, that shall dare to offend; like a good shepherd, he will protect the people, which are his flock;[9] And like David, will smite even a lion, that shall presume to break into his hold.

If the magistrate through fear or cowardice should betray his trust, he disarms the laws of their force, their life, and sting, and makes his own authority, which is, and ought to be sacred, contemptible and ridiculous. Whereas if he exerts his courage in the execution of[10] the laws, and that time, by whomsoever violated; he preserves their power and design, and makes himself, and office, worthy of esteem and reverence: he reflects such a luster upon the dignity of his office, that, in some measure,[11] he will seem to deserve that glorious title, which the scriptures give to magistrates, where it says of them, "I have said ye are gods." And therefore to rule in the fear of God implies that the magistrate should, to the utmost of his power, endeavor by all his actions, to advance his glory. For he that fears God, as he ought to do, doth not entertain a slavish and unworthy fear of him, as of an arbitrary and tyrannical master; but a filial awe of him, as of a kind and indulgent mother; and consequently will, as much as he is able, strive to pay him that respect and homage, which is most justly due to him; and therefore will, with all his might, promote his glory. The most effectual method of doing which, is for the magistrate to give countenance to piety and virtue, and to rebuke with all authority, irreligion and profaneness; to put the laws of man in force against all those that violate the laws of God, and to protect his sacred religion, and all that belongs to it from the virulent tongues of lewd and presumptuous libertines: and by thus advancing the honor and glory of God, he will advance his own; for God will honor those that honor him; whereas they that despise him shall be lightly esteemed.

To these qualifications, I have already mentioned, we may add or rather reduce those of a public and generous spirit; a hearty zeal for the love of justice; affability and condescension, to those of low degree, pity and compassion, bounty and liberality to the poor and distressed; for all these virtues and graces, both recommend and adorn the magistrate; and represent justice as full of sweetness and love, as of majesty and terror; and give that public person in whom they shine, a just right to say with Job: "I put on righteousness, and it clothed me; my judgment is as a robe and a diadem." From what has been said, give me leave to make a brief application to those who bear rule and authority. And likewise to those who live under; and enjoy the benefits thereof.

To apply what has been said to the First, although there are some magistrates, who think it sufficient to receive honor from the high stations to which they advanced; it must be owned nevertheless, that there are others, who by their wisdom and justice, have added reputation to the honorable places they have filled; to such as these, I hope I am now applying my discourse: And hope I shall not be thought impertinent, if I desire you to be careful, to discharge the several duties of your respective stations, with diligence and patience; with an upright heart, and well tempered zeal; aiming at the glory of God in maintaining his sacred laws; and the welfare and happiness of men, in preserving, with all your might and strength, piety—justice—and peace amongst them. Nor should I offend you, if I should observe, that the outward marks of honor, which are appropriated to your offices, should make you consider whose divine image and [illegible] you bear: and that a serious reflection or your own character should make you dare to do anything assiduously because of it; and only fear and scorn to do anything which is beneath and[12] unworthy of it.

As to those who live under and enjoy the benefits of a good magistrate's rule and authority: though subjection is a duty difficult to be believed, and more hard to be practiced, by corrupt nature, man being as Job expresses it, born like the wild asses colt, in regard to the rudeness of his mind, and the rebellious temper of his passions, hating, through pride and stubbornness of heart, all superiority and restraint, yet considering the great advantages of government, and the miserable confusion and disorder, which without it would necessarily ensue: considering these things, I presume,[13] (without laying before you the term of the divine, as well as human law, denounced against the disobedient) that it would be no difficult task, to animate you to a ready and cheerful compliance to all the just commands of your superiors; and to excite in your hearts a spirit of gratitude towards God; and those whom he has commissioned to bear rule over you.

But if these considerations will not prevail, I shall desire you seriously to consider, how sharply St. Paul reproves those that[14] despise government, that are presumptuous, self-willed, and are not afraid to speak evil of dignities; And let the Apostle's reproof excite us to behave, as to deserve none, yea, rather, let it excite us so to behave, as may entitle us to those great rewards which are reserved in heaven for all those, who live in obedience to the just laws of man, and the holy laws of God. For to such, will the great judge eternal at the last day pronounce well done good and faithful servants; enter ye into your Master's joy—which may God of his infinite mercy say to us all through.[15]

This sermon was delivered at St. Philip's on two occasions. The initial delivery was in 1761 and the second in 1771. This sermon is indexed by Smith as #101 Session, and he credits Wilder as a printed source.

II

On the Importance
of Religion to Society

Proverbs 14:34
Righteousness exalteth a nation.

THE PROVERBS OF SOLOMON may justly be considered, as containing a collection of the wisest sentences, drawn from his own Observation and experience. They indeed contain in them instructions necessary for the direction of our moral conduct in every state and condition of human life; in our public as well as in our private capacity.

They are indeed suited to all ranks and orders of men. They, by the most happy combination, are calculated at once for the lowest, as well as the highest and most cultivated understanding; for they are not founded on an airy and ideal system, but are fixed on this most firm basis, on the most solid principle, the fear of the Lord. Nor are they the worse for being destitute for the most part of any connection or coherence with one another,[1] as they are set down just as they accidentally came into the mind of the divine penman, or as some extraordinary occurrence presented them to his observation.

Out of that great variety of matter, on which Solomon has treated, the words chosen for the subject of this day's discourse contain in them this important truth, "that righteousness tendeth to the prosperity of the people."

By righteousness in this place, must be signified a due sense of the religion; that is, an acknowledgement of an overruling Providence, the Rewarder of good men and the Punisher of the evil. If the words of the text be thus explained and understood; the subject naturally resulting from them will be the importance of religion to society.

Now in order to confirm that doctrine it will be requisite to consider in the first place the great defects which society must labor under without religion; and the next to point out the confusion in which the world in consequence of those defects would be involved.

It is, I apprehend, universally allowed, that the principle motive[2] which induced them to unite together in society, was that they might avoid those evils marshal violence, rapine and slaughter which of necessity must have abounded amongst equals in a mere uncultivated state of nature. Society therefore from the very nature of its institutions must certainly have been instituted as a remedy against every species of rapine and of violence to which men as has been observed, might in the rude state of nature have been exposed; and to secure to every individual even the meanest of the community, those mighty and hereditary advantages, to which everyone has equal right.

But another, and that no mean or trivial advantage arises from its being calculated to provide much better for the accommodations and conveniences of life,[3] than could be done in a state of nature.

These advantages, it is true, might not have been thought of, when society was first instituted; for we will know that evil felt hath a much stronger impression on the mind, than good imagined; and that the means of removing the one is much more easily discovered, than the way to procure the other. It is therefore highly reasonable to suppose that these great advantages resulting from society were by no means thought of on its first institution, but that they sprung up as it were spontaneously from the purport and nature of the institution itself.

But allowing which indeed cannot be well denied, that many considerable ends are answered by thus uniting together, and entering into society; yet its plan is still most certainly defective in many respects. On examination it will be found quite ineffectual for remedying many disorders of the most fatal tendency, and which eventually might destroy the happiness if not the very existence of the community, without some assistance far superior to that, which a contract hastily entered into betwixt individuals of different passions, and different humours, and different pursuits could possibly afford.

In the first rudiments indeed of civil society, if the expression may be allowed, open and intended violence, when apparently so, may be restrained; the insolent may be quelled, and the outrageous crushed. But this is by no means sufficient to secure the safety of any community whatever. For in time, fraud and artifice will take place in place of open and avowed violence, and whatever mischievous designs, though carried on in secret, though attended with the utmost danger to society, may not only escape public opposition, but even public observation. For it is certain, there is a great weakness and inefficacy in every human society simply and abstractedly considered. For strip it of its dependencies on matters which at first may seem foreign to it and it will be found hardly equal to the task of enforcing an obedience to the moral duties. The reason of this is evident. Society considered merely of itself wants the grand sanction of reward, which is the necessary, the master hinge on which every form of government amongst men must turn, and without which it cannot be supported. Now this reward cannot be expected[4] from society, because must in many respects be ignorant of many dark frauds, many secret villanies, which may be committed. The expectation then of reward, and the prevention of such crimes must come from a much higher tribunal, than any earthly one.

In such cases, men must fear some superior power, in such cases men must be restrained either by their own consciences, or not at all. But what force, let us ask, can conscience have in a state, where no religion, no sense of an overruling providence prevails? Without this the force of conscience would soon be diminished, would soon dwindle into nothing. But here perhaps it will be said, What? Is not virtue of itself lovely and beneficial, and as such cannot it influence us without the sanction of religion? In answer to this, let us only well observe that even though virtue be in its own nature ever so amiable, yet considering the great and flagrant corruption of human nature, its power would by no means suffice without that of religion. For to be guided by the rules of right reason; to be influenced by the charms of moral excellence, undoubtedly requires a more elegant and refined taste, than can possibly be attained by the general herd of mankind.

In confirmation of the doctrine, which we have advanced, it must universally be allowed, that we, all of us, are capable of being moved by rewards and punishments. These indeed are motives suited to all national beings, because they are equally addressed to the passions of hope and fear, those two mighty springs which actuate and enliven human nature. But for the sake of argument let us suppose, that a community of people might live together without a sense of religion. Let us even suppose that it might subsist under the most excellent form of government, which the ingenuity of man could devise: yet alas! How precarious would be the obligations in the case of both of those who governed and of those who obeyed? Under these circumstances, those who governed, and those who obeyed, would be activated not by the fear of God, but by the fear of each other.

It is a most solemn truth, and the experience of every age and nation shows it, that the laws of society and religion are hardly sufficient by their united efforts to restrain men from turning into confusion.

How much less efficacious then would these laws of society be, were they to be deprived of that necessary sanction, religion? How could our lives, our property? How could everything dear and valuable to man be secured to us without it? How would fraud and falsehood universally take place and prevail! What a scene of perfidiousness and hypocrisy would ensue? In short, what a deluge of abominations, what an inundation of iniquities would overflow, would break down the banks of all society. In one word, as force will sometimes defy, and cunning often elude, the best regulated laws and the completest systems of human government, it is therefore evident, that without some further, some superior aid, they would be almost totally deficient and ineffectual. But religion, useless it is too often deemed, prophaned as it too often is, amply supplies this defect, by teaching us, that there is a being, who ruleth over all the children of men, and all the Kingdoms of Earth; who understandeth all their works and all their devices; and who accordingly will punish or reward them hereafter. This then is the grand basis of society, this is the chief hinge on which it turns, and in this sense therefore it may be said according to the words of the text "that righteousness exalteth or supporteth a people."

Having thus in general shown the vast importance of religion to society, I should now proceed to show the great, the mighty advantages, with which the Christian religion is in particular attended. I should now proceed to point out, how admirably this religion is calculated[5] to promote the social bliss of man, and to advance the universal good of every particular community. But as these matters would carry me into a very enlarged, and too extensive a field of argument, I shall only (now) employ your attention, whilst I deduce an inference or two, from what has been hitherto advanced. Is religion then, from these arguments and the state of mankind in general, allowed to be of importance to society? If it is, it surely, it surely most unquestionably must be the duty of everyone, who deems himself a worthy member of it, and who wishes to confirm and establish its authority to fix it on a sure and certain foundation, which may be superior to all human laws, and indeed the higher a man stands in the opinion of his fellow members of any community, the greater opportunity he has of swaying and directing the hearts and affections of mankind.

In this case piety and goodness will not only prove an ornament to themselves, but will likewise be the glory of that society, to which they may belong. And it will not only be their glory, but it will likewise be attended with good and happy effect, that they will have the consolation, the glorious consolation of reflecting, that their endeavors they set an example for others to follow, and show them, as the wisest of men observes, that those, who are exalted above all others, should be able to scatter away evil with their eyes.

Now this certainly can be no otherwise effected than by the influence of a good example, which certainly speaks more loudly, and with a more enforcing authority, than the strictest and severest laws. For as the sun diffuses through this material system of the universe, both life and heat, and by his powerful and genial energy diffuses life, motion and action throughout the whole creation, so the example of the good and the religious man, animates informs, actuates, and enlivens every part of political society. Whereas on the other hand, if those, who are advanced above their fellow citizens, and who may be deemed as the luminaries of the world, should fail to dispense the salutary influence of a good example, and by their behavior stamp as it were a credit on the vice and irreligion, then the destruction, the dissolution of a community is as much to be expected, as the end of nature itself, when the Stars of Heaven shall withdraw their splendor and their influence from the sublunary regions.

Most highly therefore doth it import all good men, to consider that they are not[6] acting for themselves alone; but that the welfare of the whole community, in great measures depend upon themselves.

But it is not to be imagined, that this duty is alone confined to those, who may be advanced above their fellow citizens, to those who are high in office, the guardians of our community,[7] but it is likewise the concern, the duty and the interest of every member of society to promote, strengthen and encourage religion. For when religious restraints are once broken through, what can be expected, but that men should abandon themselves to every vile passion, to every criminal indulgence. As the contempt of religion increases, it may be relied on that a dissoluteness of morals will prevail, and that real probity, public spirit, honor and honesty will very soon be totally extinguished in a state, and when these virtues once expire, liberty, that boasted, that inestimable privilege of man, will soon expire too.

This solemn truth may easily be deduced from the history of all former ages, which are replete with the strongest proofs of this alarming and most melancholy truth—that sin is not only the reproach, but that it will likewise be the destruction of a people; or according to the words of the text, "that righteousness exalteth a people."

Let us all, my friends and brethren, if we have any the least regard for that community, of which we are members, for those our fellow creatures and our fellow Christians, to whom, we are connected by every sacred, and endearing tie, be convinced, that it is our duty to discountenance every species of vice and irreligion, and to promote the practice of virtue and godliness to the utmost extent of those abilities, which the God of Heaven and Earth in his great goodness has bestowed upon us.

This important truth let me once more exhort you, friends and brethren, well and seriously consider, be assured, that though at all times it is our bounden our indispensable duty to discourage vice and immorality; yet it is more peculiarly so and in these perilous times,[8] when we are continually exposed to every hazard and every danger, which can beset mankind. By these means, we shall secure the blessing of God on all our endeavors here below, and as a reward for our perfect adherence to his cause, we shall through mediation of our blessed Savior and Redeemer, be entitled to everlasting happiness hereafter.

Which God of His infinite mercy, etc., etc., etc.

This sermon was delivered first while Smith was banished to Philadelphia. He gave it at Christ Church in Philadelphia in 1782, at St. Peter's in Philadelphia, and as his first sermon after he returned to Charlestown on June 1, 1783. He also delivered it twice more to the General Assembly, in October 1784 and again in January 1789. The sermon is indexed by Smith as #101, and he credits Martyn as an original source. Smith supplied the sermon's title.

III

"Keep All My Commandments Always"

Deuteronomy 5:29
O that those were such an heart in them, that they would fear me, and keep all my
commandments always, that it might be well with them, and their children forever.

WERE THERE NO OTHER EVIDENCES of the Being and, Providence of Almighty God, than those which observation and experience point out, the manifestations of a wise and merciful superintendence are very clear and demonstrable. God hath not left himself without a witness in any part of his creation, in the wonderful contrivance of the universe—and the wise disposal of its several parts; in support of that nature he commanded into being; and in his care of those creatures he called forth to life and happiness.[1]

In speaking of the operations of almighty power we talk indeed of nature, and natural causes as if independent of providence, but what is nature but the hand of God—and natural causes, but secret affects of omnipotence. Directing us in the most striking and intelligible manner to the first efficient cause of all.

But lest the notices of Providence should either be overlooked or forgotten by us. Almighty God in his great mercy to mankind set up the Jewish peoples as a standard to the several nations of the world; giving us those by a monument of his care and circumspection; and teaching us a lesson we seem extremely averse to learn, how impotent and insufficient we are without it. The favor and guardianship of Heaven[2] are so necessary to communities and individuals, that if they are but withdrawn, prosperity and happiness are withdrawn with them; and yet so vain and foolish is the heart of man, as to forget or disregard the important truth. We form schemes of happiness, and deceive ourselves with a weak imagination of security, without ever taking God into the question; no wonder then if our hopes prove abortive, and the conceits of our vain minds end in disappointment and sorrow. For [we are] inclined to attribute our prosperity[3] to the wisdom of our own councils, and the arm of our own flesh, we become forgetful of him from whom our strength and wisdom are derived; and are then betrayed into that fatal security, which ends in shame, in misery and ruin.

As a curb therefore to the arrogance of man, in the Jewish history, God hath declared his power over, and government of, the world; instructing us, that apart of his blessing, vain is the counsel and the help of man: that with it the most improbable means can administer happiness, and afford security. And that the way to obtain this blessing is by fearing him and keeping his commandments.

The part of scripture[4] under our present consideration (which are the words of God himself) is very express to this point. He declares, that if they fear him, and keep all his commandments always, that it should be well with them, and their children forever. From this declaration the deduction is natural and easy—that if they did not fear him and keep his commandments, it would <u>not</u> be well for them, and their children forever.

As the article of fear he lays great stress when it, because it is in a great degree the support of Religion, and accordingly tells us, when Ephraim spake trembling, he exalted himself in Israel, but when he offended in Baal, he died. As to the observation of his commandments, he insists upon it as a duty both general and perpetual, that we should keep them all, and that always. And we are bound to it under the strongest penal sanction: "for those that honor him, he will honor; and those that despise him, he will lightly esteem." It is not my intention to enlarge upon the doctrine of fear and obedience, because they are of themselves pretty obvious—neither does the occasion of this day's solemnity require it—but should anyone ask,[5] "why is the Almighty so concerned about the conduct or behavior of men: or what need he concern himself whether they fear or obey him or not?" The question is sufficiently presumptuous, but the answer is plain, "that it is his <u>goodness</u>, not his <u>interest</u>, which prompts him to it." And if he expresses himself with a desire that shows something of uneasiness when considered in a human light, it is only because he is earnest that we should avoid that punishment, which rigorous justice will of necessity demand. His desire of obedience is that we should be saved and if he calls upon us to observe his laws, it is because his judgments are ready to vindicate any contempt that may be cast upon them. It is remarkable of the Israelites, that after every general revolt from God, we find them groaning under [illegible] afflicted by tyrants, oppressed by conquerors. When they repent, God hears their prayer, and sends them a deliverer. If at any time they rest themselves upon Egypt, and rely upon human policy more than upon a divine promise, his indignation to them is equal to their prevarication with him. If, again, they become sensible of their error, and humble themselves by a submission proportionate to their crime, his favor is restored thereon. We may observe, that their great Lawgiver, Moses, took great pains, to prevent them being misled by a false notion of God Almighty's Mercies. He was ever warning them, that they were not to conclude themselves the favorites of heaven, because that favor was merely conditional; that they might forfeit all by disobedience, and would become as miserable as they might otherwise be happy. When he reminds them of the mighty things that God had done for them in Egypt it was always to stimulate them[6] to such a conduct as would show their gratitude. He taught them to look back to their first original, and to recollect how inconsiderable they were, when the Almighty first distinguished them. He bids them remember how he preserved and protected them when they were a wandering family and were glad to sojourn where they could find admittance. "A Syrian ready to perish was their Father," and "he went down into Egypt with a few." This was the solemn confession they were obliged to make every year. Yet such was the regard of the Almighty to their perishing Syrians, and to his Father's destitute family that he suffered no man to do them wrong but reproved even Kings for their sake.

We have taken a short view of the wonderful mercies that were shown to this extraordinary nation. The question that now occurs, is, "What could be the meaning and design of all this?" Why was this magnificence bestowed, and all these favors heaped upon them? Was it merely an act of the divine will, without any end or reason proposed? Was it not rather a lesson to all mankind, to convince them of the Almighty's power, and to show us that notwithstanding such miraculous distinctions, yet we shall no longer continue the favorites of God, than while we fear Him[7] and keep His commandments. For we must observe, that this very people no sooner rejected the counsel of God, those they were given up by him in to the hands of their enemies they fell by degrees from Empire to Slavery, tell at length they were scattered over the face of the earth, and continue to this day the monuments of divine judgment to every incorrigible people.

The history of this unfortunate people, is a lesson of concern and instruction to us. Let us then from their example, take particular care, lest iniquity be our ruin. And in urging this argument may we not take up the wish of the text, "that these were such an heart in them that we would fear God and keep his commandments, that it might be well with us and our Children after us."[8]

Happy were the people of Israel, while they retained allegiance to the Lord their God. While their manners and integrity were of that stamp, which the divine goodness could not fail to bless with favor and protection.[9] And happy will be any other people while they continue virtuous and religious; for all the kingdoms of the earth are God's; and he ruleth alike in all. He bestows and he withdraws his mercy, not with an arbitrary or partial hand; but by the strictest pale of unbiased equity. He confers his blessings on those alone, who by true desert, and moral worth, are proper objects of it. Under a strong conviction of this great truth, and sensible that the success of all events depend on God. I hope it is, that we are here met together, to search and try our ways, that the iniquity of our hearts obstruct not the protection we have so much reason to implore.[10]

But it would be injustice [illegible] to this providence not to acknowledge the seriousness with which we have implored the divine aid; an earnest [illegible]. I trust, that you will certainly obtain it. You have truly joined in owning the necessity of this day's supplication and prayer; that as differences have arisen between our Mother Country and us; not on our part. I hope so some would insinuate[11] through the unreasonable [illegible] of power, or factious discontent, but in the sole defense of undoubted rights, we should beg the Almighty to bless our endeavors and grant that peace, unanimity, harmony and love with healing in their wings, may again be established between us.

And thus far all is well. In acknowledging the absolute power of God, our dependence on his mercy, and unworthiness of it, we have acted a proper and becoming part; but let us remember this, that we have ill answered the intentions of this public call, if we rest the duty here; confine it to the church and closet, to acts of mere devotion only; and extend not the reflections, reflected by this solemn occasion, to our principles and manner; to every branch of our conduct, both in public and private life. If this be not the consequence this days devotion, will be like the devotion of too many persons on a sick bed. We whose business it is to attend people in that melancholy circumstance, are often witnesses to their sorrow for a life ill-spent, their dreadful agonies under the apprehension of God's justice, their fervent and earnest desire of pardon, and above all their solemn promise of amendment, if God would be pleased to restore them to their former health. But we have likewise the grief to be often, too often, witnesses of those people returning to their former habits as soon as it pleased God to restore them. Then piety depended on the continuance of their distemper; and the fervor of their devotion rose and fell with the irregular beatings of their pulse. If then we are serious in thus humbling ourselves[12] before God for our past offences, and if engaging his blessing by a future amendment of life; If we mean well to our country and are in earnest in our wishes for its happiness we must, in the language of scripture cease to do evil, and learn to do well; we must acquire those virtuous habits and dispositions, which alone can recommend any people to the God of uprightness, and effectually secure them his protection. And as national virtues are the only efficient means of securing national felicity —and as national virtues are but the virtues of individuals collected; it is the duty of every private person, as a member of that society in which he dwells, to be very cautious lest his misconduct, joined to the misconduct of many[13] others, be the fatal bar to the divine protection.

Being therefore in the hands of one, who requireth truth in the inward parts; who is privy to all our thoughts, and spieth out all our ways; may it not be proper for each on this occasion, to retire within himself and ask his heart these important questions; Am I the very person I would appear to be; concerned for my own and the public good? Are my pretensions to virtuous and religious practices, sincere and real;[14] or being the daubings only of outward garnish, do they hide the deformity of a fool heart, of iniquitous deed, and base design? In my several relations in[15] life, do I pursue that conduct —do I follow that design, which alone can answer the end of providence in divine glory to God, and good to Man.

Whatever is my part in life, do I act it well, and contribute my share to public happiness? As a member of the community,[16] a parent, a master, or a servant; is my behavior such as the eye of heaven can approve? Are my intentions upright, my sentiments benevolent, my behavior exemplary, my professions sincere; or frustrating the ends of

God's moral government, and confounding the order intended by providence, do I offer every selfish, and sordid passion to rule my breast without control? In fine, is the end I aim at a right and laudable one; or have I not considered whether in every passage through life, I have proposed to myself any end or no.[17]

Should a review like this appear distasteful, we may well suspect there is something wrong within. For why should we desire an acquaintance with the world, and its[18] almost every trifling object; and shun by far the most important of all, an acquaintance with that little world[19] our own lives and hearts? Is it because the interview would give us pain? Perhaps we dare not talk within, because we cannot with complacency.

As we of America were long blessed with signal marks of God's forbearance; our gratitude to heaven should have borne some proportion to the mercies vouchsafed. Disobedience under our circumstances was doubly heinous, and will greatly increase the offences punished. For how did God surround us with blessings on every side; while other countries were the seat of war, and felt all the miseries of sword, of fire, and famine? While we were secure, and free from danger, populous cities were consumed, and fruitful countries destroyed, so that as the seas encompass the land, the protection of heaven blessed us on every side.

What returns we made for these [illegible] things of our tranquility does not indeed appear—no suitable ones at least—and will not God visit[20] for these things—yes he will and that speedily—for alas! a day of darkness and gloominess (if I may be allowed the expression) hangs over our heads and perhaps waits only for the effect of this days humiliation, before it closes upon us with a night of clouds and thicker darkness. There is no knowing what the desires of heaven are with respect to sinful people; how long they may stand, or when fall, is had from the age of man; but of these one may be assured, that a sincere repentance and solemn humbling themselves before God, is the only way to avert or prolong the date of their pain. Let us then upon this solemn occasion turn unto the Lord, and he will have mercy upon us, and to our God who will abundantly pardon. Let us take this opportunity to begin our amendments,[21] we have many follies to restrain, many vices to subdue; and though there appears not that daring impiety of which some complain; yet that religion has lost much of its force amongst us, is very evident: from that disregard for worship, that love of dissipation and of pleasure, and that dissoluteness of manners which is daily before us. Instead of that cordial affection which as Christians should unite us with the closest bands, how often are the smallest differences in sentiment made the weak foundations of a confirmed aversion for each other. And the noble benevolence of the Gospel forgot amidst contentions for childish opinions and indifferent rites.

How often are the moral, those essential duties of our religion, which alone can make us good and useful men, exchanged for shadows, chimeras, nothing.

To a God of truth and purity, practices of this kind must be highly odious. As the only means then of securing that divine protection, we should earnestly resolve[22] to put away the evil of our doings, to fear God, and keep his commandments, cherishing those virtuous and religious principles, which will ever add to our real welfare. When virtue and true religion flourish in a state it is happy and prosperous; when they decline, the strength and glory of it declines also; and avarice, luxury and effeminacy lead to the way to ruin. It is the genius of true religion to inspire the mind with every noble virtue; the love of our country, generosity, fortitude, temperance. But it is the genesis of irreligion to instill, narrow, selfish principles; a contempt for everything great and noble; monopolizing avarice and mean cowardice. The different tendencies of these principles should surely then, direct us in our choice of them; and our own experience of this influence, should confirm us in it. Can we then hesitate a moment which to prefer? But as we have now acknowledged our folly, and notice most solemn manner vowed better obedience; let us in earnest set about the great work of a reform. Let each of us in our sphere and station contribute our share, let these on whom a kind providence has lavished her favor.[23] Men of large fortunes and extensive influence[24] lead the way, and thousands will catch the fashion from them. Let them be examples of every noble and virtuous requirement, of love for their community, temperance, moderation, fidelity and honor, let them reverence that Almighty Being on whom they depend for all things; and they will find the advantage of so wise a conduct—they will find it in the willing obedience of their children; in the duty and faithfulness of their dependents; in the constancy of their friends; in the proud approbation of their country; and the admiration and fear of their enemies. Nay their fame shall reach beyond the ends of the earth, shall mount up to the battlements of Heaven and become the praise and admiration of angels.[25]

As those whose circumstances and station in life may not, perhaps give them much influence over others—I must inform them, that they may do something towards averting God's judgments, by reforming their own families and themselves, which can hardly fail of having some affect on true acquaintance; however it will give them an interest with the Almighty. The lowest of us may be just, temperate, honest, and pious. Even the beggar, though clothed in rags, can have his mind adorned with the robes of righteousness. He can send up his prayers for his country with as much faith and ardency as the greatest upon earth, and his prayers will soon be accepted at the throne of heaven. In a word—as the sins of a community are made up of the sins of individuals, and can no otherwise be diminished than by the reformation of individuals—And as it is in every man's power to reform himself, this also in every means, power to contribute something towards appeasing God's wrath and procuring His protection, and consequently toward saving himself and country from ruin. Instead then that neglect[26] of the Almighty Father of all, and profanation of his sacred innocence; that spirit of envy and hatred; of trifling and impertinence, that love of pleasure and of pride which prevail among us, let the love of God and of each other, the virtues of generosity and candor; of fortitude and public spirit take place in our practice. Then may we hope with confidence that our Israel will be safe under the protection of the most high and that it will be well with us and our children forever.

To conclude—

Having then, my brethren, so many motives, and lying under so many and so sacred obligations, if there be any virtue, if there be any promise, think of these things. Forsake your sins, be religious; be virtuous; be firm, waiting patiently for the Lord: And humbly implore his favor and assistance ever acknowledging your dependence on him, and constantly trusting in his goodness and power. As these conditions may entertain good and certain hopes, that God will finally bless us; and that we shall at last be delivered out of all our troubles; and thenceforth continue long to flourish in peace, in plenty,[27] and in liberty.

"Preached before the Commons House of Assembly and the Members of the Provincial Congress at the request of the House and members of the said Congress, on Feb'y 17th 1775, observed as a day of festival and reconciliation, on account of the unhappy differences between Great Britain and her Colonies." This sermon is indexed by Smith as #049, and he credits Munton and Rogers as printed sources.

"By the Fear of the Lord, Men Depart from Evil"

Proverbs 16:6
By the fear of the Lord, men depart from evil.

I N THE WORDS THE WISE MAN HATH TAUGHT US, that if in all our proceedings we have an awful regard to God, and a religious dread of his displeasure, we shall by the means not only avoid everything that is evil, but thereby likewise escape that punishment which otherwise would follow us. Nor can anything operate more strongly on us than this fear of God. It must indeed be of all principles the most active and forcible, as it proceeds from a dread of offending that being, whose power is infinite and irresistible.

By the fear of the Lord in this place we are by no means to understand that servile terror[1] which results from the mere consideration of his justice and his power, but rather such a filial awe as is accompanied with love and reverence, such an awe, as either reason hath suggested, or the scriptures have revealed to us. In those sacred oracles of eternal life, we are excited both to love and fear him, for we are there instructed that he will reward us for our good deeds, and punish us for our wickedness: that his eyes are open upon all the ways of the sons of men, to give everyone according to his ways, and according to the fruit of his doings. We there learn that he is not only a just, but likewise a merciful God, that he will render to every man according to his deeds: to them who by patient continuance in well-doing, seek for glory and honor and immortality, eternal life: but unto them that are contentious and do not obey the truth, but obey unrighteousness; indignation and wrath.

Having thus explained the words, I shall in the prosecution of my discourse endeavor to show, that such a belief, as I have already mentioned, is absolutely necessary to induce men to live agreeably to reason and religion, and to make them as well good subjects, as good Christians. Without this fear of the Divine Being, no human laws how wisely soever they may be contrived, how carefully soever they may be executed, will prove a sufficient security against the enormities, which too often disturb society, and which every civil institution is intended to prevent.

Laws, which do not immediately depend on the divine authority itself, cannot be considered as a complete and adequate rule of righteousness, and consequently must be in some measure[2] ineffectual without this divine sanction.

It is true indeed that all laws are of themselves a rule for human actions, and the measure, whereby the righteousness of men is often estimated; yet they are by no means a complete rule, unless they are so continued that they may extend to every particular of duty, but this is far from being the case, that although he who offends against one human law, may for that reason be deemed unrighteous, yet, though he should be obedient to them all, it by no means follows that he should on that account alone be deemed a righteous man for the strictest observer of the law may possibly be guilty of many sins, with respect to which human laws may be entirely silent. For unless human laws can be supposed to take in the whole compass of our duty, and to direct us in our conduct, not only as members of society, but likewise as the creatures and the redeemed of God, they must of course be a defective rule for human actions, and consequently insufficient to make men truly righteous so evident is it that by the fear of the Lord, and of him only the men depart from evil.

But let us consider this matter a little more closely. More human laws, however excellent they may be, are not always calculated to regulate men's actions[3] in so extensive a manner, as might be required of them; for as human laws, they will be often[4] found incapable of directing us in the exercise of their duty, which we are to God, to our neighbors, and ourselves.

With regard to our duty towards God, this, though a matter of the highest consequence, as being the grand foundation on which all other duties rest, yet this is not to be learned from human laws. To them we are not indebted for this knowledge, which we have of the Supreme Being, or that worship which is acceptable to him in the divine lessons. We are to be directed by the Almighty himself, who for this very purpose hath in the Holy Scriptures declared his will unto us. In this respect then, after sincere and due examination, we must be directed by whatever we may meet with in those sacred records.

But yet notwithstanding all this it must be confessed that many parts of our duty towards God are subject to human regulation. The civil magistrate may very justly and most wisely as is often practiced in our own happy constitution[5] enforce those things which are made known to us by the revelation of God. But then it is to be observed that the right which the magistrate has in this case to our obedience is founded on a supposed agreement betwixt what is required by God, and what is enjoined by man. The rule of righteousness in this case must be fetched from the divine law, which is equally the guide of the magistrate and subject.

But besides this, mere human laws will not be found equal to the direction of every man, in the duty which he owes to himself. In this case we are not subject to the regulation of human laws. For this duty consists in our governing ourselves to the rules of reason and religion with respect both to our spiritual and our earthly part. With regard to the temper and disposition of our minds we are hereby required to subdue our passions, and keep them within the bounds which the Book of Life has prescribed to us. Hence, we should never suffer ourselves to be puffed up with pride, to pine with envy, to burn with anger and revenge, to be disquieted with the cares of life, to be restless and impatient under any afflictions, that may befall us, or to indulge our impure desires, our[6] unlawful appetites.

But can we in these things be subject to the direction of human laws? Can our passions and desires be regulated by clauses and by statutes, or can actions and indictments lie against what passes privately in a man's own bosom? But the matters we now speak of are such as are transacted within a man's own breast such as are known only to God and his own conscience, and which consequently are liable to no censure or control but from them. Thus even from the consideration of those duties[7] which we owe to ourselves, it will be found that the fear of the Lord, and of him only men depart from evil.

But besides this, human laws are many times found as incapable of directing men with respect to what they owe one to another, as they are with respect to those duties which we have just spoken to. It is true the notorious and flagrant violation of justice is seldom suffered to pass with impunity. Civil government will by no means permit those who are subject to it to be oppressed or destroyed without taking due vengeance on the head of the offender. Yet at the same time that it guards against open violence, it leaves room enough for mankind to be guilty of the most abominable crimes. Though they are restrained from acts of apparent injustice, yet they still may be griping an inhospitable, insolent and censoring, treacherous and uncharitable, not only with impunity, but even with the most triumphant security. Thus it once more appears that human laws cannot be a complete rule of righteousness, since the hateful violations of moral duties are neither prevented nor forbidden by them.

But for the sake of argument let it be supposed, that laws merely human might by the extraordinary wisdom of a legislator be so constructed, as to extend to every particular odd duty, yet even then they would by no means answer the ends of good government, or secure the dependence of the subject, unless the fear of the Lord should cooperate[8] with the fear of the temporal punishment, and men should be persuaded that by offending against the just laws of man, they offended the laws of[9] God also. Mere human laws, as I have already observed, have no real, no intrinsic authority of themselves: the authority which they have, is immediately derived from those obligations, which arise from the law of God, as made known to us by reason and revelation.

But let me not here be understood, as if I would by any means deny the power which civil government has to exact the most strict and scrupulous obedience, or to disannul that obligation, which the subject is under, of showing all due submission to the laws of the community. I speak with the greatest deference, with the most sincere regard to the laws by which we are governed. It is with admiration and rapture that I contemplate our glorious, our envied constitution, and my intention is to fix the authority of human laws upon its true, its most lasting foundation. And when I assent that human laws are immediately derived from the divine laws itself, as evidently appears from reason and from scripture, it is my intention to place it on the firmest basis on which it is possibly can rest.

The mighty advantages which result from the due and equal distribution of justice,[10] and the confusion which continually arises from the want of it, are as strong an argument as reason can suggest in support of civil government, and at the same time the declaration of scripture, that by God things reign, and Princes decree justice; and that there is no power but of God, and that the powers that be, are ordained of him, bear that testimony to the necessity of it, which cannot be controverted.

But if we suppose this authority to be derived from the nature of civil government itself, and necessarily to result from it, without a superior law of reason and religion, the foundation must be weak, treacherous and imperfect, and consequently unequal to the structure, which should be raised on it. For if it should be argued, that a subject is bound in gratitude and justice to support those laws, by which he is protected, it may on the other hand be retorted, that gratitude and justice[11] are but mere names, are but empty sounds to anyone, that does not acknowledge the being of a God, the obligations of morality, and a future state of punishments and rewards. It may be said to that when subjects have once given a promise of obedience, and pledged themselves in the most solemn manner for the performance of the promise, that this lays them under an obligation that cannot easily be broken through; yet this plea will avail but little till men are thoroughly convinced, that they are under a necessity of abiding by their engagements of this nature; which they will hardly be persuaded of, so long as they believe nothing of that divine law, which is antecedent to all moral obligations, and which is founded on the eternal reason of things, and the unchangeable nature of the Godhead. The want of sufficient power therefore in every civil government to exact obedience from the subject, in case the authority of God and the divine law should be rejected, is another strong proof that the belief of a future state of punishments and rewards is absolutely necessary to secure the honor of human laws, and to accomplish the good purposes of government.

But besides this, human laws cannot be so calculated as absolutely to prevent men from disobeying their injunctions. Though the civil Governor my be justly authorized to require obedience to the laws, yet if the power to enforce that obedience is wanting, he will find that his commands will have little regard paid to them, and that this power is too frequently wanting, will manifestly appear, if we consider that the penalties inflicted by the law are not always sufficient to answer the intended purpose. They are neither so certain in their execution, as not to be often eluded, nor so insupportable, that men should choose to avoid them, sooner than forego those temporal advantages which may arise from the transgression of them. The hopes of escaping punishment by cunning and dexterity, or of bearing it with less uneasiness, than it would cost them to subdue their unruly appetites, will oftentimes get the mastery over mens fears, and make them transgress with as little concern, as if it might be done with absolute impunity.

Since the human laws cannot be considered as a complete measure of righteousness; since they cannot fully point out to us our duty either with regard to our God, our neighbors, or ourselves, since they are invested with no sufficient power to exact a perfect obedience, it inevitably follows, that by the fear of the Lord and of him only, men depart from evil, that is, the fear of Him, who is able both to save and to destroy, procured due obedience to human laws, secures the peace of the world, and prevents us from being overwhelmed by that torrent of vice and wickedness, which has so long threatened to burst upon us.

Having thus ascertained the point which I undertook,[12] I shall now draw such inferences from what has been advanced, as may serve at once by way of application and conclusion.

If the doctrine which I have deduced from the text, be true, it will evidently appear, that it is highly worthy the attention of every government to curb, as far as possibly it can, the growth of impiety and irreligion, and to restrain all attempts that may be made to weaken the evidences of religion, or to bring the obligations of it into suspicion.

Those great legislators, from whom we are derived, were so sensible of the importance of religion, of the belief in God, and a future state of punishments and rewards, that they made their very laws to depend on the obligations of religion, and required obedience to be paid as much from the fear of God as of the magistrate and in consequence of this, it was the case to frame many excellent laws for the very purpose of restraining men from profaneness, immorality and irreligion. Yet notwithstanding we have adopted these very laws, a most audacious spirit of irreligion still so far prevails, that many not only absent themselves from all religious societies, from every kind of divine worship, but even carry their impiety so far as to exercise themselves in necessary and worldly business on that day which should solemnly be set apart for the worship of Almighty God. Hence the vigilance and best endeavors of the magistrate are now more than ever necessary that all such flagitious proceedings, all such gross enormities may be discountenanced and suppressed, lest at length our holy religion should by corrupt and wicked practices be undermined, and the peace and security of the civil government be totally subverted.

When punishment becomes necessary, it must be used against those bold and profligate offenses, whom the fears of God and eternal perdition cannot restrain within the bounds of their duty. This is a power which must necessarily be lodged in the hands of the magistrate, who could not be a security to the good, if he were not a terror to evil doers, by punishing the wicked as they deserve, that others may fear and do no more so foolishly. In vain the wisest deliberations would be held, in vain the legislative body would enact laws and interest itself in the welfare and prosperity of the community, in vain would our own petitions be offered up at the throne of grace that the Almighty would be pleased to direct all their consultations to the good of his church, the honor of our sovereign, and the welfare and prosperity of the province, if those, in whose hands the laws are lodged, do not cooperate with the legislature, and use their utmost endeavors that peace and happiness, truth and justice, religion and piety may be established amongst us. And how can this be affected, unless they, to whom this charge is entrusted, make it their peculiar care, that those laws which are justly framed, are as vigorously executed.[13] But this execution of the laws then is a trust, my brethren, which is committed to many of you by God and your country, and the importance of it is so great that it requires the most conscientious discharge. But I cannot better explain the nature of it than by reciting to you two most excellent admonitions which are found in the Holy Scripture, the first of which is left us by Jehosophat King of Judah, and the last by the Apostle Paul.

Take heed what ye do, for ye judge not for men but for the Lord, who is with you in judgment. We hope for now let the fear of the Lord be upon you, take heed and do it, for there is no iniquity with the Lord our God,[14] nor taking of gifts. And what cause soever shall come to you of your brethren between blood and blood, between law and commandments, statutes and judgments deal courageously, and the Lord shall be with thee. But he that doeth wrong shall receive of the Lord's hand for the wrong that he hath done, and there shall be no respect of persons.

May these sentiments be ever written on the tablets of your hearts, and may the Almighty God prosper all the good and pious endeavors which you may use for stopping the progress of vice and immorality, for advancing the just power of the laws and for protecting and maintaining true religion and virtue.

This sermon was delivered twice, both times at St Philip's, in 1766 and on October 19, 1773. This sermon is indexed by Smith as #327, and he credits Warren as an original source.

V

"Let No Man Seek His Own, but Every Man Another's Wealth"

1 Corinthians 10:24
Let no man seek his own, but every man another's wealth.

WE HAVE HERE COMMENDED TO US A DUTY which is of the greatest excellency and advantage to mankind. To seek the good and wealth of theirs, to be of a public spirit, is a noble character; it affords pleasure to hear it mentioned, and is the distinguishing mark of a generous mind. Men of this temper and frame, under Divine Providence keep up the being and dignity of communities and are some check[1] and antidote to the mischievous influence of those partial and narrow souls who are only lovers of themselves. The Apostle's command in the text is preemptory, "Let no man seek his own, but every man another's wealth." Which this rule will hold good[2] in all of several relations men can have to one another; being an instruction in whatsoever situation they are placed, to seek the common interest.

I shall consider it at this time with regard to ourselves, as constituting a Christian community, in which to act with a public spirit is a duty most reasonable, and of absolute necessity.

By public spirit is not be understood, such a diffused and indifferent regard to all as excludes a preference of, and a peculiar concern for some men more than for others. This, in my opinion, Christianity does not strictly bind us to. For though it does demand of us a love and good will to mankind in general, yet since our want of abilities and of constitution of things is such, that we cannot be equally serviceable to all, but must on several occasions prefer some to others, we are therefore warranted; both by reason and revelation, to pay the greatest deference to those of the same society with ourselves. Nor is there any way proposed to men, by which they can be more useful in the world, than in endeavoring to be good patriots of their country, and to consult by all due and lawful means the welfare and prosperity of that community to which they belong. And did this excellent spirit universally prevail, the condition of mankind would be so much more blessed and happy than it is. For, as public spiritedness in other words, is, a seeking of God of the society we live in, that is preferring its good to any worldly satisfaction of our own, so as in any competition of interest to determine on the side of the community. So it includes a desire, and suitable care that every member of the society may enjoy so much true happiness and prosperity, as is inherently in his power, and is consistent with the good of the rest. Let no man seek his own, but every man another's wealth. But may not a man seek his own good, and his own wealth too? Yes, certainly he may, and he ought to do it. But the Apostle would have that self concern to be grounded on a just and equitable principle, to be restrained and limited in its measure, and not to be a person's whole and only care. No man ever yet really hated his own flesh, or did not desire his own good. All men equally covet happiness, and in that sense may be said all equally to love themselves, and do all alike propose some self satisfaction, first or last, in what they undertake. But that which distinguishes as criminal self-love, from that which is allowable, is this, that he who is guilty of the first, aims at the gratifying himself. Though it may be never so much at the expense of others; in his actions regarding himself[3] alone, and so he be pleased and prosperous, cares not what his brother suffered; whereas the public spirited person and lover of mankind is so framed from the excellency of his constitution and sense of his duty to make the true happiness of his neighbor his own happiness and the general good of mankind the spring and motive of his actions. He curbs or stifles all such motions, as may carry him to act anything prejudicial to another. And he takes the same pleasure in benefiting his neighbor and brother, as the self lover does in gratifying and being beneficial to himself alone. This is a generous and noble principle of acting which all should endeavor to gain, and resolve to govern themselves by scarce anything but a general concern for the benefit and good of men, can qualify anyone for such a disinterestedness as is requisite in this matter a universal benevolence is the principle upon which it is grounded; so that the more truly Christian any man is, the more is he disposed to be of a public spirit. Whereas on the other side, self-love in all its branches is criminal and sinful, and as contrary to Christianity, as it is prejudicial to society: Which by the way shows the general benefit and usefulness, or rather the absolute necessity of religion to the good of mankind.

But the more particular properties and distinguishing marks of this amiable quality[4] are visible in our carriage towards others, and in our personal conduct as to ourselves. As to our carriage toward others. Everyone who sincerely desires the public welfare approves himself solicitous by all fitting ways and means to countenance and encourage all those good works by which the common good and benefit of mankind are promoted. Such are the erecting and endowing of alms-houses, for support of the needy and afflicted. And of the building and establishing schools for the education of children and consequently reformation of the corrupt manners of this present age. There are perhaps no fruits of a public spirit more beneficial and of greater extent, than those that attend the religious education of youth, who are the fruitful hopes of the people the most capable of impoverishment and most likely to receive an impression for a national good. And therefore to encourage and contribute to the foundation and maintenance of all such schools and nurseries, where the young plants may receive growth and cultivation, to be removed and placed afterwards as freedom shall require, for the ornament and supply of a country, is an eminent instance and affect of a public spirit. Again, the principle we are now upon in the ground of grief and concern for the wickedness, and corruption of the age wherein we live; which a lover of the public cannot think of with indifference. Rivers of tears run down mine eyes, says the psalmist, because man keep not thy law. No man who has any tolerable measure either of conscience or humanity can stand by unmoved, and see his fellow creatures owing to ignorance, or want of education[5] drawing down Divine vengeance on their heads by their iniquity and not be willing to interpose and save them from destructiveness. This is what all will do, who have the true temper and spirit of the Apostle: Not seeking his own profit, but the profit of many that they may be saved.

As to what more immediately regards a man's self, a public spirit produces in every one of us an extraordinary obedience and industry, in the discharge of the duties that belong to our respective posts and stations. It is not enough to be indifferently careful and active in business just to avoid the punishment of the law, or the hazard of losing an employment: Nor this will not come up to what we are commanding; for a truly public spirit will not let a person think any pains and labor too great that may be advantageous to the public in the rank and place that he fills up: nor even to suffer that his riches should stagnate and be dead in coffers which ought to be set a going for common use, and the support of indigence.

But it is not my design to mention all that may be required in everyone, who desires to live as becomes a member[6] in society, it is evident there is some thing in it which cannot be founded on temporal and political regards alone; but is supported by a more noble principle, a principle of religion, a tender love for, and regard to mankind. This plainly appears to be the will of God; if we call to mind the end and design of Divine Providence in forming societies which evidently was the common benefit of mankind. In short, men were originally designed for society, to love, to be kind to one another. The different excellencies and perfections, which different persons show that they ought to unite and exercise them for the common advantage, that is the deficiencies of some in one kind may be supplied by the qualifications of others. And this indeed was the very end and purpose of their entering into society, to promote their mutual good, and the true interest of all those who compose that body; and therefore in all reason it ought to be the care of every member, to further and promote that end.

These general principles so naturally lead to the good work, which occasions the present solemnity, that it is almost needless to mention the application. The mere

naming of this good design pleads powerfully in its favor, awakens every tender sentiment of pity and compassion, and suggests every argument of humanity, reason and
religion.

For this work we are met together in the house of God, to acknowledge the divine
goodness in that success which has already appeared; and to implore his blessings from
whence cometh every good and perfect gift, for further assistance and encouragement.

With no view can men be better connected together;[7] no purpose can a society be
more usefully framed; or more agreeably to the intentions of the great creator, our
common Father, than to alleviate the distress of the widow, and lessen the calamities to
which fellow creatures are subject: and the more severe the heavy these calamities are,
and the less ability the needy have to rescue themselves; the united endeavors of persons in a happier condition become still more laudable and beneficial: and every condescension, from a higher exaltation to the lowest degrees of misery, is justly entitled
to a distinguished applause.

If so, enter the wretched abodes, where both poverty and sickness dwell! Can you
behold helpless children with their afflicted mother, shedding their unavailing tears
around a meager spectacle of pain and diseases; crying for bread for themselves, and
health to the once support of the family! All their hearts fainting within them! Did you
behold but one such scene of misery, and God only knows how many such there are
what tender emotions must it raise in your breasts?[8] Could you hear the melancholy
sound of bitter cries, the piercing groans of real distress; could you see at once, all this,
aggravated by the cutting anxieties of destitute poverty; good God! What a moving
scene would this sad assemblage prove! Whose heart could bear the miserable sight?
What bowels would not melt? Whose eyes would not dissolve in tears?

What have you felt yourselves? What have you seen your friends, your children,
endure under the severe anguish of an acute distemper? How afflictive, how torment-
ing have these sensations proved, though free from the dismal fears of perishing for
want of necessaries! Recollect what you yourselves have suffered, even without the disadvantages of poverty; when your sorrow was not like unto their sorrow: And being in
the body, subject to the accidents and calamities of this changeable world, suppose
yourself, or nearest relations, groaning at once under the united weight of sickness and
indigence; and the revolutions of providence how soon may that unhappy time appear? What would you then wish should be done unto you? Would you not then desire
comfort and consolation?

Go therefore to the house of mourning; or carry even your thoughts into the dismal chamber but of one dying;[9] dying for want of that kind assistance which you may
now, and perhaps only now, administer! Could you see the departing wretch, with
eager wishful looks, praying for some friendly relief, but finding none; could you look
upon the honest, poor, neglected creature, struggling with the agonies of death; in
anguish inexpressible, for want of timely help, breathing the last gasp of miserable life;
with what passion would you wish to have contributed, as you now may to his health
and preservation!

But besides these motives in favor of this charitable work, the great instability of temporal affairs, and constant fluctuation of everything in this world, is a very powerful argument likewise in favor of it. For what by successive misfortunes; so many surprising revolutions do every day happen in families, that it may not seem strange to say. That is the posterity of some of the most liberal contributors here, in the changes which one country may produce, may possibly find shelter under this very plant which they now so kindly water. Nay, so great is the mutability of things, and[10] so quickly sometimes has the wheel turned round, that many a man has lived to enjoy the benefit of that charity which his own piety projected.

I might proceed to instance many reasons for the furtherance of this good work, but shall confine myself to one drawn from the present[11] season, in which we have been communicating the great love of our Savior Jesus Christ: the consideration of this stupendous instance[12] of compassion, in the Son of God, is the most unanswerable appeal that can be made to the heart of man, for the reasonableness of it in himself. It is the great argument which the Apostles use in almost all their exhortations of good works, "Beloved, of Christ so loved us," the inference is unavoidable; and gives weight to every thing else[13] which can be urged upon the subject. And therefore I shall beg leave to apply it;[14] that at least for their sakes, who enjoy the benefit of this charity, we might be left to the full impression of so exalted and so seasonable a motive. That by reflecting upon the infinite labor of our Savior, in the instance of his death, we may consider what an immense debt we owe each other: and by calling to mind the amiable pattern of his life in doing good, we might learn in what manner we may best discharge it.

And indeed of all the methods in which a good mind would be willing to do it, I believe there can be none more beneficial,[15] or comprehensive in its effects, than that for which we are here met together. The proper education of poor children being the groundwork of almost every other kind of charity, as that which makes every other subsequent act of it answer the pious expectation of the giver. That part of it in particular which includes the education of children. For experience evidently evinces the necessity of giving youth an general[16] early tincture of religion, and bringing them up to a love of industry and a love of the laws of and constitution of their country. And if experience shows the great importance of the proper education to children of all marks and conditions, what shall we say then of those whom the providence of God has placed in the very lowest lot of life. Utterly cast out of the way of knowledge, without a parent, sometimes may be without a friend to guide and instruct them; but what common pity and the necessity of their sad situation engages. Where the dangers which surround them on every side are so great and many, that for one fortunate passenger in life, who makes his way well in the world with such early disadvantages and so dismal a setting out, we may reckon thousands who every day suffer shipwreck, and are lost forever.

If there is a case under Heaven which calls out aloud for the more immediate exercise of compassion, and which may be looked upon as the aggregate of all charity, surely it is this: And I am persuaded there would want nothing more to convince the greatest enemy to these kind of charities that it is so, but a bare opportunity of taking a nearer view of some of the more distressful objects of it.

Let him go into the dwellings of the unfortunate, into some mournful chamber, where poverty and affliction reign together. There let him behold the disconsolate widow—sitting—drowned in tears; thus weeping over the infant, she knows not how to succor, "O my child, thou art now left exposed to a wide and vicious world, too full of snares and temptations for thy tender and unpracticed age; driven out naked into the midst of them, without friends, without fortune, without instruction. It is true our pittance was small, but large enough to have made thee virtuous[17] for we had piously resolved to have spared even something out of that pittance, to have set in the pathway of knowledge and instruction. But alas! The staff of our support is gone."[18]

Let the man who is the least friend to distresses of this nature, conceive some disconsolate widow uttering her complaint even in this manner, and then let him consider, if there be any sorrow like this sorrow, wherewith the Lord has afflicted her? Or whether there can be any charity like that, of taking the child, and rescuing her from the apprehensions. Should a heathen, a stranger to our holy religion and the love it teaches, should be, as he journeyed, come to the place where she lay, and saw, would he not have compassion on her? God forbid a Christian should look upon such distress, and pass by on the other side.

Rather let him do, as his Savior taught him, bind up the wounds, and poor comfort into the heart of one, whom the hand of God has so bruised. Let him extend his saving arm to her helpless child, and make him live by the bounty of his charity, on one hand to be brought up into this world, to a love of honest labor and industry as all his life long to earn and eat his bread with joy and thankfulness: and on the other to be trained up to such a sense of his duty, as may secure him an interest in the world to come.

Much peace and happiness rest upon the head and heart of everyone who thus brings children to Christ. May the blessing of him that was ready to perish come seasonably upon him. The Lord comfort him when he most wants it, when he lays sick upon his bed, make thou, O God! all his bed in his sickness; and for what he now scatters, give him, then, that peace of thine which passeth all understanding, and which nothing in this world can either give or take away.[19]

This sermon was delivered on three occasions, all at St. Philip's. The first delivery was on April 17, 1759; the second, with a significant revision, was in April 1764. Finally, with additional revisions, the sermon was delivered on April 21, 1772. The final version is represented here. This sermon is indexed by Smith as #070, and he credits Tennison, Bishop Aseph, and Stone as printed sources.

VI

"Love One to Another"

John 13:35
By this shall all men know that ye are my Disciples, if ye Love one to another.

THE CUSTOM OF SERMONS being preached before public communities, as it is of ancient date, so it is of pious and laudable intention. It shows a becoming regard to the honor of God and Religion; it serves to keep up an awful sense of Divine Power, who governs and presides over all orders and Societies of Men. It activates and enlivens a true Spirit of Devotion, whenever men are thus mindful of paying their first tribute of supplication to God, before they proceed to the vigorous prosecution of their respective business, or the innocent recreation of festive gladness.

It is doubtless a comely sight to behold large bodies of men agreeing to address themselves to God with <u>one heart</u>, and <u>one voice</u>, and <u>walking together to the House of God as friends</u>. This is the best method that can be taken to strengthen the types of union and <u>brotherhood</u> between members of the same voluntary Society; it tends to preserve a mutual harmony, and good understanding one among another; and helps greatly to promote all the good offices of love, joy, peace, benevolence, and affection, not only to particular persons, but to mankind in general. In short, religion and piety are the best foundation, whereon to build the most lasting hopes of unity and affection, and are the very nerves and sinews of all society.

That I may then contribute my mite to this glorious work. My business at this time shall be to recommend to your attention, the most noble and Christian duty of love and benevolence. A subject proper for all particular persons, but perhaps more especially to be recommended to a Society whose professed characteristic is if I err not[1] embodied and met together to do honor to God to promote peace and unity, and to set an example of <u>good will</u> and <u>good works</u> towards men: Agreeably to which design, I have made choice of the words of my text. <u>By this shall men know that ye are my Disciples if ye have love one to another.</u>

Permit me then from these words, to present to your consideration. First, the nature and excellencies of love and benevolence. And—secondly, the motives that persuade to this duty. Now the nature of love will be best known by its acts and its objects. As to the acts of love, it comprehends all those things whereby men may be beneficial and useful to one another. It reaches not only to the body but to the soul of man, that nobler and better part of us; and is conversant about those things whereby we may be serviceable to the temporal or spiritual good of others, to promote either their present, or future and eternal happiness. In short it resolves the doubtful minds, comforts the weak, heals the broken-hearted, relieves the afflicted, weeps with those that weep, and mourns with them that mourn.

But all these are no more than branches and parts of this great duty. It must not stop here. No! Love doth not altogether consist in sending a liberal supply to the wants of the poor and needy, but also in restraining our innocent and lawful freedoms, in condescension of the weal and wavering: Nay! This God-like love sometimes shines with more commanding luster in acts of severity, than in a general and unlimited indulgence and there is frequently more mercy in the execution than in the remission of punishments, provided they be not inflicted to feed a wanton or revengeful appetite, and to satisfy the cravings of malice and ill-will. For, love does not study to gratify the palate, but to recover the health of the languishing criminal. It is often bitter in the first taste, but sweet in the after relish: A rigid mercy and an austere kindness; a good conveyed in a vehicle of frowns and severe discipline; such are the correction of children, the reproof of friends, and the sentences of the law: The rod and ax are as instrumental to love as honor and reward. Open rebuke, says Solomon, is better than secret love: And parables of Scripture, and the gainful fictions of Divines, will tremble at the thoughts of an inexorable judge, and an unrelenting law. They will consider whether they can escape the punishment, if they commit the crime; and not run on madly to transgress, —seeing nothing is to get by the attempt, but shame and everlasting remorse.

Thus far, I have briefly treated of the nature and excellency of this duty from its acts: proceed we now to consider it in relation to its object. When Almighty God put the Jewish nation under the discipline of the law, he taught them by a kind of hieroglyphical and symbolical Divinity; and it seemed good to his wisdom to lead them in the ways of virtue, and hold them at a distance from vice, by allowing or disallowing them the use of such creatures and customs, as showed then the beauty of the one, and the deformity of the other. Thus God taught them that the sensuality and prophaneness were sinful, by denying them the use of swine's flesh, which was emblematical thereof. He condemned hypocrisy and corruption of doctrines, by forbidding garments of mixed matter, and sowing fields with seeds of several kinds. So he forbid them idolatry, by commanding a perpetual war with the nation of Palestine, which was deeply immersed in that sin. But upon this the old[2] Jews looked upon themselves as perfectly separated and freed from all the obligations of kindness to the rest of Mankind. They thought they had been born to animosity and hatred; and that they had quarrels entailed upon them, like their lands had so many nations made over their hereditary, legal, and commanded hatred.

But our Savior has restored this law of laws, this duty of love, to its natural and original extent. And the Christian is not allowed to count any sort of people his enemy. He has commanded us to bear an amicable and friendly disposition to all men, and taught us that our brethren are not only those of our own kindred and nation, but those of the same nature. The old law taught us to love our neighbors, but the new law teaches us that all the world are our neighbors; not only those whom we know, but those whose distresses we are acquainted with, though their persons are strangers to us. This doctrine our Savior has revealed and explained in the parable of the wounded traveler, and the good Samaritan. Be him then an Arabian, or an Indian; Nay! Though a Jew, or a Mohammedan, or an Infidel; not only an enemy to the common faith, but one to me; he has not lost his humanity, though he has lost his religion and goodness. He may cease to be our friend but cannot cease to be our brother; for all are descended from the same loins. And though Esau may hate Jacob, and Jacob may supplant Esau, yet they once lay in the same womb; and therefore the saying of Moses may be extended to all mankind, <u>Sirs, ye are Brethren, why do ye wrong one to another</u>? The word enemy therefore ought to be a mere notion, an empty name in the Christian religion, and to be applied only to our sins, to Satan. The <u>disciples</u> of the philosophers were distinguished by the various opinions of their masters; those of the Pharisees by certain traditions observations; but <u>Christ</u> would have no distinction amongst us. <u>This</u> only is to be a mark to us, that we are <u>Christ's disciples</u>, if we have Love one to another. Therefore those that hate their brother be it on what pretense soever, are not <u>Disciples of Christ</u> but of the Synagogue.

And thus I have treated of the nature of this duty, as to its object, all Mankind in general, even our enemies. But to this large and comprehensive notion of it, I find it necessary to subjoin two cautions. The first is, that no Rule of love obliges us to love our enemies so, but we may be allowed to secure and defend ourselves against them. We must <u>love</u> our enemy, but not so as to hate ourselves: We must love him as ourselves; but then, by that rule, our love to him is but a copy, that to ourselves the original, and ought in the first place to be secured. Love indeed darts it rays to remotest distances, but its neighborhood feels it's warmer and most refreshing influence. We are not to give up our Religion, Lives and Estates tamely, without the best and justest opposition we can make, whenever the hands of violence would wrest them from us. And though we are commanded, when our <u>Enemy hungers, to feed him</u>; when he thirsts to give him drink, yet not when he hungers for my estate, or thirsts for my blood.

The second caution is this, though charity obliges us to love all men, yet we are not to love all men alike. Our Heavenly Father, who is to be our pattern in general beneficences, does not so. Though his love be universally to all, yet it is not alike to all. He shows himself a common Father to all, yet a <u>gracious Father</u> only to the righteous. <u>He loveth the Gates of the Lion, more than all the Dwellings of Jacob</u>: And so we ought to conduct our <u>limited Love</u> by the same rule. We should shed our common influences on all mankind, but if they cannot reach to all, to give the preference to those of our own brotherhood and fraternity. I come now secondly, to consider the motives of this duty. The first motive which I shall mention, is the example of our heavenly Father, who, out of mercy and compassion towards us, when we were in open rebellion against him, and <u>the thoughts of the imagination of our hearts were only evil continually</u>; when he had nothing in the object to move him to it; when we were so far from being good or just men, that we were profane, profligate, and blasphemous sinners. Then God sent his only begotten Son Jesus Christ, in testimony of his Love, to die for us, and to obtain, by the shedding of his most precious blood, pardon of sins upon our reformation and amendment. If any motive can be more prevailing, this dying redeemer in his last moments bequeathed this advice, as his last legacy, to his disconsolate <u>Disciples, that they should love one another</u>.

The advice of a friend should be always listened to with attention, and, if good and profitable, be obeyed with cheerfulness. But, when it comes recommended to us with this engaging circumstance, that it is the advice of a dying friend, our hearts must be as unrelenting as the nether millstone, if we do not treasure it up in our memory, and when opportunity serves, let it burst forth into action. What should make it still more prevalent is, that it is the advice of a dying friend who, whilst we were enemies to him, and rebels to his just and merciful authority, submitted to the most cruel and ignominious death, that we might live, and by that means become heirs with him of an eternal inheritance in the Heavens. And can we then be so unjust to ourselves, so ungrateful to our Redeemer, so rebellious to our God, as once to dispute the equity and necessity of this command? A command so just and reasonable in itself, so perfective of our happiness both here and hereafter, that we must as perversely oppose our own interest, as Divine Authority, if we do not cheerfully and constantly submit to it. And this leads to[3] a—Second Motive—as it is the only expedient to make this life agreeable, and Heaven a state of happiness.

God at first created man a sociable creature; He wove into his composition a kind prosperity towards acts of love and beneficence, and adorned him[4] with every perfection that might dispose him to consult the good of the whole human race. And he can no more divest himself entirely of this friendly passion, than he can shake off his nature. That this intercourse between man and man might be constantly upheld he has made us all mutually dependent on each other for support and happiness. For this reason we are ranged and disposed into bodies and communities,[5] that we may the better answers the end of our creation, which is to set forth the Glory of God, by living together in love, and affording each other, as far as possible, mutual help and assistance. Thus the whole world is but one <u>grand</u> society, and we are all members of it; only for the more easy and orderly government, we are formed into lesser numbers and bodies, to which every member does more particularly belong, and for whose Welfare they are in a more immediate and especial manner concerned. But as mankind cannot subsist without the help and society of one another, so neither can any Society or body of men subsist without mutual love and unity. Without these it would be no better than a bedlam of men, a confused chaos of discordant and jarring individuals. Nay! One member that shall thwart and oppose the joint interest of the whole is like the instrument out of tune in a consort of music, which disturbs the harmony of the whole, and must interrupt the progress of the wisest and best concerted designer. Love and unity are the bonds, the cement, nay the very foundation of society. Without these it must stand upon a very precarious and sandy bottom, and whenever the winds of opposition shall blow, and the waves of contention be lifted up against it, inevitable must be its fall. You are then, my brethren, the advantages and necessity of these excellent virtues: whether we consider ourselves as members of one great community, or as members of lesser societies, it is these that support and maintain the whole. For as sure as love and unity are the great bond, so sure are strife and divisions the bane, of society. If such evil dispositions as these generally prevailed, who sees not that society would be a curse instead of a blessing? Upon this supposition, the best and wisest thing that man could do, would be to break up and disperse, to fly to solitude as the only refuge, and herd with the tamer beast of prey.

But, there is another motive still behind, and that is, that Love makes Heaven a place of happiness. God is love, and heaven is the seat of perfect[6] love: This was from everlasting, and will be to everlasting the same. Its birth was older than the world, and its life and duration runs parallel with eternity; before even the mountains were brought forth, it was founded in the nature of God; and when this frame of things and all its glories shall have a period, it will survive and triumph over this disjointed edifice, and constitute the happiness of Saints and Angels. What the Psalmist saith of God, may be truly applied to Love, The Heavens shall perish, but thou shalt remain; they all shall wax old as doth a garment, be folded up and changed, but thou art the same, yesterday today and forever. The time will come when faith shall be swallowed up in light, and hope be lost in fruition. But then, when all this scene of things is vanished away,[7] Love shall still keep the stage, and be the everlasting exercise of our glorified natures. You have heard, my friends,[8] the nature and excellencies of Christian Love explained; you have heard the motives which should prevail with you to practice it, laid before you unadorned indeed with the flowers of rhetoric, and arts of persuasion; but the extract of this virtue is so divine, its blessings so extensive, that it must shine sufficiently bright in its own native simplicity, without borrowing any light from human eloquence. You have heard also, that it is the only bulwark of society, and therefore cannot scarcely be too strongly enforced, or too carefully maintained: But waving the general application, permit me particularly to address myself to you, a band of brothers, my much respected brethren.[9] Any encomium of mine upon you as a Society[10] would be superfluous. I leave you to the esteem to the applause of your own consciences, a recompense that cannot fail you in this world; and which will not fail you in the next,[11] if you <u>continue rooted and grounded in Love one to another</u>, the characteristic of Christ's true <u>Disciples</u> and distinguishing mark if I augur aright, of you my respected friends.[12]

But here give me leave, seriously to advise you, not as jealous lest you should do otherwise, but as sensible how variable a creature man is, and as sensible of the subtlety of our <u>grand adversary</u>, who will not fail his utmost endeavors to blast every excellent work; to carry on your glorious plan, and if unfortunately begun, healing them with Brotherly Love and forbearance,[13] with <u>unanimity</u> and <u>love</u>; and to manifest you do so by pursuing it <u>with one heart</u> and <u>one soul</u> carefully avoiding all beginnings of contention, and if unfortunately begun, healing them with brotherly love and forbearance. Then will you securely outbrave all the storms of opposition, and stand firm and unshaken, though thousands should join hand in hand to pull down your superstructure. But what need I dwell on this topic, and studiously endeavor to urge the advantages and necessity of love and unanimity, they have ever been the <u>boast</u>,[14] and I trust will continue to be the <u>ornament</u> and <u>support</u> of this venerable Fraternity. I trust the success of your future <u>zeal</u> and <u>benevolence</u>, to the grace of God; and make an end as I begun in prayer[15] to him for your <u>perseverance in well-doing</u>.

I make an end with reasonable hopes, that such <u>zeal</u>, and such <u>perseverance</u>, will have a persuasive force with everyone, to find out the great, the important secret of <u>raising</u> to himself Friends of the Mammon of Unrighteousness, that when he fails they may receive him into everlasting habitations. I make an end, with strong assurance, that no censorious reflections, no distant surmises, and no baneful intemperance, will cloud or disturb this your Feast of Love, and in this assurance, dismiss you with love and friendship, sobriety and temperance.[16] <u>Go thy way, eat thy bread with joy, and drink thy wine with a merry heart for God accepteth thy works.</u>

This sermon was preached before the Freemasons at St. Philip's in 1771 and 1787. This sermon is indexed by Smith as #004.

VII

"Love Not the World"

1 John 2:15
Love not the world.

THERE IS CERTAINLY NO GREATER ENEMY to virtue and all true religion, and consequently to our best and truest interest than a love and fondness of temporal things. For the great treasures and design of virtue and religion is, to purge and purify our minds from all gross and sensual affections from whence, as from a fountain proceeds all that great and horrible wickedness we see in the world. To inform us of the worth and dignity of our souls, and of the nature of their chief good and happiness; and by calling off our thoughts from false and fading joys, to raise and fix them where true and durable ones are only to be found; is the great design of virtue and religion: and to countermine and make ineffectual this design is the natural and necessary consequence of loving this world. Because the love of this world which cannot make us happy necessarily renders us regardless and unmindful of those things which can; necessarily puts us upon those actions and enterprises which make us unworthy of our proper happiness; and so indisposes and vitiates the mind, as to disqualify and unfit us for lasting and relishing it, though it were put into our mouths.

Absolutely necessary therefore is it, that men should often be cautioned against the love of this world: a vice so fatal in its effects; and an object so powerful in its temptations; for if in the very days of Christ and his Apostles, when with regard to the evidence and assurance of a future state, men may be said to have walked by sight and not by faith: and by the doctrines which they heard, and the miracles they saw, to have had heaven, and the glories of another world, laid open to their view: if under these advantageous circumstances men still stood in need of being cautioned against a deluding and ensnaring world: much more needful is the caution now. For whether it is that Christians have really forgot that there is another and a better world than the present;

or that they think the pleasing of God, and the recommending themselves to his favor; is very consistent with indulging their unbridled lusts and passions; whatever, I say, their inward thoughts and imaginations may be, more sensuality, more worldly-mindedness, in their lives and conversations cannot be. Nay, had God made the loving of this world a necessary condition of obtaining heaven; and expressly told us, that whosoever doth not love life[1] and riches, honor pleasure more than himself, cannot be his disciple; we could not, I think, generally speaking, be more careless and unmindful of God, or more greedy and fond of those worldly things, than we are at present. But since the whole scope and tenor of the Gospel speaks the contrary and since it is the concurrent voice of reason and all revelation, that God has made this world, not to be a rival to himself, by withdrawing our affections from him; but to serve as a test and touchstone of our love and allegiance to him; since these things are so very plain; it is highly necessary that men should be often called upon, be begged and entreated, as they love God and their own happiness, "not to love this world."[2]

But it may be asked, and a very reasonable question it is, whether the love of this world, in every sense of the word love, is a crime? To which, it may be answered very safely, no surely. For this will be running out of one extreme into another; a weakness that rash and inconsiderate man is very liable and incident to. We must not understand the Apostle by these words, "love not the world," as forbidding us to have that regard and value for temporal things which the present state and condition of our lives make necessary. For though earthly things are by no means the proper materials of rational delight and felicity; yet they are the kind provisions and remedies that a most good and gracious creator has given us against our bodily wants and miseries: and therefore are to be received with thanksgiving, though not looked upon as our happiness. Providing for our well-being here is a branch of the first law of nature, self-preservation; and so for it is a duty and a virtue, as well as providing for our well-being hereafter. And there is, in truth, no other difference between the error and misbehavior of the mere worldling and the cloistered saint, but in degree. They also infer from the Apostle's forbidding us to love this world, that therefore we should hate it, make a very unnatural and a very impious conclusion. I had almost said, deserve to want the comforts and accommodations of this world. For were there really anything criminal in diligence and industry in acquiring; or in frugality and temperance in the enjoying of worldly goods; it would then be a sin to be flesh and blood. And in this case, every man would have good reason to say to his maker, why hast thou made me this? Since therefore it appears to be the bounden duty of all to provide for their temporal, as well as for their eternal welfare; we must not, we cannot, suppose the contrary of this to be enjoined by an Apostle, a preacher of universal righteousness. Consequently it is not the loving of this world, in every sense of the word love, that the text forbids.

In order therefore to conceive aright of the nature and extent of this prohibition; we must first of all consider what we are, who are here forbid to love, and what this world is, which is here forbid to be loved by us. That is, we must endeavor to understand the design of our maker in the formation of this world; and for what ends and purposes he has placed us in it. For it is from hence only that we can come to any determinate and satisfying resolution of the real worth and value this world is to us; as this depends entirely upon the will and pleasure of our common Creator, and upon nothing else. For that the worth and value of this world is really more to man, than it is to angels; but less than it is to brutes; this is resolvable into nothing else, but the mere good pleasure of God.

Now God's principle design in our creation seems to be that of making a creature, capable of enjoying himself, and of living and being with him in a manner at present inconceivable to us; and probably to fill up the stations of other beings, from thence they by transgression were fallen. In order then to this advancement[3] and promotion, some things seem to be absolutely necessary, as requisites and qualifications. Which I apprehend to be, such dispositions of virtue and holiness; such an inward, and I had almost said, inborn rectitude of mind and will, as is no other way attainable, but in a state of trial and probation.

For this end and purpose God seems to have put us in place and condition we are now in; to have clothed us with a body and sensual appetites; and to have placed us in this world, in order to train us up for heaven and himself. And that the law in our members might yield sufficient scope and occasion for the law of the mind to exercise and exert itself, "God has made all things in this world very good for every way fit for a probationary state; fit to answer his purpose, both in providing a supply for our natural and innocent desires, and also a temptation to our unreasonable and lawless ones; that we might prove our adherence and fidelity to himself." And in this sense, the forbidden fruit, the tree of knowledge of good and evil is growing still.

This being observed and considered, it is very easy to apprehend, when the love of this world becomes criminal. And this it certainly doth, when it prevails on us to do anything, that disqualifies us for the presence and enjoyment of the best and most perfect of all beings. When we so far forget ourselves of this world, as to look upon it, and desire it, as a sole, or principle good; or put in practice any at least fraud or violence, to procure anything in it: when we possess this world's goods, and yet use and suffer our fellow creatures to be miserable through a want of them; or are unwilling to leave this world, whenever, or by what means soever, God in his providence shall call us out of it: When the love of this world betrays us into any of these impieties, we not only love it better[4] than we ought to do, but, in reality, better than we do ourselves. And this world, with all its greatness and glory, could we possess them, would make us a very poor amends, for what we shall lose by this foolish fondness.

For always to have God before our eyes, as our sole or principle good; to be just and merciful towards our fellow creatures; and with a cheerful resignation to say to him, who knows best what's good for us, "My will be done;" these things are all great and indispensable points of duty. Virtues that this life, and this world, are designed to practice and perfect us in, by their being temptations to the contrary. They are some of those necessary qualifications to happiness which are sent here on purpose to acquire which we can never see the face of God in glory. Is that this world is so far from being an object that we should be fond of as, or even free with; that on the contrary it is what we should look on with a most watchful, and a most wary eye. Or, if we must love this world, it should be only as heroes do dangers and difficulties, and the champion his antagonist, because the conquest of them leads to reward and glory.

But it may be asked; is not the supposition of this world's being designed as a tempter to evil an exciter and provocative of unreasonable and lawless desires, an impeachment of the goodness and holiness of God. To which it may be answered: That God's principle design in the making of man, as was before observed, seems to be that of making a creature to be with himself. But before man can see, and be with God, it is necessary that he be holy; and to be holy he must be bred. This makes some such state as we are now in this world, to become necessary; where the motives and inducements to virtue and vice are so widely qualified, so duly proportioned, as that our preference of either may be a matter of mere choice, and determination of a free agent. And this setting of evil as well as good before us, and consequently, putting it in our power[5] to make ourselves miserable as well as happy, is so far from being anything particularly hard in man's case, that it may be safely affirmed, that this either now is or has been, the case of every revealed intelligent being besides man; and that there is no creature now in heaven, where good and virtuous men[6] shall be, but has gone through some such state of trial and probation, as good and virtuous now do in this world.

Let us therefore consider, often and seriously consider what we are, and for what we are here, and for what God has breathed a reasonable soul into a sensual body: and placed us here as in a pleasant garden indeed but with forbidden fruit in it! Not surely for us to eat until we are surfeited and die; but rather to refrain and live. Not that we should let go our integrity, and sell our righteousness, for what in time of need and distress cannot profit us; our birthright, like man, for a morsel of bread: but to let it appear by all our thoughts, by every word, and by every action, that the approbation and favor of God are more dear to us than gold, yea than much fine gold; and the doing of our duty sweeter than honey, and the honey-comb.

The motives of religion ought at all times,[7] but more particularly at this holy season when the blessed Jesus made expiation for the sins of the whole world to have so much[8] influence upon us as to prevail over the temptations of sin and it is not our [illegible] they do it; our passions and appetites; nor employment, our company; our youth or our age; the examples of those we converse with or the fashionable customary vices of our country;[9] these, and such like, are temptations, which it is the business of religion, and the proper trial of our virtue, to overcome. And if our passions hurry us, or our company seduce us, or the customs and fashions of the world lead us carelessly and inconsiderately into the ways of destruction; it is not our excuse, but our condemnation that "we have followed a multitude to do evil, that we have prevailed upon more by the shame of men, than by the fear of God;" or that our affection and love to sin has been so strong, that our reason and religion have been able to subdue our appetites. How far the truth of this charge may hold true as to ourselves, a single reflection on our behavior and on the one which we have entertained ourselves during this solemn season of Lent. For whatever the worldling may advance, or the Atheist pretend. The Church, sensible of the frailty of human nature, has wisely appointed the forty days of Lent the time of humiliation generally observed[10] by Christians; Easter, the great festival of our Savior's resurrection on which especially to recollect our thoughts and wean our affection from the things of this world.

An institution so fit, so reasonable, so pious, one might think could meet with no opposition from any who call themselves Christians especially such as affect to be thought good Christians, and exemplary patterns of piety! Alas! What punishment must[11] such hypocrisy, and lip-service expect; a stammering tongue, a quivering lip, and a throbbing heart, and a trembling stance, are but feint sketches of what they must undergo, before the dreadful sentence overwhelm their souls in utter perdition. A wise and serious person would think that if then through indiscretion or vicious temper have abused this season, he for his part is the more concerned to restore it to its proper use;[12] and by his exemplary conduct on this occasion, both to express his own humility, and to edify the Church of Christ. I am naturally led to these reflections, from the late prostitution of this holy season[13] at a time when all things within, and all things without us conspired (one would have thought) to a contrary behavior. For what with our own iniquities, the torrent of which, if it has not altogether, broke its bounds, it is very nigh full, even up to the brim. And what with the gloomy prospect which presents itself to view, of savage murders, wallowing in the blood of our fellow creature man. When the devouring sword is come near us; permitted by the Almighty, perhaps totally to destroy us. Methinks when judgment is so near, we should, instead of reveling in licentiousness, been humbling ourselves in dust and ashes, and but no time in our application for mercy. The favor of God's mercy hangs over our [illegible]. And have we at least a plea to offer that the shame may be averted; have our behavior for some time been truly Christian. No. For many who are of too delicate a texture to visit this place of a rainy day, or plead an excuse of indisposition for not doing it can dare the inclemency of the air; and visit those places, as the rakes of the town, in consequence of which must think that they are as bad as themselves, and that it is not the sense of the sin, but rather of some temporal inconveniences, or want of opportunity, which restrains them from being like themselves.

To conclude, let us all be exhorted to put up our prayers to God, first for the negligent, that they may see their error, repent of their sin and folly, and do so no more. If neither [illegible] but our prayers may reach them and God may have mercy on them. Secondly, let us pray to God for the whole province that he would but lay these sins to our charge, but try and spare us a little longer. Never was there a greater occasion for this than now. Do we think that there is a God? And that he is the Creator and the Governor of the world and all that is therein? Can we think that he will always be thus mocked, insulted and provoked? That he will suffer his glory to be given to another, and his praise to the devil, his greatest enemy? And that he will not at last show his resentment and indignation? The prophet Jeremiah saith that when such wonderful and horrible things are committed in the land, and the people love to have it so, then God exert his authority: "shall I not visit for these things, saith the Lord?" And shall not my soul be avenged on such a nation [illegible]. That he would hide them under the hollow of his hand until his indignation is over-past. And that whenever he is pleased again to visit us in mercy and lift up the light of his countenance upon us, and give us peace, the sense hereof may work such a reformation[14] in our hearts, that we may no longer be guilty of such provocations but we may devote ourselves to his service, like such as are preserved by him. To conclude, let us all pray to God to give us his grace, that we may delight ourselves in his commandments and say with holy David, "I hate vain thoughts, but thy law do I love."

According to Smith's index, the sermon was delivered once, in 1761. This sermon is indexed by Smith as #092, and he credits Dorman as a printed source.

VIII

"Be Not Conformed to This World"

Romans 12:2
Be not conformed to this world.

THE APOSTLE IN THESE WORDS cautions his converts against a too easy compliance with the customs and manners of this world; and though this advice was addressed to a particular set of Christians under particular circumstances, yet it may be considered as containing matter of general utility to all Christians in every age and country;[1] and perhaps there never was a time, since the Apostles' days, where it could with more propriety be insisted on, than now; whether we consider, on the one hand the great corruption of manners, which prevails among us: Or on the other, the more than ordinary fondness, which most men show for conforming to the course and way of the world, without regarding whether such a compliance is consistent with the rules of our duty or not.

Be not conformed to the world. First, I will endeavor to state the bounds and limits, under which this prospect is to be considered.

Then, I will offer some considerations in order to show the great reasonableness of it.

And in the last place, I will make some remarks and observations, which may prove useful to us in point of practice.

As to the bounds and limits, under which this precept of the Apostle is to be understood, we may observe that when he directs us not to conform to this world, he does not mean, that we should yield no compliance—that we should conform in no instance whatever to the humors and dispositions of those, with whom we live and converse, since such a conduct as this would deprive us of all the pleasures and advantages of society, for the enjoyment of which, man seems to be in a particular manner designed, and without which he would be the most forlorn and miserable of all beings.

Nor again is the caution of the text to be understood so rigorously as if the Apostle intended that we should not comply with the innocent customs, and manners of the world, or conform in things of an indifferent nature and of no importance—such as dress, behavior, conversation, and all the little intercourses of human life. For in these cases a certain deference as due to custom; and though there may be some color of reason to depart from the multitude in some particular, yet a man ought to sacrifice his private inclinations and opinions to the practice of the public, and to do otherwise argues an unreasonable degree of pride and arrogance. Besides, such an affectation of singularity in matters of importance, and which are in their own nature indifferent, will render us extremely ridiculous and contemptible, and utterly unqualify us for being of any moment or consequence in the world. But as there is more danger of our paying no regard at all to this caution of the text, than of our observing it in too rigid[2] and scrupulous a manner, as there is more danger of our being too easy in complying with the customs and manners of the world, than of our affecting a blameable singularity by not conforming at all, I shall spend no more time in fixing the bounds under which this precept is to be understood, but proceed in the second place to show the great reasonableness of it, when confined within the limits just now marked out.

And first then it was reasonable that the Apostle should caution us against a too easy compliance with the customs and manners of this world, because we are extremely apt to imitate that, which is most prevailing and to persuade ourselves into a belief that it ought so to do, or at most that there can be no great harm in it.

It is in practice as in opinion, what most men hold, we consider as true, and so what most do, we take to be right and proper to be done. And indeed there are many, who have no other rule to go by. Many, who being unable to think and judge for themselves, are obliged to consider the general practice of the world as the only proper standard to follow, and even those, who are wiser can hardly refrain from following it, as nothing comes so great authority with it as the example of a multitude, and though we may perhaps think ourselves wiser and better able to choose than any one of them, when taken singly; yet when we look at them as united into one body, we are apt to feel a secret awe and reverence for them, and can hardly think it possible that so many should be mistaken. On such occasions it is rational to suspect our own judgment, and to conclude that that must be right, concerning which so many are agreed. That there can be no ill in that, which so many do, and which is received, as it were, for a law and custom all the world over.

This is the reasoning, which most men make use of on this occasion, and which commonly prevails on us to conform to the way and course of the world.

But if we should think that the generality are in the wrong—if we should really believe that the customs and manners of the world are not such as would become a good and conscientious man to follow, yet still we should be apt to comply, for fear of incurring the censure of singularity which is, it seems, so heavy a charge, that few, very few have the courage and confidence to encounter it.

Besides there are many, who do not think it at all necessary to run this risk, since though custom will not entirely justify vice, yet it will, they imagine, much lessen the guilt of it, and therefore, if they do remiss in following the general practice, it is at most but a sin of infirmity, which God will take no notice of. They are ready enough to own that men's manners are much depraved, and that there is but little of true piety to be found among them; but then they add, this is the general practice, this is the way of the world, and he cannot be very guilty, who does only what others do.

These are some of the grounds and principles, on which we inclined to conform to the course and way of the world. We either think that the multitude have right on their side, or if we are of opinion that they are in the wrong yet still we conform, either because we are afraid of incurring the censure of singularity, or fondly imagine that general custom will excuse us in the sight of God.

And as we are extremely apt for these reasons greedily to fall in with that, which is most prevailing, whether it be good or bad. It was highly proper that the Apostle should put us on our guard by cautioning us against a too easy compliance with the customs and manners of the world.

So again, this advice will appear still more proper, when we observe that it was addressed to Christians that is to persons, who had renounced all the pomps and vanities and follies of this world, and had in the most solemn manner engaged to live, not according to the loose manners and notions which obtain among men, but according to the strict rules and precepts of the Gospel.

And as this consideration suggested to us a good argument for the propriety of this precept of the text, so also does the great reward, which sincere Christians are entitled to.

If we had hope only in this life, it might perhaps be difficult (I had almost said impossible) to comprehend the necessity of many of the precepts of the Gospel; and none would appear more strange than these in which we are exhorted not to conform to this world, but to look down with scorn and contempt on the pleasures and pomps of it, and to wage a continual war as it were with our natural appetites and passions; but when we are assured of a future recompense and are taught that it will not consist in sensual gratifications, but in pure intellectual joys, nothing can be more reasonable for persons in these circumstances not greedily to follow the corrupt customs and manners of this world, but to obstruct themselves as far as they can from the pleasures of senses, and by this means to prepare their minds for a due relish of those joys, which eye hath not seen, nor ear heard, nor hath it entered into the heart of man fully to conceive.

Thus have I examined the limits, under which the precept contained in my text is to be understood, and shown likewise the great reasonableness of it. Let us now try in the last place whether these reflections will not afford us some use in manner of practice.

And first then, we may observe that the multitude is not a safe guide to follow, that the measures of right and wrong are not to be taken from the consent of the majority, since it appears from what has been said, that vice has always had the greatest party on its side, and yet it is vice still. Indeed the only safe way in all cases is to consider not what is the prevailing custom, not what is the general practice, but what is duty, and to make that the only rule of our conduct; always remembering that virtue, like truth is not the less so, because she happens to have but a few followers, and that it is the nature of actions, and not the number of actors, by which a wise and thinking man will regulate his behavior.

And as the multitude is not a safe guide to follow, so again they, who happen to have the majority for their particular way of thinking and living, must not conclude from thence, that they are certainly in the right, since we find that it is natural for men to join themselves to that party, which is most prevailing and they therefore, who consider this circumstance as an argument of a good cause, show that they do not understand the world and are strangers to the general temper and inclination of mankind.

Further, it will not be improper on this occasion to make some remarks on the hazards and inconveniences to which a love of conforming to the customs and manners of the world, or what is the same thing, a desire of not appearing singular, will expose us, when carried to excess.

He that has not courage and confidence enough to resist the power of custom and example will often be obliged to live in a manner, that he does not approve of and be betrayed into many things, which are by no means proper for a person of his station and rank in life.

But such a temper and disposition will not only make us do such actions as are indiscreet, but very often such are highly criminal. For he that is possessed of this false modesty, complies with everything, and is fearful of nothing but what may look singular in the opinion of those, with whom he lives and converses. Such an one falls in with the torrent, and is ready for every action, every discourse, how unjustifiable soever in itself, so it be in vogue.

But this dread of appearing singular, this love of following the multitude, this false modesty, or whatever name it is called by, will not only betray us into many things that are indiscreet, and highly criminal, but will restrain us oftentimes from doing what is truly good and laudable.

Your own thoughts will suggest to you many instances under the head: However one there is, which I cannot omit on this occasion, and that is the manner in which many of us behave in matters relating to religion. It is no uncommon thing in this loose and profane age for persons to conceal all serious sentiments of their natures, and to affect to be greater libertines, than they really are and this is done merely because they have not courage and confidence enough to bear those absurd jests, which light and unthinking persons are apt to cast as virtue and religion, and on all, who pretend to have a regard for them; and some carry this matter so far that they are almost ashamed of being seen at the exercises of devotion and piety, lest they should be reckoned precise and hypocritical; and this humor increases so much on us, that instead of hypocrisy, which distinguished the last age, we seem now to be in danger of falling into the other extreme open impiety, and of the two, the second is worst: for though hypocrisy is a most detestable vice, yet it is better than open impiety. They are both equally destructive to the person who is guilty of them, but with respect to others, barefaced irreligion is certainly the most pernicious. The true mean in this case is to be sincerely good and virtuous, and not to be afraid to let the world see that we are so.

And that we may have this Godly courage and confidence, let us remember that nothing[3] can be more base or unworthy a mark than to desert the cause of virtues for fear of incurring the idle censures of an ignorant and corrupt world. But above all, let us remember that such a conduct is particularly blameable in a Christian who is called openly to profess his religion and faith and accordingly there is not a more severe sentence in the Holy Scripture[4] than that which is denounced against Christians of their character—against those who are ashamed before men in a manner of such unspeakable importance, and I cannot better close this discourse than by repeating the very words themselves.

Whosoever says our Savior shall be ashamed of me and of my words, in this adulterous and sinful generation, of him also shall the Son of Man be ashamed, when he cometh in the glory of his Father with the holy angels.

According to Smith's index, the sermon was delivered at least four times, in 1772, 1779, 1784, and 1795. This sermon is indexed by Smith as #162, and he credits Stokes as an original source.

IX

"Love Your Enemies"

Matthew 5:43–44
Ye have heard that it hath been said thou shalt love thy neighbor, and hate thine enemy.
But I say unto you, Love your enemies, bless them that curse you, do good to them that
hate you, and pray for them which despitefully use you, and persecute you.

THE JEWS HAVING READ that their ancestors were commissioned by God as ministers of His justice, utterly to destroy the seven nations that possessed the land of Canaan before them, to blot out the remembrance of Amalech under Heaven and to have no peace with the Amorites and the Moabites, their declared enemies; considered not that these were special cases, the divine command and grounded upon reason both of state and religion, but drew from them very falsely a sanction both to their[1] own private and personal quarrels; and advanced it into a maxim that in general they were to love their neighbors, yet not only might, but ought to hate their enemies, especially such as were enemies to their law, and to their manner of worship. This their doctors taught with much assurance, and the people received it with a malicious readiness.[2] But our Savior in his sermon on the Mount, endeavored to correct their mistake, and prescribe to his followers, the very contrary habit of mind; "ye have heard that it hath been said, thou shalt love thy neighbor and hate thine enemy, but I say unto you, love your enemies, bless them that curse you, do good to them that hate you, and pray, for them that despitefully use you and persecute you."

This is descriptive of the duty given by our Savior of loving our enemies. The first step towards which is discharging our minds[3] of all rancor and virulence toward them; for where the least particle of this is, it will soon discover itself in our words and actions. Upon this account the scripture calls it very significantly the leaven of malice; which being of a spreading and fermenting nature, will in time diffuse itself through the whole behavior.[4] Nay, should we suppose (which is very seldom found) that a man has such an absolute command over himself as to stifle his disgust,[5] and to manage his actions in a constant consideration to his affections; and yet all this is[6] but a mastery of dissimilation, and acting in a diffusion which cannot long be worn. Enmity is a restless thing[7] and not to be dissembled without some torment to the mind that entertains it: and therefore we may presume that he who is resolved to hate his enemy and not to show it, has turned his hatred inward and becomes a tyrant and an enemy to himself; nor can he wish his most mortal enemy a greater misery than to possess a mind ever ready to burst, and yet never to give it vent.[8] Are we then persuaded that both our duty and interest require that we should deport ourselves with all tokens of love to our enemies?[9] Let us but take this easy course, to entertain the things in our heart which we would manifest in our converse, and then we shall find small difficulty in the next instance of our love to our enemies which is blessing them that curse us.

The word which we render bless, implies not only our showing them a personal civility, but avoiding any malicious invectives in their absence, uttered to deprecate and vilify them. And therefore though they reproach, revile and slander us, and then presume with the most contemptuous and insulting, the most scurrilous and bitter language; and when absent make it their business to lessen and defame us;[10] our conduct, is to be decidedly the reverse of this. We must answer them in the most civil, courteous, obliging terms; and whenever we have occasion to speak of them, to conceal their faults, where[11] justice do not require us to discover them. We must put the best construction upon all their actions, and be ready to publish whatever we know virtuous and commendable in them, even tough they will acknowledge no such quality in us; for thus the Christians behaved of old., "we are fools" says St. Paul, "for Christ's sake, but ye are wise in Christ; ye are honorable, but we are despised; being reviled we bless; being persecuted, we suffer; being defamed, we entreat." What harmony, what beauty, what perfection must there be in such a temper as this! What command over his passions must we suppose in such a person. And how amiable does it look to see him unmoved by abuse, and invincible by reproach, returning good for evil, and gracious wishes for base and horrid imprecations! This certainly is one of the best arguments of a great and generous mind, for according to the observation of the wise man, "he that is slow to anger, is better than the mighty, and he that ruleth his spirit, than he that taketh a city."

Again, to love an enemy[12] is to do him all the real offices of kindness and beneficence, that opportunity shall lay in our way. Has providence, for instance, put any of our enemies' concernments, his health, his estate, his preferment, or any other thing conducing to the convenience of his life under our power or influence? In all this it affords us an opportunity to manifest whether we can reach the sublimest height[13] of this precept. Is our enemy sick and languishing? Is it in our power to preserve him, or neglecting the means of preservation to destroy him: Christianity here commands us to be concerned for his weakness, to rescue him from death and the grave; and to preserve that life, which perhaps would once have destroyed ours. Or do we see our enemy defrauded and oppressed, we must contribute[14] our assistance to discover the fraud, or repel the oppression; and be as ready to preserve him from poverty as we would to relieve him if we were in it. Is it in our power to interrupt or injure his business or interest,[15] to give him a secret blow that shall strike him to the ground forever? Can we by our power obstruct his lawful advantage and preferment and so reap the diabolical satisfaction of a close revenge! Can we do him all the mischief imaginable [illegible] successfully and to applaud an [illegible] and power, our evil, our subtle contrivances? Yet all these practices by rising by the fall of an adversary are to be detested as infinitely opposite to that innocence and clearness of spirit; that openness and freedom from design which becomes a professor of Christianity.

But the last and crowning instance of our love to our enemies, is to pray for them; for by this a man[16] acknowledges himself, as it were, unable to do enough for his enemy, and therefore he calls in the assistance of Heaven, and engages omnipotence to complete the kindness. Prayer for our own prosperity is indeed a necessary duty, but if we consider it narrowly, it is but a kind of lawful and pious selfishness; but when we pray as heartily for our enemies, as for our daily bread, we reckon his felicity among our own necessities. When we recommend him to God's infinite power and compassion to restore his health, relieve his wants, and supply him with all needful things, even at the same time that he is injuring and persecuting us; we then follow that divine pattern of perfect charity, who in the midst of the most barbarous and contentious usage, made both this prayer and apology for his murderers, "Father forgive them for they know not what they do."

This then, is the perfection of Christians choosing to be kindly, affected not to our friends and benefactors only, but to our enemies and persecutors. It is a good degree of charity to speak them fair and civilly when they are reviling and reproaching us; it is still a higher degree of it to confer real benefits upon them and to contribute what we have to their happiness and welfare; it is the height[17] and perfection of it to recommend them to God, who can do them more good than we can; can grant them the grace of repentance, which we can only wish them; can bestow upon them that pardon for their faults, which we can only request for them, and make them as great and as happy as he pleases, both in this world and the next.[18]

But if all this is to be done for our enemies, where is the difference between those that have done us kindness, and those that have done us wrong? The most we can do for our best friends and kindest benefactors, is to love them, to bless them, to do them good, and to pray for them: if therefore we are obliged to do all this for our enemies, there is plainly nothing more left to be done for our friends. Now, though benevolence in general[19] is to be extended to all mankind, even to those that hate and injure us, as well as those that do us good, yet that particular and special[20] friendship, i.e., the loving one person above another is still as commendable as ever. We have an instance of our blessed Savior himself who, though he was continually teaching and instructing, healing and doing good to an ungrateful people; and he came into the world to die[21] for his enemies, (which is the strongest effort of love that can be made even for our dearest friends) yet nevertheless, he had his twelve disciples with whom he conversed with more intimacy; whom he instructed with more diligence and freedom, and prayed for in a particular manner, with more than ordinary tenderness and concern; and even in that number, three of them were singled out for special confidences and favors; and of these three, St. John is eminently distinguished as his bosom friend, and the disciple whom he loved; which makes it evident that however the Christian religion may require a very extensive charity, yet it has still left room for the obligations of particular friendships and relations. We are bound to relieve our enemies if we can; when they want; but we are not bound to give them extraordinary presents, or to make them inheritors of our estates. We are required to love our enemies, to wish and do them all possible good, but it does not from thence[22] become necessary that we should take them into our bosom, and give them the same place in our most secret thoughts and purposes, that is due our most familiar friends, and though we are to deny our assistance to none, yet when friend and foe stand in competition, and both cannot be served at once, the Apostle I think has clearly[23] determined the preference: "for as we have opportunity," says he, "let us do good unto all men, but especially to them that are of the household of faith, and by purity of reason, especially to those of this household, that are bound to us by a nearer tie of consanguinity and friendship."

But the greatest objection against the practice of this duty arises from the vast difficulty that is supposed in it. What, love an enemy? Embrace a wretch that would take away my life, had he a secure opportunity? As well may you bid me pull up[24] the mountains by the roots, or stop the sun in its daily[25] course. The thing is impossible, and the whole tendency of nature is against it. To forgive injuries, and tamely put up affronts, are lessons proper for the weak and pusillanimous, for such as want power, courage or[26] opportunity to express their resentments; but they badly comport with a man of spirit, and worse with a man of honor. To silence this objection, we cannot do better than proceed[27] to some of the motives and arguments that may recommend the love of our enemies and reconcile us to the practice of it.

Would we be impartial and lay aside our prejudice, we might, perhaps discern several great and good qualities in the person that hates us: and even in an enemy, whatsoever is lovely, whatsoever is of God's report, should not be without its due praise and acknowledgement. Nay, suppose the worst, that he is never so much an enemy, and never so immoral a man, yet still he is joined with us in the same society, and communion of the same nature, and partaking of the image and superscription of our Heavenly Father: and we paint him in false colors,[28] when we think him capable of affording us no benefit at all; since by him we may be admonished of our faults, which our friend would be unwilling to mention, or too tender in reproving. By him, and the fear of his censures we may be restrained from those liberties which if we had taken, might have proved a snare and temptation to us; and by him and his injuries have an opportunity given us of improving our virtue and thereby of increasing our happiness. In him indeed there is no such intention, and all that he does is hostile against us;[29] but still we are to consider him as an instrument in God's hand, without whom appointment or permission nothing can befall us; and consequently, not fix our eyes with indignation upon him, but have always an awful regard to the divine providence that employs him.

This enemy of ours perhaps, at present may create us some uneasiness; yet hereafter he may become (what reconciled enemies usually are) our most cordial friend.[30] And to bring about this event, what can we imagine as so prevailing as a continual series of kind and good offices, to those that bear us ill will. For if to see an impaired person when insulted by outrageous malice, not only patient in bearing it, but quietly passing by all other methods of revenge besides that of a generous contempt, if such a sight as this, I say, cannot but fill, even him that does the injury, with secret shame and confusion, what operation may we not expect it to have. When the same innocent and injured person, not contented only to forbear and forgive, pursues his very persecutor with courtesy and kindness, and endeavors to reduce him by all possible overtures of reconciliation, and invitations to friendship. Such resolved goodness must be sufficient to subdue[31] the most obstinate ill-nature, and can hardly fail of the effect; of which the Apostle gives us this assurance, "if thine enemy hunger feed him; if he thirst give him drink; for in so doing then ye heap coals of fire upon his head;" coals not to burn and to consume him, but melt him into easiness[32] and compliance; to refine him from his unsociable fashions, and fit him for your partiality and friendship.

But if this event should not follow, nay, if we are even assured, that the malice our enemy bears us, is so settled and implacable, that no love or kindness on our part can work on his temper and regain his friendship; yet herein is the great advantage of this duty, that in loving our enemies, we really exercise and express our love to ourselves. By loving an enemy, notwithstanding his hatred to us, we free our minds of those barbarous passions of anger, hatred, and revenge, which put the minds into an unnatural ferment and tumult. By not being[33] easily provoked, we blunt the edge of the weapon, wherewith he seeks to hurt us, and by returning good for evil; we have it in our power [illegible] be revenged of him. It must soften them to see so much goodness in those they hate; it must mollify them to see a generous return to an unworthy provocation; and in short we must quiet shame[34] and confound them by showing ourselves to be, in all the contention between us, much the better. The worser and the greater persons. How pleasing a prospect[35] must it be to the meek, the humble, and the patient mind, whenever an enemy approaches, to perceive himself placed, as it were, on an eminence above him, and that he is able to keep himself undisturbed, notwithstanding all the attacks that are made upon him. Nor can it but continue this pleasure, to conceive some probable hopes of vanquishing the stoutest oppression of an enemy, by courtesy and kindness, and like a great and wise general[36] by art and stratagem, by skill and conduct, by patience and delay, to make an end of the war: without even putting it to the hazard of a battle.

By our Lord's authority we may continue to carry the practice of this duty to a still higher pitch of commendation. For as love for love is but justice and gratitude; love for no love, favor and kindness; so love for hatred and enmity is a most divine temper, and that whereby we may become the children of our Father who is in Heaven: for He maketh His sun to rise on the evil[37] and the good and sendeth His rain on the just and unjust. Who then can think it beneath him to pass by an injury or to put up an affront, when he sees that God, the sovereign Creator and Lord of all things, whose power no creature is able to resist, does nevertheless spare and pressure us, who provoke him every day; and by our continual abuse of his forbearance and long-suffering call for the severest vengeance upon us? Who can think it unbecoming his dignity or greatness even to buy sustenance with his neighbors, who has done him wrong, by doing him, as he has opportunity, all offices of goodness and kindness, when he has before him the example of God himself, entreating us to be reconciled to him; and not withstanding our manifold provocations, desirous at any rate, to purchase our friendship. When we have the example of the Son of God, our crucified Savior, who did no sin, neither was guile found in his mouth; and yet when he was reviled not again; when he suffered, he threatened not. When we have the example of His Apostles,[38] who, in all things approved themselves as the ministers of Christ and His faithful followers, in honor and dishonor, by evil report and good report. When we have the example of the church in the best ages, who prayed for all that were unjustly their enemies. When we have God's gracious promise of recompense to be made us, for all that we suffer: for blessed are ye when men shall revile you and persecute you, and say all manner of evil against you falsely for my sake: rejoice and be exceeding glad, for great is your reward in Heaven. And lastly, when we have his severe threatenings, that without forgiving our enemies, we can have no remission of our transgressions: for if he that is but flesh nourisheth hatred,[39] who shall entreat for pardon of his sins? Therefore, remember corruption and death,[40] and abide in the commandments; remember the commandments and bear no malice to thy neighbor; remember the covenant of the Most High, and wink at ignorance.

This sermon was delivered three times at St. Philip's (1765, October 3, 1773, and July 1793). Smith also delivered it at Christ Church on March 8, 1767. This sermon is indexed by Smith as #191, and he credits Pearce as an original source.

X

"I Will Have Mercy and Not Sacrifice"

Matthew 9:13
But go ye, and learn what that meaneth; I will have mercy, and not sacrifice.

T HESE WORDS ARE ORIGINALLY the Prophet Hosea's, wherein God Almighty represents to the Jews the nature of that obedience which is most acceptable to Him; and consequently what he chiefly requires of them.

It is not so much a scrupulous observance of positive instituted parts of religion, which he insists on, as a conscientious obedience to the duties of the moral kind.

"I desired mercy," saith He, "and not sacrifice; I desired not only your observance to the positive duties commanded you, but to the laws of justice, temperance and mercy."

It was the want of these, and the practice of some notorious vices, of which God frequently complains in the prophets, that unhallowed their obedience, rendering all their oblations abominable in his sight. "Be what purpose is the multitude of your sacrifices unto me, saith the Lord. I am full of the burnt offerings of rams, and the fat of the fed beasts. I delight not in the blood[1] of lambs or of goats. Your new moons, and your appointed feasts, my soul hateth. I am weary of them."

Nothing could give a more lively representation, of the Almighty's dislike to his non-institutions, when attended with a violation of his moral laws, than that variety of expressions which the Holy Spirit has more use of in this place. Where[2] it is not meant that He prohibited all obedience to his ceremonial law, but that he was desirous, that those duties, which were enjoined only as marks of obedience to him, without any other consideration to recommend them should give place to such, as are of substantial benefit, and in their nature always obliging.

The design, therefore of the words, of the law, is not to make void the obligation which lay upon the Jews to obey the positive institutions of God, but to convince them that the duties of natural religion, were the principal things mankind were ever bound to observe; that they are so far from being set aside by revelation that they are always to be performed with, or before them, and that the obedience paid to God in the positive commands, without the performance of moral virtues, are so far from being acceptable, that they prove the objects of his displeasure and detestation.

To enforce the truth of these propositions, is the intent of the following discourse.

First, then, the duties of natural religion were the principal things mankind were ever bound to observe. By the duties of natural religion is meant a performance of those duties relating to God our neighbor, and ourselves, which are obvious to every man from the dictates of his own mind, or the right use of his natural faculties, without the help of an extraordinary revelation. Such laws are the ground work of all religion, and the foundation of every duty which God requires of mankind.

Of this nature is the belief of a God, the creator of all things, whom we are to worship with all that reverence which is due to his infinite majesty. This belief will infer the persuasion that He is infinitely perfect in truth, in goodness, and in power; which perfections require our confidence in his mercy, our obedience to his commands, and our gratitude for his benefits. Of this kind again are the duties of temperance with regard to ourselves; of justice and mercy towards others. These are such like duties, every man's unprejudiced reason will convince him of the obligation he is under to perform, without any further light, or means of knowledge afforded him.

Now revealed religion supposes the establishment of these, and is built upon them. This is evident from the dispensation of the Jewish, and that of the Christian religion at this day. In neither of which we find the moral laws of nature to be altered, but only improved and carried to perfection.

The revelation vouchsafed to Moses, though it consisted of many positive precepts, peculiar to that people; yet we find that it insists on moral duties as the main and fundamental part of their religion. This is evident from our Savior's answer to that question put to him, concerning the first and great commandment of his law: "Thou shalt love the Lord thy God, with all thy heart, and with all thy soul, and with all thy might, and thy neighbor as thyself."

This also is plain from another passage of the New Testament wherein our Savior tells the Jews, that He came not to destroy the law of the prophets, but to fulfill; that is, to establish and confirm them.

These moral performances we find are styled by our Lord, the weightier matters of the law, which it is true, they ought first to have done, though at the same time they were under an obligation, not to leave the other undone.

In like manner the prophet Isaiah observes that nothing could be more hateful to God, than observance of the ritual law, so long as his people indulged themselves in the practice of immorality. "He that killeth an ox, is as if he show a man; and he that burneth incense, as if he blessed an idol. They have chosen their own ways; and their soul delighteth in their admonitions."

Thus in the Jewish revelation the practice of virtuous actions was preferable to the most exact observance of external rites; which were of no value without the performance of the other; upon which alone their religion was founded, and in which it did princi-pally consist.

The same may with a greater degree of justice be affirmed of the Christian dispen-sation, which it must be owned, is the perfection, both of the natural and mosaical law. Our Savior's design, was to establish and reinforce the practice of these laws with argu-ments unknown or at least in a great measure so in the two former dispensations. He gives promises of eternal happiness, for man's encouragement in the ways of virtue; and threatens eternal misery to deter them from those of vice and folly. He enters upon his sermon, with promises of blessedness to the practice of humility, meekness, purity, righteousness, patience, and mercy: duties of a moral nature, and incumbent on all men; always essential in religion, and to continue such while that remains among man-kind. For till Heaven and Earth shall pass away, not one jot or tittle of the law, the moral part of it, shall pass, till all be fulfilled.

To that natural religion is the foundation of that which is revealed. They are indeed the same, only delivered at different times, and in different manner.

My next proposition is, that the duties of natural or moral religion are so far from being made void or set aside by revelation or revealed duties that they are now made stronger on mankind,[3] and are always to be performed with, if not before them. Moral duties such as I have observed God has originally planted in our nature, of which we can come to the knowledge by the dictates of conscience, and the right use of our natu-ral powers, are of immutable and eternal obligation. Of this kind are the laws of the two tables, which God distinguished from the other by giving them in writing; a token of their indispensable and perpetual obligation; not upon the Jews, but upon all future generations. The observance of these is what he principally required[4] of that people, who were always reproved for their violations of them, without any notice taken of their other defects, with regard to their efficiencies, or other parts of God's instituted worship.

The case is the same under the Gospel Dispensation; the greatest part of which, we may perceive, is made up of moral virtues, heightened and exalted by this revelation into evangelical graces. Every duty of morality remains the same, or is vastly refined by the gospel. So that the Christian religion, which is the most perfect revelation, that God ever made to mankind, is so far from taking away the necessity and obligation of moral virtues, that it enforces the one, and binds the other more strictly on mankind, and so included in it every precept of morality; and likewise affords the best helps and means that were ever offered to the performance of it.

This we may infer from the clearness and perfection of the discovery of those laws, to which it obliges mankind; from the means of grace, and the hopes of Glory; the cer-tainty of which depends upon no less foundation than the truth of God, who has given his express and repeated promise of them. So that the necessity of moral virtues is so far from being made void by the revelation of the Gospel, that it is now made stronger upon mankind; and obedience to evangelical duties the more strict and incumbent.

This, then, being the doctrine of the holy scripture, and the practice of our church, which regards the essentials of religion, namely faith and obedience, more than the instituted and ceremonious parts of it, how unjust it is to charge which accuses our church of laying the greatest stress upon the circumstantials of religion; neglecting in the meanwhile, like the Jews, the more weighty and substantial matters of the law.

An accusation as groundless as it is uncharitable: as if our church had not a high regard for the necessary and substantial duties of religion, as any of those who think proper to separate from our communion. One as if the set up the observance of rites and ceremonies above the practice of the Christian law; and had as great a regard to the practice of such things, which she owns in their nature to be indifferent, neither commanded nor forbidden, and subject to alteration and change, as to the essential and immutable laws of nature and religion.

These we assert are certainly first to be done; and yet the other ought not to be left undone; because, though they are not bound upon by any express command of God, yet as they serve to the decent and orderly performance of God's worship, and are therefore commanded by those who have the rule over us, whom we have ever thought it our duty and happiness to obey; they cease, by virtue of that injunction, to be quite so indifferent, and rather become matter of duty and obedience.

From what has been said we may conclude,[5] that the obedience paid to God in his positive commands, without the performance of moral virtues, are, so far from being acceptable, that they prove the objects of his displeasure and detestation. Nothing can justify a willful transgression of them. Not even that pretense, that good may come, or of doing God service by it.

Moral duties, such as honesty, justice, truth fidelity, mercy, sobriety, charity, and of such Christianity chiefly consists, oblige always, at all times, and in all circumstances. Nor can it be shown by anything our Savior either spoke or did, that he ever designed to release his professors from their obedience to them. He came not to destroy the law but to fulfill it. He declares, that he will have mercy rather than sacrifice; and tells us, that unless our righteousness exceed the righteousness of the Scribes and Pharisees, because we have better means and opportunities of doing it, we shall in no case enter into the Kingdom of Heaven. The practice of moral virtues, improved and bound upon mankind more strictly by Christianity, is the one thing needful; without which faith, though never so exalted; the Holy Communion, though never so often attended, and prayer and fasting, though never so devout and rigorous, will never be of any use or benefit. For faith without works is dead; the prayers and mortifications of the wicked are an abomination; and a participation of the sacrament, without obedience, will only aggravate the guilt of the communicant, and increase his misery.

And, while any one places his religion in the observance of these only, without practicing the more weighty and essential parts thereof, he may justly expect that severe reproof of the prophet. "To what purpose is the multitude of your sacrifices unto me? Who hath required this at your hands? Bring no more vain oblations to me. But put away the evil of your doings from before mine eyes. Cease to do evil; learn to do well. Seek judgment. Relieve the oppressed. Judge the fatherless. Plead for the widow.

"And ye be willing and obedient, ye shall eat the good of the land. But if ye refuse and rebel; ye shall be devoured by the sword of God's wrath. For the mouth of the Lord hath spoken it."

From which wrath, we beseech thee, O Lord to deliver us all, for the sake of Jesus Christ, thy Son, our Savior.[6]

This sermon was delivered one time, at St. Philip's in January 1774. This sermon is indexed by Smith as #261, and he credits Wilton as an original source.

XI

"The Fruit of the Spirit
Is Love, Joy, and Peace"

Galatians 5:22
But the fruit of the Spirit is love, joy, and peace.

THE FEAST OF PENTECOST among the Jews was likewise called the Feast of Harvest, because they were then obliged to bring the first fruits of the land into the House of the Lord their God. This ceremony was designed to include the indispensable obligation men were under, solemnly to acknowledge the benefits they receive from the bounty of God,[1] and to declare openly that it is to Him they have all the blessings they enjoy, and success of their works and the fruit of their labors.

The Christian Pentecost requires something like this from us:[2] we must not now, any more than the Jews, heretofore, appear empty before the Lord, but ought to then and bring forth the fruit of that Spirit, to whom this Holy Festival is dedicated.

St. Paul enumerates them distinctly in this chapter to the Galatians; but the fruit of the Spirit, saith He, is love, joy, peace, longsuffering, gentleness, goodness, faith, meekness, temperance. Not as if there were no more than these, for all the virtues and graces accompanying salvation, are the fruit of God's Spirit. But because these, thus enumerated,[3] stand in direct opposition to those works of the faith which are recited in the foregoing verses.

At present we shall consider only the three first of these, love, joy, and peace. The first fruit of the Spirit here taken notice of by the Apostle is love, by which is meant both the religious homage we have to God, and likewise the benevolence and affection which are due from one man to another. So that it comprehends all the duties which are implied in the two great commandments of the law, and are expressed by a loving God with all our souls, and our neighbor as ourselves. This love is the fruit of the Holy

Ghost, because he is necessarily[4] the author of it. He produces the love of God in our hearts, by suggesting to our minds the excellency of the Supreme Being, and the greatness of His goodness toward[5] us. The merit of a person, and the good we receive or expect from him, is that which generally attracts our affection, and faces our inclination in His favor.[6] How great then ought to be our love of God, when we consider the infinite and incomparable perfections of His nature, His immensity, eternity, and wisdom, omnipotence, majesty and glory. And when to these we add the consideration of His unspeakable goodness to us, and while many blessings which He daily bestows on us, and reflect that it is to Him we are indebted for our redemption, justification and sanctification here, and for the hopes of a glorious immortality hereafter, it is impossible that we can do otherwise than to admire so excellent a being, and love so gracious a benefactor; saying it with the Psalmist, "I will love thee O Lord my strength; the Lord is my strong rock and my defense: my Savior, my God, and my might in whom I will trust, my buckler, the horn also of my salvation, and my refuge."

And whosoever thus loveth God, must of necessity love his brother also, and do him all reasonable service, upon every proper occasion. It is our duty to instruct the ignorant, to comfort the afflicted, to warn them that are unruly, to support the weak, to be patient toward all men, to assist the distressed, and to relieve the necessitous, because these obligations are laid upon us by the express command of God, and therefore we cannot love him, unless we thus love our neighbor likewise. That these duties were the principle objects of St. Paul's thoughts in this place, appears from the catalogue that follows my text, and which contains only these social virtues, which are the cement of society, and unite men with one another: such as peace, longsuffering, gentleness, goodness, and meekness. These will be attended to us with the happiest consequences for[7] the trust and confidence of being reconciled to God, must needs inspire man's heart with inexpressible joy and pleasure, and make him cry out with the Blessed Virgin, my soul doth magnify the Lord, and my Spirit rejoiceth in God my Savior; for He that is mighty hath done to me great things, and Holy is His name. When He can say with the Apostle, "who shall lay anything to the charge of God's elect? It is God that justifieth, who is He that commandeth? It is Christ that died, yea, rather is risen again, who is even at the right hand of God, who also maketh intercession for us." Besides a consciousness of doing our duty in the fear of God, is always attended with the greatest inward satisfaction. For it is joy to the just to do judgment, saith Solomon. And St. Peter takes notice of it as the peculiar privilege of Christians, that they rejoice with joy unspeakable and full of glory. For this reason St. Paul joins together the two exhortations to rejoice evermore and to pray without ceasing, as being reciprocally the causes and effects of each other. And when to recommend alms-giving, he tells the Corinthians, that God loveth a cheerful giver; he plainly intimates that cheerfulness and true charity are inseparable.

Again, the consideration that we dwell under the defense of the most High, and abide under the shadow of the Almighty; and that we enjoy the favor and are under the protection of a most gracious and powerful God; this persuasion, I say, must be a never failing source of comfort and satisfaction. This was the foundation of the Psalmist's joy when he saith, "I have set God always before me, for He is on my right hand, therefore I shall not fall. Wherefore my heart was glad and my glory rejoiced, my flesh also shall rest in hope." This supports the good Christian under the weight of those calamities which damp and sink the spirits of other men. This it was that made the Apostles exceeding joyful in all their tribulations, and rejoice that they were counted worthy to suffer shame for the name of Jesus. And so the primitive Christians counted it all joy when they fell into diverse temptations; and took joyfully the spoiling of their goods, and met even death itself with a cheerful countenance.

But above all, the thoughts of that glorious inheritance which is promised and re-served in heaven for the faithful, cannot but inspire their souls with the most exquisite delight. Rejoice said our Savior to His disciples and be exceeding glad, for great is your reward in heaven. And when Paul bids the Romans to rejoice in hope, he does not mean so much to recommend a particular duty, as to declare the natural consequence of that well grounded hope and certain expectation which is given us in the Gospel; that when our earthly house of this tabernacle is dissolved we shall have a building of God a house not made with hands eternal in the heavens, and that our light afflictions which we endure upon the Earth, and are but for a moment, work out for us a far more exceeding and eternal weight of glory, with which nothing here below is worthy to be compared.

Thus, we see that joy is a fruit of the Spirit, and the genuine effect of pure religion and undefiled before God. It is a slander falsely cast upon duty and virtue to say that they make men fallen and morose; sour their tempers, or disturb their joy: on the con-trary, there are none that have so much reason to rejoice as good men; and nothing that is so productive of real contentment and tranquility of mind, as a true sense and prac-tice of religion: that is to say, the fear of God, and benevolence and goodwill towards men. For this reason, the Apostle places joy between love and peace. The fruit of the Spirit saith He, is love, joy, and peace.

In fact, men of turbulent spirits, maligners, backbiters, and the whole tribe of them can have no joy, for they are enemies to peace. For they are like the evil one in the[8] book of Job, who went to and fro upon the Earth, and walked up and down it, seeking oppor-tunities to do mischief, for this diabolical employment must needs be attended with a great deal of trouble and uneasiness. Whereas he that is friendly and kindly-hearted[9] lives easy and undisturbed, because as his conscience bears him witness, that he has no ill will to anybody, so he has reason to believe that nobody owes him any. He may sometimes be mistaken, and the knowledge he hath of the uprightness of his own heart, may lay him open to the craft and the artifice of wicked and designing men. But all that caution and suspicion which is necessary to guard against treachery and deceit, is too full of torments, to be harbored in his peaceful breast; and he rather chooses to be sometimes deceived, than to be always in a state of war. By this means his sleep is sweet and easy, and his waking hours undisturbed, and he fears no evils because he knows none.

And this is the peace, which St. Paul had principally in view in the text. Not only the peace of God, nor yet only the peace of conscience; but chiefly that friendly correspondence with one another, whereby we keep the unity of the Spirit in the bond of peace. For we may observe that the Apostle opposes in this place, the fruits of the Spirit, to the works of the flesh as therefore he had in the preceding verses reckoned among the works of the flesh; hatred, variance, wrath, strife, envyings, murders, and the like; so we may conclude that by the fruit of the Spirit, love and peace, he means that brotherly love and charity by which men are disposed to avoid all contentions, to interpret favorably the words and actions of their neighbors: and as much as in them lies to live peaceably with all men. Not that we are obliged to compliment away our sense of reason, much less to sacrifice our faith and honor for the sake of peace. This would be to purchase friendship at too exorbitant a price. But we may always avoid everything that savors of bitterness, heat, ill nature, strife, and malice; and ought to put on (as the elect of God) bonds of mercy, kindness, longsuffering, forbearing one another, and forgiving one another. So we shall approve ourselves the temples of the Holy Ghost, who is not the author of confusion, but of peace. As in the vision of the prophet Isaiah, God was not in the strong wind that rent mountains and broke in pieces the rocks, nor yet in the earthquake or the fire, but in the still small voice; so his Holy Spirit will never abide with those haughty, turbulent, fiery tempers, whose chief delight it is to send diversions and foment quarrels; and to disturb, perplex, and confound mankind: and whose breasts are in a continual agitation. Like the troubled sea when it cannot rest.

If, therefore, we desire that the Holy Ghost should dwell in our hearts, let us fit them for the reception of Him, that they may be such habitations as he delights in. We read in the Acts, that he came upon the Apostles when they were all with one accord in one place. From whence we may learn, that love and charity, unanimity and concord, are the best dispositions to invite this heavenly guest, and to keep Him where He is already. Let us therefore, highly value and diligently practice those virtues and graces that are most agreeable to Him: and carefully guard against the opposite vices and passions, which grieve and drive him away from us. Particularly let us follow after the things which make for peace; remembering the words of the Savior, that blessed are the meek for they shall inherit the Earth; the merciful for they shall obtain mercy; the peacemakers for they shall be called the children of God.

Let us in case of any unhappy disagreement[10] not only heartily accept the tenders of reconciliation, but even be the first to offer reasonable terms of accommodation. Let us diligently seek after peace when it is lost, and carefully preserve it when we have it: let us freely forgive them who have offended us, and gratefully acknowledge the favors of those who have done us good. Let us tenderly love our friends, and even our enemies as Christians ought to do, that we may be the children of our Heavenly Father, for he maketh his Sun to rise on evil and on the good and sendeth his rain on the just and on the unjust.

Thus, cultivating the fruits of the Spirit, love and peace, the God of love and peace shall be with us. He will fill our hearts with all the comfort and joy, which they are capable of receiving in this vale of misery, until He brings us at last to the possession of a happy eternity, wherein love, joy, and peace will be completed and perfected. When we shall love God with all the faculties of our souls, enjoy an everlasting peace and tranquility both of body and mind, and be satisfied with that fullness of joy which only to be had in God's presence, and the pleasures that are at his right hand for evermore. To the possession of which God of his infinite mercy brings us through Christ.

This sermon was delivered four times at St. Philip's: 1766, 1770, 1788, and 1798. It was delivered at St. Paul's on May 30, 1784. This sermon is indexed by Smith as #295, and he credits Duberdu as an original source.

XII

"Blessed Are the Merciful"

Matthew 5:7
Blessed are the merciful; for they shall obtain mercy.

THESE WORDS OF MY FATHER naturally divide themselves into two parts; containing[1] an inquiry. First, who are to be understood by the merciful? Secondly, the nature of the reward here promised to them. I shall begin with the former, who are to be understood by the merciful? Now the merciful man may be denominated so from the different objects about which the quality attributed to him is employed.

As every person is an object of love; so far as mercy imports beneficence, he is a merciful man who contributes to their relief according to his ability[2] and to the rules which prudence directs: or even if he has no opportunity of exercising any acts of beneficence, by reason of his narrow or indigent circumstances; yet his inclination, in case it be real and sincere, shall recommend him to the favor of God and the promise here annexed, as if he had actually exercised them: according to the apostolical rule; if there be first a willing mind, it is accepted according to that a man hath, and not according to that he hath not.

It is however a happiness when men can experimentally discover the effects of their good dispositions in this and all other cases, both, as it is an evidence of their sincerity, which, as the heart of man is deceitful above all things, is very desirable; and as it makes them the exemplary instruments of doing honor to God; and at the same time discover the power which religion really has over them: so that others seeing their good works may at once be more effectually excited to glorify God and to go and do likewise.

To show how much, and on how many accounts, mercy in this sense is a Christian grace and duty there is no occasion. It is required upon a common principle of humanity; upon the natural principle of doing unto others, as we would under a supposed change of circumstances, they should do unto us: it is recommended by the example of our Lord, and from the obligation we are under to imitate God, as far as we can, in all his imitable perfections, upon which account we are commanded to be merciful, as our Father who is in heaven is merciful. It is made the particular and distinguished character of a genuine disciple of Christ. It is the necessary effect of that love to our neighbor into which one half of the law is resolved: it is of so great office in the sight of God, that he is said to be well pleased with such sacrifices; and it covers a multitude of sins.

These words are capable of another sense; importing[3] that a man of a beneficent disposition, in judging of other persons will be candid and favorable, and rather inclined to cover and conceal their thoughts, than ascribe to them such faults as they are not guilty of; or to aggravate those which cannot be either concealed or dissembled. Or, by covering a multitude of sins we may understand that a man of a beneficent and generous disposition of mind, when he is really accused and censured himself, will find the greater favor and tenderness from other persons in their judgment of him, both as the circumstances of the crimes he is charged with, and in reference to other crimes wherewith in strictness he might perhaps be really chargeable.

But, as so man's promises of mercy are made to the merciful man in the Holy Scriptures, and as the design of them is to represent to us that God will be in some special manner propitious to him, it is reasonable to conclude that if on that account God does not actually justify him, when charged with the guilt of other sins, yet the good disposition he is in, and the good works he has done, may be a means of recommending him as an object of God's sanctifying grace; and in consequence of his pardoning grace. Time would fail me to enumerate all the motives to this duty, and all the proper acts and [illegible] of it. It is in a word of so great influence and extent as to our religious conduct that a person is simply denominated righteous from it.

The threats denounced in Scriptures against obdurate persons, who are without pity or compassion, or as they have opportunity, discover none toward the miserable, are very severe and terrifying: "He that trimmeth his face from the poor the Lord will set his face against him." But there's one threat against such persons in which all the terrors denounced; whether in the Gospel or the law, seems comprehended; and which one would think no uncharitable person should ever be able to resist the force and the influence of: and those are the words of the Apostle. "He shall have judgment without mercy that hath showed no mercy." This like the Word quick and powerful might be expected should penetrate the heart of the obstinate and insensible. Upon all these accounts the merciful man seems in a special manner entitled to God's favor and pardoning grace; not that those any more than other Christian virtues, has a direct efficiency to their end, or any merit in it which may induce God upon that consideration, to bless or pardon the merciful man; yet as there is a particular congruity in it to the goodness of the divine nature; God in a human way of conceiving things may be rather inclined to dispense his pardoning grace for that reason, or to make it one special condition of his favor, and our reconciliation to him.

But as was hinted, mercy may alas be considered as importing a disposition to for-give those that have injured us; or which does not permit us, when we have them in our power to take all the advantage which we might justly and legally take against them. The reason of this duty is founded in the divine resurrection and the conduct of God towards sinners. He is patient and mercifully long-suffering and of great goodness: he is good to the unthankful and to the evil, and causes the sun to shine on the just and the unjust. He long suspends the punishment due to us, and when he proceeds to inflict it, He punisheth us less than our iniquities deserve.

This branch of mercy is also founded in the common sense of our human infirmi-ties: those who have offended us are men of like passions with ourselves, they are sub-ject to the same force of temptation; to the same inadvertences, or accidental occasions of surprise, as to their conduct towards us. We ought then, upon a common and incon-testable rule of justice, to conduct ourselves towards them according to the same mea-sures of lenience and tenderness which, in a change of circumstances, we should have thought it reasonable for them to have done towards us.

Another motive to this branch of mercy is that God has made it the indispensable condition of our forgiveness at His hands. It's certainly true concerning the breadth of our duty in any other respect, that it will exclude us, if we continue impertinent under the guilt of it, from the kingdom of heaven, forgive and we shall be forgiven.[4] But when the duty of forgiving others is so expressly, so frequently mentioned, and in such forcible terms, by our Lord, through whom alone we have redemption from sin, as the indispensable condition of our being forgiven; it seems as if there was something in the nature of it to be considered not merely as a condition, but a proper and special quali-fication to render us capable subjects of the divine mercy.

Again, another motive to this duty is derived from a consideration of those mercies which mankind in general, or which any of us in particular, have received from a just and offended God. The overtures of grace and reason are only made to mankind (so far as we are capable of judging in the case) exclusive of all other reasonable beings. The angels that for their apostasy were cast out of Heaven, are reserved, without any medi-ator, without any means of atonement, to the judgment of the last day, then to receive sentence to an endless and unintermitted punishment. But, sinful man, through the mediation and atonement of the Son of God, who took not on him, the nature of angels, but the seed of Abraham, is admitted to terms of pardon and reconciliation; and even put into a capacity of attaining a far greater happiness than that from which he originally fell in a terrestrial paradise.

Here was an act of divine mercy, which those angels which kept their first station might well desire to look into; and on account of this distinction which God made in favor of mankind, and the passing by of their fellow-creatures, might justly put the question with the Holy Psalmist, "Lord, what is man that thou art mindful of him, or the son of man that then so regardest him;" this so signal, so glorious an act of the divine mercy toward sinners, and which still heightens our admiration of it; upon the method whereby it was declared and affected, the mediation of the Son of God, his personal appearance here upon the Earth, his perfect obedience throughout the whole course of his life, and at last his suffering and death. And can we after this, find ourselves in no disposition to forgive others, men of like passions with ourselves, for the injuries they have done us, real or imaginary? Certainly, in consequence of such a reflection we should rather infer that there is something great and Godlike, something that brings human nature to a still nearer resemblance with the divine, in being merciful as our Father who is in Heaven is merciful.

Let us proceed secondly, to consider the nature of the reward here annexed, "for they shall obtain mercy." The question is, whether this reward relates only to the spiritual state of man, to the pardoning grace of God, to the blessings of another life; or whether it may not be interpreted to signify some temporal advantage in this life present.

Now without considering their proposition, "the merciful shall obtain mercy," as the subject matter of a promise; but taking it only as a plain and naked declaration of truth, it may very naturally be accounted for. The merciful man, in regard to both the characters mentioned of him, takes the most probable method to obtain mercy from other men, whenever he may become a capable object of it. If we consider the merciful man as exercising acts of beneficence and liberality, nothing does more naturally recommend him to universal love and esteem; and it is often matter of wonder to see man who affect nothing so much as to draw the eyes of the world upon them for some shining and laudable qualities, very profuse on occasions that really do not conduce to this end, and yet seldom employ the proper means thereto, which would render them not only esteemed, but what is much more preferable, would render them universally beloved.

For this reason, one would be tempted to think it does not proceed from covetousness, that we have so few extraordinary instances of generosity among men, who are ambitious of nothing more than a great reputation; for the sake of which their will in other cases being extravagant in their expanses; but from a certain malignity of temper, stronger in them upon the competition than their vanity, which will not suffer, that others should share in any degree with them, those advantages upon which they have set their hearts, and wherein they place their sovereign happiness; or perhaps they imagine on one hand, that while munificence will contribute to their reputation, it will lessen the homage commonly paid to them on the other, by making the objects of their favor less dependent.

And yet acts of mercy in this kind have not always the effect that might be expected from them, not in relation even to those who directly share the benefit of them. For this, as most other moral sayings related to the conduct of human life, is not to be understood as universally, but only as for the most part true; so that the sense of the words is, that the merciful man, where the design of his mercy is not abused, or the natural fondness of it by some means obstructed, takes the best method, whenever he may be a proper subject of it, to find mercy himself.

The same might be observed concerning the other part of the merciful man's character: as it denotes a forgiving temper there is something so [illegible] and generous in it, as cannot fail of recommending a person to the same favor, should he happen at any time, or by any accident to do an injury to other persons. The reason of this may be confirmed from the general character of good nature, which disposes a man to forgiveness, and always procures a favorable disposition towards him in others.

If we consider the words in their principle design, as containing a special promise of mercy, they may relate to those acts of mercy which God dispenses to sinners in this life, by his patience, his forbearance, his pardoning grace: or to that final sentence of mercy which shall pass upon men at the hour of death, and be confirmed in the day of judgment; for at that day indeed our trial will proceed, according to the spiritual state and disposition wherein we died. After death no further overtures of mercy will be made us, but we shall be judged according to the works done in the body. The last judgment therefore should teach us, while we have opportunity to exercise all proper acts of beneficence and forgiveness, because it will not be properly a dispensation of mercy, but of strict justice. Especially when we reflect that our Lord in describing the last judgments solely proceeds upon an inquiry, what good man had here done, or omitted to do, in acts or offices of mercy.

This, therefore being the Christian doctrine about mercy, it only remains, my brethren, that in the meantime, as we knew it, we should do it. The second command in the law of nature, obliges us to be merciful and he who is not, is inhuman. It's again commanded in the Scriptures by a voice from Heaven, and he that is of God heareth the words of God. According to the law of Christ it is presented to us; not by threat or measure, but as the desire and delight of our souls, to be always practiced toward all men according to the example of his infinite mercies and compassions. There is nothing he so much recommends and inculcates to us in his Gospel as this blessed spirit and temper. By how many parables doth he set forth the mercy of God to us, for our imitation; by the parable of the Prodigal Son, of the Good Samaritan, and the servants to whom he forgave ten thousand talents.

God, grant that we may all consider these things and let them so influence our future life and conversation, that we ourselves may obtain mercy at the last day, through the merits of our dear Redeemer, Christ Jesus, to whom, with the Father and the Holy Ghost be ascribed. Amen.

This sermon was delivered five times. It was delivered at St. Michael's in 1762; at St. Paul's, October 1777; and at St. Philip's, November 1785, June 1788, and July 1796. The sermon is not indexed by Smith.

XIII

"Bear Ye One Another's Burdens"

Galatians 6:2
Bear ye one another's burdens, and so fulfill the law of Christ.

I
T IS WITH GREAT PLEASURE I take the part here assigned me by a Society formed upon the principles of charity, and regulated by those of true religion and virtue. A task indeed somewhat[1] difficult, charity being a subject which has occasioned so many excellent and useful discourses, that it is impossible to treat of it without following the beaten road. The springs of eloquence seem in great measure exhausted; and the beautiful passages of scripture relating to beneficence have been frequently repeated, urged and explained so that the hearer generally anticipates what the preacher has to say. But then we have this satisfaction reserved—that the repetition of the argument makes no abatement of the practice. Pious inclinations, the often whetted and encouraged, are by no means tired or worn out. I[2] hope the good seed already sown will take a deep root in your hearts, spring up afresh in your lives[3] and yield a fair prospect in the harvest approaching. Indeed charity is the peculiar favorite of heaven, and has the most liberal promises annexed to it, both in this and the other world. And that I may contribute some little towards keeping up of this laudable spirit, and render the very small mite I am throwing into the cauldron so useful to the purpose as I possibly can, I shall treat the subject with all decent plainness.

The great end and design of true religion is to make man happy both in this world and the next. The latter of these, as it is the great concern of all mankind, so it is in the power of all to secure to themselves by a life of piety and virtue. But as happiness in this life is for wise reasons put more out of our power. Our enjoyments here are at the best[4] mixed with crosses, troubles and disappointments, the better to prove our faith and virtue. The best of men are exposed in common with the worst to sickness, pain and losses, and are brought into want and misery by accidents which neither industry nor prudence could prevent. Yet still in such circumstances religion is a sure source of consolation, and brings with it the best succors and support that can be had; by not only fortifying the mind with patience and resignation, extending our prospects and hopes into another life, and assuring us there of a happiness proportioned to our steadfastness and perseverance in well-doing, but by deriving to us likewise the compassion, assistance and relief of our fellow Christians and neighbors: who are bound by the religion they profess, above all things to have fervent charity towards their brethren; to have the same care one for another; and if one member suffers, as members of the same body, to suffer with it.

If then it be the intention of religion to procure the happiness of mankind; all such designs as are directed to this end are so far acts of religion: and when entered upon with a true Christian temper and from a principle of charity, will certainly be accepted as such; as instances of duty and obedience to God. It is therefore, I think, an appointment of great propriety and decorum in the present and all other like charitable societies, to meet thus at times in a religious manner; to offer up our vows oblations of charity to heaven; and to beg the blessing of God on our pious endeavors.[5]

It is indeed a pleasure to see while so many parties and meetings are daily forming for pleasure and idleness, for the support it may be of fashions and uncharitable distinctions, and often for nothing better than reveling and riot, that these are not wanting some which have a nobler end for their object; and which it is no way unworthy of our character as men or as Christians to join in. This praise I think we may assume to the present Society: The design of which in its infancy was and in its maturity is[6] by the joint and united efforts of many, to guard against and repel the evils which are alike incident to all; and which, every one singly and unsupported may not be able to bear. This is in a very proper sense to bear one another's burdens; to share freely and willingly the misfortunes, the infirmities, wants and troubles of others: and is so far an act of charity, and a fulfilling the law of Christ. But it is farther at the same time[7] an act of prudence too, as it is a providing for every one's own wants and those of his family; it is throwing his own burden into the common stock; and purchasing by the relief of ministers to others a title to the same relief in his turn. Both these principles then conspire to promote the present institution; as far as you are influenced by the latter, which thus limited, though it doth not deserve[8] the name and character of charity, it is a commendable act of duty. It is a Christian prudence to arm ourselves by a provident foresight against the evils of life; to prepare ourselves for a cheerful submission to the deprivations of providence; and to lay up for the benefit and security of his family, every man, from time to time, some little, as God hath prospered him.

But I doubt not all of you are actuated by the nobler and more extensive[9] principle I have mentioned; and take a generous pleasure in preventing not only[10] the wants of your brethren, and in resolving that not only none of your friends and associates in this labor of love, shall be destitute in his distress of any helps and assistances you can give him but that as far as your power and ability permits, the widow and the orphan shall find[11] an asylum under the branches of this your spreading vine, and partake largely of its salutary and refreshing shade.[12] This, as I have said, is true Christian charity, and is in the best sense fulfilling the law of Christ, the royal law of love, as the Apostle calls it: which enjoins no duties so much as those of tenderness, gentleness, compassion, feeding the hungry, clothing the naked, assisting the sick, instructing the ignorant and unlettered, and whatever else is generous, kind, beneficent and good natured; whatever tends to promote the happiness or to lessen the griefs and sorrows of mankind.

This is so considerable a part of our Christian duty, that it is frequently in Scripture spoken of as comprising the whole. Love, or charity saith the Apostle, is the fulfilling of the law. And whosoever loveth his brother hath fulfilled the law. It is certain there are other duties, all that are comprehended under piety and temperance, equally necessary and indispensable with these. But it is here supposed that the duty we are speaking of cannot consist in all its extent and latitude without enduring the rest. The same benevolence of mind, which leads us to love not only those who are endeared to us by relation, friendship, or kindness received, but even those who are most estranged from us by a difference of religion, party or even by resentment and ill-will, will certainly lead us to love God, the fountain of all good, who made us what we are, and give us all that we possess. The heart which feels for the misery of others, and melts with pity even at the distress of an enemy will surely overflow with gratitude towards the common Father of being, who provideth for all things living with plentiousness; whose compassions never fail; and whose mercies are seen over all[13] his works. And that diffusive charity which carries us at it were out of ourselves, and interests us in the welfare of all mankind, is in its whole nature opposite the narrow principle of self love; and can taste but little pleasure or happiness in self indulgence, or the gratification of appetite and sensual inclination. How it is that love or Christian charity is said to be the fulfilling, to be not a part but the sense and spirit of the whole moral law. The same spirit which leads you to concur in the good work will, if opened and unfolded into all its consequences lead you into all righteousness; to fulfill the duties you owe to God and yourselves as well as those to your neighbor. And it is with pleasure, that I observe a proper attention paid to these in the regulations under which this Society is governed, and by which its meetings are modeled and conducted. These are so well calculated for all the ends that can be answered by such an institution, that I have little left me but to commend to your constant practice the charity, piety, and sobriety which they inculcate; and to exhort you to extend these principles farther, into your whole life and conversation.

And first as charity is the ground and foundation on which this our Society is built, this as we are taught in the text, is fulfilling in a particular manner the law of Christ. For charity is in a peculiar manner the command of Christ. "A new commandment," says He, "I give unto you that ye love one another. By this shall all men know that ye are my disciples, if ye have love one for another." This then is so necessary to the disciples of Christ, that we cannot take to ourselves the name or character of Christians without it. And as we have above seen that charity in its largest extent, can scarce consist without the practice of the other Christian duties of piety and temperance, so it is certain that we cannot in any good degree pretend to these virtues without that charity, which I am recommending. If any man, saith the Apostle, say I love God, and loveth not his brother, he is a liar: for he that loveth not his brother whom he hath seen, how can he love God whom he hath not seen? And again, whose hath this world's good and seeth his brother have need and shutteth up his compassion from him, how dwelleth the love of God in him? That is, how can such an one pretend to piety and religion, when he is wanting in a common duty bound upon him by nature and reason, and the common ties of humanity; but more especially recommended and more earnestly than almost any other by the precepts of the Gospel? In like manner in vain do we pretend to that command over ourselves, that subordination of our appetites and passions to reason, in which the virtue of temperance consists, when self love still contracts our hearts, and shuts out all charitable care and concern for others. It is therefore with great propriety that charity takes the first rank amongst the Christian graces, as it is necessary in some degree to qualify us for the very name of Christians; and as it springs from or begets in us that temper of mind which is naturally productive of every other virtue.

I might proceed to enlarge upon several other Christian graces linked with this Queen[14] of them all, but as this would carry me to considerations foreign to the occasion of our meeting; I shall therefore not to detain you from the business of the day, beg leave to offer a motive or two for us the bearing one another's burdens in this labor of love, this our work of charity.

The first of which shall be drawn from the present season in which we have been commemorating the great love of our Savior Jesus Christ. The consideration of this stupendous instance of compassion, in the Son of God, is the most unanswerable appeal that can be made to the heart of man, for the reasonableness of it in himself. It is the great argument which the Apostles make use of in almost all their exhortations to good works. Beloved, if Christ so loved us—the inference is unavoidable; and gives weight to everything else which can be urged upon the subject. And therefore I shall beg leave to apply it: that at least for their sakes who enjoy the benefit of their charity, we might be left to the full impression of so exalted and so reasonable a motive. That by reflecting upon the infinite labor of our Savior in bearing our burdens, in the instance of his death, we may consider what an immense debt we owe each other: and by calling to mind the amiable pattern of his life; in doing good, we might learn in what manner we may best discharge it.

And indeed, of all the methods in which a good mind would be willing to do it, I believe there can be none more beneficial[15] or comprehensive in its effects, than that for which we are here met together. That part of it in particular which includes the education of children; for experience evidently evinces the necessity of giving youth in general an early tincture of religion and bringing them up to a love of industry, [and giving them reading and writing] which are wanted in the very lowest stations. With regard to [the first] instruction in religion,[16] it was one great business, as well as mark of our Savior's mission, that the poor had the Gospel preached to them. The end of his coming seems to declare the glad tidings of salvation unto all the nations of the earth; and the whole purpose of his teaching, was to make all men wise unto salvation. The rites he instituted are few, and plain, and pure: the law he gave, is universal and beneficial to all orders and degrees of men, [open to general examination] adapted to all capacities, designed[17] for all ages, and all people, all stations and conditions of life; and he commanded it to be communicated freely to all mankind. Look now upon the forsaken and neglected poor; left without notice or pity, in a wretched state of rudeness and barbarity, little distant from that of the beasts that perish: and consider, what may be done to cure the misery and guilt that generally oppresses them. You see them often become stupid and senseless of all duty; or tumultuous and unquiet or rapacious and desperate.[18] Most men are made what they are, good or evil, useful or not, by education. The children of the poor have seldom the means of education, but often the seeds of corruption from their parents. The parents through ignorance or depravity, are unwilling and indifferent; or through constant necessary labor and indigent circumstances, are unable to train them up in the way they should go. Want of education occasions want of business, or a reluctance to it: and idle habits mixing with the sullen or violent passions of an uncultivated mind, produce the most flagrant crimes. When their parents neglect or forsake them, shall we not take them[19] up, with that authority and affection, which is placed in parents? Shall we not fulfill the law[20] of Christ, by thus having one another's burdens? Shall we not use those methods of instruction which may lead them to religion? Shall we not show them the arts of life, and teach them by honest industry to be of service to themselves and the public?[21] I say of service to the public, because it is out of this class of life that those poor persons are drawn without whom no community can subsist—here the king expects his soldiers[22] the merchants expect their labors, the tradesmen and merchants their apprentices. It is certainly much to be derived, that these should carry with them, into their respective trusts the principles of religion, the seeds of virtue, Christian benevolence, fidelity and industry; the fear of him whose eyes sees their most secret unwitnessed actions; the dread of him who knows all their thoughts and covert designs, the assurance of an overwatchful providence over them, the hope of a blessed recompense of reward, the terror of fire which will never be quenched were these principles early planted and engraved on their tender minds, it would require time and pains to erase them; but if they were carefully cultivated afterwards by those under whom they serve, we might appeal to find a very happy charge among us. But our poor people, as I before observed are generally too much engaged, and too ignorant to instruct their[23] children themselves, and have therefore need of further assistance. And I could wish for their sakes—for your own sakes, who feel the sad effects of an abandoned, undisciplined youth—for Christ's sake whose kingdom seems vanishing apace out of this world. In these accounts I wish I was able to persuade all men to express their sense of our private unhappiness with general corruption of good manners by joining in with this our labor of love for the establishing and endowing a school for our poor children which is attended with such

vast disbursements, such as our present funds will by no means answer. The very clothing of a number asketh a considerable supply, but when it is proposed further to clothe
their minds with righteousness, to embellish their manners to give them a subsistence
in the world by making them serviceable in it;[24] and through an honest and useful life
lead them to heaven, we must let our hands grow more acquainted with our hearts, and
give in proportion as we wish success. The public is as much interested in the education of poor children, as in the preservation of themselves. This last, we are legally
bound to provide for. The former is left amongst other works of charity, neglected by
many who care for some of these things, and to be carried on by such only as think it
their concern to be doing good. Some are able and in a situation, to assist in it in an
eminent degree by countenancing and recommending it; and all by contributing[25] to
its maintenance. In what manner and degree then[26] it belongs to you, to me, to any
particular person to help it forward, let us all consider seriously, not for one another,
but each of us for himself.

And may the blessing of Almighty God accompany this work of charity, which he
hath put into and the hearts of his servants in behalf of poor children: that being now
trained up in the way they should go, when they are old they may not depart from it.
May he, of his mercy, keep them safe amidst the innumerable dangers of this bad world;
through which they are to pass, and preserve them unto his Heavenly Kingdom.

*The sermon was delivered to the Carolina Society in 1768. This sermon is not indexed
by Smith.*

XIV

"Love Your Enemies"

Luke 6:27
But I say unto you which hear; Love your enemies and do good to them which hate you.

T HE FORGIVENESS OF INJURIES, and the loving of our enemies, though a doctrine enforced both by the Old and New Testament is yet perhaps less practiced, than any that our Bible enjoins us.

By some it seems either to be unknown or not allowed. By others, though confessed, yet thought to be allowed to be attended with such sufferable difficulties that it never[1] is likely to be put into execution. And indeed it must be owned to be a difficult task for the perverseness of human nature in its depraved condition is such, that whatever most strongly contradicts the passions, is most vigorously opposed; however the prescription may carry life along with it by the most salutary advantages yet it is rejected whenever it is found to be [illegible] or distasteful. And accommodating to the variety of tempers, and the different turns of the mind, and so is the opposition likewise to this doctrine, various and different.

There are some that upon the first surmise of an affront or injury, that is offered them, start immediately forth to vengeance, without any reflection upon what they are doing, or giving anytime for a more cool and deliberate consideration. The affair is so far from being weighed duly as it ought its favorable circumstances that the worst interpretation is generally first upon it at first view; and a single spark that falls on such a combustible temper; blows it up and sets it in a sudden and immediate flame.

While others ruminating upon the injury received, make it worse; they aggravate every minute particular and by telling it sink deep and gradually into the soul suffer it by these means to take such a strong and lasting hold that it scarce ever is to be ruled out; it lies cankering at the heart; and their blank imaginations like bodies of the same color retain the heat by smothering and confining it within.

In short, most people are extremely ready to take in an affront, and very backward in forgiving it; quick to resent, slow to pardon; impatient in feeling injuries and more impatient still have cruelly revenged them.

But however this may be the too common practice of mankind, much to be lamented that is so, yet is the command of my text expresses against it, and the doctrine of loving and forgiving our enemies, most clearly delivered both in the Old and the New Testament. This doctrine delivered by our Savior appears to be the same as that enjoined by Moses; and he chose on this occasion to propose it anew, that he might render it more explicit, and clear it from the false glosses of the hypocritical scribes and Pharisees. For we see by the words of our Savior that their dictate was, Thou shalt love thy neighbor and hate thine enemy; where the latter words, and hate thine enemy, are manifestly a false gloss of their own and directly contrary to the law of Moses as appears by what has been already quoted.

Here then was a proper occasion for our Savior to revive this law and having thus explained and cleared it, he justly makes it his own and inserted it among the injunctions of the Gospel. This doctrine thus appearing to be embellished both by the New and Old Testament. In the further prosecution of this subject I shall endeavor to show:

First, under what bounds and limitations this doctrine is to be taken.

Secondly, what reasons and motives there may appear to induce us to the practice of it.

First then, we must not be supposed in loving our enemies, to forget ourselves; charity may begin, though it should not end at home; and though we are commanded to love our neighbor as ourselves, yet no where are we enjoined to love them better. Self-love and defense are principles implanted in every breast and dictated by nature and reason for the preservation of individuals. Whatever injury therefore is offered, we are not only allowed, but obliged to repel; and the blow that is aimed against us, may be warded off, though it should not, except in cases of necessity be returned. In matters of lesser concern we should even recede somewhat from the rigor of our right in order to maintain, if possible, unanimity and concord; though in other cases to show a tame submission to a full insensibility of the grossest injuries is only opening a larger field for new and greater; and to neglect in such a case is to invite an insult. Such a procedure would be setting up ourselves as a public mark to be shot at by the petulant malice of every invader and the leaving ourselves purposely naked and defenseless; is no better than setting open the gates to the enemy that besieges us and calling in our own distinction between a love of approbation and a love of charity and benevolence; and the latter will remain always due though the first may often be withdrawn. It is impossible that we should have the same love and esteem for the wicked and profligate that we entertain for the good and virtuous. Nor is the same place to the heart to be given to a professed enemy, and a generous friend. But nevertheless, we ought to have still left even for our enemies the love of Charity when they persist to injure us though we are not to lay ourselves open to their insults, yet are we to pray for them; to wish and endeavor their amendment and reconciliation, to be ready to do them acts of kindness and humanity, and in short, though we hate the vices, yet to show a compassion and benevolent disposition to the person of our adversaries. As a father still looks with a tender and affectionate regard on his child wishes his amendment and prays for his good, though his vices and immoralities, though his stubbornness and disobedience may have justly raised his resentment and indignation.

The doctrine of the text, being considered within such bounds and limitations as have been mentioned we may proceed in the second place to consider what reasons and motives may occur to induce us to the practice of it.

The first is that universal charity, that benevolence and philanthropy, which is one of the first principle laws of nature. That it is the very cement of all human society in general and what holds together the more particular relations of affinities and friendships that intervene between mankind. And as in these latter relations we readily see and acknowledge the obligations we lie under to be kindly affectioned to, and to promote the good and interest of those that more immediately approach us, and are more nearly connected with us by the ties of consanguinity; so ought we to extend our view to a greater distance and by one diffusive thought take in the whole extent of human nature. For even there, in the very farthest extreme, relation still subsists; and though it may not be in so great or intense a degree as in the nearer objects of our regard, yet it is in so due, and sufficient a proportion, as always to keep it alive and active. We all come out of the hands of the same gracious creator; we are all the children the sons of one Heavenly Father, and whatever regions the streams may run through; whether the dry deserts of poverty and disgrace, or the fertile plains of wealth and greatness, yet are we all derived and flow from the same living fountain. Why then, being brethren should we pursue each other with rancor and revenge? Why should we forcibly break the ties of the universal relation which is calculated to keep us all in harmony and order. We counteract the will of our Almighty Father and the plainest dictates of reason when we pursue our resentment with an unrelenting fury; and when men refuse to act as such and deny to show humanity.

The very brute creation might teach us another lesson; for though animals of a different species harass and destroy each other, yet those of the same tribe and kindred are generally speaking, known to have a certain benevolence (if I may so say) to each other; and however savage to an alien race, never keep up and perpetuate enmity and malice, hatred and resentment against themselves,

But farther, this principle of benevolence will oblige us to sacrifice our resentments for the public good and advantage of society. Benevolence as before hinted is the very cement and support of all states and collective bodies of men; whatever therefore counteracts and opposes this principle in some degree tends to the unsettling foundations, and disuniting the connection of the whole. But sure an unforgiving temper and relentless malice direct opposition to that benevolence should dictate, and the one should absolutely aims at the undermining that goodly fabric which the other is endeavoring to build and establish. Was each individual in a state to act separately from the good of the whole, and be conducted by nothing but his own private passions, what would be the event, but anarchy and confusion? Whereas a proper regard for the public good and the common advantage of our fellow citizens would naturally introduce peace and tranquility; and the laying aside our own private resentment, would necessarily procure the unity and consequently the firmness and stability of the whole

The beginning of strife is as the letting out of water; no one knows where it will stop; or what harvest it will make. Now a forgiving temper is a preservative against this evil; it checks strife and quarrel in the very beginning, and stops the original streams of fury and indignation which, if let loose, might spread destruction like a deluge.

Was every one to revenge and no one to forgive, what a perpetual round would be of insult and injury, of doing and returning evil; what a continued intercourse of the most shocking and most iniquitous transactions. Whereas from a benevolent and forgiving tempest the very reverse would happen; one constant and uniform flow of interchangeable kindnesses and affections. Mercy and truth would meet together; righteousness and peace would kiss each other; nor would there be any complaining in our streets.

Farther, by forgiving we in some sort disarm our enemy and gain a victory by retreating as a blow loses its force against a yielding body which would be increased, were one a more hard and obstinate nature to resist it. By forgiving, we manifest a certain sublimity and greatness of soul for the more extensive our benevolence when it reaches enemies as well as friends, the greater must be our generosity. Hence to get the better of our resentment, may be more glorious than to conquer cities, and a much juster triumph to shut up than to open a way to rage and fury.[2]

The last and most prevailing motive that I shall mention, are the great examples drawn from scripture to induce us to pursue this doctrine and as far as in us lies, to follow the glorious patterns, that are set before us.

First then, let us consider God himself, the Father of all mercies; how is it that we treat him, and how does He deal with us? The accumulated multitude of our own transgressions rise up to heaven, and not only call[3] for, but even wrest vengeance from the Almighty; and yet it falls not as might be expected on our devoted heads. Many a time says the Psalmist of the children of Israel, many a time did they provoke him in the wilderness and grieved him in the desert; but He was so merciful that He forgave their misdeeds and destroyed them not; Yea many a time [illegible] his wrath away and would not suffer his whole displeasure to arise; for He considered that they were but flesh and that they were even a wind, which passeth away, and cometh not again. And even we (I am afraid of their ages) have little reason to boast ours a people less stubborn or stiffnecked than the Jews; we continue to provoke him every day but his mercy is over all his works.

When we consider the nature of sin, that a voluntary and open breaking of his laws, is an affront upon his majesty, and a denial or at least an impeachment of the attributes of his justice and omnipotence, to think[4] that He has either no ability to punish or no regard to justice that commands it, if we consider farther that the offenses in proportion to the dignity of the person who is offended. As on the one hand our sin must be exceeding sinful; so on the other, what a surprising instance of goodness and long suffering of mercy and forgiveness must it be; to pass by our gross iniquities, and blot out the remembrance of our audacious transgressions. The wicked might justly expect to be immediately cut off was not God's forbearance greater than their faults; and his mercies more extensive than their crimes.

For this reason it is that He undistinguishably shows his favors both to enemies and friends; that He maketh his sun to rise on the evil, and on the good, and sendeth rain on the just and on the unjust. The same sea is safely sailed over by the impious pirate as it is traversed by the honest trader; the same earth affords her fruits and plenty in rich profusion to him, that with the earthly mind seems rooted to it and never once looks up to heaven, and to him it owes the blessing from above with a grateful piety and devotion adores the creator of them both.

The very atheist who denies the being of his maker is suffered to say foolishly in his heart that there is no God, still length of time may clear his darkened understanding, and at last bring him to the knowledge of him who giveth him the very breath, with which he blasphemes. In how eminent a degree then doth forgiveness belong to the Lord our God; and with how much long suffering does this endure the vessels of wrath fitted for destruction.

In the next place, let us consider the incomprehensible mystery of our own redemption. Say this we are not only pardoned, though open to profess to enemies, but are bought with a price; the price of a Savior's blood, and redeemed from being wretched captives in the chains and servitude of sin.

We are not only forgiven[5] that execution our demerits called for, and graciously reprieved, but promised on our repentance and amendment a life bless and immortality. It exceeds the utmost stretch of the imagination to conceive the surprising condescension and benevolence of our redeemer in leaving Heaven itself and the bosom of his Father to put on frail mortality, and suffer every thing to reconcile lost mankind with their creator; and reinstate them in the favor of Heaven which they had forfeited. If we review his whole life as answerable in this first and great design, it was one continued [illegible] of benevolence and forgiveness; where he was reviled, not again He blessed them that cursed, did good to them that hated, and prayed for them that despitefully used and persecuted him.

In how pathetic a manner does He commiserate as well as pardon the insults and stubbornness of the Jews: and "Jerusalem, Jerusalem, thou that killest the prophets and stonest them that were sent unto thee. How often would I have gathered thy children together, even as a hen gathereth her chickens, and ye would not." And when at last the rancor and the malice his enemies prevailed so far against him as to bring him to an ignominious death; even then in the last scene. He continued it, and when expiring, breathed out nothing, but love and forgiveness. "Father forgive them for they know not what they do."

If then (to sum up all), we are any ways sensible of the obligations arising from that general charity and benevolence that is due to all mankind; if we regard our own peace and quietness; if we can be touched by such examples of goodness and forgiveness; as an sign by God the Father of all mercies; the Savior and Redeemer; let us endeavor with diligence and sincerity to practice the doctrine of my text; above all, remembering that our own trespasses are no otherwise to be forgiven; then as we forgive the trespasses committed against us. Be we, in short, the Apostle admonishes, kind to one another, tender hearted, forgiving one another, even as God for Christ sake hath forgiven us.

This sermon was delivered once, at St. Paul's in April 1776. It is not indexed by Smith.

XV

"A More Excellent Way"

1 Corinthians 12:31
And yet show I unto you a more excellent way.

THERE BEING EVIDENTLY A COMPARISON in the text between the more excellent way and something before mentioned or intended, it is necessary to look back to see how the relation stands, and what the thing is, to which the more excellent way is compared and preferred. The whole chapter is upon the argument of spiritual gifts; where the author, their end, their diversities, and their value are all distinctly laid down. As they all came from the self same Spirit, who divideth to every man severally as he will, so the end and design of them was the profit and edification of the church. Their respective value therefore may be estimated from this consideration; each was better than as it most promoted this end. As to their diversity, let it be sufficient to observe that it was very great; there was a subordination of them, as there is of the members in the human body.[1] For "to one was given by the spirit the word of wisdom, the faith and doctrine of the Gospel which is the wisdom of God; or such a mouth of wisdom in the defense and confirmation of it, as all their adversaries were not able to gainsay nor resist; to another, the word of knowledge enabling him to understand and explain all the mysteries, and all the knowledge of the Old Testament; to another faith, so vigorous and active as to manifest itself in miraculous and supernatural effects: to another, the gifts of healing all manner of diseases; to another the wording of miracles, a power of performing operations still more miraculous, as casting out devils and raising the dead to life; to another, prophecy; to another, discerning of spirits, highly necessary when many false seducing spirits were gone out into the world; to another diverse kinds of tongues, and to another, the interpretation of tongues."

These were gifts and powers of a very extraordinary nature,[2] and yet the excellent way spoken of in the text, is preferred before them. What way that is appears from the next chapter, which is wholly taken up in the description and commendation, viz. charity. The nature and extent of which at large I come now to consider.[3]

Charity is one of those words which through length of time has suffered some alteration in its meaning. It often signifies now in common use no more than giving of alms, though that at best, and when it proceeds from a principle of charity, is but one effect of it; and when done, as it may be done, upon selfish motives, or out of mere simple good nature, is no effect or argument of it at all. If this will not help us to the true notion of charity, much less shall we find it in any personal or party passion; where our love to part is generally so strong and eager, as to destroy our benevolence to the whole. Even the love of one's country, though laudable surely when under proper regulations, whenever it exceeds its due bounds, may become a source of many mischievous effects. If the Jew could not extend his goodwill beyond the limits of his country, and the professors of his religion; did not too the politic parts of the heathen world represent the rest of mankind, rather under the image of barbarians than men? In consequence they thought it scarce murder to destroy them.

But Christian charity, in its widest acceptation, is neither more, nor less, than universal love, distinguished by its object in Divine and human; the one productive of all Holy obedience to God, the other active in doing good to men. It is to the latter of these that our attention is now directed, both by occasion and subject. For though we need not say that St. Paul excludes the love of God in what he says of charity in the context, yet it seems plain from the qualities he there ascribes to it, that he had principally in his view the love of our neighbor. Who that neighbor is, our Lord has taught us in his parable concerning a good Samaritan, who relieved a person in distress, with whom he had connections but the common tie of humanity; when two others, under greater obligations to assist him, had passed by without compassion, and left him to expire of his wounds, though an object by the by, which must have drawn relief from any whose hearts were not as hard as adamant, and whose natural affections were not frozen up with an insensibility as cold and rigid as death. Our neighbor then is any man, or every man, to whom we have an opportunity of doing good. And love consists in that goodwill towards men, that habitual disposition and readiness to do them any good offices, which in a change of circumstances, we could reasonably expect from them;[4] which is, in effect, loving our neighbor as ourselves.

As we are, at best, but indigent beings, our liberality and bounty must be limited; and is but reasonable perhaps that they who stand nearest us, should most amply partake of them. St. Paul, who commands us to do good unto all men, that is, as much as in us lies; immediately adds, and especially unto them that are of the household of faith. But though the power of doing good be limited, the disposition and desire of doing it should be more extensive, and our benevolence universal, though our bounty be confined. Indigent as we are, our love may be unbounded, and we may wish the good we are unable to produce. One caution, however is always to be remembered, very needless it may be with regard to good men, but necessary to be mentioned in justice to the subject we are upon; and that is that good wishes will not stand for good deeds, when it is in the power of thy hand to do them. And if some persons have thought that Christianity itself is but a kind of Divine philosophy in the mind, it is not impossible but others may imagine that Christian charity is but a sort of sedate benevolence in the heart; much pleased with the contemplation of itself, but of little benefit to others, and consistent with great indolence, if not with great vice. But St. James and St. Paul have determined in another manner, "If a brother or sister be naked, and be destitute of daily food, and one of you say unto them, depart in peace, be ye warmed, and be ye filled; notwithstanding ye give them not those things which are needful for the body; what doth it profit?" And St. Paul is so far from considering charity as a mere inactive affection, that he represents it as the sum and substance, and fulfilling of the law. Ye owe no man anything, but to love one another:[5] that is, all the duties which man owes to man, are comprehended in this of love or charity;[6] for he that loveth another hath fulfilled the law. For surely he that loves another will not require him, either in his bed, person, property, reputation, or so much as covet anything that is his; he will neither commit adultery, nor kill, steal, bear false witness, nor covet; an the contrary he will serve and assist him in all these respects as opportunity offers, or occasions require, and therefore by just consequence, he that thus loveth another, hath fulfilled the laws. For all these duties relating to our neighbor, and if there be any other commandment of thy kind, it and they, are all briefly comprehended in this saying, namely, thou shalt love thy neighbor as thyself. Particular duties and particular virtues have indeed distinct names of their own, but still, they are all but parts and branches of this Royal law. And all transgressions of duty are, in reality, transgressions of this same law of love, however they may be marked by various demonstrations. For all the law is fulfilled in one word, even in this; thou shalt love thy neighbor as thyself. The extent of which, as before observed, is universal, equal to the magnitude of the object, which is all mankind.

Having observed this much[7] concerning the nature, extent and influence of love or charity: give me leave briefly to show upon what accounts it is so highly commended, which considerations without further application, will be (I hope) deemed sufficient to convince all of the indispensable duty of practicing it.[8] And first, it is worthy of all commendation, and of that high preference which the Apostle has given it, because it is a divine perfection; and in the possession and practice of it, contains our noblest imitation of God himself; For God is love. St. John has been accused, very wrongfully, of stealing his doctrines from Plato; which he learned at the feet of a more heavenly teacher. But this sentence of his puts one in mind of the theology of that sublime philosopher, who represents the Supreme Being under the name and notion of pure goodness. There is little difference here but in names; for there is no goodness without love and benevolence: And St. Paul has joined them together in one emphatical period, where he prays for the Thessalonians, "that God would fulfill towards them all the benevolence of his goodness." The instances and the arguments of the goodness of God are commensurate with the creatures of his power, and his tender mercies are over all his works. Were the inanimate parts of the world, through no proper objects of goodness, yet, considered in their use, are arguments of it. If we rise one step higher in the [realm] of beings, and contemplate those which are endued with life and sense, we shall find an ample provision made for them, that they may be able to preserve the one and gratify the other. Man, who was made in his Creator's image, still more largely partakes of his bounty: and though the good are his friends and favorites in a particular manner, yet are the ordinary blessings of his providence promiscuously dealt amongst the children of men. "He causeth his Sun to rise on the evil, and on the good; and sendeth rain on the just, and on the unjust."

And as for the evils which are sown in life, though they checker this delightful landship, and darken the scene a little; yet they cast no imputation of cruelty upon God, when it is considered, that in the end "they work for us a far more exceeding and eternal weight of glory"; giving scope and occasion in the meantime, for the noblest exercise of virtue, and affording the most instructive examples, as of the bravest suffering virtues on the one hand, so of the most active charity of the other. The rich and the poor, the sick and the sound, meet here, and are intermixed together, that like the members of the human body, they may have the same care one for another; and when one suffers, the rest may sympathize with it, and relieve it. But what room could there be for this fellow-feeling and compassion, the most amiable part of our nature, and deservedly called humanity, if all the members were exempt both from weakness and disorder?

Again, charity or love is more excellent than the gifts before mentioned, because it is more beneficial to the possessor himself. A man may speak with the tongues of men and the Angels, and yet be no better than sounding brass, or a tinkling symbol. Nay, he may enjoy all those gifts and graces in their full latitude and perfection, and yet after all be himself a castaway. But he that walks in the more excellent way shall never fail. With regard to present happiness,[9] he has within himself a perpetual source of delight, as he has the art of making other men's satisfaction productive of his own, and cannot do a good action to another, without at the same time doing one to himself. And highly just and true in this sense is the maxim of our Lord's, "It is more blessed to give, than to receive."[10] It affords more self satisfaction, more true joy of heart, when that heart is inflamed with love, to confer a benefit than to receive it. Then, a person of this benevolent temper is free from those pestilent passions,[11] which are the troubles of human life, corroding cases, and fearful forbodings, with those infernal furies, bitter strife, blessed passion, brutal revenge, jealously of jaundiced eye, fell hate, pining envy, rapacious appetite, and pale remorse. Whenever he turns his view inwards, he finds all regular within; he finds a little image of heaven in his own breast; he finds all that harmony of affections, and all the rectitude of will, in which the first Adam was created, and which the second came to restore. There can be little doubt as to the future happiness of a person, who has arrived to so great a degree of Christian[12] perfection: he seems to have a clear title to obtain that mercy, which he was always ready to show; and the natural frailties consistent with this exalted state of charity, will surely be covered by it, for it will make him the boast of human nature, and the favorite of heaven.

And, as love or charity is more excellent than the other gifts and graces upon a personal, so is it also upon a public account; it being not only more beneficial to the possessor, but likewise to the rest of mankind. Nothing is more self-evident, than that we are a system of beings,[13] related to, and dependent upon one another. We cannot subsist, in any order, or with any comfort, without one another's concurrence and support. And though self-love and private interest might prompt us to afford it in several instances, yet upon the whole, we need not scruple to affirm, that they would prove defective. We have it much oftener in our power to occasion the misery, than to increase the happiness of our fellow creatures, and were there no love or charity amongst us, we should almost always have it in our will. Without this, personal accomplishments would be dangerous to the public, as they give the possessor greater scope to execute his mischievous designs; and amongst all animals, none is more mischievous than that, which is defined to be rational, "when he hath once left off to behave himself wisely, and to do good." Let us then suppose a number of men endued with all the qualifications of an Apostle, but utterly void of that spirit of love, so conspicuous in those of our blessed Savior. And it is more than probable, that we shall find them inflicting diseases, instead of healing them; and sending men to the grave, instead of raising them from it. And as these gifts, without charity, would be destructive of public happiness, so faith and hope which are better than these, would not at all promote it.[14] For these are acts of the mind, which terminate in a man's self, and have no aspect and influence upon the rest of the world. Whereas the reverse is true of charity, which streams forth in good offices upon all occasions to all persons. It exerts itself in pity to the miserable, in protection to the distressed; to the ignorant it administers counsel, to the indigent, relief; it comforts those who are upon the bed of languishing,[15] and giveth medicine to heal their sickness. It is, in short, the source and spring of every social virtue, and a faithful discharge of all the relative duties is its genuine effect. Upon this account it is said to be of the same importance in the moral world, that motion is in the natural; for as the material world is either harmonious or out of order, recording as the Catholic laws are either observed or transgressed; so is the moral world either happy or miserable in proportion as the laws of universal benevolence are embraced or rejected. Our happiness or misery rise or fall according to this election; and we are in a state of peace,[16] or a state of hostility, as the spirit of love, or the spirit of hatred, reigns in our hearts.

But farther, charity is more excellent than spiritual gifts upon the score of its duration. For, "Whether there be prophecies, they shall fail; whether there be tongues, they shall cease; whether there be knowledge, it shall vanish away; and though now, for the present, abideth faith and hope, yet shall they hereafter be swallowed up and lost, if the one in sight the other in a blessed enjoyment. The former were a sort of temporary engines, erected like scaffolds in a building to serve a present end; and when that was attained, or at least the building was so far finished that the rest could be carried on without them,[17] they were taken away. But charity never faileth. Instead of being extinguished in heaven, it will glow with greater fervor, and as the spirits of just men shall be made perfect in all other respects, so shall they likewise in this of love.

To conclude, as charity is more excellent than the gifts before mentioned upon the score of its duration, so is it likewise with regard to its extent; being confined, as to no centuries of years, so to no rank or number of men, but the common privilege and perfection of every Christian. But all could not at first, and none can now, be Apostles, or prophets, or inspired teachers, or workers of miracles, or have the gifts of healing, or speak with tongues which they never learned. The more excellent way of charity still lies open, and every one that will may walk in it. And certainly it must give pleasure to every man, of a good and elevated mind,[18] to reflect that it is in his power to acquire and possess a quality, which is the perfection of his own nature, and makes him become partaker of the Divine.

Many practical influences and observations might be drawn from what has been offered, but I trust it needless to this auditory. I have endeavored to show the more excellent way, a path which I hope will be deemed suitable upon this occasion, if just impute my error to your own decree my pen is guilty, but my heart is free.

This sermon was delivered twice at St. Philip's: December 27, 1762, and December 1784. This sermon is indexed by Smith as #102, and he credits Horberry as a printed source.

XVI

"Let Your Light Shine before Men"

Matthew 5:16
Let your light shine before men, that they may see your good works,
and glorify your Father, who is in Heaven.

A PRECEPT THIS, which is necessary indeed at all times: because men are always too little inclined to the practice of holiness: but, more especially so at present; when virtue is so often put out of countenance by vice; when to have any serious sense of God and goodness is to become the object[1] of ridicule; when to be loose in principles, and licentious in practice is too plainly the distinguishing character of the modern age:[2] When this is the case, and God knows this is too much the case at present, it is more especially necessary to recommend and enforce the duty contained in the text, and to exhort men to let their light so shine before men, that they may see our good works, and glorify the Father who is in Heaven, to support if possible, the sinking cause[3] of virtue and religion, a Christian, so set before the world an example of holiness in his life and conduct; so that it may indeed appear that he is a true servant of God and a faithful disciple of Christ; so that from hence, man may be excited, to give glory to God, their Father, who is in Heaven.

In these words of my text then, we have two things worthy of our notice and observation: A duty required; and an argument to enforce this duty. First, the duty required.[4] As there are too many who are through a wicked fear of being ridiculed by profane men; that dare not be religious, or at least, frequently dare not to own themselves advocates for religions; so, on the contrary, are these others, who, through a warm and hypercritical show of it, endeavor to catch the applause the mankind; and would be thought really good from a vain[5] ostentation of holiness: though, at the same time, perhaps, they have set little or no true love for God and goodness; all their religion consisting only in the external appearance of it; but could never reach so far to influence their souls.

Between these two extremes; the one of not daring to be religious, in our outward behavior; and the other, of being so with vanity and ostentation, true religion shows its cause, and it is into this path that our text would guide and direct us.[6] As to the first of these crimes, the fear of being good: it stands condemned by our being required to let our light so shine before men that they only see our good works—the other—by the end and warmest profession in doing this, the promotion of God's glory, and glorify your Father which is in Heaven.

The men then, who has a true sense of religion, however he does not with the Pharisee put on an ostentatious show of it loosely to catch[7] the praises of men; yet it be careful to recommend himself to God and his own conscience: zealous for the honor of his Maker; and therefore, is still careful to let his light so shine before men, that they may see his good works; and glorify his Father who is in Heaven.

Although he does not, with the hypocrite, pray standing in the synagogue: in places of public concourse, and in the corners of the streets, to be seen of men; yet still does he not forget to enter into his closet, and pray to his Father which seeth in secret: and, upon all, attends the public worship of God in the congregation of his saints; and there behaves, though free from affectation, yet with that solemnity and gravity which becomes the house of God, the important duty he is performing, and which naturally flows from a soul truly sensible of devotion.

But yet, his religion is not confined to the narrow compass of his devotions, whether they be of a public or private nature; but he still remembers that he is a Christian, at all times and in all places; and is therefore careful to let his conversation, and his behavior, be as becometh the gospel of Christ. Studious to set consistently with that noble character he bears, cautious, of reflecting any disgrace upon it, and therefore daring to do every thing that does become it, and nothing but what does, he is not to be laughed out of his religion, but he can despise the scoffs of profaneness and infidelity: and if anything gives him uneasiness it is that such men should thus dishonor what he so much esteemeth—his God and his religion: and should take no more pity upon themselves.

But yet, as he knows his cause to be good, and that it is built upon the strongest foundation, however profaneness may be the prevailing fashion of the age, still is he not ashamed to set before it, the luster of good example, the beauty of Christian life: not ashamed to be pious and faithful to his God, just and merciful to his neighbor, sober and temperate towards himself. Still does he live, nay he believes as a Christian; and does not as some pretenders to a more refined reason than other men, dare to deny the doctrines of religions, because he cannot, by the short line of his reason, fathom the depths of the divine dispensations; but is modest and religious enough to assent to them for this convincing argument, because God has revealed them. Thus, behaves the man, who has a true sense of piety and goodness; who complies with the duty required in the text, to let his light shine before men, that they may see his good works.

The exemplariness of his Christian faith, adorned with and productive of all the beauty of Christian holiness, plainly convinces us, that he is a faithful servant of God, and a true disciple of Christ. And it is to be wished, greatly indeed to be wished, that all of us were careful to tread in these steps, and each of us, to let our light so shine before men, that they may see our good works.

To excite us to which, I come now, in the second place, to point out some reasons and encouragements. And here, the first argument I shall make use of, to excite us to this duty, of setting before the world an example of holiness, is drawn from the great good it will produce amongst men; and the great mischief that will attend the contrary practice.

Example, as we all know, has very great influence; more, generally, than precept. A good one, strongly allures to what is good; and a bad one, as strongly to what is evil. And therefore, it is the duty of every one, each to set before his neighbor, and good pattern; to win him over if possible to the cause of holiness; and, to abstain from wickedness, lest he seduce him to the party of vice. But as the examples of men, in a more eminent station of life, who are raised above the common rank of mankind either by their riches or honors, have a much greater influence than the example of those who are in a lower condition; therefore, this argument is more particularly applicable to them. If they show a good pattern in their lives, they are of the greatest benefit to mankind and to Christianity: but if a bad one, they do the greatest injury to both. For the inferior part of men generally take such persons for examples after which to frame their lives; and commonly as the great and rich behave, so do the poorer and lower sort of people. It is therefore more especially the duty of persons in a more exalted condition of life, so to be strictly careful of their conduct and behavior; lest their example should influence those beneath them to what is bad.

And let it not be thought, that holiness is any dishonor to greatness: nay, there is no real greatness without it; but, wherever these two center and unite in the same persons, they mutually adorn, and reflect a luster upon each other. Neither let it be imagined that riches can give their owners[8] any liberty to be more wicked than others, however some think or at least act, as if they thought they did.[9] For this is certain, that the more wealth anyone has received at the hands of God, the more thankful he ought to be to Him for it. And, the more thankful he is to God, the more obedient he will be to his laws; and consequently, the more holy and better man.

Another argument to excite us to this duty, mentioned in the text is, that by not complying with it, we plainly show that we are more afraid of man than of God. For, when the Almighty has commanded as to perform such a duty, and we, through the fear of being scoffed at by profane and wicked men, abstain from doing it, it is plain and evident, that we dread their censures more, than the displeasures of God.

But what says our blessed Savior? Be not afraid of them that kill the body, and after that, have no more that they can do. But I will forewarn you whom ye shall fear. Fear Him, who after He hath killed, hath power to cast into hell. Yea, I say unto you, fear Him. Although, then, men were even to put us to death and to kill this our body, yet still there is the greatest reason to fear God more than men; inasmuch as God can destroy both body and soul forever. But when the severest treatment that we can expect at the hands of men, and that only of profane and the worst of men for our leading holy lives, is only to be scoffed at and ridiculed by them, we have then much greater reason to fear God more than them: And if we suffer their ridicule,[10] which we ought to despise, to get the better of our fears, and obedience to God, we shall be utterly without excuse. And here, as the abstaining from a holy and exemplary life on this account, proves that we fear men more than God; the absurdity and impiety of this is sufficient,[11] one would think, to prevent anyone from being guilty of it.

The last argument I shall make use of, to encourage us to this duty, is the promotion of God's glory, drawn from the words of my text, and glorify your Father which is in heaven. Now holiness and exemplariness of life hath this effect; first, by our promoting it ourselves; secondly, by encouraging others to do the same. With respect to the doing it in our own persons, it is manifest and evident, that holiness has this effect: for what is holiness, but an obedience to the laws of God: a submission to, and owning of his authority and dominion over us?

And here, that we have reason thus to glorify God, will appear, if we consider that He is the most perfect, the greatest, best, and most glorious of beings: And especially, if we reflect upon the character and relation He stands in to us, that of a most kind benefactor, and of a most tender Father. For it was He who called us into being, out of nothing: it is the same, who still upholds and preserves this our being; although the snares of death compass us on every side, from our first entrance into life, until our departure out of it: it is the same kind and indulgent God, who giveth us all the good things that we enjoy, and poureth down his benefits and mercies daily and hourly upon us: it is the same compassionate God, who, out of his abundant mercy, sent his well-behaved son, to die, to redeem us, and his Holy Spirit, to purity and make holy our nature.

These are blessings great indeed, blessings that deserve the utmost returns of love and gratitude: and if we truly love and thank Him for them, we shall be very careful, by a good and holy life, to praise and honor Him; this being the best expression of our love and gratitude to Him.

But holiness of life, will also excite others to praise and glorify God. For they, seeing the beauty of holiness, the benefit that arises from it to mankind in general, the joy and solid comfort that it affords to him who professes it, the possibility of practicing it, and the glorious prospect that it affords in the other world, will be apt to grow enamored with it; and from hence, be strongly excited to copy after it: they will be thankful to God for making so great a blessing to mankind our duty, and for giving us power and strength to attain it.

I have now done with the two heads I proposed to treat of, the explanation of the duty, and the arguments to excite and encourage us to it. And here then, let not any of us, through a vain fear of being thought over religious, abstain from what is our duty; but let our light so shine before men, that they may see our good works. Let the holiness of our lives bespeak us to be, what we profess ourselves to be, Christians. Let not the wicked fashions and customs of this world be the rule of our life and behavior; but the word of God be so. For we may assure ourselves, that although it be never so much in practice among men, to be neglectful of their duty, and vicious in their lives, yet this plea will not avail us in the awful day of judgment, for we are expressly commanded, not to follow a multitude to do evil. Let not the censures of profaneness affright us from our duty; but let the authority of God command us, or his goodness and mercy win us over to it. Ever bearing in mind the goodness of our cause, which will fill us with true, Christian fortitude. It is the cause of God against profaneness and impiety that we undertake; a cause to which if we continue faithful and constant, we shall have the testimony and feast of a good conscience to comfort us here, and shall be rewarded with honor and glory and immortality in the kingdom of God hereafter. For, whosoever shall confess me before men, saith our Savior, him will I confess before my Father who is in heaven. But whosoever shall be ashamed of me and my words, of him will the Son of Men be ashamed when he cometh in his glory hereafter.

This sermon was delivered five times, all at St. Philip's: 1760, 1767, January 28, 1770, August 11, 1776, and July 1784. This sermon is indexed by Smith as #231.

XVII

"The Imitation of Christ"

Acts 14:22
Confirming the souls of the disciples, and exhorting them to continue in the faith,
and that we must through much tribulation enter into the kingdom of God.

THE DUTY AND PERFECTION of a Christian consists in the imitation of Christ; in the imitation of every part of his spotless example, as the passion as well as the active graces, in which he abounded.

Both sides of his character are highly useful and instructive to us. Both are at different times and for different ends, alike necessary to be attentively considered, and closely followed by us. But some occasions, some times there are, when that part of Christ's example, which relates to the sufferings he underwent, and the manner in which he bore them, is principally regarded by Christians.

The words you see will give me a proper occasion of explaining two great truths, always fit to be inculcated to Christians.

First, that the Christian state is certainly a state of suffering.

Secondly, that the sufferings of Christ afford us a plain argument why we also should expect our share of sufferings, and withal a powerful motive to support us under them.

And first, I am to show that the Christian state is a state of suffering.

This is a hard saying, and will not easily gain adherence with the great, the rich, and the prosperous. With those who are clothed in purple and fine linen, and fare sumptuously every day, and yet as unwelcome as the doctrine may be it is very clear and certain. We can scarce open a page of the Gospel, without finding it either laid down in the express words of his Apostles, or recommended by their practice.

Even hereunto are we called; all that will live Godly in Christ Jesus, shall suffer affliction,[1] and we must through much tribulation enter into the Kingdom of God.

It is true, these and many other passages of like import, in the New Testament are chiefly to be understood of the times when they were first spoken,[2] the infant age of

Christianity, when the standard of the cross being set up, all they who repaired to it, were engaged in a continual opposition to the powers of this world, and persecutions, afflictions, distresses, attended in every step of their conflict. And the sufferings of Christians were designed to promote the faith of Christ, and the seed of the Word sown, was to be made fruitful by the blood of martyrs.

Then indeed was it most remarkably, most imminently true, that the Christian state and profession was a state of suffering.

However, though this be not the general lot of Christians, although the instances be now rare, in which we are thus called upon to witness a good confession, and to resist even to blood, yet still I say, there is a sense of the assertion in which it holds good, and will hold good to the end of the world. Still the doctrine of the Gospel in the doctrine of the cross, and he who would be a true disciple of Christ, must even now deny himself and take up his cross and follow him. Can we doubt of this truth, if we consider the solemn engagement unto which we entered when we first listed in his service at our baptism. That we should manfully fight under his banner against sin, the world and the devil, and continue Christ's faithful soldiers and servants to our lives end?

Are these enemies so weak and contemptible as that we should hope to resist them with ease? Can this combat be maintained, this warfare be accomplished by us, without great difficulties and troubles?

The good Christian is not of this world, even while he lives in it, and therefore the men of this world, whose life is not like his, whose ways are of another fashion, will be sure to slander and traduce and perhaps despise him. Because he runs not with them to the same excess of riot, they will charge him with affection, at least with singularity. They will daily mistake his sayings, misconstrue all his best actions, misrepresent his brightest virtues. His humility and lowliness of mind shall be called meanness of spirit; his patience under injuries and affronts, insensibility and folly. His exactness in the performance of religious duties, his conscientious abstinence from whatever has the appearance of evil, his holy severities and mortifications shall furnish ample matter for the ungodly disdain. The proud will have him exceedingly in derision, he will be as a Tabret unto them, and a by-word of the people.[3]

But further, the sincere Christian cannot deny or dissemble the faith, when a proper occasion bids him stand forth in its defense. He cannot flatter wickedness in high places, fall in with false and prevailing opinions, or follow the multitude in wickedness. And he who cannot bend himself to a compliance in such cases, must not expect to continue unmolested, but to reap the proper fruits of his stubbornness as they will call it.

Or should the course of this world in which he lives run smoothly on, should he be ruffled and discomposed by no enemies, no accidents from without, yet still there are inward anxieties and sorrows, perplexities and troubles that attend him.

He has unruly appetites to mortify, strong passions to tame, and the struggle with these even after they seem vanquished must sometimes be renewed, and such a struggle is no ways joyous, but grievous.

The fear he has of offending keeps him under a perpetual alarm, the sense he has of guilt. It is quick and pungent, and subjects him whenever he falls into great remorse and uneasiness. How doth his own wickedness, how do his very errors and infirmities correct him, and his backslidings reprove him.

Or could we suppose him to have no occasion thus to suffer for his own sons, yet will he never want one of suffering for the sons of others.

The good Christian cannot be an unconcerned spectator, of any great degree of wickedness, even while he himself stands free from the detection of it.

The tender regard for God's honor, for the interest of piety, and the good of souls, makes him lay to heart the crying iniquities of that people, amidst whom he dwells; and grieve for those who do not grieve for themselves.

When he observes the scandalous progress of infidelity, the open growth of profaneness, the emulation and strife, the oppression and injustice, the hatred and cruelty in the world. In a word, when he sees the most immoral practices and pollutions of the heathens, reigning among those whose name the name of Christ, such a scene of sin and misery strikes him to the heart, and fills his soul with unspeakable sorrow. Rivers of waters run down his eyes because men keep not God's law.

The Christian state then, even setting aside the extraordinary case of persecution for the name of Christ, is certainly a state of suffering for hereunto are we called, as many of us as would have obedience to Christ, and profess to believe and to live, as he hath taught us, because that Christ also suffered for us, leaving us an example that we should follow his steps.

Which brings me to the second place to consider how the sufferings of Christ afford us a plain argument, why we also should expect our share of sufferings, and withal a powerful motive to support us under. And it is well they afford us both these for the one without the other would be an uncomfortable consideration.

The Apostle we see proposes the example of Christ on the suffering side, as if that were the chief view we were to take of it, that the great end and design of his being made an example to us.

The most difficult parts of our duty is to suffer well, and therefore we stood most in need of a perfect pattern in this respect to direct and encourage us, and what we wanted most Christ who came to make good all our defects and to heal all our infirmities took most care to supply us with. And therefore from his birth to his death, this is the character under which he appears.

His sufferings indeed were finished upon the cross, but they began when he first entered on his state of humiliation; when dismantling himself of all his majesty, he took upon him to deliver man and in order thereto did not abhor the virgin's womb.

Under this view if we consider him, and withal consider, that it is our duty and owe happiness to resemble him; what hopes can we have to escape the sufferings of this life? Nay what reason totally to decline them? How can we possibly, without suffering, be like him, who himself did nothing but suffer.

The infinite dignity of his person, hindered him not from taking our nature upon him, with all its meanest circumstances, and with all its most afflicting accidents. And who is there then among the sons of men, so distinguished from the rest by his greatness of prominence, as that it should always become him to learn the great lesson of humility. but that should be ashamed to practice it?

Forasmuch then as Christ hath suffered for us in the flesh, let us arm ourselves with the same mind, with a resolution to imitate him, in his perfect submission resignation of himself to the divine will and pleasure in his contempt of all the enjoyment of sense, of all the vanities of this world, its allurements and terrors; in his practice of religious severities, in his love of religious retirement; in his making it his only study and delight, to work the work of him that sent him; his choosing for the end, want before abundance, shame before honor, pain before pleasure, death before life; and his preferring always, a laborious uninterrupted practice of virtue to a life of rest and indolence and ease.

Let the same mind, in all these respects, be in us which was in Christ Jesus, who suffered for us, leaving us an example, that we should follow his steps. The task indeed is hard to flesh and blood, the difficulties that lie in our way are exceedingly great, and would be altogether inseparable; had not he who set us an example, so far above the level and pitch of human nature, enabled as well as commanded us to follow it.

For by the merit of those very sufferings which Christ proposes to our imitation, he has purchased for us all such extraordinary aids and assistances as are requisite to support us under them.

By what he underwent for our sakes, in his life and at his death, he obtained of God, not only a release from the punishment of our sins, but then powers to qualify us for a further increase in virtue; not only the pardoning but sanctifying grace of his spirit; by the means of which he can now crucify the flesh, with the affections and lusts mortify and subdue all our irregular passions, undervalue pleasures, rejoice in afflictions and walk even as he walked in humility and patience, in purity and holiness.

Who then shall separate us from the love of Christ? Who or what shall hinder us for obeying his precepts, and from transcribing his practice? Shall tribulation, or distress, or affliction[4] or famine or nakedness, or peril, or sword? Nay, but in all these things we are more the conquerors, through Christ who loved us.

Let us therefore imitate him, to the best of our power, in all the stages and conditions of life; in what he did, and in what he suffered.

Let us set him before us in every case, and say, would our Savior have thus or thus behaved himself in these circumstances? Would he have yielded to such a temptation? Or declined such a conflict would he have resented such an injury, or felt the least discomposure of mind, upon such an affront. Would he have seen elated upon such a success; have sunk under such a pressure? Or consulted with flesh and blood on such an occasion? Why then should we have his example to guide, his promise of an exceeding reward to encourage, and his grace to sustain us?

But particularly let us, when opportunity offers,[5] resort to that lively affecting representation of his death and sufferings, the servant of his body and blood which he hath instituted for us. There, should we move ourselves[6] to the contemplation of Christ crucified, and to the contempt of the vain glories of this world, which were, together with him, nailed to the cross. Where should we endeavor to instruct ourselves in those holy lessons of resignation, humility, patience, and perseverance unto death, which he in his Gospel hath taught us, and to furnish ourselves with such spiritual supplies of grace, as may enable us to trace the suffering example, which he hath set before us; that so resembling him in meekness, piety, and purity here, we may also resemble him in happiness and glory hereafter.

The version of this sermon that appears here is the one delivered in 1778, which used a different text from the first delivery. The first delivery used 1 Peter 2:21. This sermon is indexed by Smith as #151, and he credits Stokes as an original source.

XVIII

"According to His Will, He Heareth Us"

1 John 5:14
This is the confidence that we have in him that if we ask anything according
to his will, he heareth us.

IT NEED BE NO PART OF MY PURPOSE in discerning from the words of St. John to consider at present the obligation or necessity[1] of the duty of prayer within words which have been read to you plainly enough imply both inasmuch as they were intended to show that our want of success in such addresses was not owing to any want or defect in the duty itself, but to a wrong and undue performance of it only.

Ye ask and receive not, because ye ask amiss—where the very reason and grounds of their not receiving are taken from their not having asked aright. Give me leave therefore in what follows. In discoursing then upon these words, I shall endeavor to point out to you some of those qualifications, and circumstances[2] that are in a peculiar manner requisite towards rendering our petitions acceptable in the presence of God[3] and without which, all our prayers and all our applications at the throne of Grace must be at least vain and useless if not rather mocking devotion; and more likely to call down the displeasure of God upon us than his favor. Of the qualifications which everyone ought to be furnished with before he presumes to engage in the holy work of prayer the primary and most[4] obvious is an nimble and uniform obedience to the laws and commands of God, or at least an earnest endeavor of living agreeably to the rules of our duty as far as our weak and frail nature will permit. Without such a degree of holiness as this,[5] what title have we to expect any favor at all from the hands of God. All are sensible that the best grounds in which to found any hopes of success in the common requests between man and man are our good or at least our well manifested obligation to loving services and that nothing can be more idle or extravagant than to ask a favor of one whose interest we have either offended or but coldly espoused. And the case is just the same with regard to God, then, as we are said to do him good service, and such as he will be most graciously pleased to accept and reward to promote the cause of[*] virtue and religion, let no one that neglects to take these steps which can alone entitle him to the divine favor[6] and protection alone render him a fit and suitable object of his regard, expect to receive[7] anything of the Lord. For God heareth not sinners, said our Lord, but if any man be a worshipper of God, and doeth his will, him he heareth. It is the effectual fervent prayer of a righteous man, that availeth much and the eyes of the Lord are over the righteous, and his ears are open unto their prayers, so is his face against them that do evil. Would you therefore knock and have it opened up to you? Would you ask and not be rejected? Keep the commandments of the Lord, thy God, and pray everywhere lifting up holy hands. And then whatsoever you ask you shall obtain: especially if you are duly careful in the next place to kindle in your hearts a lively faith and confidence towards God.

Let him, says the Apostle, ask in faith nothing wavering he that wavereth is like a wave of the sea, driven with the wind and tossed, let not such an one think he shall receive anything of the Lord.

A lively faith and confidence, then, towards God are qualifications no less necessary than that to which he just mentioned. And this will farther appear, if we consider what an impiety it is to offer up our petitions to God with doubtful and mistrusting hearts, since we thus suppose him either unable or unwilling to fulfill our requests and so suspect his power and goodness.[8]

It is common in and of themselves for man to say that the doubts and apprehensions they have upon such occasions are not owing to any undue conception they have of God but to a sense only[9] of their own great unworthiness. All are subject to many kinds of failings and infirmities. Even the just man falls seven times a day. A consciousness then say they of these secret sins and inevitable miscarriages, inseparable from human infirmity is what makes them doubt and mistrust and hinders their hearts, from being warmed with this godly hope and confidence.

But let us not thus deceive ourselves. For it is not a confidence built on our own good deeds and deserts, that it is here meant to enforce; it is not a confidence of this kind, but such only as arises from a strong and mature sense of the divine goodness and benevolence; such as is wisely poised between the dangerous extremes of servile fear on the one hand, and presumption on the other. We should not fly altogether from God, despairing that creatures unworthy, shall be able to obtain any thing at his hands, nor should we come trusting in our own righteousness, but in his manifold and great mercies. We are indeed not worthy so much as to gather up the crumbs under his table, but he is the same Lord, whose property is always to have mercy. A consideration then of God's great compassion, ever inclining him to pardon and forgiveness should raise and encourage us, should give animation and confidence to all our prayers and devotions.

Nor am I prescribing any thing too difficult for human weakness for did not many, as well as Jews as Gentiles attain considerable degree of this holy trust? Was it not the first thing demanded by our Lord of all such, as were desirous of becoming converts to his doctrine, or sharing in any of the advantages of his mission. Though neither could the one have attained it, nor would it have been demanded of the other, were it not a very easy and very profitable endowment. Hast thou faith; said He. Again be it unto thee according to thy faith and behold he was healed in the self same hour. Great, is the success everywhere promised to a mind thus fervent in the spirit as it pleases the Lord. We only do what He did, but even greater things. Nay should we say unto this mountain, be thou removed, and be thou cast into the midst of the sea, it shall be done, and all things, whatsoever we shall ask in prayer believing, we shall receive.

But I pass to another qualification of acceptable and successful prayer which is a fixed and composed demeanor.[10] This is most certainly of utmost importance, nay it is indispensable. Without it, it would indeed be vain and absurd for anyone to hope to arrive at the least degree acceptableness in this duty. My heart is fixed (says David) O God my heart is fixed—I will sing and give praise—He enters not on the divine praise till he finds himself in such a posture and under such a composure of mind as suits with that holy employment.

My heart is fixed (says He) O God my heart is fixed—then and only then is it time for him to go on and say, I will sing and give praise. If we would therefore learn to perform these solemn offices with due attention and a devout fervency of soul, let us imitate this great pattern of true piety and devotion. Let us try like him to prepare and qualify ourselves in the best manner we can, and enter not on such spiritual exercises, till we have roused every faculty, affection and power of the soul, and are by that means well able to maintain our attention throughout them. For otherwise is the behavior of every man! Nor is anything more common than to see men coming into the sanctuary immediately from some worldly business with alienated and divided minds, full of the interest, the pleasure, or amusement of common life which [illegible] close to them, engrosses their hearts, [illegible]. Would it not be profitable for such [a thing] to retire for a season and not venture upon these awful solemnities, till the busy swarm of vain images that so besets them, were thoroughly disposed, and the scattered thoughts could be so collected as that would be warmed with a [illegible] flame of [illegible] holy feeling.

Another requisite to the end under consideration is universal charity, that is, such an happy temper and disposition of mind as makes us wish ill to no one, but on the contrary most powerfully inclines us to procure and promote the general welfare and happiness of all our fellow men.

This is not only necessary but essential. Not only is this [illegible] fit and becoming such as it would be better to have, than not to have, but such, as without which it would be impossible for our prayers and intercessions to gain any access at the throne of grace. Hear us this Christ our Lord, what our Lord Jesus Christ [illegible]. If thou bring thy gift to the altar, and there remembrest that thy brother has ought against thee; leave there thy gift before the altar, and go thy way; first be reconciled to thy brother, and then come and offer thy gift. That this admonition in the next chapter is if anything still more full and express: When having instructed his audience, in some particulars relating to prayer, he thus concludes. For if ye forgive men their trespasses your Heavenly Father will also forgive you; but if ye forgive not men their trespasses, neither will your Father forgive your trespasses.

There are other circumstances besides those several qualifications which every one should be furnished with before he presumes to address his God in prayer and supplication, which in order to the acceptableness of our approaches to the throne of grace claim our careful attention. While then let me here remark gravity and seriousness of deportment are an indispensable accompaniment of every sincere supplicant's devotion, yet never be allowed here.[11] For we do not approach God in order to melt him into compassion by our eloquence and soft speeches. We can never hope to impose upon him by the arts of rhetoric and study, or expect to bring him to consent to our requests by tropes and figures. Such ornaments are now out of character and impertinent for it is not an earthly Prince before whom we stand who might perhaps be touched and worked upon this way, but it is the great Lord and Father of us all. And He is not a man, the he should be deceived, or the son of man that he should be thus persuaded.

We are to assume for the sake of appearance no studied formality of manner or of language. Our prayers should be uttered with no design of attracting the [illegible] observation of others upon us, or any view to advance ourselves in the good opinion and esteem of mankind. True devotion seeks not the applause of men, but God—consists not in the outward marks and gestures, but has its seat in the heart. Accordingly our Lord forbids us to rest in any outward manifestation of our [illegible] and bids us in holy retirement and seclusion and such holy retirement and seclusion we may if we [illegible] in the [illegible] and prostrate ourselves before our Father, which is in secret, and then our Father, which seeth in secret, shall reward us openly.

And as all ostentation is offensive in acts of prayer [illegible], so likewise is all assumption on their account of holiness. The representation of the two men who went into the temple to pray, is here opposite to and instructive. In the scene there places before us the man who demeaned himself in an humble submissive manner, went down to his house justified rather than the other. And the reason there alleged is because everyone that exalteth himself shall be abased and he that humbleth himself, shall be exalted. The equity of the determination is too plain to be disputed. For surely to bow ourselves low before God, and bewail our wretchedness, must be a behavior much more suitable and becoming than to view our past conduct with [illegible] complacency, and to despise the rest of mankind as if we were more righteous than they.[12]

It is further a circumstance of the highest importance in this matter that our petitions have what is agreeable for their object nothing which [illegible].

Says John, this is the confidence that we have in him, that if we ask anything according to his will, he heareth us. And we may then be said to ask according to his will, when the whole tenor of our petitions is the averring to that which is good in their sight who is of human eyes than to some good end or design.[13]

We ought never it should be remembered except with great caution to pray for any particular worldly advantages and this obviously because we cannot say what advantages of this kind are fit for us, or most conducive to our true interest. Those comforts that we aspire and fret for which we may most eagerly to desire, may be entirely improper to be granted us or if granted us, will have no blessing. And on the contrary those sufferings which we may be most apt to shrink from and to deprecate, may in reality be useful to us, and make on the whole the highest benefits. Holiness is the gift of God, in that we certainly turn to the Lord for it. It is the true riches, the noblest treasure, the highest honor, and God's best and choicest gift. To the acquisition of this therefore and the advancement of the affluence and dominion in ourselves and others, ought all our prayers chiefly to be directed to the first and most important object of prayer may be enjoined with other things such as God in his wisdom may see to be expedient for, such as health, peace and tranquility of mind, the blessings of Heaven upon our understanding when about to engage in enterprises of virtuous interest belief in lessons of trouble and affliction when assertion of any special transmission, pardon, or when [illegible] to any suit the security of his interposing face and the constant compassion of God towards us as at unprofitable servants and his assistance to render us less and less unworthy of his favor. But such an enumeration need not be fruitless. The heart of every Christian prompted by faith approach him in prayer, but knows scripture and can best guard lips from really uttering anything before God, or offering any petition unworthy of himself or of the [illegible] in Heaven. In the spirit of such faith and such confidence with habitual endeavoring to obey the will of God, with fixedness of thought and feeling, with charity towards all men, and in community with God let us be then our own temporal safety and future salvation, together with the temporal safety and salvation of other men.

Our own salvation is doubtless a proper subject[14] for our prayer to God. For self love being that principle which most powerfully inclines us to wish for and endeavor after our own private happiness, it cannot be but very strong in every man, especially when he considers of what infinite worth his soul is. That is not like the body made for a few years only, to continue a short time, and then to molder away, but is intended to last throughout endless ages, to all eternity. When I say, anyone reflects upon this, a mighty eagerness and concern to save and preserve it, must needs arise, and make him very urgent and very importunate in all his prayers and applications to the great Lord and Savior of Souls. And such applications can never be displeasing or impertinent in the sight of God, because they are the natural suggestions of that principle, which God's own right hand hath planted in the breast of everyone, for many good and wise purposes, amongst which this is not the least that we should be from thence excited, not only to a due vigilance and concern for our peace and happiness in this life, but for the eternal welfare of our souls also in that which is to come.

As our own eternal welfare is a subject fit for our prayers and intercessions to God, so is the next place is the salvation of other men. Self love was the principle which prompted us on in the former case, and it is the express command of our Lord that enjoins us here. For we are called upon to love our neighbor as ourselves, and this love when improved to all the heights of which it is capable, cannot be supposed to respect his temporal concerns only. No. We must aid and assist him in the weightier matters of his soul also. We must pray for his everlasting salvation and heartily beg of God to fill up whatever is wanting towards perfecting it by fresh supplies of his grace and assistance.

Our own temporal safety and future salvation, together with the temporal safety and salvation of other men are of all the most proper to be dwelt upon in our prayers and address to God. Are such requests, as he will hear with pleasure and grant with freedom, and such therefore as we may ask with confidence, because we do then, we are sure, ask according to his will.

Now all that remains is to beg of God to give us grace to observe his divine directions, and that we may obtain our petitions, make us always to ask such things as shall please him.

This sermon was delivered twice with the original text, James 4:3, at St. Philip's: February 17, 1761, and November 4, 1764. On the Sunday following the British bombardment of Sullivan's Island, June 30, 1776, Smith delivered the sermon with a different text, 1 John 5:14. He again delivered the sermon at Johnson's Fort (Charlestown Artillery), March 12, 1779. He delivered it a final time at St. Philip's on October 20, 1793. This sermon is indexed by Smith as #175, and he credits Warren as an original source.

Addendum: Statement on Sullivan's Island Bombardment

Delivered after Sermon XVIII

Let this ever be remembered by us, and though beset with dangers, and surrounded with enemies, let us recollect the promise of the Almighty, and know that he is able to save either by many or by few.

Let us then look up to him with confidence and sincerity, never doubting, but that our righteous, and our earnest petitions will be both heard and granted.

What said I! Will be heard and granted? The merciful and omnipotent God hath (we trust) already heard us; for to him, to the God of Heaven and of Earth, to his blessing on our armies is most justly owing the defeat of our blood thirsty enemies in the woods of Beaufort, by a band of our heroic citizens, composed partly of this battalion. When our tyrannous foes vaunting in the pride and haughtiness of heart, thought totally to have destroyed and crushed us; when pouring their vengeance on us in floods of fire, when havoc and destruction stared us in the face, the Lord, who is mighty to save stretched forth his arm and covered us with a shield.

The intrepid behavior of our fellow subjects, our fellow citizens, and our fellow soldiers, on that day have furnished us with a most glorious example for our imitation. Warmed, and animated by the sincere love of liberty; by the warmest affection for their country they boldly despised the danger they were in; and with a most glorious intrepidity withstood our enemies.

All the praises we can bestow on them is not more than their heroic bravery has deserved. Assaulted by force superior to their own, and even that force composed of veterans and picked men they greatly repelled the insulting foe, and gained the victory.

May this prove to be an auspicious omen to the cause of liberty. May the spirit of freedom, even of that glorious freedom, which we are now contending for, pervade the whole state. May every man engaged in this most noble cause think that our safety, and his own depend on his single arm, and may every man be determined to act accordingly.

The present moment calls on us for all our vigor; all our exertion.

Great indeed has been the success of the American Armies; and may the Lord God Omnipotent, even that God, in whom we put our confidence—that God who will hear us, if we ask according to his will, still continue to protect and defend us.

On the Sunday after Smith had taken up arms and defended Fort Moultrie on Sullivan's Island from the British attack, he made this impassioned statement to his congregation at the close of his sermon.

XIX

"We Bring Our Years to an End as a Tale That Is Told"

Psalm 90:9
We bring our years to an end as a tale that is told.

T HIS IS SUPPOSED TO BE a psalm of that great prophet Moses, composed not long before his death, when he had seen the wilderness strewed with the dead bodies of that numerous army which forty years before he had led out of Egypt. The men that were numbered at their departure were considerably more than six hundred thousand: these had provoked God in the wilderness, who therefore swore, they should not enter into his rest. Moses had seen the fatal execution of the sentence, and must moreover have had a just sense of his own approaching ends; which for his distrust in God was threatened, and of which he had certain earnest and assurance in the death of so many thousands that fell before him. This makes him reflect on the uncertainty of life on which we can have no dependence, for tho' life appears beauteous as the gay verdure of the field, yet shall it fade away suddenly like the grass. In the innocent morning of our days it is green and growth up; but when guilt has spread its evening round, it is cut down, dried up and withered; and then he may well cry out in anguish of heart, "we consume away at thy displeasure and are afraid of they wrathful indignations. Thou hast set down our misdeeds before thee, and our secret sins in the light of thy countenance; for when thou art angry, all our days are gone, we bring our years to an end as a tale, that is told." This comparison of our lives with a tale that is told, will hold good.

If we consider that they are a kind of amusing little story, soon related, and as soon forgot, I know no observation better calculated to persuade men of the vanity of great projects, unjustifiable means, and painful pursuits after the things of this world than this is; we are but telling the same old tale, that our fathers have told so often before. To be convinced of this, let us my brethren, call to mind the many of our acquaintances who have finished theirs already: let us cast our eyes around, and view our crowded burial-places, heaped up with the carcasses of those, who were once as wise, as great, as good, as rich, as gracious, as we are. Let us step century after century back and learn from all that ever flourished in them, now idle and trifling a business the story of life is. To what purpose was all their care of solicitude? Where is that wit; that learning, that beauty, that wealth, they so labored after, and so prided in? How embittered and vexatious were their lives in quest of these vanities? How disappointed were most of them in their pursuits? How transient was the profession? How ridiculous is the remembrance.

Let us seek the ennobled, the mighty dust of emperors and heroes, and then determine whether or not it shines distinguished from the inglorious soil with which it is mixed? What avail them now their miraculous successes, their boasted triumphs, and their conquered worlds? All, all are vanished. Their very Empires are moldering away. Their strong places are broken down; the iron, the clay, the brass, the silver and the gold are broken in pieces, and like the chaff of the summer threshing floor, are driven away. Let us then with the calm and dispassionate eye of reason contemplate the vain and ridiculous ambition which harassed and perplexed them; the idle hopes and real fears by which they were so often agitated; the unceasing toils, the intrigues, and dangers, to when they were perpetually exposed. All these things when we have contemplated, how unconcernedly do we survey the bustle that once employed the world, and smile at the short and foolish farce which these emperors and heroes once played. But let us now the pageant of their life is over, attend them to their grave. There perhaps we shall find these mighty conquerors resting with the conquered, or perhaps their ashes undistinguished from their slaves in that place, where the wicked cease from troubling and where the weary are at rest. And after this their lives should be the subject of envy, it must be the envy of madmen; for it is the contempt of the wise and the humane; and at the best a school-boy's tale.

But besides this, let us visit those dull and dreary abodes, where so many of the daughters of beauty have taken up their last sad residence. What can so many charms, that once enlivened the sprightly forms be revealed that will not the very ashes sparkle, and spread a luster around the place, and tell us here they lie! What! Are the roses and the lilies all long since faded! Are these the remains of those, whose finished features struck fire into the coldest breast, and set the very world in flames? Alas! They that once looked fresh as the morning, fair as the noon, and clear as the sun, are now passed away like a morning-cloud. Their piercing and ensnaring eyes no longer are taught to roll; the melodious tongue, so tuned to utterance, is forever silent. Vain are all the Kings of his life; But the vainest of them all is Beauty for where that is the only praise, it vanishes quick as the breath of the mouth, and the remembrance is as ridiculous as the tale ill told.

If we are not yet satisfied with regard to the vanity of human life, let us seek out the oracles of science; let us consult the wise, the eloquent and the learned, let them tell us, what mighty benefits, what substantial pleasures they have derived from all their learning and from all their eloquence. What avails them their uncommon, their exalted genius, their unvaried labors, their wakeful vigils and their midnight studies? With all their learning and with all their eloquence, so far from knowing how to thin out the story of their lives longer than the most humble and the most illiterate, the very excellencies they professed have full often been the means to cutting them off in the very flower of their age.

Go then lettered pride; lay the foundation of thy own immortality, fortify thyself round with the volumes of the learned, and of that solid basis rest thee: but ask thyself where are all the authors of them? Vanished, as thou wilt soon, these names are already forgot. And consider too, that thou, instead of a serviceable life to mankind, hast perhaps wasted thy days on a laborious idleness, hoarding up unprofitable knowledge, already buried with the dead: and filling all thy pages with transcribing the tales of the lives of others, hast found no room to tell thine own.

And if the glory of these I have mentioned was so transitory and so trifling; what shall we say, to the bulk of mankind; to the ten thousand times the ten thousand nameless and forgotten who rose like bubbles on the stream of life and are now as though they had never been? To what purpose was that great anxiety, with which (from a survey of the present world) we may reasonably presume they consumed their days after wealth and honor, when their posterity know nothing of them? The honors they attained, have not descended to their families, and their riches have fled after them. When we consider how few can trace the real history of their ancestors, for above three or four generations, and in this country for above one or two, that great families are daily sunning to decay, and little ones bring out of their ruins, to take their turn for a short season, and then drop again into their original obscurity? It must strike a damp to our ambition, moderate our solitude, after worldly pursuits, teach us to commit ourselves and our concerns to the wise disposal of providence and to be careful for nothing, but in everything by prayer and supplication with thanksgiving, so let our request be made known unto God.[1]

Besides this, the comparison in the text may teach us to be cautious how we furnish others with materials for telling the story of our lives when we are gone.

The approbation that attends on various actions is so amiable, for the relation it bears to virtue, that many forgetting the reason of its agreeableness, have ardently sought it for its own sake. These indeed frequently miss it,[2] but so eagerly pursuing it, and even in the attainment find but a delusive, visionary reward. Fame is airy and insincere, unless it consists much of virtue, which gives it substance, and solidity, that only affords us a lasting credit and refutation. Without it, we can at best but procure an empty, momentary praise, but generally, a juster consequence of our actions, perpetual contempt of infamy.

Turn over the registers of fame: behold her consecrating the memories of great and mighty robbers and destroyers of mankind. See pride—vanity—and ambition driving on their triumphal cars. View them like malignant pestilences, scattering death and desolation over the face of the earth; —unpeopling states—sinking human nature into vassalage and growing immortal by the slaughter of millions: the groans of the dying—the widow and the orphans tears—and the sorrowful sighing of the prisoners, complete the sad inglorious tale. Oh! Distinguished infamy! What honest heart but condemns the impious triumph, however blazoned out by ingenious pens of poets and historians? Enjoy your pernicious greatness, your heroic madness, ye plunderers of the earth, ye destroyers of mankind, unenvied and despised: but know, that ye have not fallen[3] on the path which leads even to real glory in this life; much less to eternal happiness in that which is to come.

But let us turn our eyes, my brethren, from a picture odious and disgustful to humanity, and view those real heroes. Heroes who have devoted themselves to death, not to ruin, but to save their country—whose ambition was to have understanding hearts to judge a people uprightly—who wept, not that there were no more—worlds to conquer, but that a day had passed without conferring a benefit. To these we pay a willing honor—it is not in our power to refuse it and we yield them with pleasure the place they challenge and deserve, the first of human kind.[4]

But besides this, even in the learned world—how unhappily are they employed, who, too eager in the pursuit of fame, are the industriously recording their dishonor in their own writings, and transmitting their memories down as long as their works shall live for the derision and contempt of future times. To these men a party or a faction may give present credit—but unprejudiced prosperity will do them better justice. Who envies those venal, yet ingenious men, who have often prostituted their genius in defense of tyranny; or endeavored to subvert the very foundations of Christianity, the most simple and yet the most perfect religion, that ever was presented to mankind? And on the other hand, who does not consider with sincere esteem, and bestows their warmest approbation, on those who have advanced the useful Arts and Sciences, or contributed to the support of true virtue and religion? It is indeed a truth, that our memories can never live without contempt, unless a real uncounterfeited virtue lays the foundation of our fame. And whatever honors and wealth may guild the passage of our lives, we shall bring our years to a shameful end, if the tale that is told of them, raise distaste and abhorrence in the hearers—Nay, though our names should be forgotten,[5] and the story of our lives unknown. We can cast our thoughts back to the crowds that have gone before us, and frame to our imaginations some that have spent a long laborious life, to purchase to themselves riches and honors, every moment embittered with necessary fatigue and unnecessary fears, the self-denial of proper refreshments, and indulgement, nay of natural wants and appetites: and this too, at the expense of their honor and humanity, to build themselves a name, and raise a mighty family, thinking their houses would continue forever, and that their dwelling places would endure, and their lands called after their own[6] name. This in truth is their foolishness; and their posterity is lost, who only had reason to praise their saying.

Other we can extol who lived blessings to mankind; always ready to save their fellow creatures; disdaining an advantage, where honor must be the exchange; preferring their innocence to grandeur; and their integrity to wealth; and who, though now forgotten, lived and died esteemed. Nay, though they had met ingratitude, hardships, and distresses in return; the question need not be asked which of those you would choose; and which prefer.[7]

Consider then that it is now in your power to make the choice effectually, and be what you would wish yourselves to be; weigh it well, loose not the opportunity; a few days may, a few years will certainly, rob you of it forever. And to quicken you in your resolutions, the comparison in the text may suggest to you, besides what has been advanced, that there remains another day in which we ourselves, tell over the tale of our own lives, in the presence of God and his holy angels.

From these words, the first reflection taught us, is, to lessen our opinion of, and moderate our pursuits after, the things of this world; considering how trifling and insignificant the possession of them all are, and as such a consideration tends to wean our affections from the world, so it leads us to be the more easily contented, and consequently happier with our conditions; and more ready to lay down our lives, when God, in his good pleasure shall think fit to call us hence. This affects the general aim and scope of life. The next reflection seems to influence us in particular actions, and determine us in doubtful cases; teaching us, that whenever virtue and an inviting advantage are inconsistent one with another,[8] our own unprejudiced minds, and the judgment even of the wicked world, corrupt as it is, will direct us always to chose the former. And this, indeed, is so powerful a reflection, that it hardly leaves us to our choice, but puts us under a necessity, of conducting our lives with discretion, though they are brought to an end as a tale that is told. Yet it is a tale that must be told again; and it is of infinite concern to us, that we tell it with approbation.

This let us consider, and before it is too late, let us be convinced, that the life of man, though extended to its utmost length, is so short, and transitory, that it soon comes to its last fatal period. But short and transitory as the life of man may be even at the best, a thousand causes, by us unforeseen and unapprehended, may snap the tender threads of life, in our days have half run out, or our tale half told. Let us then strive to crowd as many virtues as possible into the narrow circle of our lives, that they may speak in our behalf, when neither beauty, riches, learning, or mad ambition will avail us anything. Indeed, the narrow limits of life, admit of no idleness or delay. The moments pass in such quick succession before us, that it is our duty to improve them to the utmost, and make them our own, by advancing in Godly and true religion, by which, as it were, we shall anticipate immortality.

This is more especially not only our duty, but our highest interest, as we know, when they are once past, they never can be recalled. The fleeting hours as they pass, admonish us, that life speeds quickly and imperceptively away, and that we have most important business which should be finished. The present moment is all that we can call our own. When it is once past it will return no more; and the tale of our lives must be told either to our praise or to our confusion. Today then, while it is yet day, let us lay hold on life, and consider how great—how fair—how rich—how powerful—how learned we may all be, if we make God the chief end of our happiness, and his religion the main business of our lives. Here we may give full scope to our desires and gratify the warmest wishes of our hearts. Built up on this foundation, we shall stand immoveably fixed. The strong winds may blow—the raging floods descend, but in vain they beat against us, we are founded on an impregnable rock—it is the rock of ages and can never be moved. Then may we, in the exulting—the enraptured language of the Psalmist, boldly bid defiance to all the enemies of our warfare—"The Lord is my light and my salvation whom then shall I fear—The Lord is the strength of my life, of whom then shall I be afraid."

According to Smith's index, this sermon was delivered at least once in 1779. This sermon is indexed by Smith as #195, and he credits Ridley as an original source.

XX

On the Necessity and Demerit of the Discharge of Our Duty—Part One

Luke 17:10
So likewise ye when ye have done all those things which are commanded you, say,
we are unprofitable servants; We have done that which was our duty to do.

THESE WORDS are an inference drawn from the parable immediately follow-ing. For if an hired servant, employed in the common offices of plowing, or feeding cattle, ought not to imagine, that he has obliged his master to make so much as a return of thanks; because, all his industry and diligence, be they never so great, do not exceed the extent of his duty, nor the condition of that service in which he has employed himself; so, when we have acted to the utmost of our power, it would be extreme folly to conclude that God were in arrears to us; since our very best performances come infinitely short of the exactness of the vale of our conduct; and are so far from being in themselves meritorious, that they want great allowances to make them acceptable.

So likewise, ye, when ye have done all those things which are commanded of you, say, ye are unprofitable servants; we have done all that which was our duty to do.

In which words there is,

First, support the necessity of good works; when you have done all those things which are commanded you.

Secondly, they contain an absolute assertion of their insufficiency to salvation; with the reason of it annexed—"We are unprofitable servants; we have done that which was our duty to do." These too, seem at first sight, to be very discouraging and somewhat contradictory.

For, if we are under an indispensable obligation to perform whatever is commanded us; and are yet declared unprofitable after the discharge of our whole duty, with what cheerfulness can we apply ourselves to the work, when we have so little prospect of receiving the wages? But when I shall have treated of them both in their order, these difficulties, I hope will vanish. Give me leave therefore, to prove the necessity of good works.

First, In respect to God. Secondly, to ourselves, and, thirdly, to our neighbor.

For this end God delivered us from the hand of our enemies, the dominion of sin, and the tyranny of Satan, that we might serve Him without fear, in holiness and righteousness all the days of our life. And if we consider His nature, in conformity to which the chief perfection of our own does consist; He is always employed in issuing the streams of his goodness, which is so full a plenty are derived upon us, that such a pattern must needs excite us to an imitation of it, and quicken our endeavors after as near a likeness with the divine nature as the condition of our frailty will admit.

Besides this, He is a God of spotless purity who hateth all workers of iniquity. And, as under the law, he gave the Israelites this express injunction, "Ye shall be Holy for I am Holy." So in the more gracious dispensation of the Gospel, the Apostle declares this to be the will of God, even our sanctification; and, if without holiness no man shall see the Lord, shall not be instated in the profession of perpetual bliss and happiness in heaven, the consequence will be, that the means ought not to be separated from the end; we must run, if we desire to obtain; we must use all our diligence, if we would make our calling and election sure.

If therefore the example of the Lord Himself, the consideration of His nature, or the declarations of His will, can have any influence upon our life and practice; the performance of all other duties is as necessary as the obedience of our faith; for this was the principle end of our redemption; Christ, as the Apostle saith, gave Himself for us, that He might redeem us from all iniquity, and purify unto himself a peculiar people, zealous of good works, for they are good and profitable unto men.

Secondly, they are necessary in respect of ourselves. And what we are obliged to in point of duty, will surely more strongly affect us, when it is enforced upon us by an argument, which seldom fails in other cases, that which is drawn from our interest.

Profit is generally a most powerful spring of action; it awakens all our endeavors, excites our diligence; and so eager are we in the pursuit of it, that the difficulties which we meet with, only put a keener edge upon our spirits; and we overlook all dangers, when our eyes are fixed upon the advantage, which we propose to ourselves.

And, if this be accounted a reasonable motive, when we are in quest of what is, comparatively, a very trifling concern, what shall we say of an object that is fit to engage all our faculties, and which will justify our most boundless desires. For Godliness is profitable unto all things, having a promise of the life that now is, and of that which is to come.

A life conformable to the precepts of Christianity, which requires charity as well as faith, will entitle us to blessings of the highest value; and what may seem wanting in any singular instance, will be abundantly made up in the other world; for, if we are not weary in well doing, in due season we shall reap, if we faint not. After our labors, we shall be translated into a land of rest, the celestial Canaan; and God will reward, not the merit which we must disclaim, but the faithfulness of our service. "To them who by patient continuance in well doing seek for glory, honor, and immortality, eternal life."

It is not the intrinsic value of good works which is here insisted upon; but the necessity of them, not as meritorious causes,[1] but as prescribed conditions, or appointed means, of our happiness. And so much efficacy our Lord himself ascribes to them, when he grounds our admission into His Kingdom upon this foundation, for I was an hunger, and he gave me meat; I was thirsty, and he gave me drink; I was a stranger, and ye took me in; naked, and he clothed me; I was sick, and ye visited me; I was in prison, and ye came unto me.

Here we see, what a glorious inheritance is assigned to the works of charity; whereas they who rely upon a bare faith in Christ; who prophesied in his name; and in his name cast out devils, and did many wonderful works; are utterly [illegible] or shut out of it; for then says our Savior, will I profess unto them,[2] "I never knew you; depart from me, ye workers of iniquity."

A holy and unblamable faith may lodge in the mind first with very impure and corrupt manners; but when the fruit is sound there is no danger of the tree itself being decayed.

Work, therefore, we must; it is our duty; but we ought not to place any confidence in our performances, trusting in our own righteousness; lest what we challenge from God's[3] justice; the test of which we cannot bear, shall throw us out of the comprehension of his mercy. He has, indeed, set us our task; and though He may justly punish the loiterers; yet, still it is an act of grace in Him, if He rewards those who labor in the vineyard; for, whatever we do, we do by the virtue and strength of His power; and therefore, it is impossible that we should make Him our debtor, by the effects of His own bounty and liberality. In a word, they are two very different things; to say, that good works are the cause of our salvation, which we utterly deny; and that without them we cannot be saved;[4] which we may confidently affirm, is consonant with scripture and the doctrine of the best and purest ages of the church.

Thirdly, they are necessary in respect to our neighbor.

There is one provocation which Christianity allows of, though it is a doctrine of peace; for it does exhort us, to provoke one another to love and to do good works. And, surely there cannot be a greater reproach cast upon our faith, than by supposing it to be lazy and inactive in its nature; from hence springs a shameful neglect of all moral goodness; and if I may so speak, men nail their virtues to that cross, where their sins only should be[5] fastened. They talk much of the efficacy of faith; and, so far, there is no harm, if they did not advance it to <u>such</u> a degree, as to destroy that <u>love</u>, by which it should work; and by their doctrine and example, make others very indifferent, whether they preserved the power, as long as they retained the <u>name</u> of Christianity.

There are extremes in this case, which are equally dangerous; and, therefore, ought to be equally avoided;[6] for some have become so intemperate in their assertions as to declare good works to be in themselves pernicious and utterly <u>destructive</u> of salvation; and, according to them, we ought to <u>glory</u> in the character of being unprofitable servants; and, we should best answer the <u>ends</u> of religion, by contradicting the <u>commands</u> of it.

Others, so <u>magnify</u> works, as to make them meritorious, and oblige God to <u>regale</u> them, even by the laws of strict justice.

It is not easy to determine which opinion carries[7] with it the most mischievous consequences; since the former has in it, a proper tendency to render us careless and dissolute; and the latter, arrogant and presumptuous; the one teaches us to overlook all duty as superfluous; and the other to overvalue it as meritorious.

But, God be thanked, we may safely escape <u>both</u> these rocks; for, since Christ has enjoined us in our daily petition, to pray that God's will may be done on earth; that is, the <u>commands</u> as cheerfully <u>performed</u> as the <u>afflictions</u> <u>suffered</u>, which He is pleased to send, here is an absolute obligation to duty; since by virtue of another precept, our light so to shine before men, that they, seeing our good works, may glorify our father which is in Heaven; there is <u>as</u> pressing an engagement upon us to set a good example to our neighbor; and, if we are tempted to vanity by an overweening conceit of our own performances, the Apostle's interrogation will soon abate the honor of our pride; who hath first <u>given</u> to him, and it shall be recompensed to him again.

It is a matter of our bounty, that we are able to do <u>any thing</u>; and, because, as St. Paul speaks of Philemon, we owe even <u>ourselves</u> to God, who made us, and hath wrought all our <u>works</u> in us, it is impossible we can oblige him, when, in every act that we discharge, we must of necessity be his debtors.

The sum of what hath hitherto been said amounts to this. The text observes, that when we have done all we can, we are unprofitable servants. And from thence it may be inferred, that we should much <u>more</u> deserve the title, if we did nothing.

We are called upon, to be always abounding in the work of the Lord; God commands it, our own interest prompts us to it, and the good of our neighbor requires it from us. They therefore are great <u>enemies</u> to Christianity, who set up faith in opposition to practice, and throw themselves wholly upon <u>Christ</u>, that they may be free from any personal obligation of their <u>own</u>. For we thankfully acknowledge His merits, and confess our own unworthiness, or want of desert. We entirely acquiesce in his obedience; not as it makes <u>ours useless</u>, but as it renders it more <u>acceptable</u>. We do not <u>presume</u> upon our works, but humbly beg of God to regard them, through the merits of His Son. And though we <u>must</u> be unprofitable, our prayer, is, that we may be found faithful servants, and, then, we shall enter into our Master's joy.

He that had received five talents, came and brought other five talents; saying Lord, thou deliverest unto me five talents, behold I have gained, besides that, five talents more. His Lord said unto him; well done, thou good and faithful servant, thou hast been faithful over a <u>few</u> things, I will make thee ruler over <u>many</u> things, enter thou into the joy of thy Lord.

This sermon was delivered four times at St. Philip's: 1776, 1773, 1784, and 1790. This sermon is indexed by Smith as #248, and he credits Wilton as an original source. Smith supplied the sermon's title.

XXI

On the Necessity and Demerit of the Discharge of Our Duty—Part Two

Luke 17:10
So likewise ye when ye have done all those things which are commanded you, say,
we are unprofitable servants; We have done that which was our duty to do.

IN A FORMER DISCOURSE, I proved[1] the necessity of good works; without which, our faith is utterly dead; no better than a carcass, destitute of all sense and motion, and the vigorous influences that are derived from a vital principle. Before I proceed to show their insufficiency to salvation, I would willingly remove some objections, raised by men who make so ill an use of the Gospel, as by it to destroy the obligation of the law; which it was our Savior's design to fulfill and perfect.

To this purpose, it is alleged, that when we are justified, that is, when our sins are freely forgiven, we may ever after forbear the performance of our duty; which is so much as to say, that when we are once recovered from a dangerous sickness, we need no more concern ourselves about the preservation of our health. And that this opinion[2] may appear the more plausible.

Two texts of scripture are particularly adduced in its favor:[3] which I shall severally examine and briefly explain; the more strongly to establish[4] the true doctrine of my text, by the discovery of that which will appear to be false. The first, is a passage[5] in St. Paul's Epistle to Timothy; The law is not made for a righteous man, but for the lawless and disobedient; for the ungodly, and for sinners; for unholy and profane; for murderers of fathers, and murderers of mothers; for manslayers.[6]

Now if any argument can be drawn from hence, the strength of it must consist in this, that since there is no law prescribed to the righteous;[7] they are, consequently, free from the obligation of any; they have no boundaries set to their actions, no rules of their duty; and the revelations of God's will are superfluous, when they are wholly left to the conduct of their own. This is the sense which they would force the words to speak, though you will find, that without very great violence, they cannot bear such a construction;[8] "The law is not made for a righteous man;" that is, there would have been no need of a written law, if the dictates of a nature and reason had been punctually observed; but in this corrupt state, all men's minds are not equally impressed with an awe of God, and a due reverence of His Majesty. The terrors of the law, awaken sinners out of their lethargy, by the punishment which it inflicts, and the tribulation and anguish which it denounces against every soul of man that does evil; which by no means excuses[9] the most righteous from their necessary obligations to duty, though they are prompted by their own voluntary inclinations to perform it.

The law, therefore, is <u>so far</u>, useless to them, who, without fear and compunction, square their lives according to the intention of it: and it does not <u>force</u>; but only direct them, who in obedience,[10] to the injunctions of the Gospel, fulfill the law also, in a more <u>spiritual</u> manner, then the letter of it requires.

The thunder and lightning, which accompanied the promulgation of the law on mount Sinai, will, perhaps, frighten the refractory, into a serious reflection upon <u>his</u> power who gave it; but the purity of God's nature, the charms of his love, and the certain assurances of his justice, will dispose humble minds, not to regard the law, so much for the terrors of its sanction, as the equity of its constitution.

In a word, to the Godly, the law is a light, which they cheerfully follow; but, by a kind amazement, it terrifies the sinner into a sense of that duty, which the righteous discharge with a willing and unconstrained submission. The story of God, and the ineffable beauties of his dwelling-place, are, to <u>them</u>, as well the motives as the end of their journey. To the utmost of their abilities, they perform what God commands for <u>his</u> sake, and not out of the mere apprehension of those punishments, which would otherwise[11] attend their neglect; but as St John says, there is no fear in love, but perfect love casteth <u>out</u> fear; not a filial but servile fear.

Another text of scripture, which betrays carnal men to a great security, is "they are not under the law, but under grace"; and they turn <u>that</u> strength, which is offered them to repent of sins, into an argument who they may still continue unreformed. But, surely, they stop too short, who inter such a conclusion; when the Apostle, in the verse immediately following proposes a question sufficient to quell this groundless presumption: "Shall we sin, saith he, because we are not under the law, but under grace?" God forbid.

It is as gross an abuse of our own reform, as of God's mercy, to form a larger indulgence for sinful men, out of <u>that</u> pardon, which is only allowed to the penitent; and then, to deny the necessity of good works, when we are by the assistance of God's grace, enabled to perform them. For though we have redemption through Christ, the forgiveness of sins, according to the riches of His grace; yet, there are conditions requisite on our part, to make that benefit effectual; and St. John has briefly comprehended them in his[12] saying; if we walk in the light, as He is in the light, the blood of Jesus Christ, His Son, cleanseth us from all sin.

Light is a figurative expression, and signifies the most perfect and immaculate purity, and consequently, the great obligation that lies upon Christians, not to use their holy profession as a pretence, to favor themselves, in any degree of licentious liberty; for every one that nameth the name of Christ, is thereby obliged to depart from iniquity.

Indeed, the absurdities are so palpable, that we must needs renounce our reason, before we can own a doctrine loaded with such consequences, as that because we are freed[13] from the dominion of sin, we may again enter into the same bondage; out of which we were once delivered; and that because we are created in Christ-Jesus unto good works, we therefore ought to bring forth no fruit, though we have, as it were, a new principle of life, and are furnished with all things useful to the end to which we were ordained.

Enough, surely, hath been now said to prove the necessity of works, as they are <u>declarative</u> of our faith. And, that our obligation to them, is still, in force under the gospel, appears from the purport of John the Baptist's office, which was to prepare the Jews for the first reception of it. For now, says he, "the axe is laid to the root of the trees, therefore every tree which bringeth not forth good fruit, is hewn down and cast into the fire."

I shall therefore proceed to the Second Particular,[14] namely, the insufficiency of our works, in <u>themselves</u> to salvation. For though <u>without</u> them, we cannot obtain; yet <u>by</u> them, we cannot merit a reward.

Now to make any work meritorious, all these following conditions are requisite. First, It must be entirely our own. Secondly, That we are not in strictness bound to perform it. Thirdly, There must be proportion between the work and the reward. And Fourthly, There must be in it no mixture of imperfection.

The first condition we shall find to be absolutely wanting. For, if to him that worketh, the reward is not reckoned of grace, but of debt, we can, in justice, challenge <u>nothing</u> from God; because, it is utterly impossible, that He should be indebted to us. "What <u>hast</u> thou" says that same Apostle, "that thou didst not receive? Now if thou didst <u>receive</u> it, why dost thou glory as if thou didst <u>not</u> receive it." It is God that worketh in us both to <u>will</u> and to <u>do</u>; He quickens and excites in us the principles of action, and therefore every motion must be ascribed to his hand.

Upon this account, when St. Paul professes of himself, that he labored more abundantly then all the Apostles he soon corrects the seeming arrogance of his speech, by immediately subjoining, yet not I, but the grace of God which was with me.

Our inward performances, at best, are but like paying a creditor from his own stock; and whatever sacrifice we offer to God, must be taken out of His folds. So that it would be the greatest contradiction imaginable, if we, who in every work that we do, ought to acknowledge the liberality of God's grace, should see to His justice for a reward. For Thou Lord but wrought all our works in us and without Thee we can do nothing.

Secondly, that work by which we merit, we are not in strictness bound to perform; it must be a matter of choice, and not obligation. Indeed, were we at liberty to discharge what parts of our duty we please, when God requires of us as a <u>universal obedience</u> there <u>might</u> be some pretence for <u>merit</u>. But, when the Apostle lays upon us so <u>comprehensive</u> an injunction, "whatsoever things are done, whatsoever things are honest, whatsoever things are just, whatsoever things are pure, whatsoever things are lovely, whatsoever things are of good report, if there be any virtue, if there be any praise, think on those things. Those things which ye have both learned, received, heard, and seen in we do." Could any Christian duly be named which cannot be drawn within that circle; could there be amongst the whole train of virtues, any one which God hath not commanded as to practice, <u>then</u> will it be confessed, that our performance <u>may</u> arise above our obligation; and that we may have a just title to a reward, when no antecedent necessity engaged us to our duty. Thirdly, there must be a proportion between our work and its reward. The hardest task which we have in our Christian warfare, is not worthy, in the Apostle's estimation, to be compared with the recompense which shall be made us: for our light affliction, which is but for a moment, worketh for us a far more exceeding and eternal weight of glory. Here; to lightness, an exceeding weight is opposed, to a <u>moment</u>, eternity; and if they bear no proportion, when they are put in the balance, since it is more uneasy to suffer ill, than to do well; when our afflictions cannot counterpoise the crown which we shall receive; much less, can our good works deserve that reward which God, in His mercy, will confer upon us: "as many of us as shall live godly in Christ Jesus, by walking in those laws which He has set before us." Fourthly and lastly, there ought to be no mixture of imperfection in our works. But who is there of the sons of men, that ought not to make the same declaration with Job, "if I wash myself with snow-water, and make up to hands ever so clean; yet shall then plunge me into the ditch; and my own clothes shall abhor me." As if he had said, though I were in my own, and the worlds account, innocent and blameless; yet, if God, should in strictness, judge me, my own righteousness would appear very defective, and I should detest my own imperfection.

For whitest garments are defiled with <u>some</u> stains, and our best actions are always attended with some <u>failure</u> in the <u>degree</u>, how good soever they may be in their <u>substance</u>. If, therefore, in the rigor of God's justice, every defect is punishable, we have great reason to say, as the Apostle doth, after David, Blessed is he, whose mercilessness is forgiven, and whose sin is coerced; blessed is the man, unto whom the Lord will not impute sin.

For if we faithfully compare our actions, with that which <u>should</u> be the rule of them, the commandments of God, we shall perceive our failures so <u>many</u>; that instead of making the ruler's boast; "all these have we kept from our youth, what lack we yet?" We shall find cause to address ourselves to the throne[15] of grace, in the language of our liturgy, "Lord, deal not with us, <u>after</u> our sins; neither reward us <u>accordingly</u> to our iniquities." For in the words of the Psalmist, "if thou Lord will be extreme to mark what is done amiss; O Lord who may abide it?, but there is <u>mercy</u> with thee therefore shalt thou be feared."

To conclude, St. Paul has stated the case before us in a very narrow compass, when he affirms, that "the wages of sin is death;" that is, we justly merit punishment: but "the gift of God," which excludes all our desert, "is eternal life, through Jesus Christ our Lord." "For God hath saved us, and called us, with an holy calling, not according to <u>our</u> works, but according to His own <u>purpose</u> and <u>grace</u> which was given us in Christ Jesus."

This sermon was delivered four times at St. Philip's: 1766, January 17, 1773, September 1784, and February 1790. This sermon is indexed by Smith as #248, and he credits Wilton as an original source. Smith supplied the sermon's title.

XXII

"His Mercy Endureth Forever"

Psalm 136:26
O give thanks unto the God of Heaven; for His mercy endureth forever.

THERE IS NO PART of the Psalmist's character from whose inestimable composition the words of the text are taken of which is more available or could more strongly recommend[1] him to the favor of Almighty God, than his fervent piety in the work of praise and his warm and sincere gratitude for all the mercies bestowed on him by the great Ruler of the Universe.

His adoration of the goodness of Heaven rises on these occasions to a kind of divine enthusiasm. On these occasions indeed he expresses himself with a fervor and sublimity which no other power but the God of Gods, and Lord of Lords, whose majesty name he celebrates could possibly inspire.

Noble and exalted as David is in this particular of his character; he surely must claim our regard and attention, and be highly worthy of our imitation. And this I am confident will appear to us, beyond a contradiction, evident, if we only consider the gracious benefits which the hand of this God has been continually heaping on us; benefits great, extensive and transcendent; and which only can be answered by a grateful and devoted heart; a sacrifice more acceptable to our beneficent creator, than the blood of goats and bullocks, or all the gems and perfumes of the rich and fragrant East. Instead of their idle, material, monetary offerings, we must dedicate a pure and undefiled mind; for to depart from wickedness; is a thing pleasing to the Lord; and to forsake unrighteousness is a propitiation.

Now to induce us more thoroughly so this is necessary and glorious an act of praise, of precise[2] gratitude and thanksgiving, let us only reflect on the mercies which have been internally showered down upon us, even from our earliest infancy to the present hour, this let us do. I say, and be assuredly convinced, that the God of Heaven is worthy of all adoration, and that his mercy endureth forever.

Not a single blessing, not a favorable passage, which Providence has wrought in our favor, should escape our notice or perish in our remembrance, mainly because they are so long past, that no traces of them are left on our senses and our feelings.

Thus forbid it Heaven that when we are arrived at a state of strength and maturity, we should forget him, who inducted our infancy and tender state, through the manifold dangers and disasters of human life into conflict and most hazardous periods; a succession of benefits fresh and uninterrupted, should not eradicate from our bosoms the memory of ancient ones; but on the contrary, render them more near and venerable in our eyes. There are too few amongst us, however dignified by the glorious name of Christians, but are more, much more than sufficiently mindful of insults and injuries thrown upon them. But hereafter may it never be observed to the disgrace of our holy and most perfect religion, that generally speaking it is as difficult for us to forget the injuries of our fellow creatures, as to remember the mighty[3] benefits of our Creator.

When we revolve in our minds, the favorable passages, which in the various courses of our lives, after, as well as in the stage of infancy have frequently befallen us; when we resolve in our minds the many dangers we have miraculously, or rather providentially escaped; and how the most calamitous condition of human life has often been changed into a state of joy and gladness; how the Almighty hand often delivered us from the assault of dangerous diseases; from the fatal effects of noisome and pestilential air; from the rage of open enemies and the machinations of pretended friends, then should we with all grateful exultation of mind, then should we, I say, look up to our refuge in time of trouble, to the rock of our salvation, glory, and power unto the Lord our God, for love and righteous are his judgments.

Besides this, when the ordinary effects of divine providence are in an advantageous manner presented to our view; when we consider and find recorded the seasonable reward and deliverance of suffering innocence and of just though unexpected punishment of wickedness; or when we contemplate the amazing and stupendous works of nature, and sumptuous furniture of the world, the glories of the [illegible], the fragrance of herbs, the fertility of the Earth, and all other miracles attending it, then should our hearts be affected with grateful sense, and our lips break forth in exclamation of praise, at once, rapturous and devout.

But it is not to the Lord, that our gratitude is due, merely because we breath his air, and are sustained with his food; merely because our eyes are regaled by the splendid canopy of heaven, and our feet tread this variegated and beauteous carpet of the earth, infinitely more rich and glorious than all the boasted productions of human industry. But to the Lord it is more especially, in a much more distinguished manner due because in his unspeakable goodness, he has breathed into us the breath of life, given us immortal souls, and impressed on us lasting and perspicuous characters of his own divine nature and celestial essence; because he has made us, in some degree. Partakers of his most transcendent perfections; and by an act of imitable condescension, has in some degree admitted us to a constant intercourse and familiar acquaintance with himself.

But is there nothing yet more remaining to impress the minds of man with the most ardent gratitude to this Supreme Being, and their Almighty Benefactor? Surely there is. When we consider that he to redeem fallen man from misery, and to advance him to a state of happiness, hath infinitely debased himself; and eclipsed the brightness of his glorious majesty, not disdaining to put on our frail and mortal nature, to subject himself to the conditions of humanity and even, at last, to take the bitter cup, to suffer a painful and ignominious death, to secure to us salvation, and glorious inheritance in the heavens. To this Almighty God then, to this great, this only true benefactor of ours, we certainly owe this most natural and easy, this most sweet and pleasant duty of giving thanks. And to this God, if we carelessly neglect, if we willfully refuse to pay it, it may with truth be added, that we are not only monstrously ungrateful and horribly wicked, but also abominably foolish, and deplorably abandoned. To this great, to this only patron and true friend of ours, (for the instance for the sake of having an effect upon our minds, deserves a repetition) if we do not in some measure discharge our [illegible] of gratitude, we are not only deservedly to be adjudged impious and ungrateful, but also senseless, wretched and unhappy in the extreme.

But notwithstanding the goodness of the Almighty appears so evidently to our eyes in the creation of the world, in the superb ornaments of the heavens, in the glorious furniture, with which he has so liberally invested this our mortal habitation, and above all, in the incarnation of his ever blessed Son, Christ Jesus; yet because these things are so commonly offered to our senses and reflection, we are apt to think them little worthy of our attention, and at last they become almost totally disregarded by us.

But though these things, so great and stupendous, too often lose their affect on the human imagination; and men are too apt to fall into a state of languor and irreligion, though the heavens declare the glory of God, and the firmament showeth his handy work; though day unto day uttereth speech, and night unto night showeth knowledge; yet unprovoked by this perverseness, the Almighty does not always avert his eyes from the people of his hands, but frequently in mercy and tender compassion to them, more than in the vindictiveness of inflamed justice, he brings some visitation on their heads; not to destroy, but to bring them back by a timely reprehension to repentance to him.

For this purpose, sickness, pestilence, and famine are often sent amongst the nations of the Earth. For this purpose, merciful in its effect, he sometimes speaks to them in the voice of thunder, and sometimes sends his admonitions in the tremendous flames of ethereal fire; and for this he sometimes permits even war itself to let loose all its horrors, and by its mischievous assailments to harass the children of man. Of this plague, one of the most dreadful, the most deadly, that ever disturbed the world, we sure would many years since experienced a sufficient share. But great as the calamities were which this country underwent, the sudden surprising, and almost unexpected period which was put to them, gives us more reason for wonder and gratitude than [illegible] and complaint.

The particular mercies, for which we are called upon, by authority, this day, to be thankful, are betrayed to us by the well penned pious proclamation, "When we review the calamities which affect so many other nations, the present condition of the United States affords much matter of consolation and satisfaction. Our exemption hitherto from foreign war; an increasing prospect of the continuance of that exemption;" the great degree of internal tranquility we have enjoyed; the recent confirmation of that tranquility, by the suppression of an insurrection in one of our sister states, which so wantonly threatened it; the prospect and hope that a final period is past to the sanguinary maraudings of the Indians; the happy course of our public affairs in general; the unexampled prosperity of all classes of our citizens, are circumstances which peculiarly mark our situation with indentions of the Divine beneficence towards us. In nature's state of things it is in an especial manner, our duty as a people, with devout reverence and affectionate gratitude; to acknowledge our many and great obligations to Almighty God, and to implore him to continue and confirm the blessings we experience. To render him our sincere and hearty thanks for the manifold and signal mercies, which distinguish our lot as a nation; particularly for the possession of constitutions of government which unite, and by their union establish liberty with order; and generally for the prosperous course of our affairs public and private; and at the same time humbly and fervently to beseech the kind mother of these blessings, graciously to prolong them to us; to imprint on our hearts a deep and solemn sense of our obligations to him for them; to teach us rightly to estimate their immense valor to preserve us from the arrogance of prosperity and from hazarding the advantages we enjoy by delusive pursuits; to dispose us to merit the countenance of his favors, by not abusing them; by our gratitude for them, and by a correspondent conduct as citizens and as men; to render this country more and more a safe and propitious asylum for the unfortunate of other countries; to spread among us true and useful knowledge; to diffuse and establish habits of sobriety, order, morality and piety; and finally, to impart all the blessings we possess, or ask for ourselves, to the whole family of mankind.

If we well consider the deliverances specified, which[4] we have met with, we shall find sufficient and coercive reasons for our belief in a special providence and consequently, grounds for thanks and admiration. The Lord has certainly interposed, that man may know, that it is his hand; that they may see and know, and consider and understand together, that the hand of the Lord hath done this, and the holy one of Israel hath created them.

To whom is it owing that we are met together in the house of the Lord, to celebrate the praises of the God, whose mercy endureth forever, but to him? To whom is it owing that every one can sit under his fig tree and enjoy the fruit of his labor unmolested and undismayed, but to him? To whom can these wonderful events, wonderful indeed when compared with the ordinary course of things, be inspected, but to him the great Jehovah, whose mercy endureth forever?

As these great and miraculous blessings well and seriously reflecting, let us give thanks to Almighty God, for having saved us from the many dangers which surround, and the many troubles which other nations are encountered. On these great and miraculous blessings, well and seriously reflecting, let us give thanks to Almighty God who hath protected us in the possession of our civil liberties and our religious rites, the most inestimable blessings which this perishing and transitory world can afford to the children of men; and in the consequence of this, and on full reliance on the mercy of God, though sometimes attended, with what to us may seem severities; as praise and thanksgiving and the most delightful business of heaven, may God grant that they may be our greatest delight, our most frequent enjoyment upon Earth. And may the blessed fountain of all goodness and mercy, inspire our hearts with his heavenly grace; and thereby enable us rightly to apprehend diligently to consider, faithfully to remember, worthily to esteem, and heartily to be affected with all due acknowledgement and thankful obedience for all innumerable favors, mercies and benefits freely conferred upon us; and let us say with David, "blessed be the Lord God of Israel, who only doth wondrous things, and blessed be his holy name; and let the whole Earth[5] be filled with his glory, for his mercy endureth forever."

This sermon was delivered only once, at St. Philip's on February 19, 1795. This sermon is indexed by Smith as #381.

XXIII

"A Good Name"

Proverbs 22:1
A good name is rather to be chosen than great riches, and loving favor rather
than silver and gold.

A S RICHES ARE ACCOUNTED of all things the most valuable, the wise man in order to show the great worth and excellency of a good name, hath thought fit to compare it with riches, and notwithstanding the mighty value that is set upon the latter, he hath not scrupled to adjudge the preference to the former; which cannot but afford matter of surprise to a great part of mankind. To the base and ungenerous, who are too low in their notions to think that a good name is of any worth at all, and to the covetous and worldling, who though they might perhaps be brought to give a good name the record place, yet can they never agree with Solomon in ranking it above riches. But how widely soever the generality of mankind may differ from the wise man in this particular, yet whoever will weigh, what is here laid down with a tolerable degree of care and attention, will soon be convinced, that this saying is founded on the soundest reason, and moreover that it contains a truth, that will supply us with many good and useful lessons of instruction, so that we shall not misspend our time, if we make it the subject of our present meditations.

In order, therefore, to show the truth of the wise man's assertion, we may observe that riches are equally common to the good and the bad. The worst of men may have as large a share in them as the best; the most notorious vicious [illegible] as the most eminently virtuous person. For though they are in truth secretly disposed by the most wise and just hand of Providence, yet to the outward appearance and further we cannot pretend to judge the dispensation of them seems to come from chance rather than justice, from fortune rather than merit. And this is one of the things, which the preacher complains of as a great and sore evil that all things, that is, all outward things come alike to all, that there as one event to the righteous and to the wicked, insomuch that no man can know so as to pronounce with any certainty whether he be in the love or the hatred of God by all that is before him.

But with respect to a good name, the matter is quite otherwise as that presupposes some real worth and merit. A good name being in the ordinary course of God's Providence[1] the proper effect, and by his good blessing the most certain temporal reward of piety and virtue. If there be any virtue, any praise, are the words of an Apostle: which plainly imply, that there can be no true and real praise, where there is no virtue, any more than there can be a shadow without a substance to cast it. Indeed it sometimes happens, that men obtain a good name, when they but ill deserve it, and so does it fall out sometimes, that men of real worth and probity are maligned and traduced, but this mistake is always detected sooner or later, so that according to Solomon the name of the wicked, when flattery and hypocrisy have done their best to support it, shall rot notwithstanding; whereas, the memorial of the just, when envy and calumny have done their worst to blast it, shall be blessed.

A good name, therefore, is better than great riches because it presupposes virtue, and is seldom obtained, certainly can never be preserved without some real worth and merit. Again, a good name is better than great riches because it makes us more useful in our several stations.

Riches are most undoubtedly very proper instruments for a man to promote the worthiest and most virtuous designs, but if the possessor of them has no other qualification, he will often fail of success. Whereas a good name is alone sufficient for expediting any honest enterprise, that we undertake, whether it be of a civil or religious nature, for the world is so much guided by opinion, that if we are in esteem, whatsoever we do, is well taken, whatsoever we propose, is readily entertained. Yea and our reproofs too carry weight and authority with them, by which means we are enabled to do more good, to bring more glory to God, to give better countenance to His truths than with a thousand other qualities besides.

And as a good name is for this reason rather to be chosen than great riches, so is it likewise as it is a more lasting and durable possession.

As to riches and other worldly possessions, they are of uncertain continuance, and may in a little time slip away from us, certainly we shall in a little time slip away from them, and leave them behind us. Whereas a good name is a far more lasting and durable nature, it generally continues with us all our life long, and in the hour of death stands by us and gives some sweetness to the bitterness of those last pangs. Yea and often survives us, according to the wise son of Sirach, who says, their bodies are buried in peace, but their name liveth for evermore. Have a regard therefore (says the same author) to thy name: For that shall continue with thee above a thousand great treasures of gold. For life, even a good life,[2] hath but few days, whereas a good name endureth forever.

It appears then from these instances that what the wise man has here laid down is strictly and literally true, but besides the method of showing the value of a good name by proving that it is of more worth than any worldly possession. There are several other ways of proving the same truth, and as they may perhaps appear stronger in the opinion of some, I will make a brief mention of them.

We may observe then that a good name is of real worth and excellence, as the love and desire of it is deeply implanted in the breast of every one, since it cannot be supposed, that God would give us such a strong propensity and thirsts for what is of no worth, no value.

And as the natural thirst and the appetizing after a good name is a plain indication of its worth, so shall we be able to pass the same judgment from considering the price which human laws set upon it.

There is no state or community whatever that does not guard the good name of its members by severe laws and penalties against slander and defamation, but as laws do not use to take care of trifles or make provisions against injury that, which by reason of its worthlessness is incapable of receiving an injury, we must call ourselves wiser than the law, or be forced to acknowledge that a good name is somewhat more than a mere notion, which is of importance enough to merit protection and security from the legislative power.

Thus, much then being said in order to set forth the real worth and excellency of a good name, let us see whether what has been advanced will not afford us some useful lessons of instruction, and I think it will be needless to observe how heinous a sin calumny and detraction must needs be, since the inference is so plain and natural from what has been advanced, that it can't possibly escape any one. But though it will be needless to spend any time upon this observation, yet still we can't help remarking how mightily those then do disservice to the cause of religion,[3] who endeavor to persuade us, that a good name has no worth at all in it. Nay, that it is even criminal in a Christian to be anxious about it since by this means the chief argument against slander and defamation is entirely overthrown.

A second use of the doctrine laid down will be to observe that a due sense of the real worth and excellence of a good name is the best guard a man can have over his virtue and integrity, since nothing restrains us so powerfully from doing mean unworthy actions, as a nice and delicate sense of honor, since nothing is[4] so apt to make us careful and circumspect in our conduct as an anxious concern for what the world may say or think of us. Nor will this principle restrain us only from every thing, that is mean and dishonorable, but it will push us on likewise to everything that is good and praiseworthy. Abundant proof of which may be collected from ancient history, where we find an account of many, who set so high a value upon a good name, that they readily submitted to the greatest difficulties in order to acquire it and sometimes thought that even life itself was not too dear a price to pay down for it. Hence, their mighty zeal and affection for their country; hence, their undaunted courage in any common danger or calamity; hence, their noble stands against tyranny and oppression. In a word the desire of praise and fear of disgrace was the fruitful spring of all their virtue and integrity.

And here let us stop a while, and admire the great wisdom and goodness of God in implanting these passions in the breast of man, and consider how incumbent it is upon every one of us to cherish and improve them, since as long as we keep them alive and breathing, we carry a principle about us that will not only prove[5] a strong restraint from sin, but a most powerful incentive to virtue. That will not barely keep us within the bounds of our duty, but urge us on to excel.

Thirdly, the valuableness of a good name in the judgment of Solomon will show us the weakness of that plea, which is sometimes made use of by men of great honesty and sincerity. It is usual for such to plead that as long as they stand clear in their own consciences, and are sure their hearts are honest, that they are not to regard the speeches and censures of men. There is a time, indeed, and there are cases, wherein such a plea will hold good. When men shall go about by proposing disgraces to frighten us from our duty, or endeavor to put on our names as evil for having done which was our bounden duty to do. In such cases we may comfort ourselves in our own innocence, file for refuge against calumny of others to our own consciences. These repose ourselves with security, disregarding the reproaches of evil men, and possessing with St. Paul, that is a very small matter with us to be judged of men, or of man's judgment.

But when we have an opportunity of doing more, we are not to think it sufficient just barely to satisfy our own consciences, but we must endeavor as much as in us lies to manifest our uprightness to the consciences of others. What else meant St. Peter[6] by exhorting Christians to have their conversations honest among the Gentiles? Or why was St. Paul so earnest in his own person to provide things honest not only in the sight of God, but in the sight of men also. And so earnest in stirring up others to good things by arguments drawn as well from praise as virtue, from fame as conscience.

But least what has hitherto been said should either be mistaken or misapplied, we may observe in the last place, that though the value of a good name be really great, yet it may be overrated. Though the desire of it be a good principle, and such as we should cherish and improve, yet it must not be made the sole end and design of our actions. The heathens, indeed, being deprived of the blessed hopes and immortality knew no greater good than the praise of men, and turned therefore all their thoughts and endeavors towards acquiring it, looking even upon the loss of life itself as sufficiently recompensed, if they could have their names thereby transmitted to posterity in characters of honor. But now life and immortality is brought to light through the Gospel, the praise of men must not be the sole end and design of our actions. We must not now set so great a value upon it, but must regulate our pursuits of it by those measures which right reason and divine revelation prescribe. We must remember that though a good name be valuable, yet that virtue and a good conscience are of more value, and must do nothing sinful therefore in order to gain the esteem of the world, but resolutely perform our duty, even when we are sure to be evil spoken of for so doing. And as we must take no wrong or indirect means in order to acquire a good name, so when we have acquired one we must not use it to flatter our pride or our vanity, but apply it to some good and useful ends, such as the glory of God. The edification of our neighbor, and the quickening ourselves in a vigorous performance of all laudable actions, a regard from reputation, that springs from these principles, that is bounded within these limits and directed to those holy purposes in the duty and ornament of every sincere Christian. And though such a procedure as this should not always prove successful in acquiring us the esteem and good opinion of the world, yet will it be sure to secure us from what we have much more reason to dread, that shame and confusion of face which is represented in scripture as one of the bitterest ingredients in the punishment of the wicked hereafter. Now to God.

This sermon was one of Smith's favorites. He delivered it at least six times: twice at St. James in Santee, January 19, 1766, and August 1771; once at St. Michael's, April 23, 1775; and three times at St. Philip's, June 5, 1774, February 19, 1775, and September 1800. This sermon is indexed by Smith as #398.

XXIV

"A Day Which He Will Judge"

Acts 17:31
He hath appointed a day in this which he will judge the world in righteousness,
by that man whom He hath ordained; whereof he hath given assurance unto all men,
in that He hath raised him from the dead.

THE FESTIVAL OF THE LORD'S RESURRECTION we have already celebrated; and may now therefore turn our thoughts, not improperly, to consider the chief consequence of his resurrection, as judgment to come. And as this doctrine is fully revealed in scripture, and besides, is in itself so reasonable, that no one can doubt of it, I shall not spend any time in proof of that which I take for granted you all believe, but shall inquire into two points that appear to me most practical and therefore more proper for our consideration at this time, and those are:

How it comes to pass[1] that a matter of so great importance as a judgment to come, makes so little impression on the minds of the generality of mankind, who profess to believe it, and then show in conclusion, by what means the consideration of a future judgment may have a greater influence on our minds.[2]

Now the reasons why the day of judgment makes so little impression on the generality of those, who profess to believe it, are various. The first and principle of them is the meat of[3] consideration.

We flatter and please ourselves with the thoughts that we are intelligent and considerate beings, when perhaps consideration especially as to matters of consequence is one of the things which mankind have the greatest aversion to, and can there be a plainer argument of this, than the small regard which men have to another life. For if they would seriously consider this matter, if they would lay the present and the future world in balance, the one against the other, they could not but soon discover the wonderful folly of preferring that, which this world accounts happiness, before that, which is offered to our choice in another. Since let us make all the fair and reasonable allowances that may be as to our inclinations and appetites and circumstances in this world. As to the distance, obscurity and incomprehensibleness of the joys of another world, yet every considering man, that regards true happiness, will be sure to choose that which is to come.

For supposing the happiness were equal, yet there is no proportion in continuance of them; and a considering man will be sure to choose a happiness, that can never have any end, before one that may be irrecoverably lost in a moment, and can certainly be enjoyed but for a little time, if there were any certainty at all in the enjoyment.

But the happiness of the present and future worlds are so far from being equal that no man ever placed his happiness here, but the more he considered, the more he repented his folly for so doing. Whereas no man ever placed his happiness above, but the more he considered, the better satisfied he was placing it here, where alone that good is to be found, which can make us truly happy.

But what makes a considerable difference in the choice is this, that He that looks after a future happiness doth not thereby lose any of the real conveniences of human life. Whereas He, that places his happiness here, cannot find it in this world, and is sure to be miserable in another. Indeed, if God made it absolutely necessary in order to future happiness for us to forego all the natural pleasures and innocent delights of this life, the terms would be much harder, and scarce possible to human nature. But God hath not dealt as severely with mankind. He allows us all the reasonable desires and nature and forbids nothing but what is unreasonable and unnecessary. Nothing but what is really repugnant to our well-being here; and when therefore a man [illegible] being miserable forever, for what can never make him happy here, if he had his full liberty to pursue his desires, He shows how far he is from acting like a wise, considering being. So that want of consideration is certainly one great reason why the thoughts of a judgment to come make so little impression on the minds of men.[4]

A second reason is the bewitching and stupefying nature of sensual pleasures. They who place their happiness in seasonal delights, which can never be enjoyed, when this life is ended, have but a melancholy prospect into another world. For they are shut out from the very possibility of being happy in their own sense.[5] But when they are once come to apprehend that there is no pleasure to make them happy, but what is seated in the body, they are apt to conclude, that when that dies, there is an end to all, for their imaginations are so stupid, that they can reach no farther. And the true cause is they have laid reason and conscience asleep so long, that it is very hard to awaken them; their notions of good and evil are like the confused apprehensions of men half awake; they see enough to perplex, but not enough to satisfy them; and when their fears grow upon them, they have not the heart and courage to examine them, whether they be reasonable or not, but rather choose to return to their former opiates, than undergo the trouble of an effectual cure, by a hearty repentance and coming to themselves; as the Prodigal Son in the parable did, when his hardship had brought him to consideration. We do not know, what had become of him, if he had been wise and frugal in his pleasures, if he had taken care of a good stock and plentiful subsistence; but he first came to be pinched with want, before he was awakened to repent. But we have in the scripture a more remarkable instance of the stupefying nature of sensual pleasures and that was in David, after his sins of adultery and murder. It is indeed a wonder how a man of such a tender conscience in other things, should continue so long under the guilt of these enormities, without being awakened to repentance. For he did not know these to be great sins; and did not his conscience charge him with the guilt of them? How came he to need a prophet to be sent to him, and to deal so plainly with him as to tell him, "Thou art the man." But this is a plain proof how apt the pleasures of sin are to stupefy men's consciences. And if it were thus in the case of a man, otherwise after God's own heart, we may cease to wonder how others, who walk in the ways of their hearts, and in the sight of their eyes, who allow themselves in all sensual inclinations and pursue carnal delights with greediness. We may cease, I say, to wonder how such lose at last a notion of God and religion and become so insensible of the awakening consideration of a judgment to come, as if there were no such thing.

The third and last reason, why a judgment to come makes so little impression on the generality of men is owing to their presuming too much on the mercy of God.

The first thing which sinners aim at is to think as little as may be of what they are doing, or what will be the consequence of their actions. For every thought of themselves is very uneasy to them, and every thought of God is much more so. Therefore they drive away all such thoughts by one means or other, by diversion, by drink,[6] by company and such public entertainments as rather heighten and inflame their vices than correct them.

And if all this will not do, but there will be some melancholy hours wherein conscience begins to rouse itself and to awaken the sinner to some sense of his folly. Then he is ready to hearken with pleasure to any [illegible] against religion and morality, and admires the wit of anyone who dares say a cold and sharp thing against the wisdom of all ages, and of the best men in them. Then any skeptical disputes are sufficient demonstrations to them; and the most unreasonable cavils against religion are embraced, because against the thing they hate; and even a jest against the day of judgment shall signify more with them than the strongest arguments in the world to prove it. The true reason is, they love [illegible], and hate everything that makes them uneasy in the enjoyment of them, and nothing does more so than the thoughts of a judgment to come.

But suppose after all, the terrible and frequent expressions of scripture concerning the day of judgment, joined with the reasonableness of the thing, do make such impression on their minds, that they cannot wholly shake off the fears and apprehensions of it, than their last endeavor is to loosen and mitigate them from a general presumption of God's merciful nature, and therefore they are willing to suppose, that however God to keep the world in awe, hath threatened them with dreadful severities of the great day, yet as he is full of mercy and compassion to all his creatures, it cannot be supposed say they that He will proceed at that day according to the rigor which he has threatened to use. And to comfort themselves in these hopes, they find out all possible extenuations for their sins, and then laying all together, they conclude, that great abatements are to be made in the scripture account of the day of judgment, and therefore the severity of it is not so much to be feared as some pretend. And when men have persuaded themselves by such false reasonings as these, that there is nothing in the consideration of a judgment to come which ought to give us the least trouble or concern, what wonder is it that this awful truth should have no greater effect upon them?

Proceed, we,[7] in confirmation to show by what means God's bringing us into judgment may make a deeper impression on our minds.

One very likely way of impressing this truth deeply on our minds would be to observe that the more we weigh and consider it, the better will our condition be hereafter.

There would, it must be confessed be great reason to walk in the way of our hearts, and in the sight of our eyes, and never trouble ourselves with what will happen at the great day, if the putting it out of our heads could[8] make the account the easier, when it comes. But alas! This is so far from being the case, that whether we think of it, or no, the account runs on, and we must answer to every particular at last and how unprovided shall we be, if we spend no time here in examining, stating and clearing of them as far as we are able. It is a mighty privilege. We have by the Gospel, that God allows us to clear our accounts with him in this world; for, if we would judge ourselves, we shall not be judged. If we call ourselves to a strict account for our actions, if we repent heartily and sincerely of our sins, then we may with joy and peace in our minds, think of the great day of recompense. But if we never enter into ourselves to search and examine our own actions, never look into the habits of our own minds, nor charge ourselves with the guilt of the sins we have committed, how can we hope to escape the scrutiny or avoid the severity of that day? For our account continually increases by our neglect of it, and the burden of God's wrath must be so much heavier when we have taken no care to lessen it; but after our hardness and impertinent hearts have only treasured up wrath against the day of wrath.

Another likely way of making a judgment to come have its due weight upon our minds would be to observe that our frequent considering it will prove the best means to prevent the evil consequences of it. For although we cannot hope to plead innocence; yet which is next in point of wisdom this is the most effectual motive to bring us to repentance, and that which makes us repent, makes us to grow wise in time, and to lay a good foundation for eternal life. There are many arguments to induce us to repent, but there is no one more sensible, and which touches men more in point of interest and concernment than this of a judgment to come, and therefore we cannot take a surer road to eternal life, than frequently to reflect on it, and to let it sink deep into our minds, for shall we be awakened out of our security. So shall we be roused into a timely and serious acceptance—in a word, shall we make our peace with God whilst he is to be found and our iniquity shall not be our ruin. Now to God.

This is another of Smith's most-often delivered sermons. He gave it eight times on the Sunday past Easter or the second Sunday past Easter. He delivered it at St. James, Santee, April 6, 1766, April 2, 1769, and April 29, 1770; at Prince Frederick April 22, 1770; and at St. Philip's April 17, 1774, April 11, 1779, April 1790, and April 1795. This sermon is not indexed by Smith.

XXV

"Faith without Wavering"

Hebrews 10:23
Let us hold fast the profession of our faith without wavering.

SUCH WAS THE ADVICE which the Apostle gave to the Hebrews in consequence of the promises of God made unto them in the Gospel of Christ: asserting the faithfulness of him who made the promises, upon whom therefore, as they had sufficient reason to depend, so they ought to hold fast the profession of their faith without wavering. And forasmuch as these promises are not confined to the Hebrews only; but are our privilege also, we therefore being fellow heirs with them of these promises, ought, for the same reasons as they, to hold fast the profession of our faith also.

And indeed, as it was necessary, in the primitive ages of the gospel, to encourage its profession to stand firm and unshaken in the faith, on account of the many adversaries that fought against it: so is it necessary at present also, when the attacks of infidelity upon our religion are so frequent, and so full of every craft and strategem to overturn it, we then may take unto ourselves the same encouraging motives that the Hebrews did, and being fully assured that God, who has made these promises unto us in his hands; is faithful, he therefore will perform them in due time, and therefore let us also hold fast the profession of our faith without wavering.

But perhaps you'll ask what are the grounds of this our profession and faith? and therefore why do we believe these promises of the gospel to be the promises of God? is not the Christian, you'll say, a rational being? Should he not then act upon rational principles, and be able to give a reason of the hope that is in him? Very true. And to this we answer that the evidence of Christianity is the evidence upon which our profession and our faith is built; and from the evidence which we think to be sufficient, we are led to believe these promises to be promises of God. We profess ourselves rational beings, and to act upon rational principles our faith is not founded upon enthusiasm, but upon the most solid basis of reason itself;[1] and we apprehend we can give a sufficient reason of the hope that is in us. For if we believe Christ to be the Messiah of the Old Testament, which is one fundamental point[2] of our faith, it is because the prophesies of the Messiah were completed and fulfilled in Him. If we believe that Christ is a teacher sent from God, it is because the works that he did, bear witness of him that he came from God. If we believe the Apostles preaching the same religion, it is because none could do those miracles, which they did, unless God was with them. From hence then we infer that the Christian acts upon the most solid reason in believing the truth of his religion; for it is most certainly the direction of reason to believe those truths for which we have sufficient evidence. But waving this evidence, easily drawn from prophecies, our own Savior's working of miracles himself, let us consider those worked by him for the prophesies of old came not by the will of men, but holy men of God spake as they were moved by the Holy Ghost: or in working of miracles for as the gift of prophecy so likewise the gift of miracles was by the same Spirit.[3] This I say therefore will supply a subject proper for our consideration at this time. To begin then with prophesies and first, those of the Old Testament. If you enquire into these you will find they contain many plain and clear predictions not only of the coming of the Messiah in general, but they also point out to us so many particular circumstances which should attend him. They describe the place of his birth, to be Bethlehem, the time when he should be born, before the destruction of the second temple; the person of whom, a virgin, the particular tribe from whence he should spring; of the House of David, his condition whilst in this world, a man of sorrow and acquainted with grief; the manner of his death, that he should be cut off and be taken away by a violent death, out of the land of the living; and the end of his death for the transgression of the people; and that his soul should be made an offering for sin. Now as these and many other things mentioned in the prophesies of the Old Testament as relative to the Messiah were fulfilled in Christ, and in none else, what I pray is the inference but that Christ was the very Messiah foretold of in the Prophets, and that all who admit the truth of these prophesies, should submit to him as the Messiah which was expected and in consequence of this, acknowledge his religion to be from God.

But Christ not only fulfilled these prophesies of the Old Testament and thus proved himself to be the Messiah, but he also by that spirit[4] which was given him without measure, foretold several things himself and thus he proved himself a true prophet, and consequently to be sent from God. Thus he foretold that he should be betrayed and that by one of his disciples, he foretold his death, and the manner of it, his resurrection and the time when it should be accomplished, the destruction of Jerusalem, with some very remarkable circumstances that were to attend it, and which were most wonderfully accomplished, he foretold also the dispensation of the Jews, verified to this day, and also the wonderful progress of his gospel, notwithstanding the powers of the world were combined against it. These with other things, that might be mentioned, demonstrate him to be a true prophet. And as to foresee and foretell things which depend upon mere contingencies and free actions of mankind is the privilege of that being only, from whose eyes nothing is hid, and who sees through the whole compass of nature, it must follow from hence that whosoever does thus foretell things to come, must receive his knowledge from the Divine Being, and must act by his commission, and therefore ought to be believed as such in what he declares unto us.

But our blessed Savior not only fulfilled prophesies of the Old Testament, and so proved himself the Messiah, not only foretold several things himself which were afterwards strictly verified, and thus proved himself a true prophet. But still further[5] to confirm his Divine Commission, he was armed with all the power and demonstration of miracles. A proof this the force of which may be understood and judged of by the meanest capacities, miracles are appeals to the senses of mankind. Behold him then giving health to the sick, ears to the deaf, eyes to the blind, feet to the lame, tongues to the dumb, and even life to the very dead, and that not by the intervention of any natural causes, but by a mere word, a touch or the like; and this not once but often; not in the sight of friends only, but in the midst of enemies; not in private but in the public view of the world. If you will not conclude of such a person that God is with him of a truth especially when the doctrines he teaches, and the laws which he enforces are for the honor of God[6] there is no evidence one would think could satisfy you on this head. One thing I would observe as a recommendation of our religion, that the miracles of Christ not only displayed the flower of that God who is Lord of nature, but also the goodness of that same Divine Being who is likewise the Father of Mercies. For these miracles were not instances of power only, but also of compassion towards the Sons of Men in relieving their temporal necessities whilst it laid a foundation of that religion which bringeth life and immortality to the children of men.

But our blessed master did not work these miracles himself only, but he enabled his Apostles also to do the same. A portion of his spirit rested upon them also; and more especially by the descent of the Holy Ghost on the feast day of Pentecost commemorated this day[7] when the extraordinary powers of the Spirit of God, were publicly and more largely distributed amongst them. They therefore as they went forth preaching the glad tidings of the gospel, confirmed it with signs and wonders and mighty deeds. Treading in the steps of their blessed Master both by their doctrines and by their miracles, and were endued from above by the same spirit with the gift of tongues so as to be able to speak to every man in his own tongue in which he was born. By these means they prevailed over the power, the malice, and the long rooted prejudices both of the Jewish and the heathen world. Which carried such conviction with it, and all the wisdom,[8] and power of man could not resist, or prevent its spreading. It prevailed therefore over every obstacle and spread itself with so much rapidity that it soon extended itself to the most distant parts of the Earth. The judgments indeed in this case were but weak, for the most part a few, poor, ignorant, illiterate fishermen or the like. But the power of God wants not the assistance of man. The less therefore of worldly strength and policy the more must there have been of that wisdom and power which is from God.

If then you suppose that Christianity is false, you must either assent that Christ and his Apostles never wrought these miracles, or else supposing they did, yet that this is no sufficient evidence of a Divine commission. With regard to the first of these, it is indeed a supposition made use of by modern infidels, but was utterly unknown to the first ages of Christianity. The very enemies of the gospel in those times admitted the truth of the facts, and did not venture to deny them as they were so plain and public. So that the truth of the miracles were confessed by both parties, both friends and enemies. The dispute lay upon a very different point, i.e. they differed only in accounting for them. The Christian as he justly might[9] supposed them to be from the power of God; the other asserted them to be wrought by the power of evil spirits; But the present enemies of the gospel have changed the objection, and dispute the facts though their friends, who had the best opportunity of knowing the truth in this respect, admitted them. An evidence this in favor of our religion which is so much the stronger as it comes from the adversaries of our faith.

But perhaps you allow the truth of the miracles and yet deny their sufficiency to prove a Divine Commission. Consider then that as these miracles are evidently above the power of man to effect they that wrought them must either have been assisted by the Almighty[10] himself by good beings which act in submission to his will, or evil spirits which act in opposition to it. If these miracles were wrought by the immediate assistance of God himself then the Divine Commission is clear and evident. If by the help of any good spirit it will amount to the very same. Because good spirits act in subordination to, and according to the appointment of the supreme being. If you suppose it to be by the help of any evil spirit, it must involve this absurdity in that Satan[11] fights against Satan, as our Savior replied to the Jews upon the like occasion. For the gospel[12] in confirmation of which these miracles were wrought directly tend to the glory of God. By establishing the worship of the one true God, and teaching a religion that is pure and undefiled. And to the disgrace of such spirits by destroying their power, and putting an end to their worship which was paid them by the Heathen world. Add to this that it is scarce reconcilable to the notion of Divine Providence to suppose that any Being suppose it to be in the power of that Being[13] should be suffered to work such astonishing miracles, in confirmation of a falsehood as were wrought in defense of Christianity. For was this to be the case, without any means afforded to detect their falsehood, and to know that they came not from God, men and good men more especially, could scarce avoid running into false religion. Admit then the truth of these miracles, and you must also admit the truth of the gospel. But to this we may add as a still further recommendation[14] of our faith that which is called its eternal evidence. Let us then briefly examine this evidence of our religion which is contained principally[15] in the Scriptures of the New Testament, and which were written under the influence and direction of the Holy Ghost. As they were written by the Inspiration of God. By this enquiry you will find that the religion of the gospel is that very sort of religion which the present wants and necessities of mankind did require, and is most excellently adapted to their relief and recovery. A religion which is not only worthy of that God who is of purer eyes than to behold iniquity, so likewise of that God who is also the Father of mercies and God of comfort. Such considerations as these are strong arguments in favor of Christianity. To begin then with this evidence.

And I might first instance in that excellent rule of life which it has given us in its laws and precepts, so pure and holy as to bespeak their origin to be from heaven. So plain as to be understood by the meanest capacities, such as all the wisdom of the Heathen world would never teach, nor learn. It speaks indeed the very language of holiness itself, by teaching us to deny ungodliness and worldly lusts, and to live soberly, righteously, and godly. But to what purpose are laws without sufficient motives and encouragement to the practice of them? The gospel then has set before us both the terrors and the mercies of God to this purpose. It has displayed such motives as open to us a scene of existence beyond the grave; of life and immortality to the good and faithful Christian and of eternal misery and punishment to the wicked and impenitent, and indeed has afforded every motive which can affect the nature of man. But you will perhaps yet ask to what purpose are even laws and motives if we have not strength sufficient to obey them? The gospel then considered and offered a relief for this want also. For it does not bestow upon us of these times the extraordinary gifts of the Holy Spirit, yet it confers upon us that strength and help which is necessary and sufficient that we may live as the gospels directeth. It indeed affords no grounds for those enthusiastical pretences which some have made in these days, but yet it gives whatever assistance is necessary to enable us to walk as Christians ought to walk in holiness and righteousness. But to what purpose are laws given as a rule of life, motives proper to encourage us to the practice of them, and strength to enable us for the future to obey them. When by our past offences we are already subject to the displeasure of God. Something further then is still necessary for our relief and even this the gospel has offered to us. Behold then the mercy of God displayed in that redemption which is strong through Christ Jesus, whom God has set forth to be a proposition through faith in his blood, to declare his righteousness for the remission of sins that are past, through the forbearance of God. And to propose such terms as are agreeable to the present state of our nature, which though it will admit of perfect obedience yet will it of the sincere performance[16] of our duty, of repentance when we offend, and of growth in grace. Judge now then the wants of our nature. Consider its ignorance, its weakness and corruption, its want of motives and encouragements. And also that it is already obnoxious to the displeasure of Heaven. And then reflect upon the blessings which the gospel offereth. And you will find that it relieves every of our wants and from hence you may with reason conclude, that the religion which Christ has taught us, is not only suited to our necessities, but also worthy of that God, whose mercy, though it be in general over all his works, yet is in a more especial manner towards the Sons of Men. Such a religion as this our wishes must define, and I think our reason must approve. A religion which designed to reinstate us in the favor of God, from which we had fallen by our transgression and to recover us to the practice of holiness that we might be fit objects for the enjoyment of life and immortality. A design this so great and noble that the man who is not deaf to every call of virtue and his own happiness cannot well and surely will not reject.

This sermon is not indexed by Smith. The sermon is part of the Smith Family Papers at the South Carolina Historical Society.

XXVI

"Overcoming the World"

1 John 5:4
This is the victory that overcometh the world, even our faith.

O F ALL THE CONQUESTS that can be made by man,[1] this over the world is by
far the greatest.

For, whether we consider the infirmity of human nature, or the many
allurements of the world, the difficulties of our spiritual warfare must
needs be[2] extremely great; the issue and event of it very hazardous. And when at last,
through God's grace we are conquerors;[3] the victory we gain cannot be, of all others,
the most honorable and glorious. And our obligations to virtue, we are daily carried
out to that which is vicious and sinful. In this manner St. Paul complains in the character of a sinner, we know that the law is spiritual: but I am carnal, sold under sin. For
what I would that I do not; but what I hate, that I do. And we have all of us, abundant
reason to cry out with him, and wretched man that I am, who shall deliver me from
the body of his death. But, however desperate and melancholy our condition may
seem to be, at first sight, we have equal reason with the same Apostle to thank God,
through Christ our Lord. For, what neither the law of Moses would do; God the Father
hath done effectually by sending his own son to die for us; and thereby to make us
free from the law of sin and death. We may well join[4] in that rapturous exaltation of
the Apostle, I can do all things through Christ which strengtheneth me: Or else, in the
words of my text, this is the victory that overcometh the world, even our faith.

In my ensuing discourse, I shall first show[5] the nature of the Christian faith in general. Secondly, the several essential properties of it more distinctly. Thirdly, the benefits
and advantages of it. Christian faith delivered to us[6] in the writings of the Apostles and
Prophets. And as seated in the understanding and heart of man, and considered as a
religious habit and disposition of mind, it is a rational and firm assent to the doctrines
of the gospel; together with such a serious and settled attention to them, as produces a

firm and humble reliance upon the truth and certainty of them: and this is joined with such an inviolable regard to all the precepts of it, and such a steady and uniform course of virtue and piety, as is in some measure answerable to such great and glorious expectations. For as St. John observes, every one that hath this hope purifieth himself, even as he is pure.

The right notion of the Christian faith which may be understood in this manner is such a proper sense of our unworthiness[7] in the sight of God, as creates in us a serious and awful apprehension of His displeasure on this account. But, it is,[8] at the same time, such a firm belief of God's unspeakable love to his creatures, of his readiness to accept returning sinners; as produceth in us the most affectionate thankful remembrance of these mercies.[9]

And this is joined with such a steadfast belief of all His promises and threatenings, as encourageth us to look unto Him only, for mercy and compassion; for pardon and salvation, to secure us in the hour of temptation; and to sanctify and change our natures; by inclining our wills to God and goodness. Add to this the most entire and perfect resignation of ourselves, our wills and affections to the will of God; with a sincere desire, a serious and diligent endeavor to live according to His laws; to do His will on Earth, as it is done in Heaven; to grow in grace to work out our salvation; and as far as is consistent with the infirmities of humanity to have our conversation in Heaven; to be holy, comparatively speaking, as God is holy; perfect as our Father who is in Heaven is perfect.[10]

But in order to show the nature of the Christian faith more distinctly; let us examine the several particular properties of it.[11]

The first is a rational[12] and well-grounded assent to the doctrines of the Gospel. This assent is not an enthusiastic fancy, not a groundless opinion, but rests upon[13] the solid and firm foundation of reason. And therefore, it does not, by any means, decline or shun an impartial inquiry, and a fair examination; but it freely submits its evidence to a candid hearing and equitable decision; and only desires to stand or fall, by its own intrinsic excellence.[14]

Upon which account, our blessed Savior, in His discourse with the Jews, and in His disputes with the Scribes, and Pharisees, does all along address Himself not to their passions, but to their understandings. His arguments are all drawn[15] from the avowed principles of human reason. His discourse proceeds, and His conclusions follow, according to the strictest laws and methods of arguing. He does not expect to be believed, nor that His doctrines should be received merely upon the strength of His own word; but after demonstrating their suitableness to our nation and state, to give them a better sanction and authority.[16] He constantly appeals to the prophecies concerning Him, and to the miracles which he wrought publicly amongst them.

Thus, He says, "the works which the Father hath given me to finish, the same works bear of me, that the Father hath sent me. And if I do not the works of my Father, believe me not; but if I do, though you believe not me, believe the works: that you may know and believe, that the Father is in me, and I in Him."

It seems there was so much force of reason, and strength of argument in our Lord's discourse; that several of His hearers were convinced and converted accordingly. Christian faith, then, is a rational assent, a well-grounded persuasion; perfectly[17] agreeable to the soundest principles of human reason. And as this foundation of God standeth sure, since He always abideth faithful;[18] even so is the faith that is built upon it, firm and steady.

And this is another property of it. It is not a wavering[19] unsteady principle; perplexed with doubts, distracted with fears, and tossed about[20] with every wind of doctrine: But it is a firm and settled persuasion of mind, concerning the certainty[21] of those promises and threatenings, which we meet in the writings of the New Testament. It is a steadfast[22] assurance, and humble and unshaken reliance upon the veracity, the justice, and the goodness of God.

Different degrees of this faith, undoubtedly there are mixed perhaps with some degrees of scruples such as that of St. Peter, which our Savior reproved with these words, "O though of little faith, wherefor didst thou doubt?" An unsteady faith like this, is by no means, however a sufficient principle of virtue and piety; but must needs be followed by a conduct unequal and unsteady, as that principle from which it proceeds. For as the spring cannot rise higher than its first source; neither can our obedience than the fountain, from whence it flows. Indeed the sequel to Peter's history is abundant to confirm the truth of his observation. Therefore it was, that our Lord foreseeing the ill effects of so weak a faith; said to him, just before His Passion, "I have prayed for thee, that thy faith fail not."[23]

A sufficient intimation that any defect in this divine principle is always accompanied with a proportionable failure in our duty and obedience: And as a weak faith always produces a very defective so is a lively faith constantly productive of a steady obedience to the will, and the commands of God.[24]

To confirm which observations; let us cast an eye upon the history of St. Paul's life;[25] and we shall find towards the close of it, a full assurance of and dependence upon[26] the truth of the divine promises. For, when this great Apostle was brought before Nero the second time; when he was ready to be offered, and the time of his departure was at hand; with what undaunted resolution,[27] he looks through the veil of death, into the world of spirits, to that glorious reward, which then was reserved for him. And when we consider the grounds of that confidence,[28] we shall have no reason to wonder at the boldness, which that Christian hero discovers upon this awful and trying occasion. "Nevertheless," says he, "I am not ashamed for I know whom I have believed; I am persuaded, that he is able to keep that which I have committed unto him, against that day. I have fought a good fight, I have finished my course, I have kept the faith. Henceforth there is laid up for me a crown of righteousness, which the Lord the righteous judge shall give me at that day." And certain it is that those who receive[29] the word of God with joy, who embrace the promises of the Gospel with sincere affection; will be naturally disposed to give a serious and fixed attention to those great and glorious objects of the Christian faith; which is another essential property[30] of it.

The Christian faith brings constantly to our minds, and sets before us, in the most lively and affecting manner, the things of another life. It gives us a sort of foretaste of the joys and glories of Heaven. And for this reason, it is said of our Blessed Savior Himself; that for the joy that was set before Him, He endured the cross, and despised the shame He submitted to, in the discharge of His mediatorial office.

This foresight, and desire of our glorified state, is by St. Paul called, "the earnest expectation of the creature," which waits, with a sort of religious impatience, for the manifestation of the sons of God.

It was this vanishing foretaste of the joys of Heaven, that made Him reckon all the sufferings of this present life, not willing to be compared with the glory which was soon to be revealed in Him. It was this that enabled Him to walk by faith, not by sight; to overlook the things which are seen; and to extend His view to those things, which are not to be seen with the eyes of the flesh. Thus it is said of Moses, that he had respect unto the recompense of reward: that is, He fixed His attention upon it, and kept it constantly in view. And to say the truth, a religious attention to the doctrines of the Gospel is, as I may so speak, the very life and soul of the Christian faith. Unless we keep those great and glorious objects constantly in our eye we cannot possibly walk by faith, and have our conversation in Heaven. The very moment we lose sight of them, we lose sight of our duty at the same time. This devout attention is an essential property of the Christian faith. There is an inseparable connection between faith and practice: and all the sin and wickedness, which we see in the world proceeds from the weakness and deadness of faith; and from the want of this religious attention to the doctrines of the gospel: and this can only be cherished and be kept alive by carefully reading and meditating upon the holy scriptures by considering ourselves as strangers in this world; by looking up frequently to Heaven; and by setting God always before us, and walking daily in His presence. Without all this, there is no such thing as being truly holy in this life, nor happy in the next. And this leads to another property[31] of the Christian faith; which is, that it is always productive of righteousness and holiness of life.

Christian faith is a lively active principle; that naturally exerts itself in a regular and uniform course of virtuous and good actions.

It is as St. Paul speaks, a faith which worketh by love. It is such a serious and firm belief of, and such a fixed and settled attention to, the doctrines of the gospel; as naturally disposes and inclines us, to make all possible returns to God, for this inestimable mercies to us in Christ Jesus. It is what the Apostle calls a work of faith, a labor of love, and patience of hope in our Lord Jesus Christ. It is such a faith as is fruitful of good works; such as constantly labors by all possible means, to show the most ardent and unfeigned love of God and our neighbor: such a faith in God's promises, and such a firm and unshaken hope of enjoying them, in this due time; as enables us with patience and perseverance, to wade through all the difficulties and discouragements which we often meet with in the discharge of our duty.

We must not be weary, nor faint in our minds, when we are beset with difficulties and discouragements: but we must hold the beginning of our confidence steadfast unto the end. Unless we do so, our faith will profit us nothing, we cannot possibly be saved by it. For, as St. James observes, faith, if it have not works, is dead being alone: and again, by works is faith made perfect. Faith is the great root of the Christian life: and if there be any life in the root, good works will naturally grow and branch out of it. But where these do not spring from it, it is a certain sign, that the root is dead; that the vital principle of the spiritual life is perfectly extinguished. But when the Christian faith is accompanied with good works, with uniform and universal obedience; yet even in this case, the faithful Christian does not presume upon his own righteousness, nor place any manner of trust and confidence in his own performances; he gives all[32] the glory to God, and hopes for the salvation only through the merits of Jesus Christ.

There is such a mixture of imperfection in our best services, that they stand in need of all the gracious allowances, which a merciful God can probably make. And surely there can be no room for boasting, or a presumptuous reliance upon our own righteousness. For we are so far from doing more than our duty, that we do not even so much as we are able to do. We might be, all of us, more just and charitable, more honorable and forgiving, more patient and contented, more pure and holy, more spiritual and Heavenly minded than the very best of us are. And, if God were to enter into strict judgment with us, extreme to mark everything we do amiss, and to deal with us according to our deserts; no flesh could be justified in His sight nor able to stand in His presence. And, as for that small share of holiness which we have, it is entirely the gift of God. For it is God that worketh in us both to will and to do, of His good pleasure.

Since then it is God only, that maketh us to differ from the rest of the world; and since we have nothing that is good, but what we have received at His hands; we must not presume to glory as if we had not received it. But let him that glorieth, glory in the Lord. For by grace are we saved, through faith; and that not ourselves, it is the gift of God; not of works, lest any man should boast. Well then may we say, in the words of the prophet, "Surely in God have I righteousness and strength." In our Savior shall all fruitful Christians be justified, and shall glory. He is of God made unto us wisdom, and righteousness, and sanctification, and redemption. For there is no salvation in any other: there is none other name under Heaven, given among men, whereby we must be saved.

When we consider the many feelings and miscarriages of our lives, and the manifold defects of our best services; we should cover ourselves with shame and confusion of face. We should lament the corruption of our natures, and the sins of our lives. The sense of both together is so very afflicting, that it would overwhelm us; were it not for that comfortable prospect, that bright sunshine and full assurance of faith and hope;

which our belief in, and dependence upon,the merits of our Savior doeth at all times furnish us with. For, notwithstanding that we have the most lively and affecting sense of our unworthiness and guilt, on the one hand; yet on the other, in Jesus Christ, we have boldness, and access with confidence by faith of Him. Because, being justified by faith, we have peace with God, through our Lord Jesus Christ.

Smith delivered this sermon four times at St. Philip's: April 1770, March 1774, March 1788, and April 1798. The sermon is indexed by Smith as #390. It is part of the Smith Family Papers at the South Carolina Historical Society.

XXVII

The Efficacy of National Virtue
for Securing National Felicity

W ERE THERE NO OTHER EVIDENCES of the Being and, Providence of Almighty God, than those which observation and experience point out, the manifestations of a wise and merciful superintendence are very clear and demonstrable. God hath not left himself without a witness in any part of his creation, in the wonderful contrivance of the universe—and the wise disposal of its several parts;[1] in support of that nature he commanded into being; and in his care of those creatures he called forth to life and happiness.[2]

In speaking of the operations of almighty power, we talk indeed of nature, and natural causes, as if independence of Providence; but what is nature, but the hand of God; and natural causes, but secret effects of omnipotence; directing us, in the most striking and intelligible manner, to the first efficient cause of all. But lest the notices of providence should either be overlooked or forgotten by us, Almighty God. No wonder then, if our hopes prove abortive,[3] and the conceits of our vain minds end in disappointment and sorrow. For inclined to attribute our prosperity to the wisdom of our own councils, and the arm of our own flesh, we become forgetful of him from whom our strength and wisdom are derived; and are thus betrayed into that fatal[4] security which ends in shame, in misery and vain.

As a curb therefore to the arrogance of man, in the Jewish history, God hath declared his power over, and government of the world; instructing us, that apart of his blessing, vain is the counsel[5] and the help of men; that with it, the most improbable can administer happiness, and afford security. He can smite the rock, and it shall gush out with water, He can command the heavens, and they shall rain down food; how shall a little one chase a thousand; yea, ten thousand shall fall down before him?

The part of scripture under our present consideration is very express to this point. The sacred writings inform us, that Sennacherib, the great King of Assyria, having subdued the neighboring states and nations, marched a prodigious army to Jerusalem.

Being discontented it seems, with the usual tribute which was paid him, he demanded of the people that they should deliver the city into his hands. At the same time threatening in case of refusal, to lay waste the country with fire and sword.[6] In these calamitous circumstances, Hezekiah, who then reigned over the Jews had recourse to that Being, whose protection he and his people had often experienced. He rent his clothes, and put on sackcloth; and confiding in the justice of his cause he went to the temple, and implored God's assistance against his enemies.[7]

The book of Kings is more particular in this relation, than that of Chronicles; and informs us, that he received an answer from the prophet Isaiah, full of comfort and satisfaction.[8] The man of God informed him, that the Almighty had heard his prayer and would defend his cause; he might therefore be of good comfort, and dismiss every fear concerning the strength and number of the foe.

Hezekiah had too often experienced the divine veracity, to doubt the accomplishment of this gracious promise. He therefore made everything for a serious defense. He had his people enrolled, who were fit for war; he appointed over them proper officers.[9] He provided darts and shields in great abundance, and all other weapons to defend the place and annoy the enemy. And being thus prepared with every requisite, he addressed the people in terms like these.

[illegible] with truth and equity, is able to deliver us out of their hands. I need not recount to you the many instances of the divine interposition and goodness to us. For many of you must be living witnesses[10] of the miracles wrought for our sakes. Why should I mention the wonders in Egypt, in the red sea, and in the barren wilderness? Repeated have been the instances of God's protection, so long as we were objects worthy of his notice and reform his conduct[11] without delay, that the city be not destroyed for his sake. In general, I think I can testify, for you, that your hearts and lives are right before God. We have learnt wisdom from the folly of our fathers; have turned unfeignedly to the God of our strength. Go on therefore, and prosper in the name of the Lord. Make use of the means with which Providence hath furnished you,[12] and depend on Heaven for success against your foes. For the prophet assures me, that the victory shall certainly be yours; be strong therefore, and courageous. Be not dismayed for the King of Assyria nor for all the multitude that is with him; for there be more with us than with him. With him is an arm of flesh; but with us is the Lord our God to help us and to fight our battles.

And surely, this was a most encouraging declaration,[13] that the Lord of Hosts would fight their battles; and the God of armies be their defense. Great reason had they to be strong and courageous; not to be dismayed for the King of Assyria, nor for all the multitude that was with him. Their manners and integrity were of that stamp, which the divine goodness would not fail to bless with favor and protection, with victory and with honor.

Thus happy were the people of Israel, while they retained allegiance to the Lord their God and thus happy will be any other people[14] while they continue virtuous and religious people; for all the Kingdoms of the earth are God's; and He ruleth alike in all. He bestows and he withdraws his mercy; not with an arbitrary or partial hand; but by the strictest rule of unbiased equity. He confers his blessings on those alone, who by true desert, and moral worth, are proper objects of it. Under a strong conviction of this great truth that authority[15] hath called us to this public meeting. Sensible that success depends on God; that it is He who breaketh the bow, and snappeth the spear in sunder; who pulleth down the mighty from their seat, and disappointeth the designs of the lofty; we are commanded to search and try our ways; like the iniquity of our hearts obstruct not that protection against our enemies which we have now so solemnly implored.

It would be injustice done to this audience, not to acknowledge the seriousness with which you have implored the divine rod; an earnest this, I trust, that you will certainly obtain it. You have truly joined in owning the necessity of the royal all; that as the sword hath long been unsheathed in the land; not through unreasonable thirst of empire; but in the sole defense of undoubted right; should we beg the Almighty to bless our arms; and grant us the enjoyment of a lasting peace.

And thus far all is well. In acknowledging the absolute power of God; our dependence on his mercy; and unworthiness of it, we have acted a proper and becoming part; but let us remember this; that we have ill answered the intentions of our superiors, if we rest the duty here; confine it to the church and closet, to acts of mere devotion only; and extend not the reflections, suggested by this solemn occasion, to our principles and our manners; to every branch of our conduct, both in public and in private life. If then we mean well to our country, and are earnest in our wishes for its happiness; we must in language of scripture, "cease to do evil, and learn to do well"; we must acquire these virtuous habits and dispositions, which alone can recommend any people to the God of uprightness, and effectually secure them his protection. And as national virtues are but the virtues of individuals collected; it is the duty of every private person, as a member of that society in which he dwells, to be very cautious lest his misconduct, joined to the misconduct of many others be the fatal bar to the divine protection.[16]

Being therefore in the hands of one, who requireth truth in the inward parts; who is privy to all our thoughts, and spieth out all our ways; may it not be proper for each on these occasions, to retire within himself, and ask his heart these important questions; Am I the very person I would appear to be; concerned for may own, and the public good? Are my pretentions to virtuous and religious practices sincere and real; or being the daubings only of outward varnish, do they hide the deformity of a fowl heart, of iniquitous deed, and bad design? In my several relations in life, do I pursue that conduct which alone and which in concerning the design of Providence, is the indispensable duty of a reasonable creature.

Whatever is my part in life, do I act it well, and contribute my share to public happiness? As a magistrate, a parent, a master, or a servant; is my behavior such as the eye of Heaven can approve? Are my intentions upright; my sentiments benevolent; my professions sincere; my behavior exemplary; or frustrating the ends of God's moral government, and confounding the order intended by Providence do I suffer every selfish and sordid passion to rule in my breast without control? In fine, is the end I aim at a right and laudable one; or have I not yet considered whether in my passage through life, I have proposed to myself any end or no.

Should a review like this appear distasteful, we may well suspect, there is something wrong within. For why should we desire an acquaintance with almost every trifling object; and shun by far the most important of all, an acquaintance with our own lives and hearts? Is it because the interview would give us pain? Perhaps we dare not look within, because we cannot with complacency.

As we of this state in particular[17] have been blessed with signal marks of God's protection, our gratitude to Heaven should bear some proportion to the mercies vouchsafed. Disobedience under our circumstances is doubly heinous, and will greatly increase the offenders punishment. For how has God surrounded us with blessings on every side; while other countries have been the seat of war, and felt all the miseries of the sword of fire, and famine? While we have been secure and free from danger, populous cities have been consumed, and fruitful countries have been destroyed, so that as the seas encompass the land, the protection of heaven has blessed us on every side.

What returns we have made, for these lengthenings of our tranquility, does not indeed appear—no visible ones at least. We have still many follies to restrain, many vices to subdue; and though there appears not that daring impiety of which some complain; yet that religion hath lost much of its force amongst us is very plain; from the disregard for worship, that contempt of authority; that love of dissipation and of pleasure, and that dissoluteness of manners which is daily before us. Instead of that cordial affection which as Christians should unite us with the closest bands, how often are the smallest differences in sentiment made the weak foundations of a confirmed aversion for each other. And the noble benevolence of the gospel forgot amidst contentions for childish opinions, and indifferent rites. How often are the moral those essential duties of our religion, which alone can make us good and useful men, exchanged for shadows, chimeras, nothing.

To a God of truth and purity, practices of this kind must be highly odious. As the only means then of securing that divine protection, we should earnestly resolve to put away the coil of our doings, and cherish those virtuous and religious principles, which will ever add to our real welfare. When virtue and true religion flourish in a state, it is happy and prosperous; when they decline, the strength and glory of it declines also; and avarice, luxury and effeminacy lead the way to ruin. It is the genius of true religion to inspire the mind with every noble virtue; the love of our country, generosity, fortitude, temperance. But it is the genesis of irreligion to instill narrow, selfish principles; a contempt for everything great and noble; monopolizing avarice and mean cowardice. The different tendencies of these principles should surely then, direct us in our choice of them; and our own experience of this influence, should confirm us in it. Can we then hesitate a moment which to prefer? But as we have now acknowledged our folly, and notice most solemn manner vowed better obedience; let us in earnest set about a great work of reform. Let each of us in his sphere and station contribute our share, let our magistrates lead the way, and thousands will catch the fashion from them. Let them be examples of every noble and virtuous requirement, of temperance, moderation, fidelity and honor, let them reverence that Almighty Being on whom they depend for all things; and they will find the advantage of so wise a conduct—they will find it in the willing obedience of their children; in the duty and faithfulness of their dependents, in the constancy of their friends; and the admiration and fear of their enemies. Instead

[A page is missing from the original.]

and preserve us from them that lie in wait to destroy us. Then may we be strong and very courageous, and need not be dismayed for all the host that are against us; being assured that there is more with us than with them. For though with them is an arm of flesh yet with us will be the Lord our God to help us fight our battles.

The text reference for this sermon is not on the manuscript, but Smith's index indicates the text to be 2 Chronicles 32:7–8. The first time it was delivered was in England at Royal Chapel, Greenwich, perhaps on the occasion of Smith's installation as rector of St. Philip's. As Smith notes on the manuscript, he gave the sermon at St. Philip's in 1775 with variations and different text. He delivered it a final time at St. Philip's on April 23, 1778. The first portion of the first paragraph was reconstructed from the 1759 version of the sermon. The sermon is indexed by Smith as #236, and he credits Wilton as an original source. Smith supplied the sermon's title.

Textual Annotations

THESE NOTES REPRESENT, as comprehensively as practical, the editorial changes made by Smith to the manuscript of each sermon. As discussed in the introduction, these changes were probably made either prior to the initial delivery or between successive deliveries. The latter instance is particularly likely for sermons delivered during the Revolution. At times attempted editorial changes were unreadable, and in others it was impossible to decipher where in the manuscript the changes were intended to be placed. Those instances, however, were few, and in such cases the original language was maintained.

The symbols used are in the following list. In instances where Smith replaced existing material with revisions, the cancelled material is indicated before the material that replaces it. Insertions without cancellations are listed without context phrases as long as their identification is clear in the text. Otherwise, an insertion is accompanied by the phrase that provides it context.

Symbols:
< > Cancellation or strikethrough
{ } Smith's insertion or overwrite
[ ] Editorial insertion
¶ Smith's intended paragraph

Example:
variously applied by <varied> {different} men.

The textual note that would represent the manuscript passage ". . . variously applied by different men."

When it improved readability, separate paragraphs were combined, and original paragraph breaks have been noted with "¶."

Sermon I. "Ruling in the Fear of God"

1. These words <are> {though} variously rendered and as variously applied by different men: <are yet in the general acceptation of them more particularly applied to David the pious and> some with a little change of the version understand and

2. are not only proper but highly necessary; because since <sinful> man is more apt to walk "by sight, than <to walk> by faith"

3. which we may cultivate, partly from those unavoidable evils, from which <as we hinted before> such a

4. strength to a sound and vigorous constitution of body, <not> they are either not all observed <by us>, or else

5. inestimable privileges, there is <we praise God> no national establishment in the world, better provided with laws, both wise and excellent, {through kingdoms and provinces to which we belong} and yet even these

6. the important trust committed to them with honor to themselves, and benefit to <others> {those over whom they preside}.

7. <First, that ruleth be <u>just</u>; in order to which, two things are requisite; the one that he should have a competent knowledge of all those particular statutes or laws which during the time of his magistracy, he may or shall have frequent occasion to execute. For how can he reasonably be supposed able to discharge with equity or credit, that important trust, which is committed to his care and management, who is altogether unacquainted with the rules of his duty? How should be able to decide, or to distinguish, what is right from what is wrong? Or to know what penalties are due to such or such offences; or to order the just proportion of men, who is ignorant of those laws. By which right and wrong are to be determined; and by which alone the particular penalties and their proportion are allotted to trangressors?

If such magistrates err not in their determinations or decisions, it ought to be imputed, not so much to their virtue, as to their good luck: and what a misfortune will it be to those who live under their government, to have their reputations—their interests—and all that is dear to them in this world, depend, not on the wisdom of their rulers, but on the blind ambition of chance! And as it is a requisite, that he should have a competent knowledge of those particular statutes of laws which may or shall concern him during his magistracy.

So is it, also, no less requisite, that he should execute, on all proper occasions, those statutes or laws without prejudice or partiality. For the knowledge of those laws, without a fair and impartial execution of them, will be of no other use to him, than to aggravate his guilt, and render it more inexcusable. Inasmuch, as "that servant, which knew his masters will, but did it not, shall be thought worthy of much sorer punishment, than he that shall transgress his masters will, through ignorance or mistake.">
{First, He that ruleth over men must be just; and must execute all those particular statutes or laws, which he may or shall have frequent occasion to execute, without prejudice or partiality.}

8. comfort those that do <u>good</u>; and terrify and restrain only those that do <u>evil</u>. <Nevertheless these qualifications of knowledge and impartiality are not sufficient for the magistrate, or rather the magistrate is not sufficient for them:> {Nevertheless this qualification of impartiality is not sufficient for the magistrate, or rather the magistrate is not sufficient for it: Unless,} secondly, He rules

9. great soever he be, that shall dare to offend; like a good shepherd, he will protect the people <over whom he makes rules>, which are his flock;

10. Whereas if he exerts <himself> his courage in the execution of

11. the dignity of his <function> {office}, that, in some measure,

12. a serious reflection or your own character should make you dare {to do anything assiduously because of it; and only fear and scorn} to do anything which is beneath and

13. ensue: considering <the express word of God,> these things, I presume,

14. how sharply St. Paul reproves <all> those that

15. obedience to the just laws of <God.> {man, and the holy laws of God.} For to such, will the great judge eternal at the last day pronounce well done good and faithful servants; enter ye into your Master's joy—which may God <out> of his infinite mercy <which that all.> {say to us all through.}

Sermon II. On the Importance of Religion to Society

1. fixed on this most {firm} basis, on the most solid principle, the fear of the Lord. Nor are they the worse for being destitute for the most part of any connection or coherence <together> with one another,

2. It is, I apprehend, universally allowed <amongst writers>, that the principle motive

3. provide much better for the accommodations and conveniences of <more elegant> life,

4. Now <the expectation of> this reward cannot be expected

5. Having thus in general shown the vast importance of religion to society, I <shall> {should} now proceed to show the great, the mighty advantages, with which the Christian religion is in particular attended. I <shall> {should} now proceed to point out, <to you my brethren> how admirably this religion is calculated

6. Most highly therefore doth it import all good men{, to consider} that they are not

7. advanced above their fellow citizens, to those who <may be considered as luminaries of the> {are high in office, the guardians of our} community,

8. yet it is more peculiarly so {and} in <the> {these} perilous times,

Sermon III. "Keep All My Commandments Always"

1. [The first part of the sermon is missing. It was reconstructed from the sermon delivered in 1759 on which this sermon was based.]

2. {of Heaven}

3. For [we are] inclined to attribute our prosperity

4. The <words> {part} of scripture

5. lightly esteem." ¶ {It is not my intention to enlarge upon the doctrine of fear and obedience, because they are of themselves pretty obvious—neither does the occasion of this day's solemnity require it—but} should anyone ask,

6. mighty things that God had done for them in Egypt it was always <to remind them> to stimulate them

7. continue the favorites of <Heaven> {God}, than while we fear Him

8. and our Children after us." <If the cause of God, and obedience to his laws have glory.>

9. {While their manners and integrity were of that stamp, which the divine goodness could not fail to bless with favor and protection.}

10. <It is> Under a strong conviction of this great truth, and <that people of the province are called to this public meeting, to search and try your ways, that the iniquity of our hearts might obstruct not that protection we have so much implored in this our day of distress.> {sensible that the success of all events depend on God. I hope it is, that we are here met together, to search and try our ways, that the iniquity of our hearts obstruct not the protection we have so much reason to implore.}

11. {some would insinuate}

12. If then we are serious <and earnest> in thus humbling ourselves

13. {many}

14. religious <actions> {practices}, sincere and real;

15. In my several relations <of> {in}

16. As a member of <society> {the community},

17. I have proposed to myself any end <at all> or no.

18. {the world, and its}

19. {that little world}

20. and <shall> {will} not God visit

21. darkness{.} {There is no knowing what the desires of heaven are with respect to sinful people; how long they may stand, or when fall, is had from the age of man; but of these one may be assured, that a sincere repentance and solemn humbling themselves before God, is the only way to avert or prolong the date of their pain. Let us then upon this solemn occasion turn unto the Lord, and he will have mercy upon us, and to our God who will abundantly pardon. Let us take this opportunity to begin our amendments,}

22. we <shall> {should} earnestly resolve

23. let these on whom <fortune> {a kind providence} has lavished her favor.

24. Men <who call themselves gentlemen and whose station in life constitutes them a right to that appellation> {of large fortunes and extensive influence}

25. {Nay their fame shall reach beyond the ends of the earth, shall mount up to the battlements of Heaven and become the praise and admiration of angels.}

26. {In a word—as the sins of a community are made up of the sins of individuals, and can no otherwise be diminished than by the reformation of individuals—And as it is in every man's power to reform himself, this also in every means, power to contribute something towards appeasing God's wrath and procuring His protection, and consequently toward saving himself and country from ruin.} Instead {then} that neglect

27. {all} our troubles; and thenceforth continue long to flourish in peace, {in plenty,}

Sermon IV. "By the Fear of the Lord, Men Depart from Evil"

1. that <slavish> servile terror
2. {in some measure}
3. men{'s actions}
4. {often}
5. {as is often practiced in our own happy constitution}
6. {any} afflictions, that may befall us, or to indulge our impure desires, <and> {our}
7. Thus even <in respect> {from the consideration of} those duties
8. unless the fear of <God> {the Lord} should cooperate
9. {the laws of}
10. The mighty advantages which <arise> {result} from the due and equal distribution of justice, <are as strong an argument as reason>
11. {that gratitude and justice}
12. Having thus <proved> {ascertained} the point which I undertook,
13. foolishly. <The wisest consultations must be held in vain, in vain must we then offer up our petitions to the throne of grace, if> {In vain the wisest deliberations would be held, in vain the legislative body would enact laws and interest itself in the welfare and prosperity of the community, in vain would our own petitions be offered up at the throne of grace that the Almighty would be pleased to direct all their consultations to the good of his church, the honor of our sovereign, and the welfare and prosperity of the province, if those in whose hands the laws are lodged, do not cooperate with the legislature, and use their utmost endeavors that peace and happiness, truth and justice, religion and piety may be established amongst us. And how can this be affected, unless they, to whom this charge is entrusted, make it their peculiar care, that} those laws which are justly framed, are as vigorously executed.
14. there is no iniquity with the Lord our God, <nor respect of persons>

Sermon V. "Let No Man Seek His Own, but Every Man Another's Wealth"

1. <This is and such a quality as that ought to be aimed at, as a> {Men of this temper and frame, under Divine Providence keep up the being and dignity of communities and are some} check
2. <The Apostle discoursing in this chapter concerning the lawfulness of eating things offered in sacrifice to idols, does upon that occasion exhort the Corinthians, that whatever they might imagine to be their duty in that respect, they should by all means avoid giving offense, intimating, that though it might be lawful to eat those things, so that they did not partake of the sacrifice, yet it might not be expedient, nor tend to edification. All things, says he, in the verse before the text, are lawful for me, but all things are not expedient: all things are lawful for me, but all things edify not. And from this particular instance, he makes a general conclusion, that men ought always to seek the good of others. Not barely their own private satisfaction.> {The Apostle's command in

the text is preemptory, "Let no man seek his own, but every man another's wealth." Which} this rule will hold good

3. in his actions regarding <only> himself
4. <qualification> {quality}
5. {owing to ignorance, or want of education}
6. <subject> {member}
7. <For notwithstanding the impious efforts of a slavish philosopher in the last age, it is now almost universally admitted, that man by the circumstances of his own being, and the constitution of things about him, as well as the express instructions of divine revelation, was designed and required by providence, to act under the agreeable character of a social creature: and that all the Sons of Adam should consider themselves as branches of the same family; as parts of the same general body, and members of another.> With no view can men be better connected together;

8. <There is, moreover, another very agreeable circumstance that attends this social combination. The various apprehensions of mankind, the different opinions entertained upon points of government and policy, as well as upon subjects of a higher nature, are too often apt to inflame the passions, create animosities, and produce, at best, a cold disregard; and sometimes, much rage and fierceness: but this mutual intercourse in works of charity, smooths and rubs off these asperities. A joint labor of love, by uniting in some measure the views of different persons, forma a kind of friendly cement; softens the angry passions, and abates that severe and harsh opinion, which men of different sentiments and views are too ready to entertain and propagate upon the character of another; while the same earnest concurrence in such charitable works, an equal zeal to prosecute the same good designs, naturally create a better opinion of each other, and afford just reason mutually to believe, that differences upon other masters do not take their rise from such bad principles, as are too often imprinted by angry opponents: such united acts of charity and compassion publicly confute the narrow and suspicious query can any good thing come out of Nazareth? Nor should it be omitted, that the better to answer the benevolent purpose of this society, and conciliate more friendship among its members, no other distinction is observed in the treatment of the distressed, than the reality and greatness of their distress.

Such is the constitution, and such the management of this excellent community! And are arguments requisite to gain a favorable reception to a work so truly beneficent! Can human nature need persuasion to encourage such a design; or can a Christian require any importunity thus to obey and imitate his blessed Savior? With what engaging force do religion and humanity, or reason and affections, generosity and justice, love to our fellow-creatures, love to our country, love to ourselves; the pleasure, the honor, the reward of such beneficence, all, plead the moving cause so much innocent distress.

Can the least doubt remain in any breast whether this pious and useful design, undertaken with compassion, and conduct with prudence, deserves approbation, or censure? Whether an establishment so helpful to the orphan, and munificent to the widow, should be generously encouraged, or totally destroyed? I speak it distinctly, totally destroyed. For those, who refuse a proper assistance, when it is in the power of their hand to grant it, declare aloud by such refusal, "Let this design perish and come to naught."

Indifference and disregard, or the smoother language of empty applause, with kind wishes and good hopes that encouragement may continue to arise; what is all this, but aggravating the guilt of an avaricious and uncharitable mind? What is it, but publicly owning, we ought to give, when we cruelly determine to grant no help?

Very unwilling I am to suppose, that there can be an individual person so insensible, so regardless of a duty of the highest obligation: God forbid, that there should be one heart so obstinate, so void of all the affections of a man, all sense of religion as a Christian. Are the sorrows of the distressed less genuine, is their misery less grievous because providence has kindly placed you in circumstances not convenient with scenes of woe.> Could you hear the melancholy sound

9. chamber but of one dying <man>;

10. <That we may never be inattentive to the complaints of the necessitous, and never unheard, when we implore the miseries of heaven, may the God of all truth and kindness grant!> {But besides these motives in favor of this charitable work, the great instability of temporal affairs, and constant fluctuation of everything in this world, is a very powerful argument likewise in favor of it. For what by successive misfortunes; so many surprising revolutions do every day happen in families, that it may not seem strange to say. That is the posterity of some of the most liberal contributors here, in the changes which one country may produce, may possibly find shelter under this very plant which they now so kindly water. Nay, so great is the mutability of things, and}

11. I might proceed to instance many reasons for the furtherance <and promotion> of this good work, but <further> {shall confine myself to one drawn from the present}

12. <shall> the consideration of this stupendous instance

13. and gives <strength and beauty> {weight} to every thing else

14. And therefore I shall <make it my last appeal> {beg leave to apply it};

15. I believe there can be none <more charitable> more beneficial,

16. the necessity of giving youth an {general}

17. It is true our pittance was small, <therefore we never indulged one wish to make the rich but> {but large enough to have made thee} virtuous <we would have made thee>

18. But alas! <he thy Father is gone from us, never more to return more, and with him are also the means of doing it.> {The staff of our support is gone.}"

19. {to a love of honest labor and industry as all his life long to earn and eat his bread with joy and thankfulness: and on the other to be trained up to such a sense of his duty, as may secure him an interest in the world to come. Much peace and happiness rest upon the head and heart of everyone who thus brings children to Christ. May the

blessing of him that was ready to perish come seasonably upon him. The Lord comfort him when he most wants it, when he lays sick upon his bed, make thou, O God! all his bed in his sickness; and for what he now scatters, give him, then, that peace of thine which passeth all understanding, and which nothing in this world can either give or take away.}

Sermon VI. "Love One to Another"

1. {whose professed characteristic is if I err not}
2. {old}
3. And this <brings me> {leads} to
4. {him}
5. disposed into bodies and <associations> {communities},
6. {perfect}
7. when all this scene of things is <quite> vanished away,
8. You have heard, my <brethren> {friends},
9. a band of brothers {, my much respected brethren}.
10. Any encomium of <u>mine</u> upon <this very ancient and honorable> {you as a} Society
11. a recompense that cannot fail you in this world; and <to the everlasting rewards of the Gospel, the basis of our admirable science> which will not fail you in the next,
12. {if I augur aright, of you my respected friends} <of <u>free and accepted Masons</u>>.
13. to carry on your glorious plan, <as you have begun> {and if unfortunately begun, healing them with Brotherly Love and forbearance},
14. {the <u>boast</u>},
15. and make an end <as I begun> in prayer
17. dismiss you with <the words of the Royal preacher> {love and friendship, sobriety and temperance}.

Sermon VII. "Love Not the World"

1. that <whatsoever> {whosoever} doth not love life
2. "not to love <God> this world."
3. In order <therefore> then to this advancement
4. we not only love <the world> it better
5. putting it in our <own> power
6. where good <men> and virtuous men
7. The motives of religion <as a> ought at all times,
8. when the blessed {Jesus} made expiation for the sins of the whole world <and by the shedding> to have so much
9. the fashionable customary {vices} of our <vices> country;
10. forty days of Lent the time {of humiliation} generally observed
11. What <must> punishment must

12. to restore it to its <former> {proper} use;

13. prostitution of this {holy} season

14. sense hereof may <make> work such a reformation

Sermon VIII. "Be Not Conformed to This World"

1. containing matter of general utility to all Christians in <u>all</u> ages> {every age} and <countries> {country};

2. than of our observing {it} in too rigid

3. {nothing}

4. is not a more severe <menace> {sentence} in the Holy Scripture

Sermon IX. "Love Your Enemies"

1. but drew <an instance> from them very falsely {a sanction} both to their

2. and the people received it with a malicious readiness <being naturally violent and revengeful>.

3. This is <the description> {descriptive} of the duty <that our Savior gives us> {given by our Savior} of loving our enemies. <And accordingly we shall consider further first wherein the duty consists and secondly by what arguments it may be enforced.> The first step toward{s which} <loving our enemies> is discharging our minds

4. will in time diffuse <a soundness upon a man's> {itself through the} whole behavior.

5. absolute <empire and> command over <his heart> {himself} as to stifle <forever> his disgust,

6. {is}

7. and acting <a part instead of acting a friend> {in a diffusion which cannot long be worn.} Enmity <however> is a restless thing

8. a greater misery than <this> to possess a mind ever ready to burst, and yet never {to} give<s> it vent.

9. should deport ourselves with all <signs> {tokens} of love to our enemies?

10. make it their business <daily> to lessen and defame us;

11. We must answer them in the most civil, courteous, obliging <and good natured> terms; and whenever we have occasion to speak of them, <labor> to conceal their faults, where <charity>

12. <Thirdly> {Again}, to love an enemy

13. {height}

14. Or do we see our enemy defrauded and <circumvented> {oppressed}, we must contribute

15. to <quash or promote> {interrupt or injure} his business or interest,

16. {man}

17. it is the <top> {height}

18. both in this world and <in> the next.

19. Now, though <it cannot be denied that> benevolence in general

20. {and special}

21. and he <purposely> came into the world to die

22. but it does not <presently> {from thence}

23. {clearly}

24. {up}

25. {daily}

26. for such as want power, <or as> {courage or}

27. <Now> To silence this objection, we cannot do better than proceed <secondly>

28. and we paint <our enemy then> {him} in false colors,

29. and all that he does is <pure hostility> {hostile} against us;

30. <one of> our most cordial friend.

31. Such resolved goodness <without dispute> must be sufficient to subdue

32. but melt him <down> into easiness

33. {being}

34. must <vex> {mollify} them to see a generous return to an unworthy provocation; and in short we <can> {must} quiet shame

35. How <now what a> pleasing {a} prospect

36. great {and wise} general <as ours>

37. for He maketh <the> {His} sun to rise on the evil

38. When we have the example of <the glorious company of> His Apostles,

39. for if he that is but flesh <as the son of Syrach observes> nourisheth hatred,

40. <And> Therefore <he concludes> remember corruption and death,

Sermon X. "I Will Have Mercy and Not Sacrifice"

1. <fat> {blood}

2. <When> {Where}

3. My next proposition <was> {is}, that the duties of natural {or moral} religion are so far from being {made void or} set aside by revelation {or revealed duties} that they are now made stronger on mankind,

4. <requirest> {required}

5. From <this whole discourse> {what has been said} we may conclude,

6. Christ, <our Lord to whom> thy Son, our Savior.

Sermon XI. "The Fruit of the Spirit Is Love, Joy, and Peace"

1. solemnly to acknowledge the benefits they receive from <God's> {the} bounty {of God},

2. The Christian Pentecost requires something like this from us <Xtians>:

3. But because these, <here mentioned> {thus enumerated},

4. {necessarily}

5. <to> {towards}

6. <what> {that which} generally attracts our affection, and faces our inclination <to Him> {in His favor}.

7. <These the Apostle saith, are the first of the spirit, from whence we may learn to judge most infallibly of men's religious characters. Such a one has learning, and natural and acquired parts, but he is injurious and unjust; a backbiter and a slanderer; consequently he cannot be animated by the spirit of God. Another hath a ideal for religion, but he is cruel, fierce, and hath no charity for those that differ from him; and therefore I pronounce without hesitation that this man's zeal is not inspired by the Holy Ghost. On the other hand if we see a person who lays no claim to superior talents, and pretends to no higher degrees of sanctity than his neighbors, but is peaceable, long-suffering, gentle, meek and charitable, to the extent of his power, we may safely conclude that this person lives under the guidance and direction of God's Holy Spirit. From whence it will follow that so much benevolence as there is in a man's temper, so much he hath of the blessed spirit in Him. Happy are they who thus feel the presence of the Comforter, by its sensible effects upon their hearts and minds: who are made perfect in love, and by that means are filled with joy through the power of the Holy Ghost. For that is another fruit of the Spirit: the fruit of the Spirit, saith the Apostle, is love and joy.> {These will be attended to us with the happiest consequences for}

8. {In fact, men of turbulent spirits, maligners, backbiters, and the whole tribe of them can have no joy, for they are enemies to peace. For they are like the evil one in the}

9. Whereas he that is friendly and <generous> {kindly-hearted}

10. Let us in case of <a> {any unhappy} disagreement

Sermon XII. "Blessed Are the Merciful"

1. <Misery, whether on men's souls or outward estates, is the proper object of mercy and mercy is usually set forth to us in Scripture by the affection of compassion and pity. It is the fifth grace, or Christian virtue, to which a blessedness is pronounced in the text, which may be paraphrased thus, "Blessed are they who are compassionate and pitiful towards the wants and infirmities of other men, whether of their souls or their bodies; who are apt to relieve and pardon, to give and forgive: For God shall deal with them as they deal with others; He shall answer their requests in time of necessity, and be abundantly merciful to them at the great day of accounts." ¶ Mercy is founded on its suitableness and congruity to the divine nature; which abounds with all possible perfection, and is an everlasting fountain of felicity. And as from a principle of self-love, every being is disposed to beget its own likeness; everything that is happy with the consequence be inclined to make others: and since Almighty God is happy in himself; his self love must necessarily incline him to beget his likeness on his creatures, and impart happiness to all the world, which doubtless was the reason of his making it. From this disposition to transform all mankind into his likeness, he must be tenderly affected with their miseries; and forever inclined to relieve and render them happy.

And for this reason I conceive it is that our Savior so emphatically urges it, "Be ye merciful as your Father is merciful." Mercy is also founded on its suitableness with the frame and constitution of our nature; in which God, the wise author of it, hath implanted a natural sympathy in the pains and pleasures of all that share this common nature. And this human nature is diffused through a vast variety of individuals, who are wisely separated from one another by time or place, yet as though it were all but one common soul operating in various bodies at several times and places, it feels almost in every one what the other suffers or enjoys: The sense indeed is quickest in that individual upon whom the pain or pleasure falls immediately; But all the rest as soon as notice is given them, are sensibly affected therewith. This affection then of pity and compassion, needs only actual exertion to make it a direct Christian grace and its own excellency will place it in the highest rank. It is for this reason therefore, as I humbly conceive, that of all the affections implanted in the mind of man. Our blessed Savior adopted this only into the number of his gracious beatitudes, "Blessed are the merciful, for they shall obtain mercy."> These words {of my Father} naturally divide themselves into two parts; <for our further consideration; and contain> {containing}

2. according to <their abilities> {his ability}

3. another sense; <and may be aptly enough interpreted according to it as they import> {importing}

4. <and all capacity of being> {forgive and we shall be} forgiven.

Sermon XIII. "Bear Ye One Another's Burdens"

1. {somewhat}

2. {no abatement of the practice. Pious inclinations, the often whetted and encouraged, are by no means tired or worn out. I}

3. {in your lives}

4. Our enjoyments here {are} at the best

5. and to beg the blessing of God on <your> {our} pious endeavors.

6. {and in its maturity is}

7. But it is farther <an act> at the same time

8. which <though> {thus} limited, <and therefore> {though} it doth not deserve

9. {and more extensive}

10. {not only}

11. that <the widow> as far as your power and ability permits, the widow and the orphan <if distressed, will> shall find

12. and refreshing <dew> {shade}.

13. whose mercies are {seen} over all

14. I might proceed to enlarge upon several other {Christian} graces <and attendants> linked with this Queen

15. there can be {none} more beneficial

16. and bringing them up to a love of industry, [and giving them reading and writing] which are wanted in the very lowest stations. With regard to [the first] instruction in religion,

17. degrees of men, [open to general examination] adapted to all capacities, <the ignorant> designed

18. {You see them often become stupid and senseless of all duty; or tumultuous and unquiet or rapacious and desperate.}

19. {neglect or} forsake them, shall we {not} take them

20. Shall we not <thus> fulfill the law

21. to be of service to themselves and the public <to be happy here and hereafter>?

22. {the king expects his soldiers}

23. {instruct their}

24. making them serviceable in <the world> it;

25. countenancing and recommending it; <as well as> {and all} by contributing

26. {and degree then}

Sermon XIV. "Love Your Enemies"

1. sufferable difficulties <and so violent opposition to flesh and blood> that it never

2. triumph to shut up than to open a way to rage and fury. <The heathens themselves thought it as glorious to pardon as to subdue their adversary; and when Cicero the Roman orator launches out into praise an encomiums, on the great Caesar, though he magnifies his bravery yet his magnificent clemency he places in a much stronger light, and sets a greater value on his confession and benevolence, than on all the other great and numerous qualifications that hero was posses of; And particularly in enumerating some of his great abilities and among them the wonderful force of memory (for which he was famous). He pays him a very elegant and just compliment in telling him that Caesar never forgot anything, but injuries do we regard our interest in procuring peace and tranquility to ourselves. If we do, let this be another motive to us, to love and forgive our enemies. ¶ While the passions are calm and still a certain secret complacency diffuses itself and procures an unknown happiness and enjoyment of ourselves. A continued exercise in acts of humanity is a perpetual source of joy. And though this pleasure may not show itself, like others, in outward expressions, yet it is nevertheless most sensibly felt; with the less noise it flows, the deeper will it sink; as shallow waters make the greatest murmur, while the profoundest glide serenely and calmly by. ¶ On the contrary,, if the passions are up, no wonder if there are disturbances within; the soul is immediately untuned and all that sweet harmony which was before enjoyed, is lost in discord. The mind no longer keeps its proper posture and every thing is in an unnatural tumult. But more particularly unhappy is the state of that mind that is possessed with malice and revenge. These dismal reflections will never suffer it to be at rest like scourges in the side, and thorns in the eyes. The revengeful (as

Isaiah describes the wicked) can no more rest than the troubled sea, whose waters cast up mire and dirt. He is ever working to bring about and ever in anxiety, until he has accomplished his end, constantly on the rack both in inventing and pursuing his designs and the edge of his fury is in great measure turned upon himself, and he becomes his own tormentor. This sure, if anything must be a life of misery and how dreadful must the time be spent, when a man is continually employed like a thirsty bloodhound in hunting down his prey? How gloomy must those days appear when scarce a single gleam of joy or satisfaction shines out upon the mind and when it is constantly covered with a sullen darkness, that is made by its own black reflections. ¶ Who then would not endeavor to shake off a passion that is the spring of so much inward uneasiness? In short, we should forgive and love our enemies, on this very account, that it is in effect to procure our own happiness and love ourselves. Nor will this forgiving temper procure our inward quiet alone, but also our outward peace in being a very probable means of stopping any farther insult from our enemy in soothing his inveteracy against us, and bringing him at last perhaps to a wished for reconciliation. For who that has any sparks of virtue and gratitude remaining can return evil for good and repay humanity and benevolence with hatred and barbarity when our adversary sees that when he curses we are ready to bless; to do good to him, when he hates us; and pray for him when he despitefully uses and persecutes us; this surely must make him either admire so virtuous, so winning a behavior in us, or be confounded and ashamed of himself; that heart (as Job expresses it) must be as firm as a stone, yea as hard as the nether millstone that will not yield to such continued impassions of courtesy and kindness; that stands obstinately out against all the overtures of love that are so frequently offered; and remains insensible to all the good offices that can be expected or imagined. If thine enemy hunger (says St. Paul) feed him; if he thirst give him drink, for in so doing thou shalt heap coals of fire on his head. ¶ Which words of the Apostle, though taken in a double sense by interpreters, will yet in either of them be applicable to the present argument. If (as some think) it is an illusion to the refiners and then according to this interpretation, agreeable to the sense of that we have been already showing. Our kindness and good offices to our enemy may at best touch his heart and melt it down though of the most stubborn metal into softness and compliance. If it be a phrase to denote the anger and indignation of the Almighty; still may we promise ourselves peace, and rest secure in the Lord for our avenger; who, if our enemy persists in his fury, and nothing can work upon him, will undertake our cause, and be always present to guard and protect us; he will make that very vengeance which our adversaries design against us, return upon themselves; and heap coals of fire on their own head, which if they cannot melt, must consume and destroy them. Shall therefore have we reason to be at rest, and securely follow St. Paul's advice, Dearly Beloved, avenge not of yourselves, for it is written, vengeance is mine and I will repay saith the Lord.>

    3. up to heaven, <provoke the divine anger> and not only call

4. justice and omnipotence, <for by such procedure we seem> to think

5. We are not only <not brought out> {forgiven}

Sermon XV. "A More Excellent Way"

1. as there is of the members <of> {in} the human body.

2. These were gifts and powers of a very <excellent> extraordinary nature,

3. <of> {viz.} charity. The {nature and} extent of which at large {I come now to consider}.

4. we <would> {could} reasonably expect from them;

5. Ye owe no man anything, <so the scope and sense of the place seems to require it should be rendered>, but to love one another:

6. are comprehended in this of love <and> {or} charity;

7. Having <this much> observed this much

8. convince all of the indispensable <necessity> {duty} of practicing it.

9. regard to {present} happiness,

10. "It is more <highly> blessed to give, than to receive."

11. free from those <pestilential> {pestilent} passions,

12. {Christian}

13. are {a} system of beings,

14. these, would not {at} all promote it.

15. bed of <distress> languishing,

16. and we are in a state of <hostility> peace,

17. the rest could be carried on <then> without them,

18. man, <to reflect> of a good and elevated mind,

Sermon XVI. "Let Your Light Shine before Men"

1. goodness <among the brave men of this age> is to become the object

2. distinguishing character of the modern <polite and fashionable gentlemen> {age}:

3. to <supply> {support} if possible, the sinking cause

4. A duty required; and an argument to enforce this duty. <I shall therefore, in the following discourse endeavor, first, to consider and explain the duty required in my text. Secondly, I shall point out some reasons for our compliance with it. ¶ And, first I shall endeavor to consider and explain the> {First} the duty required <in my text>.

5. {thought} really good from a vain

6. this path that our text would guide and direct us <if we would but follow its instructions>.

7. an ostentatious show of <religion> {it} loosely to catch

8. {their owners}

9. as if they thought <it> {they} did.

10. And if we suffer their <ridiculing of us> ridicule,

11. the absurdity and impiety of <which> {this} is sufficient,

Sermon XVII. "The Imitation of Christ"

1. <persecution> {affliction},

2. {were} first <uttered> {spoken},

3. {and} a by-word of the people <and the song of the Disciples>.

4. <persecution> {affliction}

5. {when opportunity offers}

6. There, {should} we <will> move ourselves

Sermon XVIII. "According to His Will, He Heareth Us"

1. <I shall not here consider the expediency> {It need be no part of my purpose in discerning from the words of St. John to consider at present the obligation} or necessity

2. {In discoursing then upon these words, I shall endeavor to point out to you some of those} qualifications {, and circumstances}

3. <sight> {presence} of God

4. must be <only one contrived impertinence> {at least vain and useless if not rather mocking devotion; and more likely <therefore> to <bring> {call} down <God's wrath and indignation> {the displeasure of God} upon us than <to appease and avert it> {his favor}. {Of the qualifications which everyone ought to be furnished with before he presumes to engage in the holy work of prayer the primary} <And in order to this I shall consider the three following particulars. First, I shall consider what qualifications everyone ought to be furnished with, before he presumes to engage in this holy work. Secondly what should be the form and manner of our prayer. And thirdly and lastly what should be the drift and tenor of them. Of the qualifications then which should be offered before he presumes to engage in this holy work, the primary and> and most

5. Without such a degree of <piety> {holiness} as this,

6. entitle him to <a share of the God's> {the divine} favor

7. object of his <care and> regard, <Let not that man> expect to receive

8. <two of his most adorable attributes> his power and goodness.

9. of God <or his attributes> but to a sense only

10. {But I pass to} another qualification of acceptable and successful prayer {which} is a fixed and composed <behavior> {demeanor}.

11. <These are some of those qualifications which everyone should be furnished with before he presumes to address his God in prayer and supplication. ¶ Let us next consider the form and method of our petitions. And here the first thing observable is, that they ought to be gravity and serious and entirely free from all that pomp and parade of words, which, how commendable soever in compositions of another kind>

{should be furnished with before he presumes to address his God in prayer and supplication, which in order to the acceptableness of our approaches to the throne of grace claim our careful attention. While then let me here remark gravity and seriousness of deportment are an indispensable accompaniment of every sincere supplicant's devotion}, yet never be allowed here.

12. as if we were more righteous than they. <Much less than like the proud Pharisee to set about a detail of our good deeds, and so instead of asking pardon and forgiveness for our manifold sins and insufferable wickedness endeavor to prove what a just right and title we have to the peculiar care and esteem of Heaven and how truly worthy we are of what mere grace and undeserved mercy alone is most graciously pleased to bestow.>

13. some end or design. <The glory of God our own salvation and that of the rest of mankind. ¶ The glory of God and his name is doubtless, and at all times a very fit subject for our prayers, as well private as public. For this is our particular province, our most glorious employment, and one great end proposed by God himself in the creation of man. As we are therefore never so well, never so profitably employed as in the promotion of it, so are we indispensably obliged to solicit God's grace and assistance in its behalf> {We ought never it should be remembered except with great caution to pray for any particular worldly advantages and this obviously because we cannot say what advantages of this kind are fit for us, or most conducive to our true interest. Those comforts that we aspire and fret for which we may most eagerly desire, may be entirely improper to be granted us or if granted us, will have no blessing. And on the contrary those sufferings which may be most apt to shrink from and to deprecate, may in reality be useful to us, and make on the whole the highest benefits. Holiness is the gift of God, in that we certainly turn to the Lord for it. It is the true riches, the noblest treasure, the highest honor, and God's best and choicest gift. To the acquisition of this therefore and the advancement of the affluence and dominion in ourselves and others, ought all our prayers chiefly to be directed to the first and most important object of prayer may be enjoined with other things such as God in his wisdom may see to be expedient for, such as health, peace and tranquility of mind, the blessings of Heaven upon our understanding when about to engage in enterprises of virtuous interest and belief in lessons of trouble and affliction when assertion of any special transmission, pardon, or when [unreadable] to any suit the security of his interposing face and the constant compassion of God towards us as at unprofitable servants and his assistance to render us less and less unworthy of his favor. But such an enumeration need not be fruitless. The heart of every Christian prompted by faith approach him in prayer, but knows scripture and can best guard lips from really uttering anything before God, or offering any petition unworthy of himself or of the [unreadable] in Heaven. In the spirit of such faith and such confidence with habitual endeavoring to obey the will of God, with fixedness of thought and feeling, with charity towards all men, and in community

with God let us be then our own temporal safety and future salvation, together with the temporal safety and salvation of other men.}

14. \<likewise another\> {doubtless a} proper subject

Sermon XIX. "We Bring Our Years to an End as a Tale That Is Told"

1. so let our request be {made} known unto God.
2. These indeed frequently \<lose\> {miss} it,
3. \<and\> {but} know, that ye have not fallen
4. deserve, \<even that of being\> the first of human kind.
5. our names {should} be forgotten,
6. their lands {called} after their own
7. those you would choose \<sic.\>; and which \<you would\> prefer.
8. advantage are \<consistent\> {inconsistent} one with another,

Sermon XX. On the Necessity and Demerit of the Discharge of Our Duty—Part One

1. of \<that\> {them}, not as meritorious causes,
2. will I profess unto \<that\> {them},
3. lest \<when\> {what} we challenge from God's
4. and that without \<that\> {them} we cannot be saved;
5. where their sins {only} should be
6. be equally \<divided\> {avoided};
7. It is not easy to determine \<when\> {which} opinion carries

Sermon XXI. On the Necessity and Demerit of the Discharge of Our Duty—Part Two

1. In a former discourse, I \<have\> proved
2. And {that} this opinion
3. \<And to put a more plausible gloss upon this opinion, \> Two texts of scripture are particularly \<brought to give it better countenance\> adduced in its favor:
4. \<that I may\> the more strongly {to} establish
5. The first, \<place of scripture that fall under my consideration\> is a passage
6. for manslayers \<and if any argument can be drawn from hence, the strength\>.
7. \<point\>, that since there is no law \<presented\> {prescribed} to the righteous;
8. they cannot \<leave\> {bear} such a construction;
9. which \<does\> by no means excuses
10. but only direct \<that\> {, them} who in obedience,
11. of those punishments, \<we\> {which} would otherwise
12. comprehended \<that\> {them} in his
13. as that {because} we are freed
14. to the Second Particular \<I propose to speak to\>,
15. find cause to address \<ours\> {ourselves} to the throne

Sermon XXII. "His Mercy Endureth Forever"

1. {recommend}
2. {of precise}
3. {mighty}
4. {specified, which}
5. <forward ever> and let the whole Earth

Sermon XXIII. "A Good Name"

1. {God's} Providence
2. even a <long> good life,
3. then {do} disservice {to} the cause of religion,
4. since nothing <as> {is}
5. will not only <presage> {prove}
6. St. <Paul> {Peter}

Sermon XXIV. "A Day Which He Will Judge"

1. <First> How it comes to pass
2. <¶Secondly> by what means the consideration of a {future} judgment may have a greater influence on <all> our minds.
3. {the meat of}
4. so little impression on <men's minds> {the minds of men}.
5. happy in their own sense <unless they would believe their Eastern [unreadable]>.
6. {by drink,}
7. <I> Proceed, <how in the second place> we,
8. out of our heads <would> {could}

Sermon XXV. "Faith without Wavering"

1. reason {itself};
2. one {fundamental} point
3. consider those worked by him <but let us consider this evidence somewhat more particularly. This will lead us into a subject proper for our meditations at this present season, at which we commemorate the descent of the Spirit by the demonstration and power of which displayed either in foretelling things to come> {for the prophesies of old came not by the will of men, but the holy men of God spake as they were moved by the Holy Ghost}: or in working of miracles {for as the gift of prophesy so likewise the gift of miracles was by the same Spirit.}
4. but he also <foretold> by that spirit
5. {still further}
6. {especially when the doctrines he teaches, and the laws which he enforces are for the honor of God}
7. {commemorated this day}

8. and {all} the wisdom,

9. {as he justly might}

10. been assisted <immediately from God> by the Almighty

11. absurdity <with> {in} that Satan

12. For the <religion> {gospel}

13. {suppose it to be in the power of that Being}

14. <Thus far you see a brief and general view of what is called the external evidence of our religion. The demonstration of the Spirit and of power displayed either in the gift of the prophesies or of miracles. To this we might add a still further> {But to this we may add as a still further} recommendation

15. contained {principally}

16. perfect {obedience} yet will it of the sincere <obedience of our> performance

Sermon XXVI. "Overcoming the World"

1. Of all the conquests that <were even yet> {can be} made by <frail> man,

2. the difficulties <and dangers> of our spiritual warfare must needs <appear> {be} .

3. it <is> very hazardous <and precarious>. And when <we are> at last, through God's grace <more than> {we are} conquerors;

4. <Being therefore not under the law, but under grace,> We may well join

5. In my ensuing discourse, <on the words> I shall first show

6. <Christian faith is an assent unto truths, indelible upon the testimony of God> {Christian faith} delivered to us

7. The right notion of the Christian faith {which} may be <more fully> understood in this manner<. It> is such a <lively> {proper} sense of <the infirmity of our nature, and> our <great> unworthiness

8. But, <then> it is,

9. unspeakable love to his <lost> creatures, <in sending His Son to die for them; of the worth and dignity of Christ's obedience and death; and> of his readiness to accept returning sinners; as produceth in us the most <devout and> affectionate <a sense, and the most> thankful remembrance of these <wonderful> mercies.

10. And this is joined with such a steadfast belief of all His promises and threatenings, as encourageth us to <lift up our eyes unto Him, and to> look unto Him only, for mercy and compassion; {for pardon and salvation} <under afflictions, and for a plentiful effusion of grace>, to secure us <from falling> in the hour of temptation; {and} to sanctify and change our natures; <and to dispose and> {by} <incline> {inclining} our wills to God and goodness. <Or in one word, this faith directs us to look unto God alone for all the means of virtue and holiness here, and of glory hereafter. This accompanied with> {Add to this} the most entire and perfect resignation of ourselves, our wills and affections to the will of God; with a sincere desire, <and> a serious and diligent endeavor to live according to His laws; to do His will on Earth, as it is done in

Heaven; to grow in grace <and> {to} work out our salvation; and as far as is consistent with the infirmities of <our nature> {humanity} to have our conversation in Heaven; to be holy, {comparatively speaking,} as God is holy; <and to be> perfect <even> as our Father who is in Heaven is perfect. <This is an imperfect copy of that Christian faith, which is fully described in the Gospel, where you will find a lively image of this heavenly virtue.>

11. {But in order} to show the nature of the Christian faith more distinctly; <by showing the> {let us examine the} several {particular} properties of it.

12. The first <property of the Christian faith is, that it> is a rational

13. but <a rational belief and persuasion of the truth and certainty of them. This Christian faith> rests upon

14. by its own intrinsic <worth and> excellence.

15. Himself <to their reason> {not to their passions, but to their} understandings. His arguments are all <fairly> drawn

16. His doctrines should be <embraced and> received <by them> merely upon the strength of His own word; but {after demonstrating their suitableness to our nation and state, to give them a better sanction and authority.}

17. <The> Christian faith, then, is a rational assent, <and> {a} well-grounded persuasion; <and> perfectly

18. abideth faithful; <and cannot deny himself, but continueth true to His promises>

19. And this is <the second> {another} property of it. <True Christian faith> {It} is not a wavering

20. distracted with fears, <and scruples> and tossed about

21. concerning the <truth of the Christian doctrines, of the> certainty

22. It is a <holy and> steadfast

23. <There is indeed a weaker and lower degree of faith,> {Different degrees of this faith, undoubtedly there are} mixed {perhaps} with some degrees of <doubt> {scruples} such as that of St. Peter, which our <blessed> Savior reproved with these words, "O though of little faith, wherefor didst thou doubt?" <Such> An unsteady faith <as> {like} this, is by no means, {however} a sufficient principle of virtue and piety; but must needs be followed by a conduct <as> unequal and unsteady, as that principle from which it proceeds. For as the spring cannot rise higher than its first source; neither can our obedience <rise higher> than <that> {the} fountain, from whence it flows. <And> Indeed the sequel to Peter's history is <abundantly> {abundant} to confirm the truth of his observation. <And> Therefore it was, that our Lord foreseeing the ill effects of so weak a faith; <especially in a person of Peter's sanguine and unsteady temper> said to him, just before His Passion, "I have prayed for thee, that thy faith fail not."

24. <Which words are> A sufficient intimation that any defect in this divine principle is always accompanied with a proportionable failure in our duty and obedience:

And as a weak faith always produces a very <faulty and> defective <obedience; even> so is a <strong and> lively faith constantly productive of a steady <and uniform> obedience to the will, and the <commandments> {commands} of God.

25. <If we look into the history of St. Paul's life> {To confirm which observations; let us cast an eye upon the history of St. Paul's life;}

26. assurance of <faith> and <an> dependence upon

27. with what <a holy confidence, and> undaunted resolution,

28. to that <exuding great and> glorious reward, which {then} was reserved for him <; then against his enemy>. <But> {And} when we consider the grounds <that he went upon> {of that confidence},

29. And <those faithful Christians> {certain it is that those} who receive

30. <the third> {another} essential property

31. And this <brings me to> {leads to} <the fourth> {another} property

32. <For the fifth property of the Christian faith is this, that a good man> {he} gives all

Sermon XXVII. The Efficacy of National Virtue for Securing National Felicity

1. contrivance <of the universe. In the contrived preservation of the several systems which compose it> {of the universe—and the wise disposal of its several parts;}

2. <existence> {happiness}.

3. {either} be overlooked or <forgot, in great mercy, to meet wonder> {forgotten by us, Almighty God. No wonder then,} if our hopes <be> {prove} abortive,

4. betrayed into that <false> {fatal}

5. his power {over,} and government <in> {of} the world; instructing us, that apart of his blessing <and protection>, vain is the counsel

6. {Being} discontented {it seems} with the usual tribute {which was} paid him, he demanded <the city and the people to be delivered, threatening> {of the people that they should deliver the city into his hands. At the same time threatening in case of refusal, to lay waste} the country with fire and sword <in case of refusal>.

7. God's assistance {against his enemies}.

8. comfort and <assurance> {satisfaction}.

9. <Rewarding then his people, he made every preparation for a rigorous defense> {He therefore made everything for a serious defense}. He had <those> {his people} enrolled, who were fit for war; <placing> {he appointed} over them proper officers <to instruct them in military exercise, and led them on in battle>.

10. I need not recount {to you} the many instances of divine interposition <in our favor.> {and goodness to us. For} many of you <are> {must be} living witnesses

11. have been the <assurances> {instances} of God's protection, <while we continue> {so long as we were} objects worthy of <it. Is nothing but disobedience will cause the Almighty to forsake his people, let every one conscious of disobedience> {his notice and} reform his conduct

12. which Providence hath <put in your hands> {furnished you},
13. a most encouraging <assurance> {declaration},
14. any other <nation> {people}
15. truth that <our generous sovereign> {authority}
16. the fatal bar to the <public happiness> {divine protection}.
17. As we of this <nation> {state in particular}

Appendix A

ORIGINAL OR MANUSCRIPT SOURCES
OF THE SERMONS OF ROBERT SMITH

# in Smith's Index*	Delivery Dates (17—/18—)	Reference	Source	SC†
101 [II]	59, 83, 84, 89	Prov. 14:34	Martyn	yes
102	61, 67, 74, 88, 96	2Cor. 12:9	Duberdu	
103	61, 66, 70, 84	1Thess. 4:3	Duberdu	yes
103 ST	71, 76, 96	Mic. 6:8	Duberdu	yes
104	60, 67, 74, 84, 88, 96	Prov. 15:3	Martyn	
105	60, 67, 74, 80, 87, 95	1Sam. 3:18	Martyn	
106	68, 74, 75, 76, 88, 94, 00	Eph. 3:17	Duberdu	yes
107	60, 66, 67, 75, 80, 01	Matt. 10:29	Duberdu	
108 (see 329)	74, 83, 94	Judg. 1:7	Green	
108 ST	63, 67, 75, 80, 88, 98	Ps. 9:16	unknown	
109	58, 61, 68, 75, 79, 96	Eccles. 12:14	Martyn	
110	59, 63, 68, 75, 84, 87, 94	Prov. 10:9	Clarke	
111	58, 61, 64, 68, 75, 83, 88, 94	Deut. 32:29	White	yes
112	57, 60, 65, 68, 74, 85, 89, 01	Job 28:38	White	
113	55, 61, 66, 75, 84, 88, 01	John 13:17	unknown	

*Number assigned by Smith in his own index, or listing, of his sermons. A bracketed number following = the sermon number in this volume; (1) = first in a series; (2) = second in a series, etc.; and ST = second text.

†= In Smith Sermons Collection, St. Philip's Church, Charleston, S.C.

# in Smith's Index	Delivery Dates (17—/18—)	Reference	Source	SC
114	64, 68, 75, 84, 89, 97	Josh. 1:8	unknown	yes
114 ST	—	1Tim. 4:15	unknown	yes
115	59, 63, 73, 84, 99	1Thess. 4:11	Martyn	yes
116	57, 75, [illegible]	James 5:12	Martyn	yes
117	60, 73, 87	Matt. 6:24	unknown	
118	59	Luke 2:10–11	Bennett	
119	59, 63, 74, 85, 89, 94, 00	1John 3:8	Bennett	yes
120	59, 61, 66	1Cor. 15:14	Martyn	
121	60, 72, 75, 80, 88, 94	Prov. 4:23	self	
122 (1)	59, 95	Luke 22:19	Martyn	
122 (2)	59, 95	Luke 22:19	Duberdu	
123 (1)	59, 74, 97	Eccles. 5:1	Martyn	
123 (2)	59, 74, 97	Eccles. 5:1	Martyn	
124	59, 72, 75, 84, 90	1Tim. 6:10	Martyn	
125 (1)	60, 67, 71, 75, 83, 90, 98, 99	Eccles. 5:4	Martyn	yes
125 (2)(see 138)	61, 72, 87, 95, 96	Mark 6:12	Martyn	
126	59, 76, 85, 89	Ps. 58:11	Martyn	
127	60, 67, 85, 89, 98	Prov. 22:6	Martyn	yes
128	67, 72, 75, 84, 89	Ps. 42:1	Martyn	
129	61, 72, 75, 87, 95	Titus 3:2	Martyn	yes
130	61, 72, 75, 84, 89	Eph. 4:25	Martyn	
130 ST	—	Ps. 15:1–2	Martyn	
131	61, 84, 90, 99	Eccles. 12:1	Martyn	yes
132	60, 72, 75, 83, 87, 95	2Cor. 4:17	Martyn	
133	60, 61	Job 2:1–4	Martyn	yes
134	84, 93, 97	John 6:14	unknown/ Tonge	
135	65	Rev. 22:15	unknown	
136	62, 76	Hosea 6:4	Duberdu	
137	60, 61, 75, 84, 87, 96	Ps. 96:13	unknown/ Tonge	
138	61, 72, 87, 95, 96	Mark 6:12	Martyn	
139	63, 66, 76, 87, 93	Dan. 9:18–19	unknown/ Tonge	yes
140	66, 87, 93	Eccles. 9:2	unknown/ Tonge	yes
141 (1)	63, 66, 70, 76, 87, 91, 99	Luke 15:7	Green	yes
141 (2)	63, 66, 70, 76, 87, 91, 99	Luke 15:7	Green	yes

# in Smith's Index	Delivery Dates (17—/18—)	Reference	Source	SC
142	63, 67, 76, 87, 01	1Cor. 11:21	Duberdu	yes
143	63, 66, 67, 71, 75, 85, 90	Rom. 2:6	Duberdu	
144	61, 72, 84	[illegible]	unknown	
145	63, 70, 75, 85, 92, 98	Luke 14:24	Martyn	
146	63, 73, 76, 79, 86, 91, 97	Luke 2:14	Martyn	
147	—	Isa. 45:6–7	Martyn	
148	64, 67, 70, 84, 90, 00	Eph. 5:16	Martyn	
149	64, 68, 75, 80, 87, 92, 01	[illegible]	Duberdu	
150 (1)	64, 65, 72, 76, 97	[illegible]	Duberdu	
150 (2)	64, 65, 72, 76, 97	Matt. 11:4–5	Duberdu	
151 [XVII]	65, 68, 74, 87, 92	1Pet. 2:21	Stokes	yes
152	67	Eccles. 12:1	Stokes	yes
153	65, 95	1Cor. 15:5	Stokes	
154	63, 66, 96	Rom. 8:1	Stokes	
155 (2)	76, 87, 95	2Pet. 3:16	Stokes	
156	64, 67, 72	Heb. 10:23	Stokes	
157	64, 70, 73, 76, 85, 98	Mark 16:19	Stokes	
158	64, 67, 99	Ps. 42:14	Stokes	
159	64, 68	James 1:22	Stokes	
160	64, 68, 97	James 4:14	Stokes	
161	[illegible]	Rom. 13:13	Stokes	
162 [VIII]	[illegible], 72, 79, 84, 95	Rom. 12:2	Stokes	yes
163 ST	63	2Cor. 7:1	Stokes	
164	63, 66, 96	Rom. 8:13	Stokes	
165	63, 67 [illegible]	13:16	Stokes	yes
166	63, [illegible]	Matt. 3:10	Stokes	
167	65, 70, 76, 88	Prov. 19:2	unknown/ Tonge	yes
168	63, 64, 76, 89, 01	Matt. 4:23	unknown/ Tonge	
169	65, 76, 99, 01	1Cor. 14:20	unknown/ Tonge	yes
170	64, 71, 73, 79, [illegible]	Acts 11:26	unknown/ Tonge	yes
171	65, 75, 88, 01	1John 5:28–29	unknown/ Tonge	yes
172	66, 71, 85, 89, 01	Matt. 22:29	unknown/ Tonge	yes

# in Smith's Index	Delivery Dates (17—/18—)	Reference	Source	SC
173	64, 76, 77, 79, 86, 89	Isa. 53:1	Warren	
174 (1)	64, 74, 79	1Tim. 5:8	Warren	
174 (2)	64, 74, 79	1Tim. 5:8	Warren	
175 [XVII]	64, 67, 74, 76, 93, 00	James 4:3	Warren	yes
175 ST	—	1John 5:14	Warren	yes
176	64, 72, [illegible]	Matt. 27:3–5	Warren	
177	64, 67, 73, 86, 89, 97	Mark 1:15	Warren	
178	64, 74, [illegible]	Rom. 12:3	Warren	yes
179 (1)	64, 79	Acts 17:22–23	Warren	
179 (2)	64, 79	Acts 17:22–23	Warren	
180	65, 76, 00	Ps. 114:71	Warren	
181	65, 93, 00	Prov. 18:14	Warren	yes
182	65, 73, 98	1Cor. 15:9	Warren	yes
183	65, 70, 76, 99	Matt. 6:34	Warren	yes
184	65, 68, 73, 99	Eph. 2:11	Warren	
184 ST	—	—	Warren	
185	65, 98	Phil. 4:11	Warren	
186	65, 73, 93	1John 3:17	Warren	yes
187	65, 95	Matt. 15:28	Warren	
188	65	Jer. 23:23–24	Warren	
189	65	John 46:47	Warren	yes
189 ST	92	Isa. 24:15	Warren	yes
190	66, 74, 99	2Cor. 5:10	unknown/ Pearce	yes
191 [IX]	65, 73, 93	Matt. 5:43–44	unknown/ Pearce	yes
192 (1)	66, 72, 96, 00	1Cor. 10:15–16	Green	
192 (2)	66, 72, 96, 00 [see #193, #200, #297 for complete set]	1Cor. 10:15–16	Entick	
193	66, 74, 96, [illegible], 00	John 6:56	unknown	yes
194	66, 71, 79, 86, 89, 96	[illegible]	unknown	yes
195 [XIX]	79	Ps. 90:9	Ridley	yes
196	67, 70, 78, 84, 88, 94	Job 19:23–24	Shackley	
197	67, 72, 78, 88, 95, 01	Rom. 6:8	Shackley	
198	67, 98	Rom. 8:9	Shackley	
199 (1)	67, 74, 99	1John 4:8	Shackley	yes
199 (2)	67, 74, 99	1John 4:8	Shackley	yes
200	67, 76, 96, 00	1Cor. 11:29	unknown/ Wilton	

# in Smith's Index	Delivery Dates (17—/18—)	Reference	Source	SC
200 ST	—	1Cor. 10:15–16	Entick	
201	64	Rom. 10:14–15	Ridley	yes
202	67, 73, 96	Matt. 7:26	Martyn	
203	67, 73, 93, 00	Ps. 62:8	Martyn	yes
204	73, 86, 96	Rom. 5:19	Martyn	
205	67, 73, 85, 94, 01	1Pet. 5:5	Martyn	
206	[illegible], 79, 84, 88, 00	Col. 3:1	Martyn	
207	67, 75	2Cor. 1:12	Martyn	
208	67, 76, 95, 00	Ps. 145:9	Martyn	yes
208 ST	—	Ps. 109:8	Martyn	
209	67, 76, 91, 00	2Pet. 3:9	Martyn	
210	68, 76, 85, 95, 00	1Pet. 2:17	Martyn	
211 (1)	65, 74, 77, 83, 87, 93	John 20:31	Drake	yes
211 (2)	65, 74, 77, 83, 87, 93	John 20:31	Drake	yes
212	60, 71, 85	Eph. 4:26	Drake	yes
213	64, 78, 86, 92, 99	Acts 10:42	Drake	yes
214 (1)	64, 66, 72, 77, 84, 89, 94	1John 4:9	Martyn	
214 (2)	64, 66, 72, 77, 84, 89, 94	1John 4:9	Drake	
215 (1)	65, 71, 79, 84, 88	John 6:44	Drake	yes
215 (2)	65, 71, 79, 84, 88	Luke 11:13	Drake	yes
215 (3)	65, 71, 79, 84, 88	Phil. 3:12	Drake	yes
215 (4)	65, 71, 79, 84, 88	Rom. 15:13	Drake	
216	66, 72, 79, 84	Prov. 12:26	Drake	
217	73, 78, 84, 90, 00	Matt. 11:3	Drake	
218 (1)	66, 72, 86	Job 22:21	Drake	
218 (2)	66, 72, 86	Job 22:21	Drake	
219	64, 70, 79, 86, 99	Eccles. 1:14	Drake	yes
220	67, 79, 86, 98	Ps. 4:4	supposedly Stokes	yes
221	67, 78, 87, 97	Matt. 22:37	supposedly Stokes	
222	67, 78, 87, 97	Matt. 22:39	supposedly Stokes	
223	[illegible]	[illegible]	Wilton	yes
224 (1)	79, 88, 00	Isa. 57:21	unknown	
224 (2)	79, 88, 00	Isa. 57:21	unknown	
225	67, 77, 92	Rom. 5:8	unknown	
226	67, 70, 78, 84, [illegible]	Prov. 14:9	unknown	

# in Smith's Index	Delivery Dates (17—/18—)	Reference	Source	SC
227	65, 79, 87	Heb. 13:5	unknown	yes
228	65, 70, 76, 87	Titus 2:10	unknown	
229	67, 70, 76, 83, 87	Luke 18:42	unknown	yes
230	67, 70, 73, 84, 97	Heb. 13:12	unknown	yes
231 [XVI]	67, 70, 76, 84	Matt. 5:16	unknown	yes
232	[illegible]	Matt. 26:41	supposedly Stokes	
233	[illegible]	Heb. 2:15	supposedly Stokes	
234 (1)	—	James 4:8	unknown/ Evans	yes
234 (2)	—	James 4:8	unknown/ Evans	yes
235	66, 70, 79, 84, 92	Prov. 20:9	Duberdu	
236 [XXVII]	75, [illegible]	2Chron. 32:7–8	unknown/ Wilton	
237	65, 67, 71, 76, 83, 84, 93	Isa. 5:12	unknown	
237 ST	—	Ps. 118:24	unknown	
238 (1)	65, 68, 73, 87	John 5:3	unknown/ Wilton	
238 (2) (see 281)	65, 68, 73, 87	Titus 3:8	supposedly Drake	
239	65, 71, 75, 86, 95, 01	Ps. 116:10–13	unknown/ Wilton	yes
240	65	1Cor. 10:14–15	Duberdu	
241 (1)	65, 70, 79, 88, 98	1John 5:4	unknown/ Wilton	yes
241 (2)	65, 70, 79, 88, 98	1John 5:4	unknown/ Wilton	yes
242	65, 70, 79, 84, 99	Luke 13:24	unknown/ Wilton	
243	65, 70, 77, 86	1Cor. 10:12	unknown/ Wilton	yes
244	66, [illegible]	Ps. 39:5	unknown/ Pearce	
245	65, 70, 84, 98	Ps. 139:7	unknown/ Wilton	
246	64, 73, 78, 85, 93	Luke 13:8–9	unknown/ Wilton	yes
247	65, 67, 71, 77, 84, 98	Rom. 14:18	unknown/ Wilton	

# in Smith's Index	Delivery Dates (17—/18—)	Reference	Source	SC
248 (1) [XX]	66, 73, 84, 90	Luke 17:10	unknown/ Wilton	
248 (2) [XXI]	66, 73, 84, 90	Luke 17:10	unknown/ Wilton	yes
249	66, 70, 79, 84, 91	Ps. 119:32	unknown/ Wilton	
250	64, 70, 79, 84	Matt. 13:8	unknown/ Wilton	
251	65, 70, 79, 87, 99	Ps. 119:15	unknown/ Wilton	yes
252	66, 75, 86, 98	2Cor. 12:7–8	Duberdu	
253	66, 71, 79, 85, 97	Eph. 6:4	unknown/ Wilton	
254	66, 76	Acts 15:18	unknown/ Pearce	yes
255	66	Ps. 122:6–9	unknown/ Wilton	
256	60, 67, 72, 85, 91	Eccles.7:29	Duberdu	yes
257	65, 76	Ps. 119:57–60	unknown/ Wilton	
258	[illegible]	Col. 3:2	Clifton	yes
259	66, 76, 87	Matt. 23:28	unknown/ Wilton	
260	65, 70, [illegible], 86, 97	[illegible]	unknown/ Wilton	yes
261 [X]	[illegible], 94	Matt. 9:13	unknown/ Wilton	yes
262	64, 75, 86	[illegible] 35:6	unknown/ Wilton	yes
263	70	Mic. 11:8	unknown/ Wilton	yes
264	—	Gal. 3:22–23	unknown/ Wilton	
265 (1)	—	Rom. 12:20	unknown/ Wilton	yes
265 (2)	—	Rom. 12:20	unknown/ Wilton	yes
266	64, 85	2Tim. 2:6	unknown/ Wilton	
267	62, 91, 98	Heb. 5:9	Stokes	
268	65, 71, 76, 87, [illegible]	Ps. 96:10	Duberdu	

# in Smith's Index	Delivery Dates (17—/18—)	Reference	Source	SC
269	65	Matt. 20:16	supposedly Drake	
270	[illegible]	[illegible]	supposedly Drake	
271	[illegible]	Phil. 3:8	supposedly Drake	
272 (1)	65, 74	Phil. 3:20	supposedly Drake	yes
272 (2)	65, 74	Phil. 3:20	supposedly Drake	yes
273	65	Matt. 25:30	supposedly Drake	
274	65	Deut. 1:13	supposedly Drake	yes
275	—	Luke 13:5	supposedly Drake	yes
276	—	Heb. 2:3	supposedly Drake	yes
277	64	Pss. [illegible]	supposedly Drake	yes
278	64, 70, 79, 87	Luke 22:44	Drake	
279 (1)	64, 73, 79	Prov. 2:30	supposedly Drake	yes
279 (2)	64, 73, 79	Prov. 2:30	supposedly Drake	yes
280 (1)	63	Heb. 4:13	supposedly Drake	yes
280 (2)	63	Heb. 4:13	supposedly Drake	yes
281 (see 238)	65, 68, 73, 87	Titus 3:8	supposedly Drake	
282	64, 96	Heb. 4:13	unknown/ Wilton	yes
283	[illegible]	Matt. 6:21	unknown/ Wilton	
284	65, [illegible]	1Cor. 2:10	unknown/ Wilton	yes
285	64, [illegible]	1Pet. 1:21	unknown/ Wilton	yes
286	64	1Tim. 2:12	unknown/ Wilton	yes
287	63, 66	Ps. 119:106	unknown/ Wilton	

# in Smith's Index	Delivery Dates (17—/18—)	Reference	Source	SC
288	64, 68, 71, 78,6 86, 92, 9	Rom. 6:21	unknown/ Wilton	yes
289	70, 75, 80	Job 1:21	unknown/ Wilton	yes
290	64, 68, 75	2Cor. 8:12	Duberdu	yes
291	60, 66, 75, 85, 96	Deut. 8:3	Duberdu	
292 (1)	64, 71	Num. 32:23	unknown/ Wilton	yes
292 (2)	64, 71	Num. 32:23	unknown/ Wilton	yes
293	61, 66, 71, 92	Ps. 139:1–2	Duberdu	yes
293 ST	60, 67, 66	Matt. 10:29	Duberdu	yes
294	61	Ps. 74:17–18	Duberdu	yes
295 [XI]	66, 70, 88, 98	Gal. 5:22	Duberdu	yes
296 (1)	66, 72	Isa. 55:7	unknown/ Pearce	
296 (2)	66, 72	Isa. 55:7	unknown/ Pearce	
297	73, 90, 97, 01	1Cor. 11:26	Entick	
298	70, 74, 90, 00	John 8:34	[illegible]	
299	—	Luke 7:13	Pearce	yes
300	70, 95	Ps. 37:37	Pearce	yes
301	72, 78, 84, 94, 00	Deut. 29:29	Duberdu	
302	71	2Cor. 3:17	Duberdu	
303 (1)	86, 95	Matt. 4:1	unknown/ Pearce	
303 (2)	86, 95	Matt. 4:1	unknown/ Pearce	
304 (1)	75, 87, 01	Acts 2:1	Green	
304 (2) (see 313)	72, 77, 84, 87, 94, 00	Phil. 2:12–13	Martyn	
305 (1) (see 332)	76, [illegible]	Luke 24:34	unknown	yes
305 (2)	76, [illegible]	Acts 26:8	Martyn	
306 (1)	[illegible]	Gal. 6:10	Martyn	
306 (2)	[illegible]	Gal. 6:10	Martyn	
307	[illegible], 95	Matt. 6:20	Martyn	
308	89, 97	Acts 16:31	Martyn	
309	74, 79, 89, 93	Ps. 103:1–2	Martyn	yes
309 ST	—	Ps. 107:27	Martyn	
310	70, 75, 83, 88, [illegible]	Luke 2:32	Martyn	
311	76, 89, 90, 96	Isa. 38:1	Martyn	

# in Smith's Index	Delivery Dates (17—/18—)	Reference	Source	SC
312	97	Ps. 29:2	Martyn	yes
313	72, 77, 84, 87, 94, 00	Phil. 2:12–13	Martyn	
314	71, 76, 85, 95	Ps. 94:12	Martyn	
315	70, 76	Matt. 16:26	Martyn	
316	79	Ps. 139:7	Warren/ Martyn	
317	70, 80, 85, 90, 97	[illegible]	Martyn	
318	70, [illegible]	Ps. 73:25	Martyn	
319	70, 74, 85, 90, 96	Matt. 7:12	Martyn	yes
320	71, 74	Ps. 39:12	Martyn	
321	70, 78, 94	Eccles. 12:13	Martyn	
322 (1)	72, 76, 93	Heb. 9:27	Martyn	yes
322 (2) ST	72, 76, 93	[illegible]	Martyn	
323	70, 73, 87, 95	Hag. 1:7	Martyn	
323 ST	—	Isa. 1:3	Martyn	
324	71, 78, 90	Ps. 104:24	Martyn	
325	71, 79, 90, 97	Job 5:7	Martyn	
326	71, 76, 90, 97	2Cor. 5:1	Martyn	
327 [IV]	66, 73	Prov. 16:6	Warren	yes
328	74, 94	Ps. 68:4–5	Warren	yes
329	74, 83, 94	Judg. 1:7	Green	
330	74, 80, 92, 01	1Cor. 9:24	Green	
331	76, 84	Matt. 27:3–5	unknown	yes
332	76, [illegible]	Luke 24:34	unknown	yes
333	76	Hosea 13:14	unknown	yes
334	76, 88	Matt. 28:19–20	unknown	yes
335	67, 74, 90, 97	Matt. 11:28–30	supposedly Green	
336	67, 79, 90	Ps. 34:17	unknown/ Wilton	yes
337 (1)	78, 87, 94	John 5:14	supposedly Drake	yes
337 (2)	78, 87, 94	John 5:14	supposedly Drake	yes
338	78, 87, 99	Matt. 12:32	supposedly Drake	
339	80, 84, 91	Jer. 28:16	self	
340‡ (see 25)	80	Hosea 6:1	self	yes
341	72, 88, 96	Acts 24:25	self	yes
342	78, [illegible]	Matt. 15:19	unknown	

‡On meeting with friends when exiled from Charleston to Philadelphia.

# in Smith's Index	Delivery Dates (17—/18—)	Reference	Source	SC
343	[illegible], 84	Matt. 6:33	unknown	yes
344	[illegible]	John 4:24	Stokes	yes
345	80	Isa. 26:9	Stokes	yes
346	79, 85, 93, 96	[illegible]	Martyn	
347	85, 95	Ps. 90:12	Martyn	yes
348	85, 90	Exod. 20:8	Martyn	
349	85, 86, 89	2Pet. 3:16	Martyn	
350 (1)	78, 85, 95	John 16:33 (altered and corrected)	unknown	yes
350 (2)	78, 85, 95	John 16:33	unknown	yes
351	67, 74, 85, 95	Luke 9:33	Green	
352 (1)	74, 78, 85, 94	Rom. 12:1	Green	yes
352 (2)	74, 78, 85, 94	Rom. 12:1	Green	yes
352 (3)	74, 78, 85, 94	Rom. 12:1	Green	yes
352 (4)	74, 78, 85, 94	Rom. 12:1	Green	yes
353	85	Rom. 12:8	not listed	
354	85, 91	1Tim. 4:8	unknown	yes
355 (1)	[illegible], 93	Luke 19:46	unknown	
355 (2)	[illegible], 93	Luke 19:46	unknown	
356	—	Ps. 16:8	unknown	yes
357	87, 94	Rom. 14:7	Lewis	yes
358	80, 92	Luke 17:17	Lewis	
359	89, 95	John 9:14	Martyn	
360	89, 97	1Cor. 15:22	Martyn	
361	74, 84, 89	Acts 2:33	unknown/ Tonge	
362	90, 95	Luke 24:26	Martyn	
363	91, 97	John 6:53	supposedly Green	yes
364	91	1Thess. 5:15	unknown	yes
365	85, 91, 96	Matt. 6:9	Martyn	yes
366	[illegible]	Heb. 6:12	unknown	yes
367	92	Acts 26:28	self	yes
368	92	1Cor. 7:17	self	
369	[illegible]	Num. 6:24–26	Duberdu	
370	65, 79, 92	John 7:46	Warren	
371	92	Phil. 2:5	Clifton	yes
372	75, 92	Mark 7:21	Warren	
373	85, 92, 99	Rom. 12:8	Clifton	yes
374	94	Rom. 3:8	Clifton	
375	74, 94	Rom. 1:16	Clifton	

# in Smith's Index	Delivery Dates (17—/18—)	Reference	Source	SC
376	94	Gen. 43:14	self	
377	[illegible]	Ps. 100:4	self	yes
378	[illegible]	1Pet. 3:18	self	yes
379	[illegible]	Matt. 22:11–13	self	yes
380	[illegible	John 3:16	Warren	yes
381 [XXII]	[illegible]	Ps. 136:26	self	
382	[illegible]	Luke 15:11	unknown	
383	97	Phil. 2:8	self	
384	74, 91, 97	Ps. 119:80	Warren	
385	99	Luke 14:51	self	
386	98	1Tim. 2:1 (of Ely)	James	yes
387	00	Acts 3:18 (collected)	self	yes
388	—	Acts 2:24	self	yes
389	[illegible]	Acts 13:36	self	yes
390 (1) [XXVI]	[illegible]	1John 5:4	self	yes
390 (2)	[illegible]	1John 5:4	self	yes
391	[illegible]	Rom. 8:26	self	yes
392	[illegible]	1Cor. 13:3	self	
393	[illegible]	Luke 8:18	self	yes
394	[illegible]	Titus 2:15	self	yes
395	—	2Sam. 12:23	self	yes
396	00	Acts 24:15	self	yes
396 ST	—	Rom. 6:5	self	yes
397	65, 00	Ps. 19:13	self	yes
398 [XXIII]	00	Prov. 22:1	self	yes
399	74, 91	Heb. 3:13	self	yes
400	67, 00	1Cor. 10:13	self	yes
401	[illegible]	[illegible] (collected)	self	yes
402	[illegible]	Matt. 3:2	self	yes
403	[illegible]	Ps. 139:7	self	yes
403 ST	[illegible]	—	self	yes
404	[illegible]	Rom. 12:5	self	yes
405	[illegible}	1Thess. 5:21	self	yes
406	[illegible]	Exod. 20:4–5	self	
407	[illegible]	John 17:3	self	
408 (1)	88, 01	Titus 2:11–12 (collected)	self	yes
408 (2)	88, 01	Titus 2:11–12	self	yes

Sources Identification

The following list identifies the likely sources to which Smith referred in the index above.

Clarke, Rev. Richard, was rector of St. Philip's Parish, 1753–1759. Smith served as assistant minister under Clarke and succeeded him as rector in 1759.

Drake, Rev. Samuel, arrived in South Carolina in 1762 and left the state in 1766.

Evans, Rev. John, became rector of St. Bartholomew's Parish, Colleton County, in 1764. He died in 1770.

Green, Rev. John, became rector of St. Helena's Parish, Beaufort, in 1762. He died in 1765.

Lewis, Rev. John, formerly of St. John's Parish, Berkeley County, became rector of St. Paul's Parish, Colleton County, in 1773. There was also a Stephen C. Lewis who was quite active in the early American Episcopal Church in South Carolina after the Revolution. However, the Lewis whom Smith cites in the index is probably John Lewis.

Martyn, Rev. Charles, was a close friend and colleague of Smith's. They lectured together on philosophy in the early 1760s. He arrived in South Carolina in 1752 as an S.P.G. missionary and became rector of St. Andrew's Parish, Berkeley County, in 1753.

Pearce, Rev. Offspring, was a charter member of Smith's Society for the Relief of Widows and Orphans. He was the rector of St. George's, Winyaw, and later rector of St. George's, Dorchester County. The source citation could also refer to Rev. John Pearce, another South Carolina Anglican clergyman of the time. When Smith and his wife traveled to England in 1769, John Pearce accompanied them on their return. A third possible identification of the "Pearce" reference could be Dr. Zachary Pearce, bishop of Bangor in the 1750s, who ordained Richard Clarke, Smith's predecessor at St. Philip's.

Stokes, Rev. Joseph, was a charter member of the Society for the Relief of Widows and Orphans. He was an Anglican clergy, but his charge is uncertain.

Tonge, Rev. John, was rector of St. Paul's, Colleton County. He arrived in South Carolina in 1759.

Warren, Rev. Samuel Fenner, is the most likely identification for the "Warren" reference. He arrived in South Carolina in 1758 as an S.P.G. missionary and served as rector of St. James Parish, Santee. He and Smith worked closely together, sharing the pulpit at St. Thomas Parish for several months while the rector there was ill. S. F. Warren was the son of an Anglican minister, Rev. Richard Warren, who lived in Suffolk, England, and the brother of Richard Warren, who became bishop of Bangor. Either of these Warrens could also be the "Warren" to whom Smith referred.

White, Rev. Joseph, served St. John's Parish, Berkeley County, 1788–1790. Another possible identification for the "White" reference is Rev. William White, who became bishop of Pennsylvania shortly after the postwar reorganization.

Wilton, Rev. Joseph Dacre, arrived at the end of 1761 and became assistant rector at St. Philip's in 1762. He died in 1767.

Appendix B

PRINTED SOURCES OF THE
SERMONS OF ROBERT SMITH

# in Smith's Index*	Delivery Dates (17–/18–)	Reference	Source
01	58, 61, 65, 73	Ps. 107:4	Wilder
02	60, 64, 75	1Chron. 29:15	Bilton
03	58, 61	Mark 13:37	Littleton
04	58	Ps. 40:12	Littleton
04 ST	61, 64	Eph. 5:15–16	Littleton
05	58	John 20:19	Smith
05 ST	60, 64, 72, 85, 88	Ps. 119:165	Smith
06	60, 65	John 9:4	Feathergill
07	60, 65, 80	2Cor. 8:21	Bishop of Bangor
08	60, 65, 74	1Cor. 1:18	Wilder
09	60, 65, 74	2Tim. 3:5	Dorman
010	59	2Tim. 1:10	Calamy
011	60	Matt. 25:19	Rogers
012	58, 61, 65, 74	Mark 8:38	Wilder
013	57	Matt. 6:12	Littleton
014	59	Ps. 18:3	Rogers
015	58, 61	Matt. 12:36–37	Littleton
016	—	Matt. 16:26	Moss
017	58, 61	Matt. 5:34	Calamy & Littleton

*Number assigned by Smith in his own index, or listing, of his sermons. A bracketed number following = the sermon number in this volume; (1) = first in a series; (2) = second in a series, etc.; and ST = second text.

# in Smith's Index	Delivery Dates (17–/18–)	Reference	Source
018	58, 61	Num. 23:10	Calamy
019	59, 66	Ps. 22:25	Moore
020	58, 61	1Pet. 4:18	Rogers
021	59	Prov. 14:9	Rogers
022	60, 64, 71	Ps. 100:2	Dorman
023	58, 66, 71, 75	Eccles. 11:7–8	Munton
024	58, 61, 66, 71, 75	Matt. 7:14	Munton
025	60, 65, 66, 70, 77, 83	Matt. 2:16	Wilder
026	—	Col. 3:2	Dorman
026 ST	61, 66, 71, 75	Heb. 10:34	Dorman
027	58, 61, 66, 72	Ps. 34:1	Munton
028	58, 64, 73, 92	Eccles. 11:9	Munton
029	59	Ps. 119:59:60	Rogers
029 ST	63	Lam. 3:40	Rogers
030	57	Heb. 12:14	Clarke
030 ST	61, 66	2Cor. 7:1	Clarke
031	57, 64	Matt. 7:12	Bolt
032	57, 61, 65, 72, 76	Prov. 12:21	Boyce ms. Uncertain
033	57, 60, 64, 73	Prov. 15:3	Dorman
033 ST	—	Prov. 5:21	Dorman
034	57, 60, 64, 73	Eccles. 1:2–3	Corybeare
035	61, 66, 71, 76	Prov. 29:18	Dorman
036	58, 62, 67, 74	Matt. 25:5	Corybeare
036 ST	—	Matt. 26:40	Corybeare
037	59	Eccles. 12:7	[illegible]
038	58, 61, 66, 72, 75	Heb. 11:13	Corybeare
038 ST	—	Heb. 13:14	Corybeare
039	58, 63, 73	2Pet. 3:8–9	Corybeare
039 ST	—	Rom. 2:4	Corybeare
040	58	Heb. 10:26	Corybeare
040 ST	63	Heb. 10:27	Corybeare
041	58, 61, 66, 71, 75	1John 3:2	Corybeare
041 ST	—	John 14:2	Corybeare
042	58, 66, 73, 80, 96	Luke 19:41	Munton & self
043	58, 61, 66	1Cor. 5:7–8	Wilder
044	58, 61	Matt. 19:17	Abbott
045	59	Isa. 5:20	Clarke
046	59, 67	Prov. 3:6	Moss
047	58, 67, 73	Exod. 20:9–10	Wilder

# in Smith's Index	Delivery Dates (17–/18–)	Reference	Source
048	58, 59	Acts 2:4	Wilder
049 [III]	58, 64	Deut. 5:29	Munton & Rogers
050	58, 63	Eph. 4:26	Wilder
051	58, 66, 73	Prov. 10:18	Wilder
052	58	Ps. 19:11	Littleton
053	58	Matt. 6:13	Lettleton
054	58	Job 8:13	Littleton
055	58	Job 27:8	Littleton
055 ST	67	Job 8:13	Littleton
056	58, 61, 67, 72, 75	Prov. 3:17	latter pt. Wilder
056 ST	—	Prov. 8:32	latter pt. Wilder
057	58, 67	Col. 3:2	Littleton
058	59	Isa. 32:17	unknown
059	58, 61	1Tim. 6:11	Scott
060	58, 61	Prov. 2:4	Scott
061 (1)	58, 61, 66, 71, 75	Prov. 30:8–9	Harvest
061 (2)	58, 61, 66, 71, 75	Prov. 30:8–9	Harvest
062 (1)	58, 66, 71, 76	Luke 18:14	Harvest
062 (2)	58, 66, 71, 76	Luke 18:14	Harvest
063	58, 61, 66	1Pet. 2:17	Harvest
063 ST	—	Ps. 33:8	Harvest
064	58, 61, 65	1John 4:9	Wilder
065	59	Ps. 98:1–3	Harvest
066 (1)	59	John 1:46	Littleton
066 (2)	59	John 1:46	Littleton
067	59, 61, 64	Matt. 9:15	Littleton
068	59	Matt. 6:9	Littleton
069	59, 63, 67, 71, 73	Ps. 144:3	Dorman
070† [V]	59, 64, 72	1Cor. 10:24	Tennison & Bishop Aseph & Stone
071	59	Matt. 6:9	Littleton
072	59, 67	Matt:11:30	Dorrington
073 (1)	57	Matt. 6:10	Littleton
073 (2)	57	Matt. 6:10	Littleton

†Society sermon.

# in Smith's Index	Delivery Dates (17–/18–)	Reference	Source
074	59, 61, 66, 71, 84, 87	Eph. 4:8	Wilder
075	59	Phil. 3:10	Claggett
076	—	Ps. 9:10	Hickman
076 ST	59, 64, 70, 75	Prov. 9:12	Hickman
077	59	Matt. 6:12	Littleton
078	59	Matt. 6:27	collected by Cooper
079	59	Ps. 33:18	Rogers & Clarke
080	59	Matt. 6:11	Littleton
081	59	John 4:24	Claggett
082	59, 64	Ps. 40:4	Rogers & Atterbury
083	59	1Cor. 9:25	Claggett
084	59	1Cor. 13:13	Claggett
085	59, 65, 71	1Pet. 5:10	Johnson
086 (1)	59, 64, 72, 75	2Thess. 4:1	Johnson
086 (2)	59, 64, 72, 75	2Thess. 4:1	Johnson
087‡	59, 63, 67, 71, 75	John 6:66–68	Johnson
088§	59	2Sam. 10:12	collected
089	59	Rom. 12:11	collected
090	60, 75	James 4:11	unknown
091	60, 65, 75, 79	Matt. 11:29	unknown
092 [VII]	61	1John 2:15	Dorman
093	61, 01	1Tim. 1:13	Wilder
094	61	1Tim. 4:16	Miller
095	61, 64, 70, 75	Gal. 6:9	Dorman
096	61	Deut. 29:29	Littleton & Swift & Atterbury
097	61	Luke 13:5	Littleton & Atterbury
098 (1)	61, 66, 73	Heb. 11:6	self & Dorman & Wilder
098 (2)	61, 66, 73	Heb. 11:6	self & Dorman & Wilder

‡There are 2 versions of the sermon and three texts.

§Collected by Smith concerning British victory in India during the 1750s colonial war.

# in Smith's Index	Delivery Dates (17–/18–)	Reference	Source
099 (1)	62, 67, 71, 75	Ps. 89:7	Feathergill
099 (2)	62, 67, 71, 75	Ps. 89:7	Feathergill
100	61, 67	1Cor. 15:58	Wilder
101 Session [I]	61, 71	2Sam. 23:3	Wilder
102 [XV]	62, 84	1Cor. 12:31	Horberry
103	63	John 5:14	Rogers & self
104	64, 71, 78, 87	John 7:24	Wilder
105	64, 72, 80, 87	Luke 24:46	Wilder
106	66, 71, 75, 79	Phil. 4:4	Batty
107 (1)	66, 71, 75, 87, 94	Prov. 14:14	Cousy
107 (2)	66, 71, 75, 87, 94	Prov. 14:14	Cousy
108	—	Ps. 100:2	Dorman
109 (1)	72, 75, 87	Gen. 4:7	unknown
109 (2)	72, 75, 87	Gen. 4:7	unknown
110	73	1Cor. 1:23–24	unknown
001	75	Luke 15:10	Munton
002	—	John 13:35	unknown
003	77	Num. 10:29	*Systems of Sermons*
004 [VI]	71	John 13:35	unknown
005	58, 60, 64, 72, 85	John 20:19	Smith
006	88	Matt. 11:28	unknown
008	89	Isa. 60:12	unknown
009	—	Luke 2:29–30	unknown
010	94, 98	Ps. 103:13	Bingham
011	96	2Kings 1:2	New York, 1771
012	99	1Thess. 3:12	Martin; printed and preached at St. Michael's 1764
013	83	Luke 7:47	self

Index of Biblical Citations

Index of Subjects and Names